THE CHOICE IS MADE IN VOL. 21, COMING APRIL 2017!

IF ONE LIFE IS LOST, THEN ANOTHER LIFE...

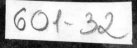

Attack on Titan 20 is a work of fiction. Names, characters, places, and incidents are the products of the author's imagination or are used fictitiously. Any resemblance to actual events, locales, or persons, living or dead, is entirely coincidental.

A Kodansha Comics Trade Paperback Original

Published in the United States by Kodansha Comics, an imprint of Kodansha USA Publishing, LLC, New York.

Publication rights for this English edition arranged through Kodansha Ltd, Tokyo.

First published in Japan in 2016 by Kodansha Ltd., Tokyo as *Shingeki no kyojin*, volume 20.

ISBN 978-1-63236-309-1

Original cover design by Takashi Shimoyama (Red Rooster)

Printed in the United States of America.

www.kodanshacomics.com

9 8 7 6 5 4 3 2 1
Translation: Ko Ransom
Lettering: Steve Wands
Editing: Ben Applegate
Kodansha Comics edition cover design by Phil Balsman

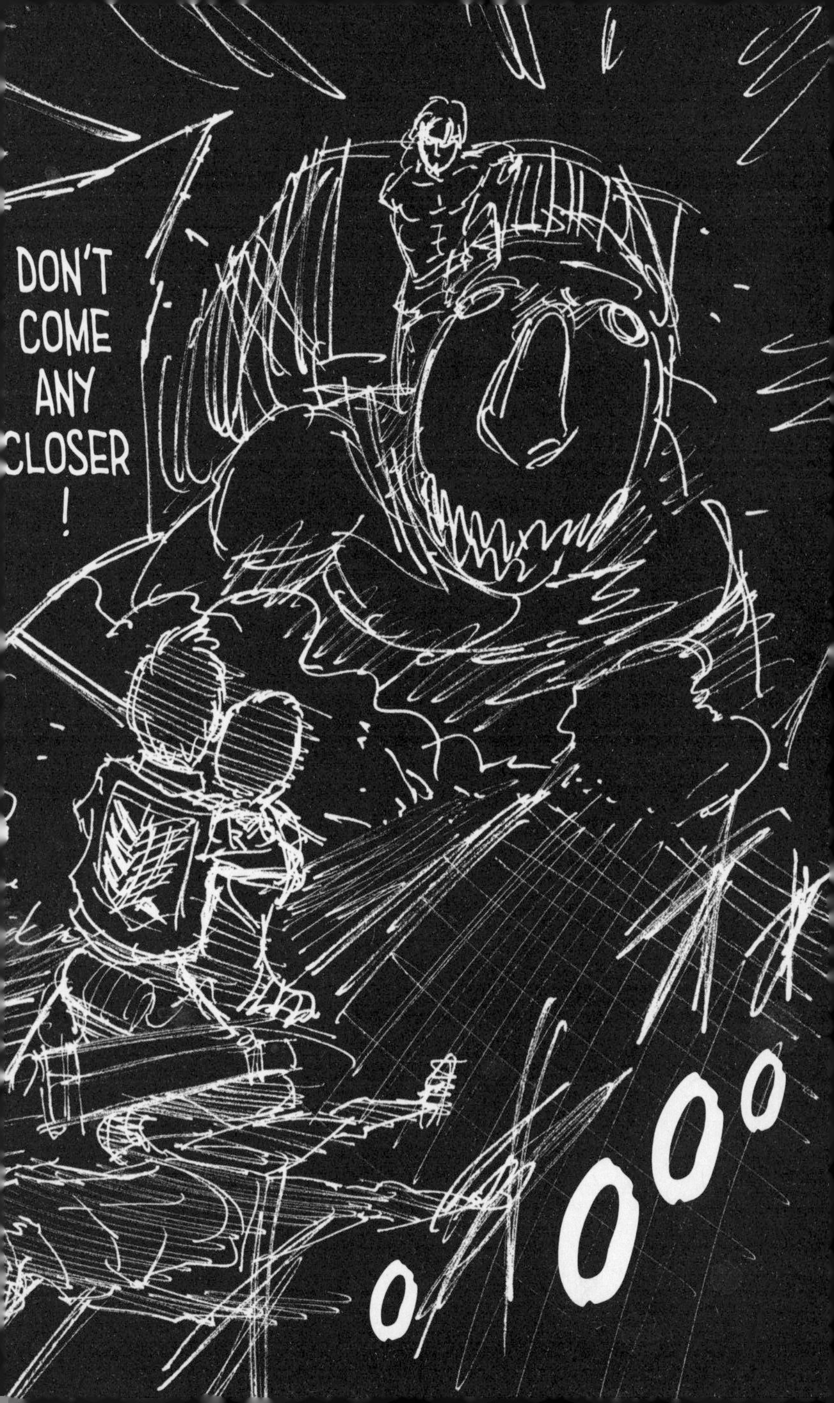
DON'T COME ANY CLOSER !
OOOO

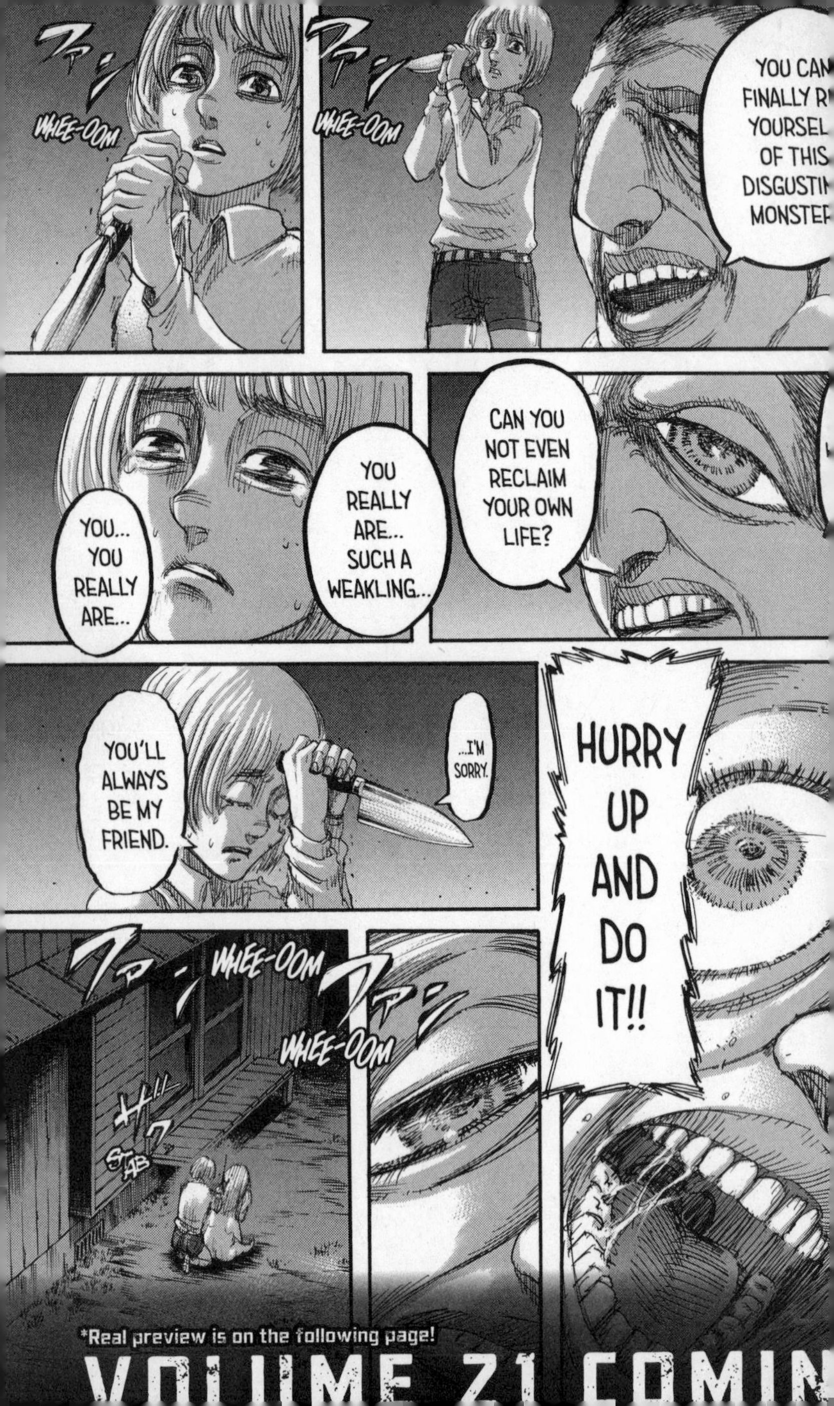
YOU CAN FINALLY R YOURSEL OF THIS DISGUSTI MONSTE
ファン
WHEE-OOM
ファン
WHEE-OOM
CAN YOU NOT EVEN RECLAIM YOUR OWN LIFE?
YOU REALLY ARE... SUCH A WEAKLING...
YOU... YOU REALLY ARE...
HURRY UP AND DO IT!!
...I'M SORRY.
YOU'LL ALWAYS BE MY FRIEND.
ファン
WHEE-OOM
ファン
WHEE-OOM
ドサッ
STAB
*Real preview is on the following page!
VOLUME 21 COMIN

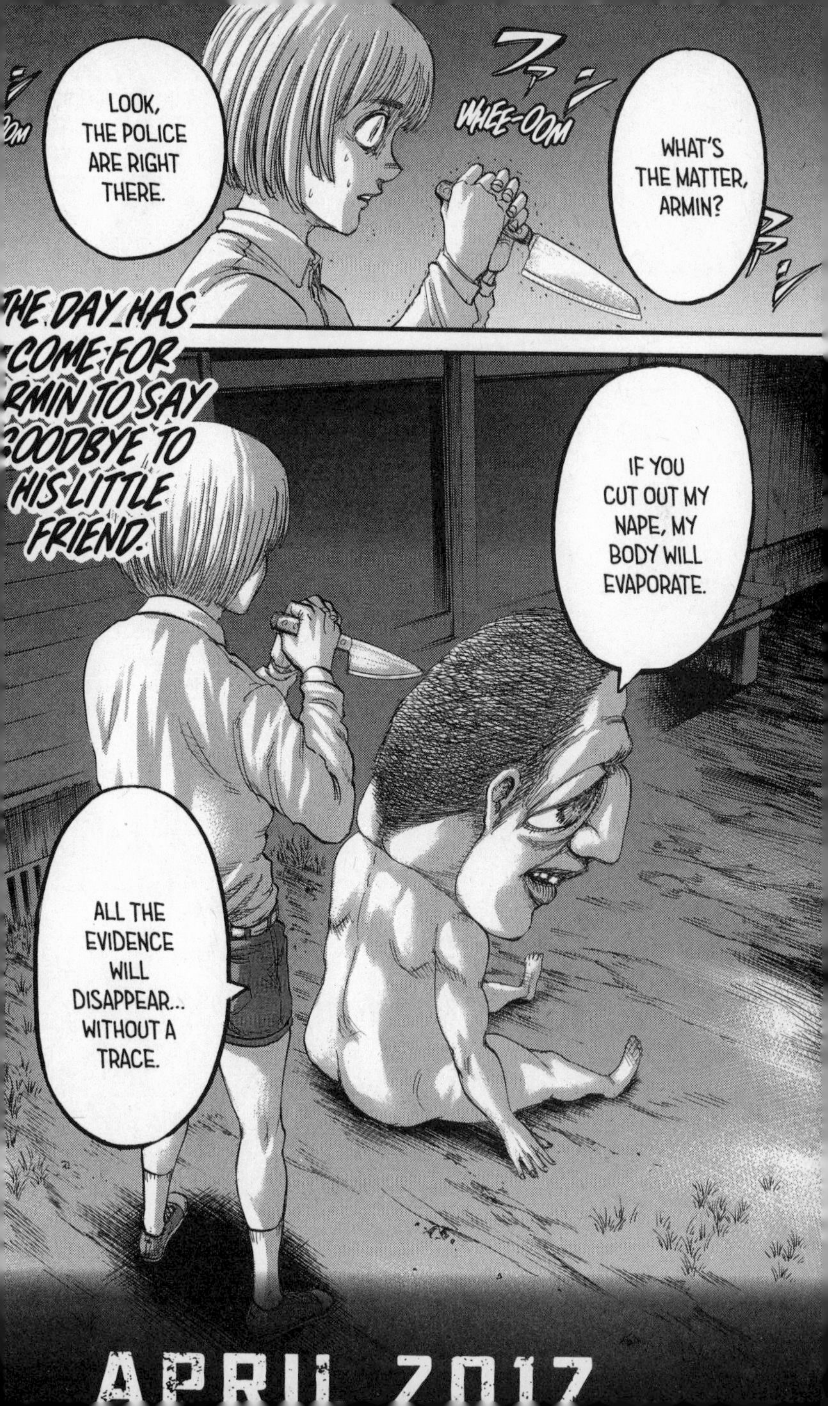
WHEE-OOM
WHAT'S THE MATTER, ARMIN?
LOOK, THE POLICE ARE RIGHT THERE.
HE DAY HAS COME FOR RMIN TO SAY OODBYE TO HIS LITTLE FRIEND.
IF YOU CUT OUT MY NAPE, MY BODY WILL EVAPORATE.
ALL THE EVIDENCE WILL DISAPPEAR... WITHOUT A TRACE.
APRIL 2017

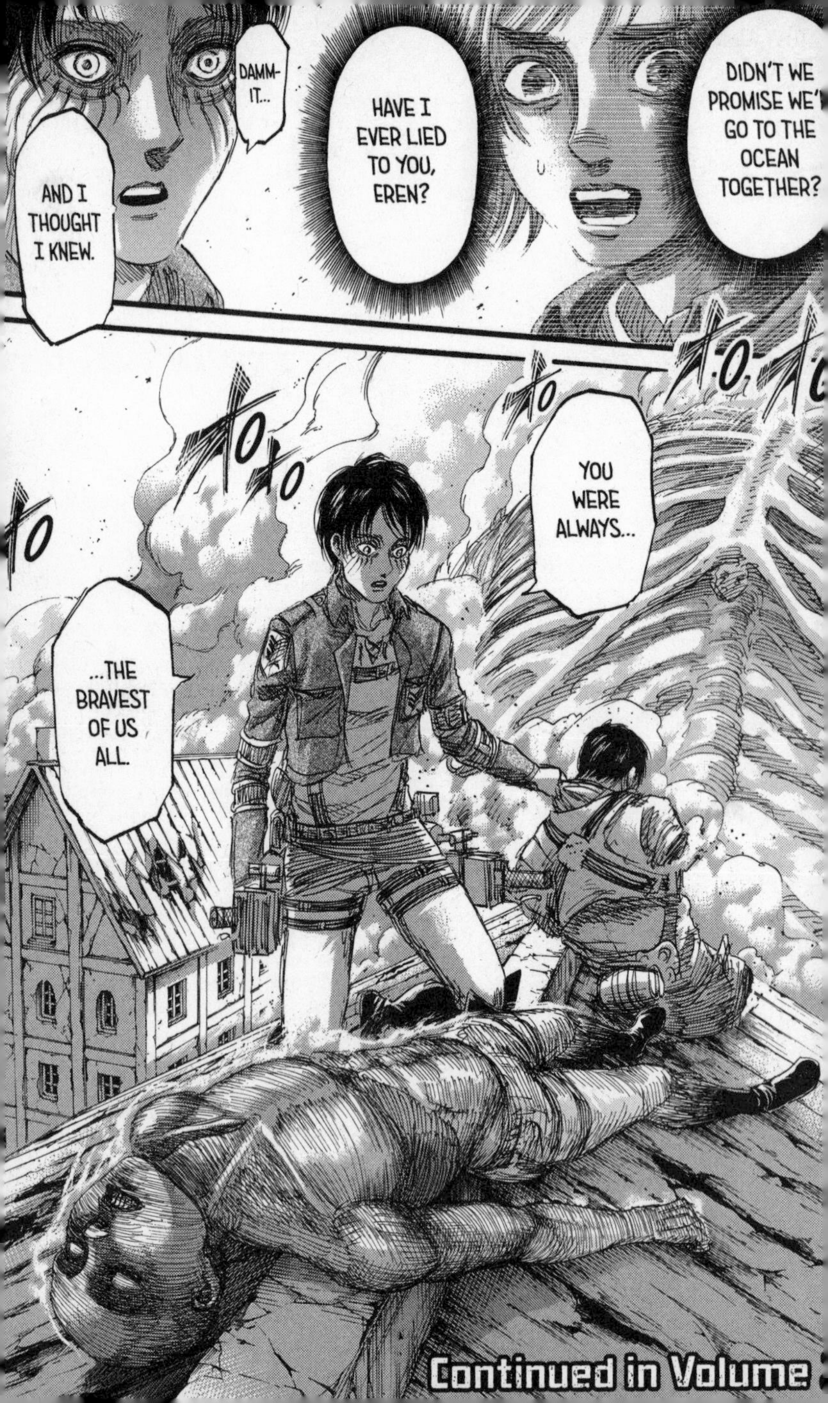
DIDN'T WE PROMISE WE' GO TO THE OCEAN TOGETHER?
HAVE I EVER LIED TO YOU, EREN?
DAMM-IT...
AND I THOUGHT I KNEW.
YOU WERE ALWAYS...
...THE BRAVEST OF US ALL.
Continued in Volume

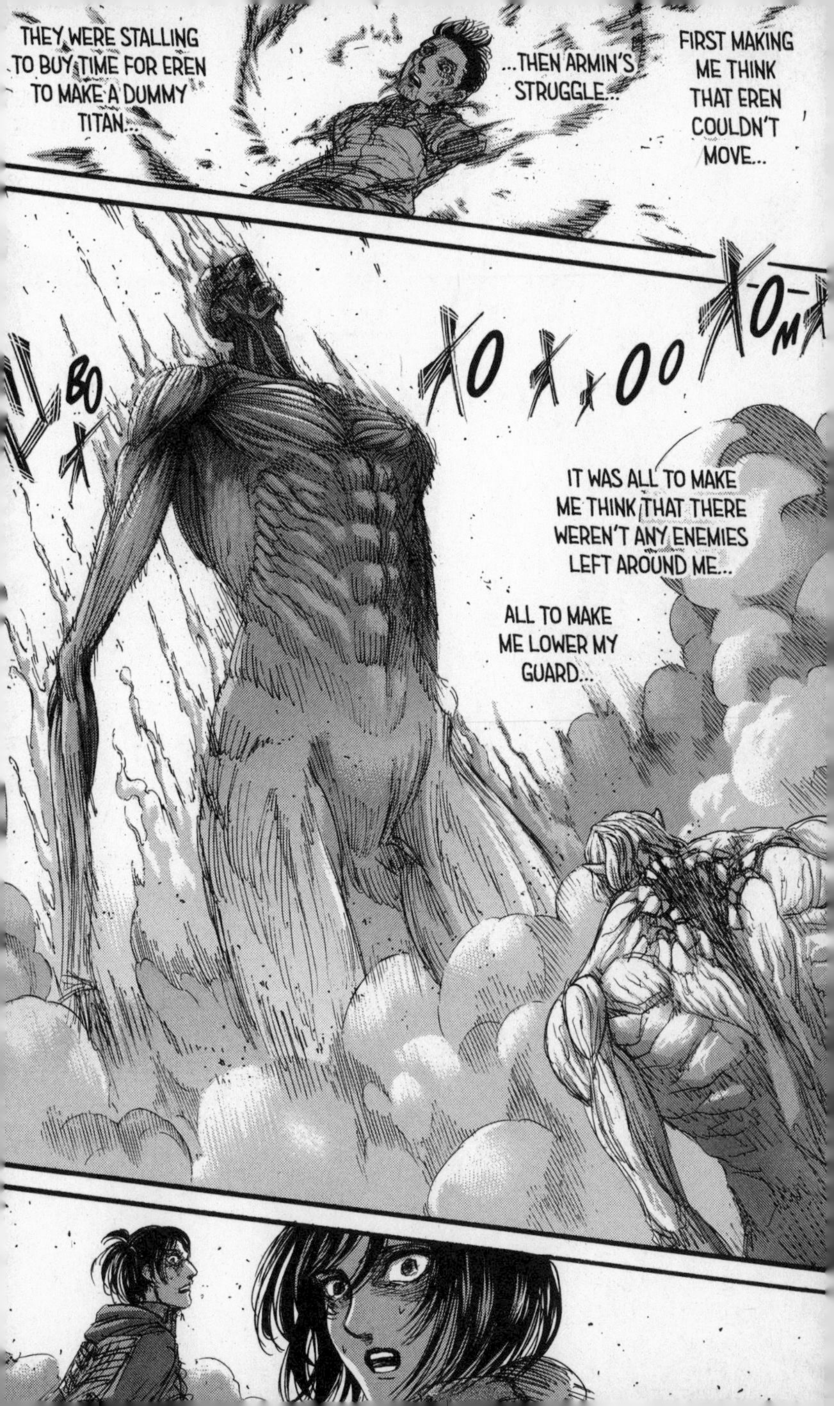
FIRST MAKING ME THINK THAT EREN COULDN'T MOVE...
...THEN ARMIN'S STRUGGLE...
THEY WERE STALLING TO BUY TIME FOR EREN TO MAKE A DUMMY TITAN...
IT WAS ALL TO MAKE ME THINK THAT THERE WEREN'T ANY ENEMIES LEFT AROUND ME...
ALL TO MAKE ME LOWER MY GUARD...

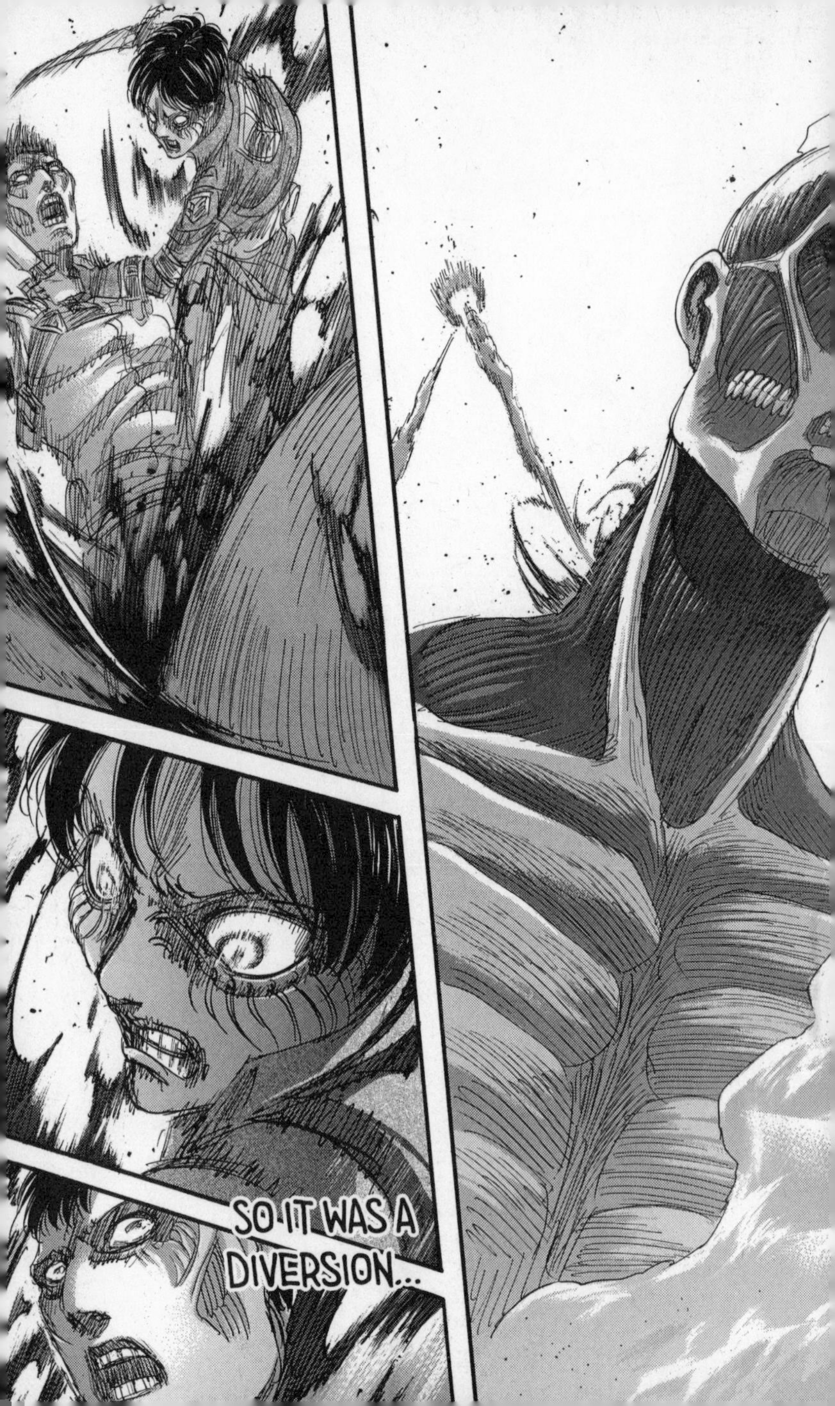
SO IT WAS A DIVERSION...

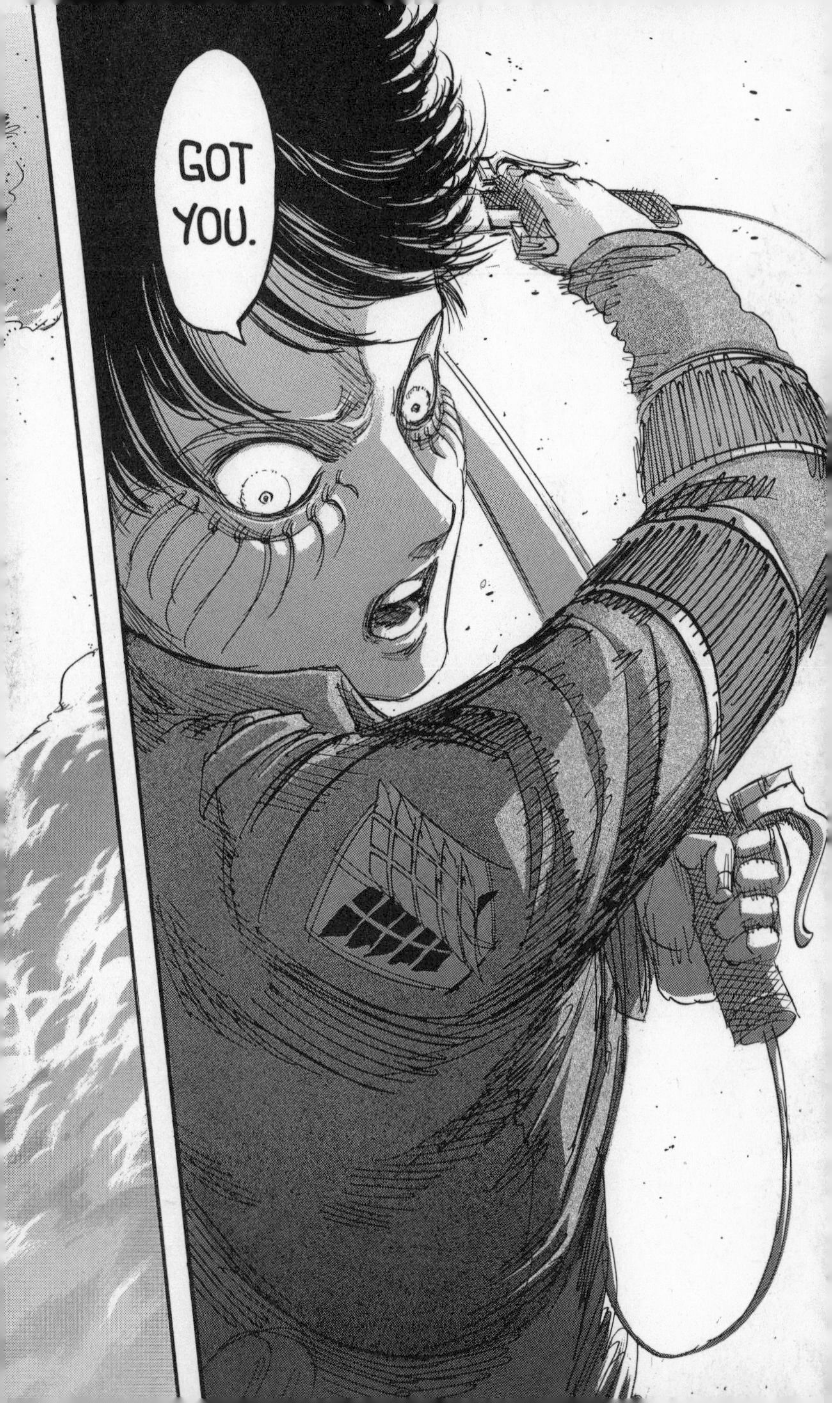
GOT YOU.

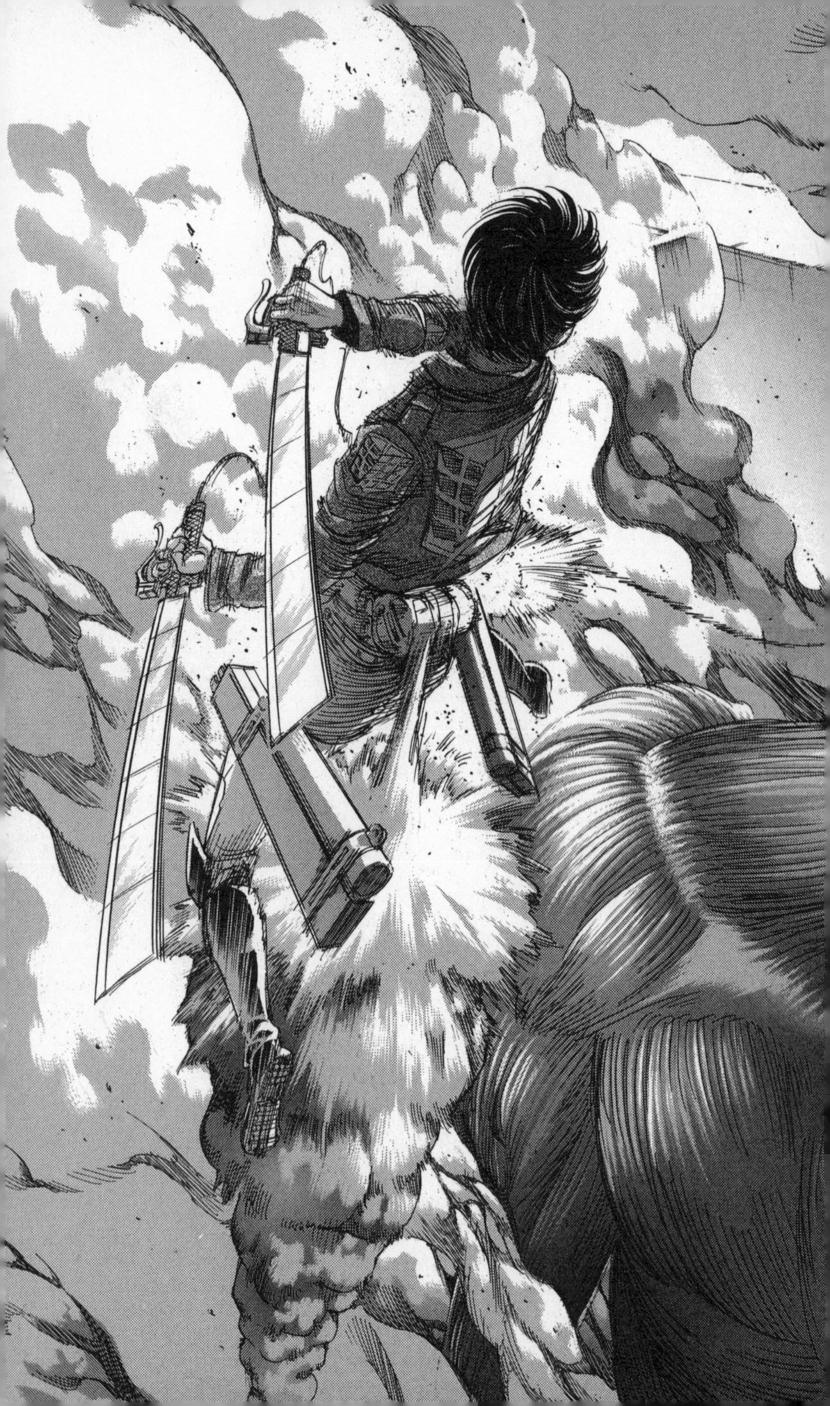

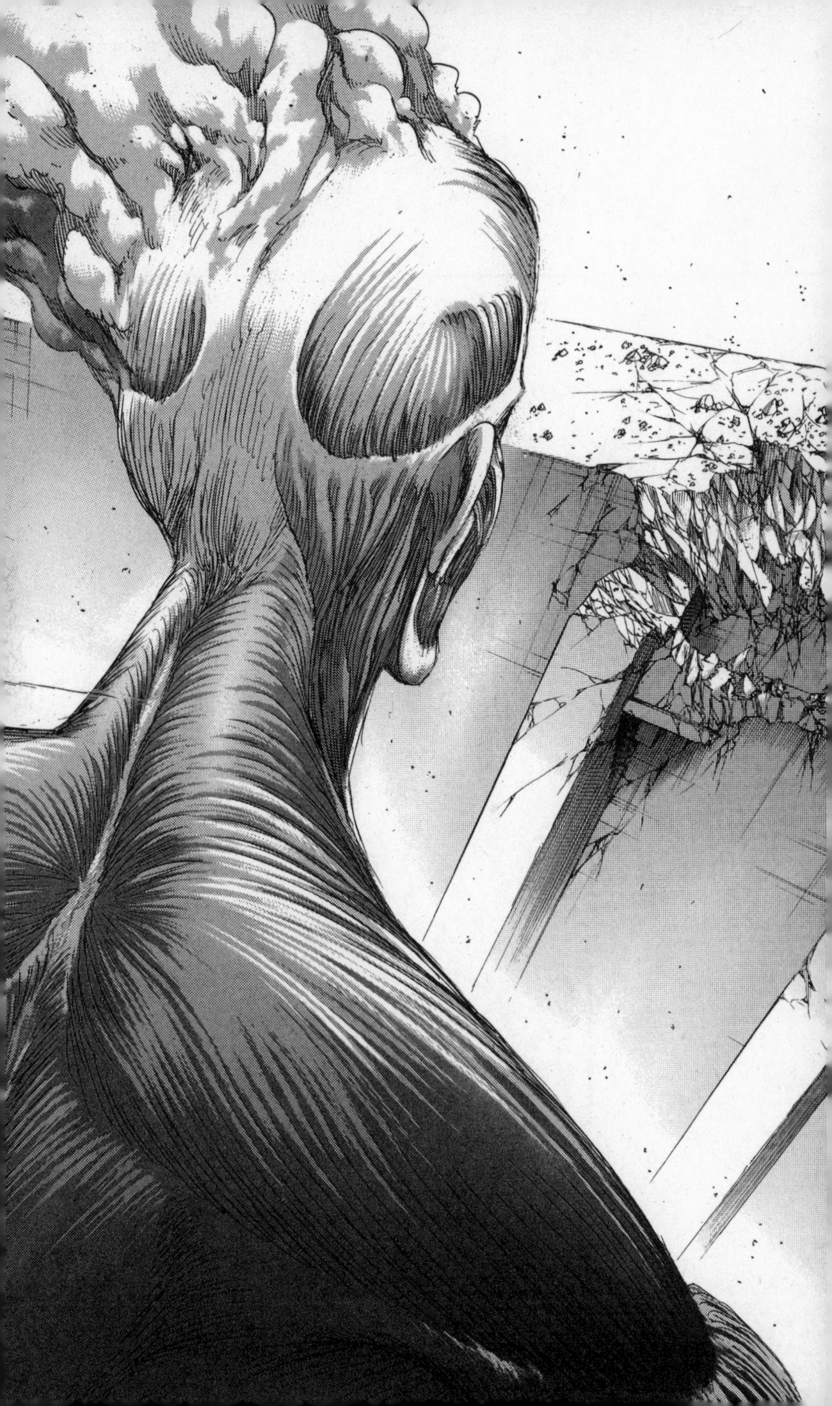

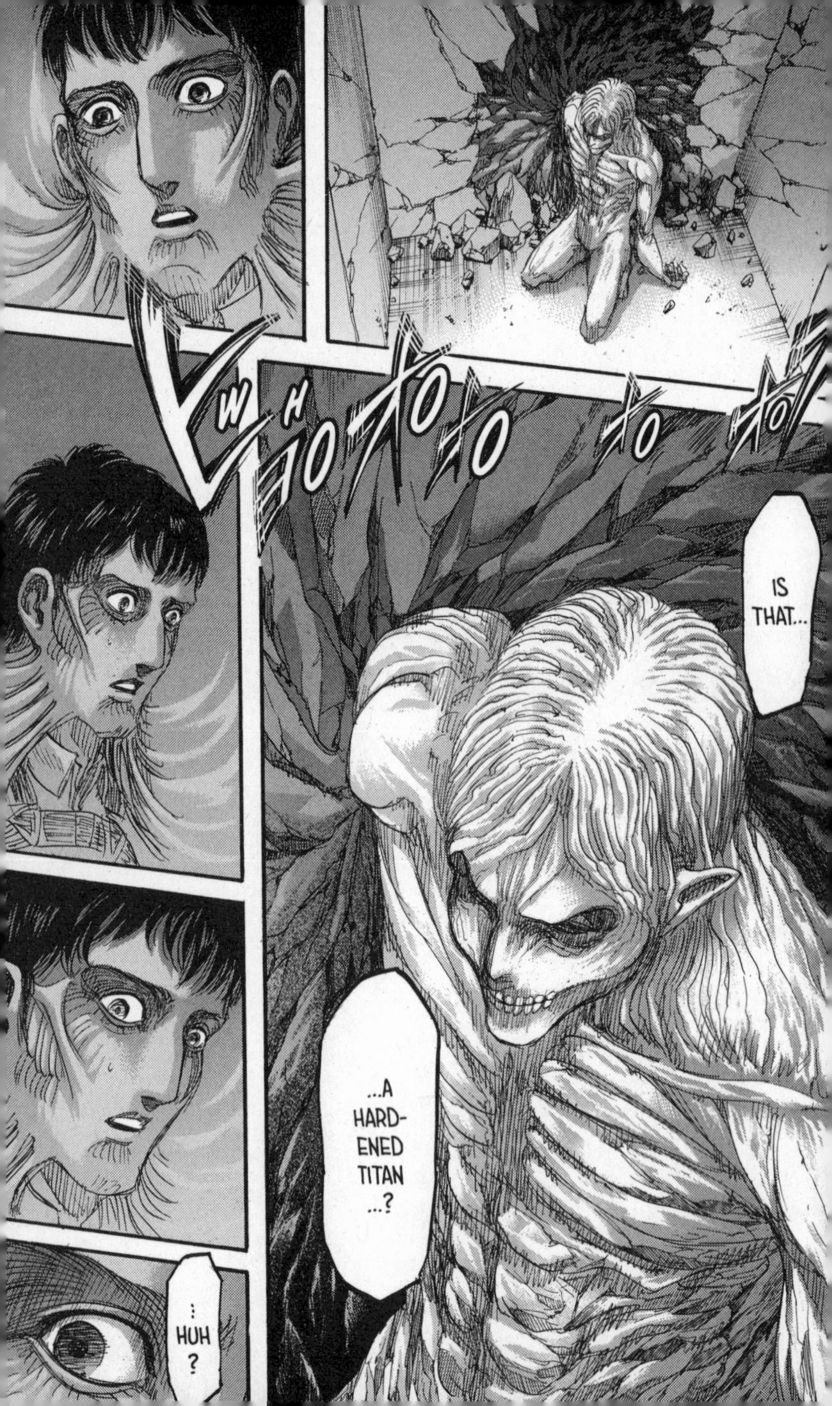
IS THAT...
...A HARD-ENED TITAN ...?
...HUH?

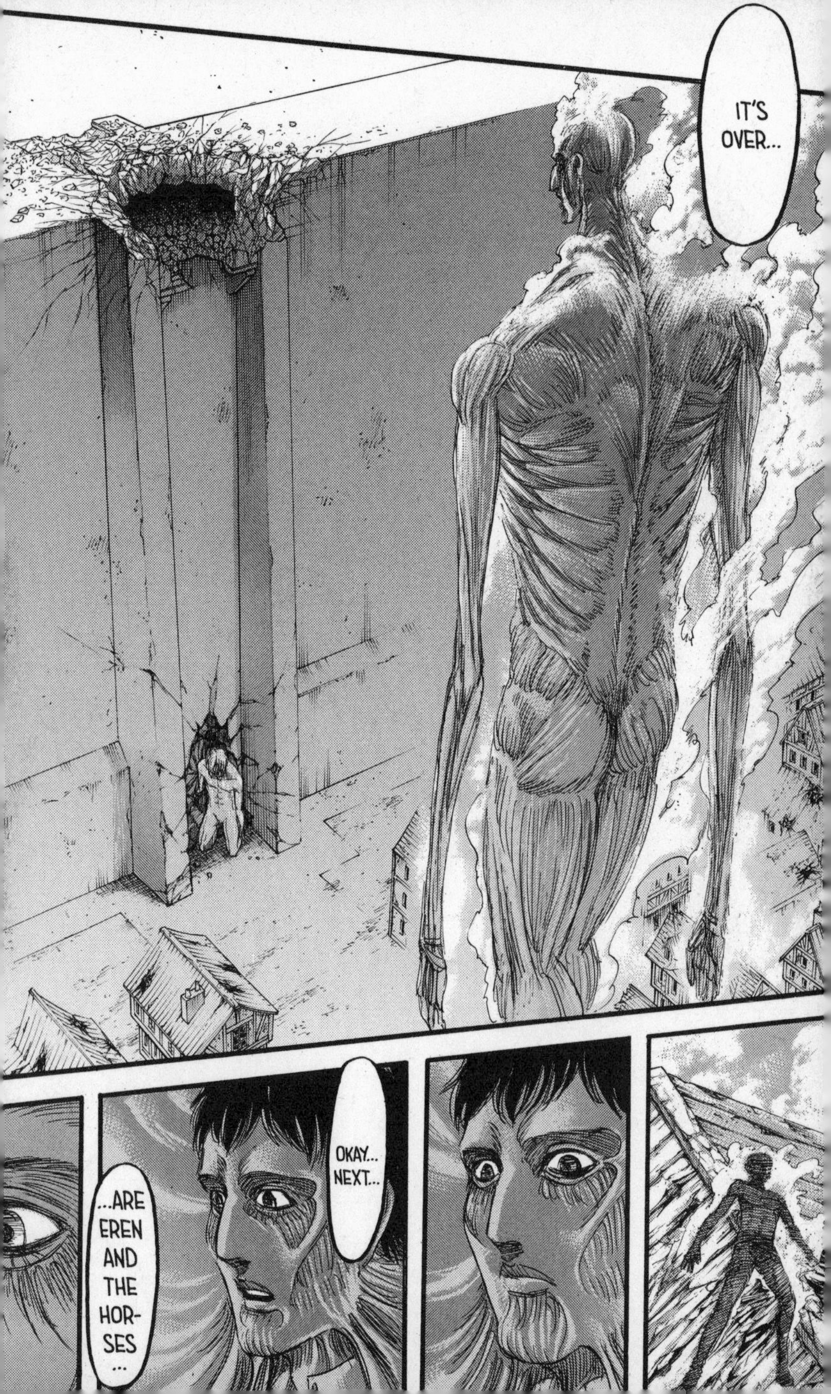
IT'S OVER...
OKAY... NEXT...
...ARE EREN AND THE HOR-SES ...

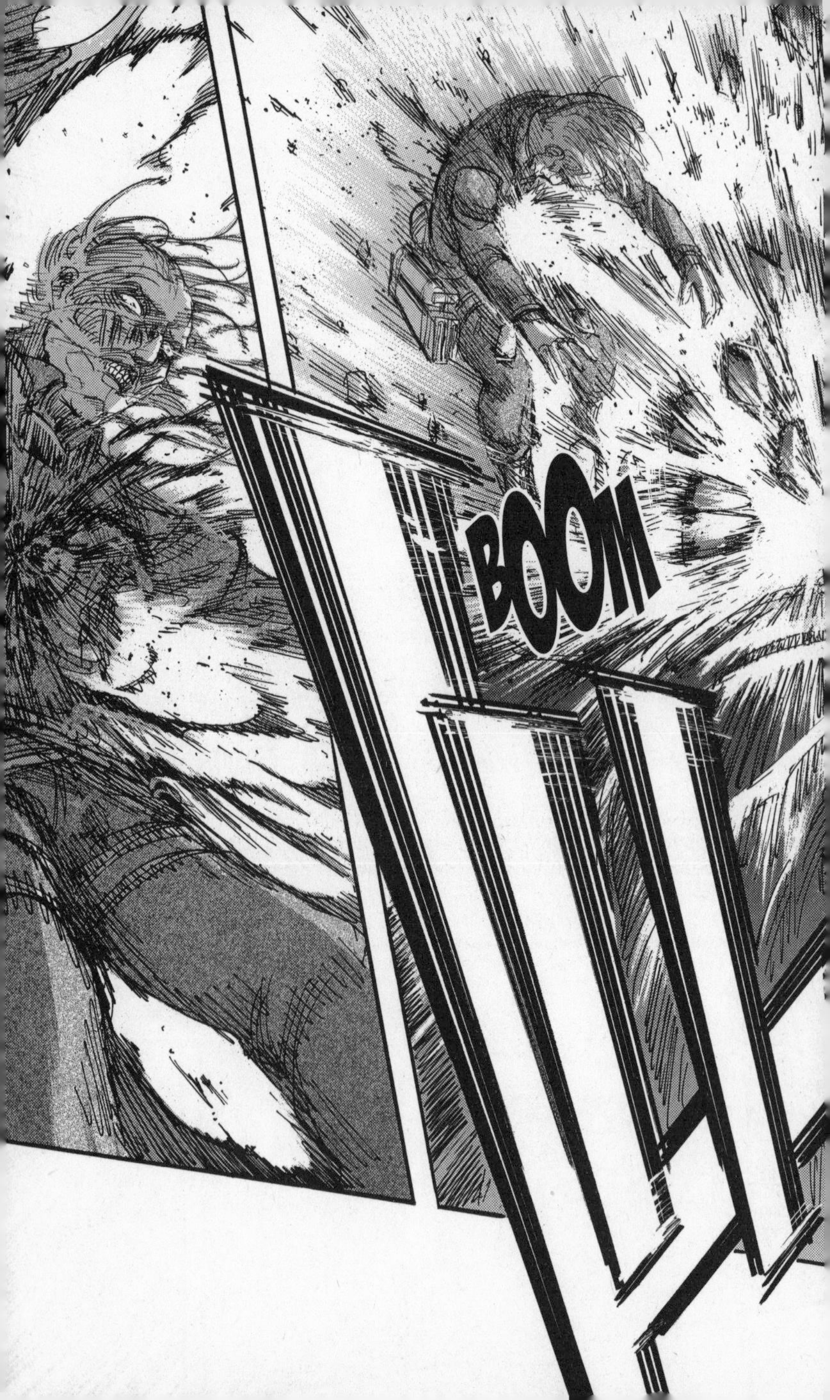
BOOM

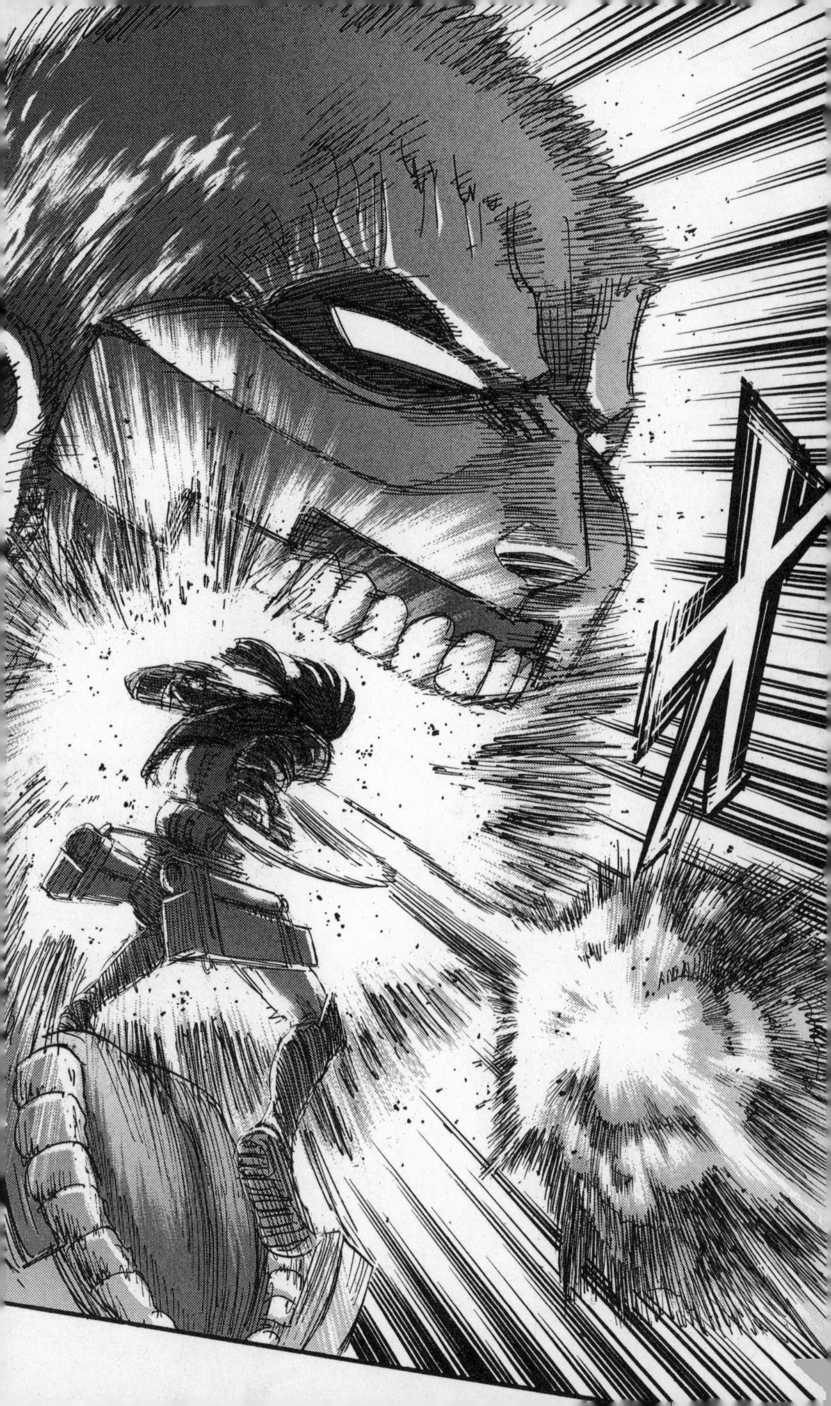

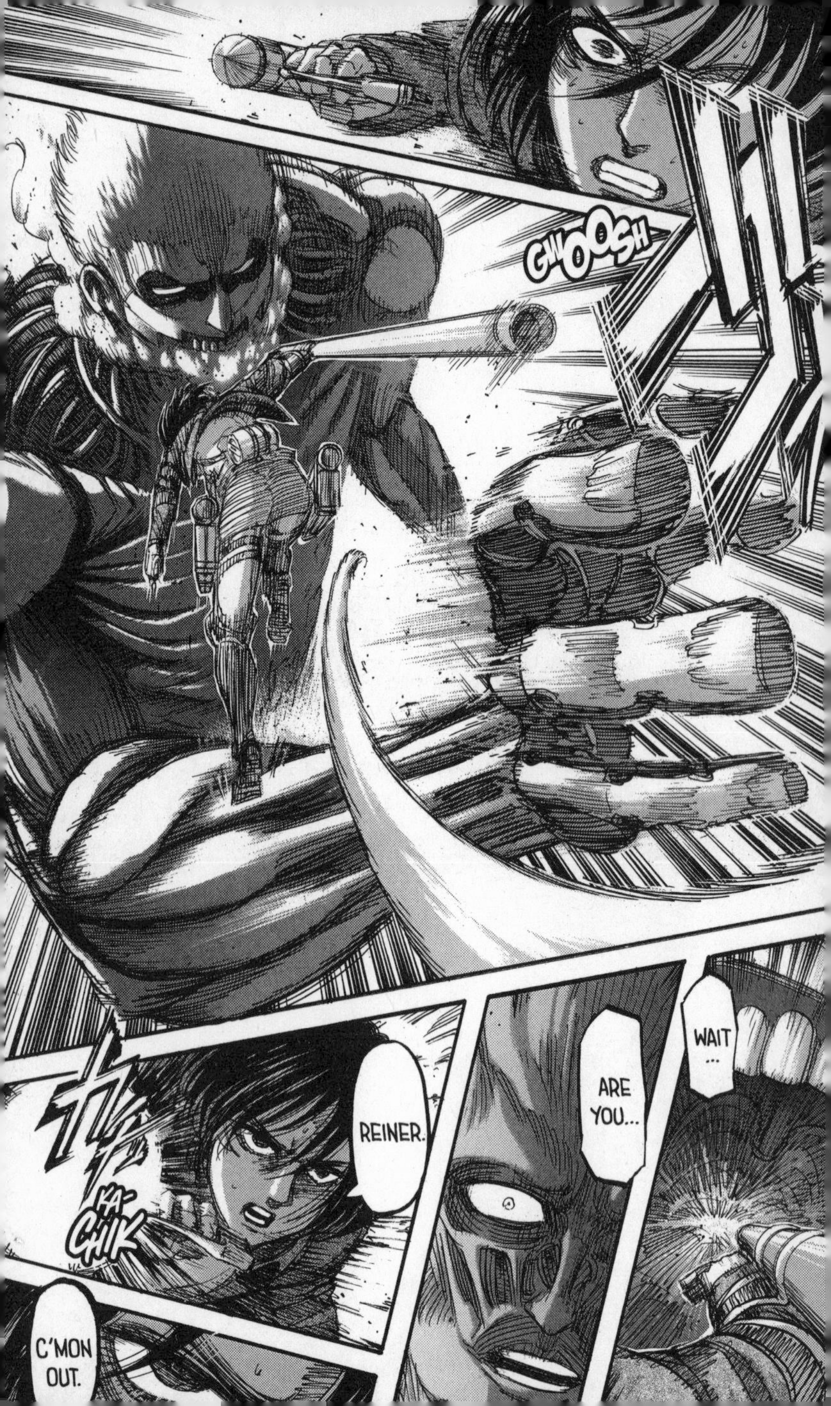
GWOOSH
WAIT ...
ARE YOU...
REINER.
KA-CHIK
C'MON OUT.

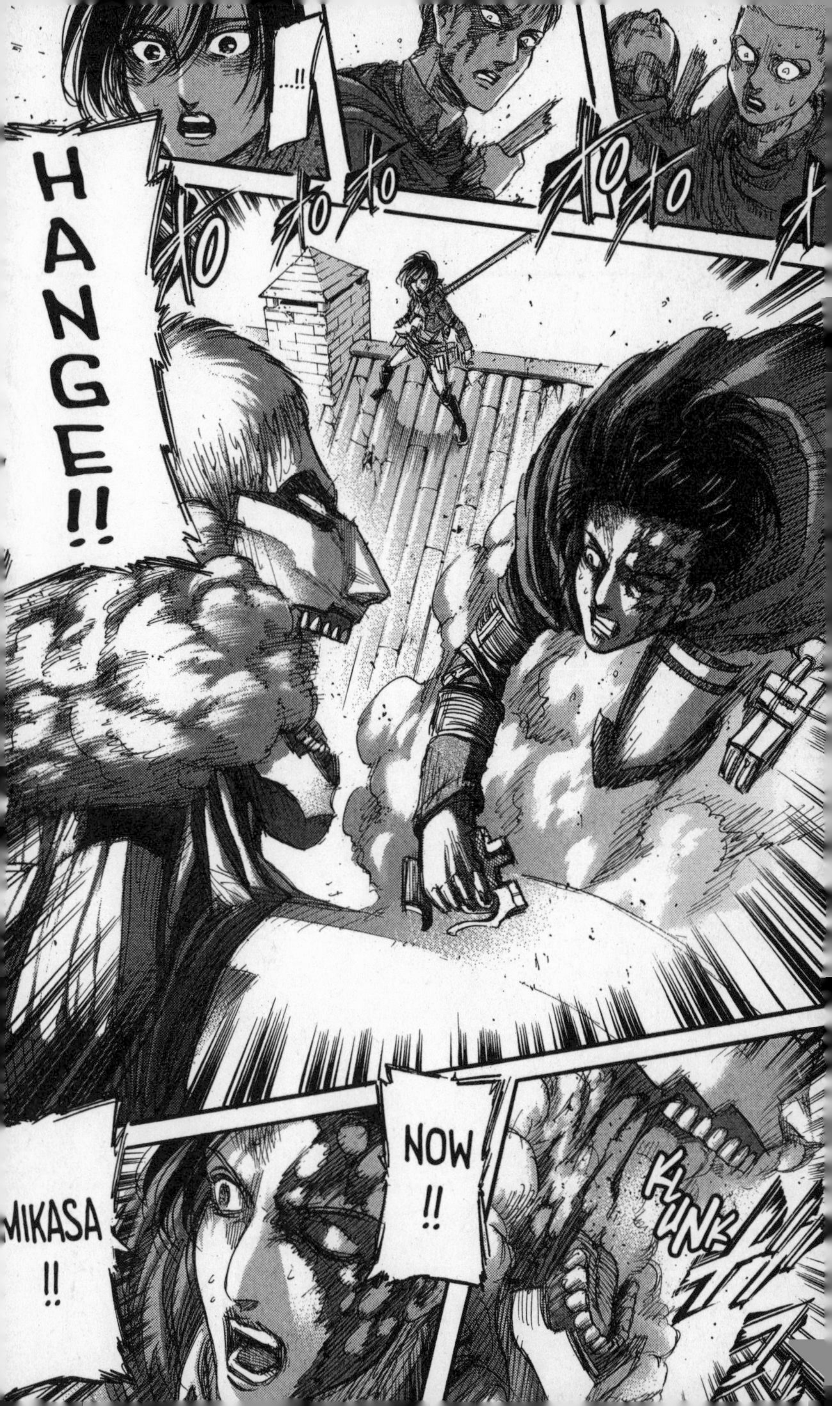

...!!
HANGE!!
KLUNK
NOW!!
MIKASA!!

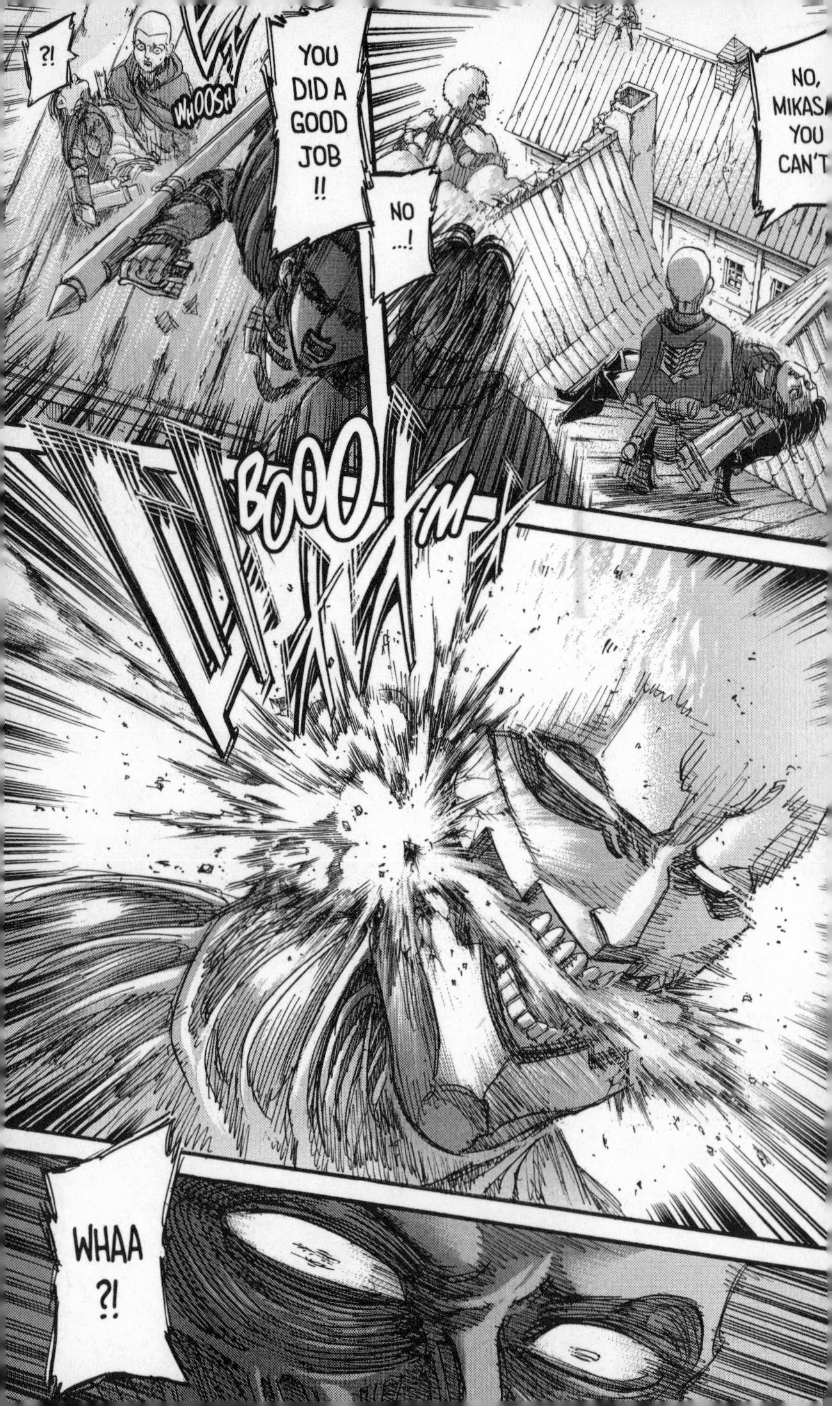
NO, MIKAS YOU CAN'T
NO ...!
YOU DID A GOOD JOB !!
WHOOSH
?!
BOOOM
WHAA ?!

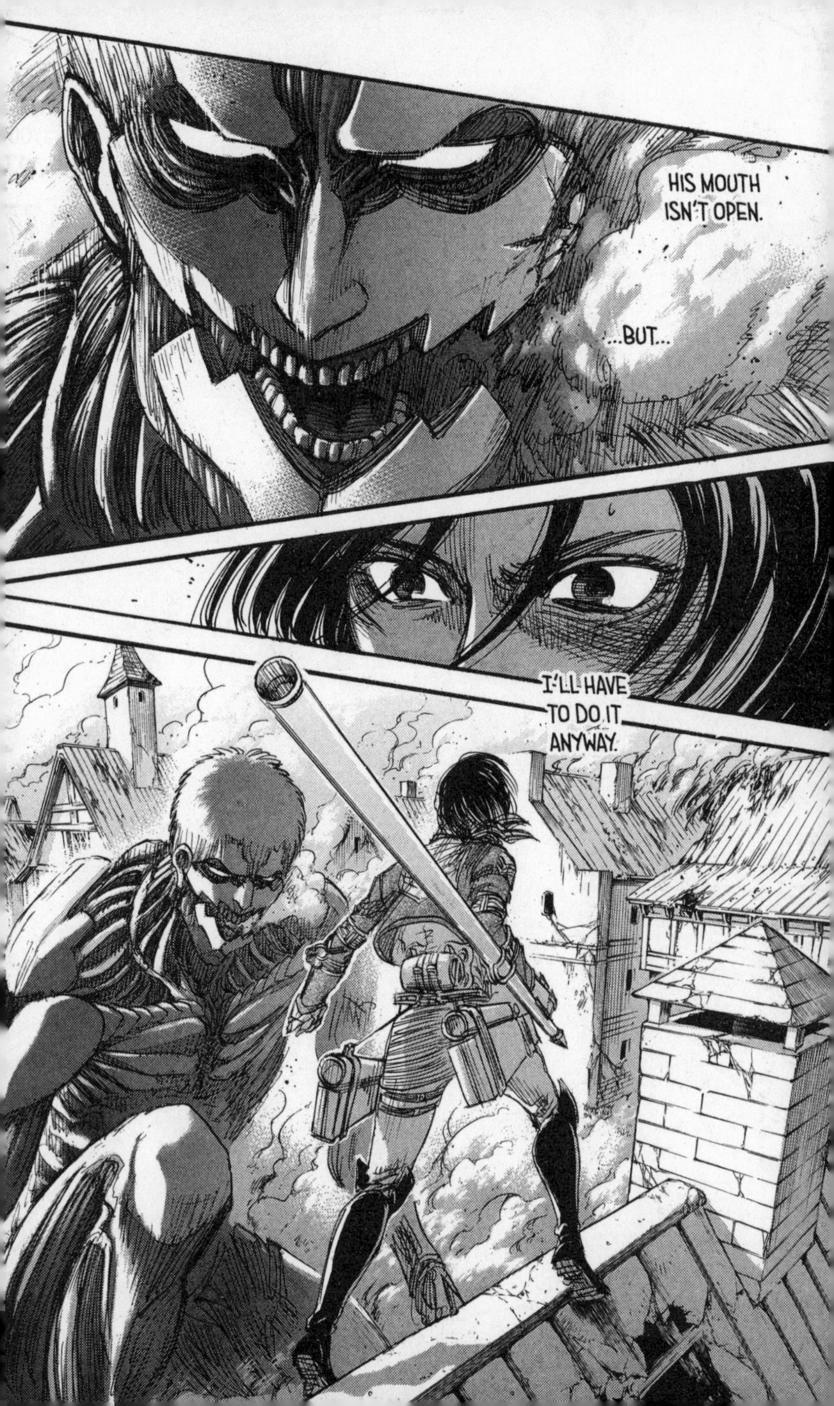
HIS MOUTH ISN'T OPEN.
...BUT...
I'LL HAVE TO DO IT ANYWAY.

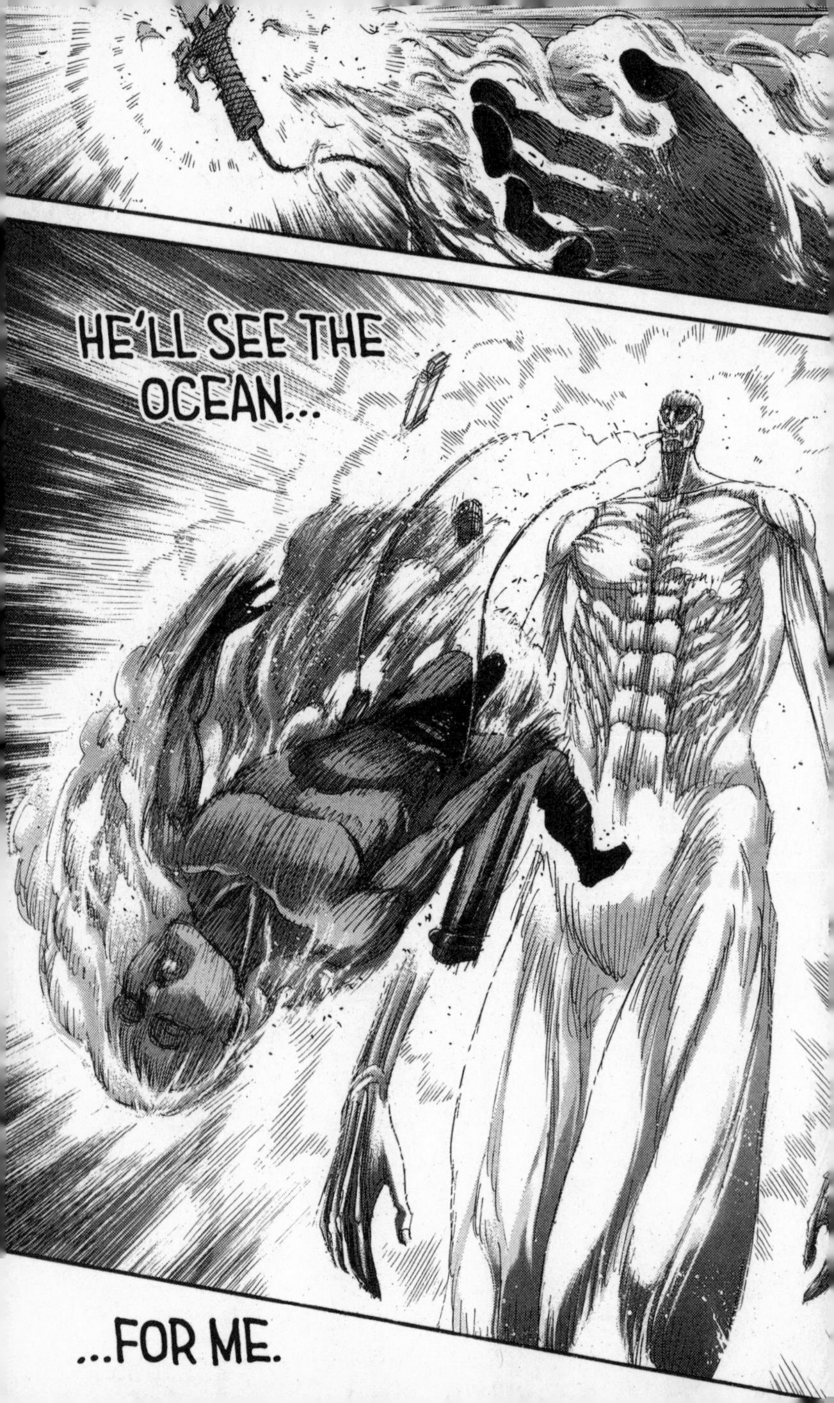
HE'LL SEE THE OCEAN...
...FOR ME.

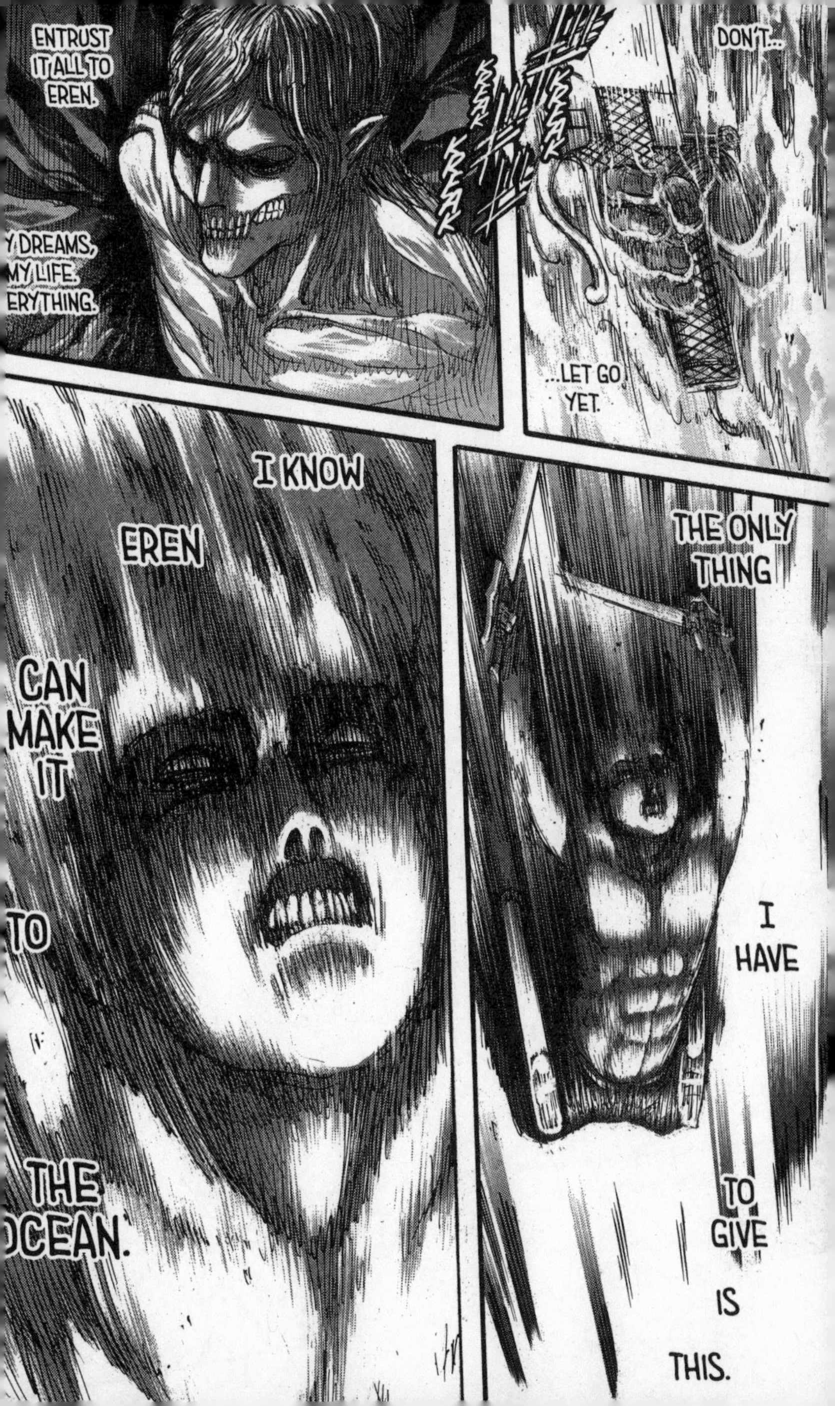
DON'T...
KREAK KREAK
...LET GO YET.
ENTRUST IT ALL TO EREN.
Y DREAMS,
MY LIFE.
ERYTHING.
THE ONLY THING
I HAVE
TO GIVE
IS
THIS.
I KNOW
EREN
CAN MAKE IT
TO
THE OCEAN.

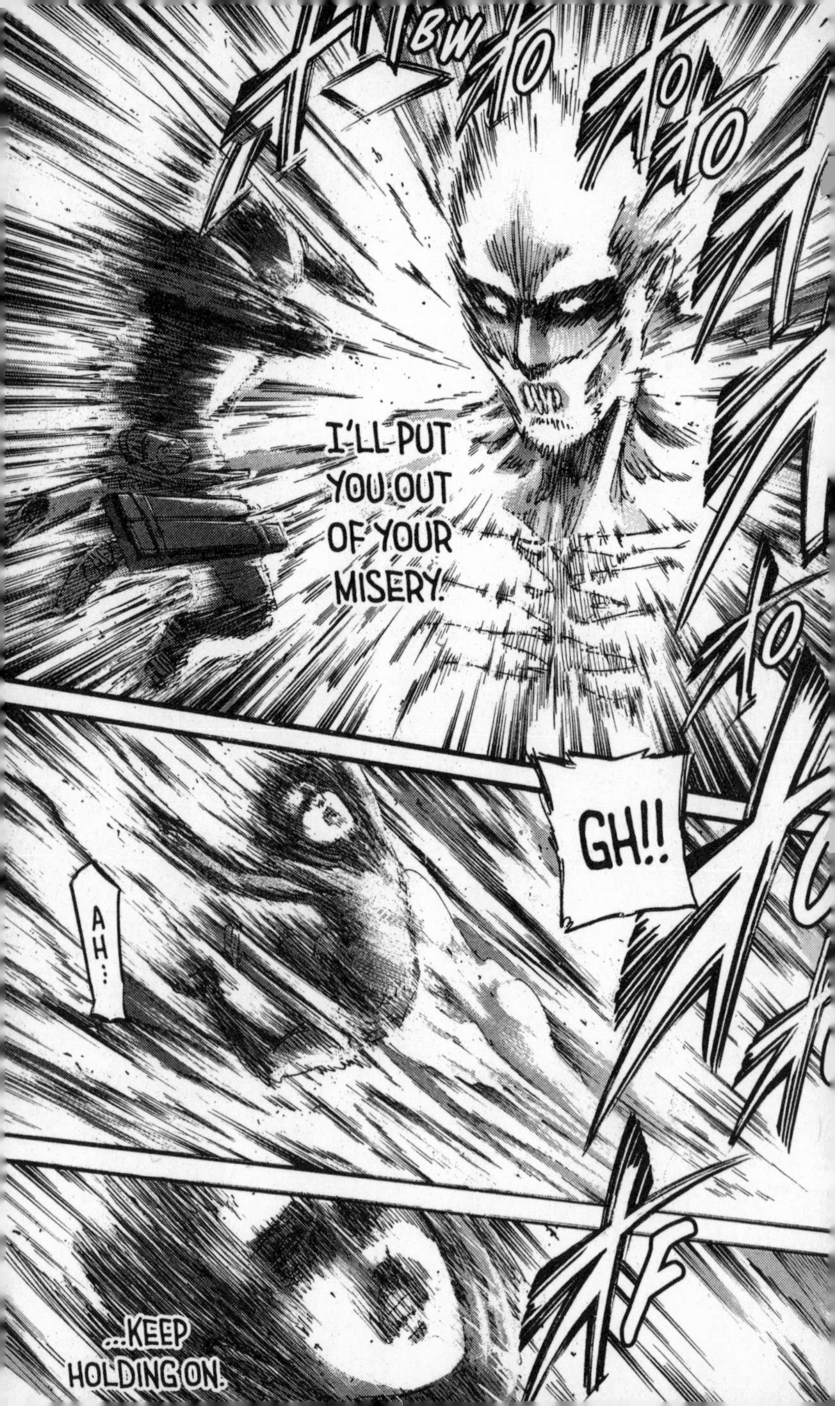
BW
I'LL PUT YOU OUT OF YOUR MISERY.
GH!!
AH...
...KEEP HOLDING ON.

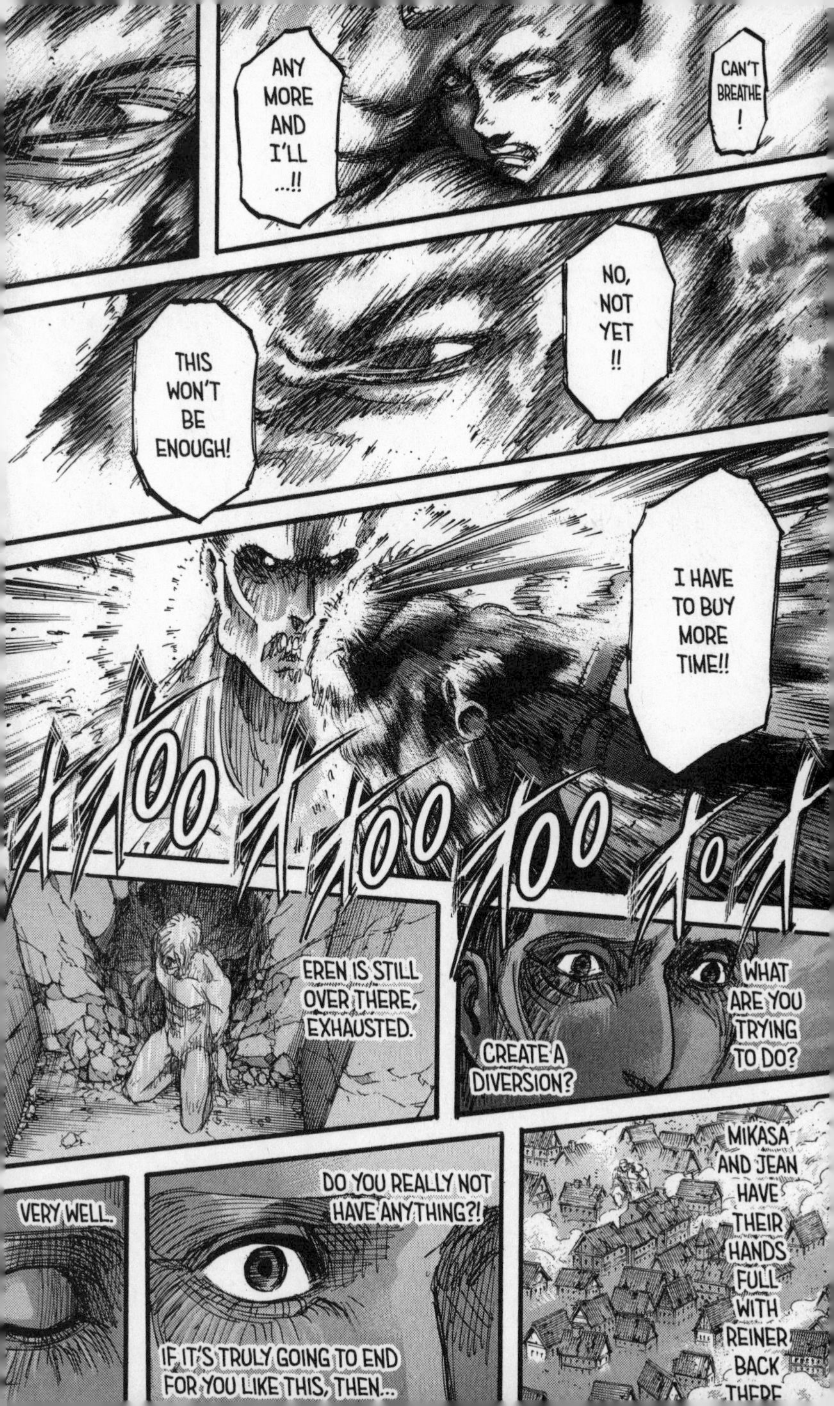
CAN'T BREATHE!
ANY MORE AND I'LL ...!!
NO, NOT YET!!
THIS WON'T BE ENOUGH!
I HAVE TO BUY MORE TIME!!
WHAT ARE YOU TRYING TO DO?
CREATE A DIVERSION?
EREN IS STILL OVER THERE, EXHAUSTED.
MIKASA AND JEAN HAVE THEIR HANDS FULL WITH REINER BACK THERE
DO YOU REALLY NOT HAVE ANYTHING?!
IF IT'S TRULY GOING TO END FOR YOU LIKE THIS, THEN...
VERY WELL.

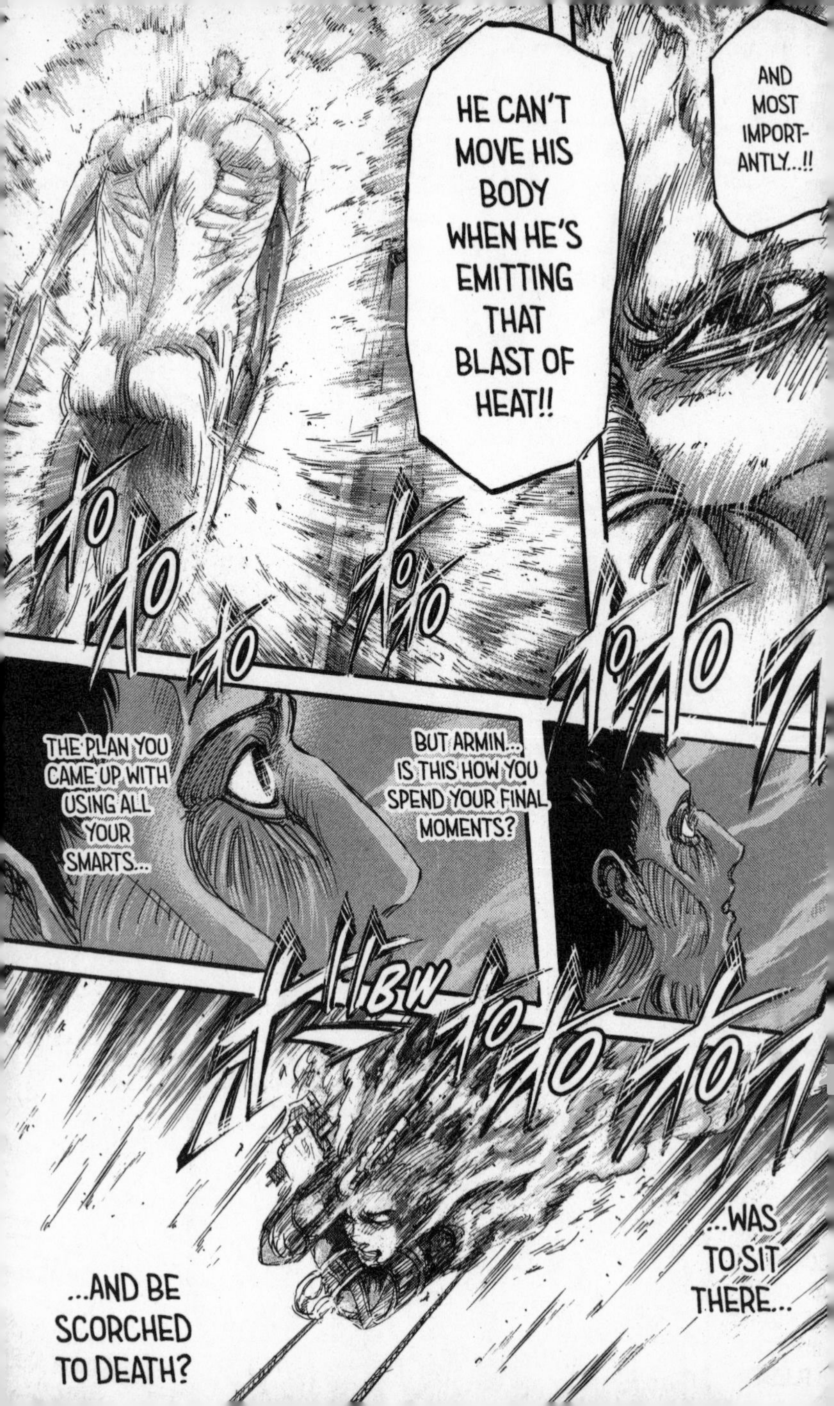
AND MOST IMPORT-ANTLY...!!
HE CAN'T MOVE HIS BODY WHEN HE'S EMITTING THAT BLAST OF HEAT!!
BUT ARMIN... IS THIS HOW YOU SPEND YOUR FINAL MOMENTS?
THE PLAN YOU CAME UP WITH USING ALL YOUR SMARTS...
...WAS TO SIT THERE...
...AND BE SCORCHED TO DEATH?

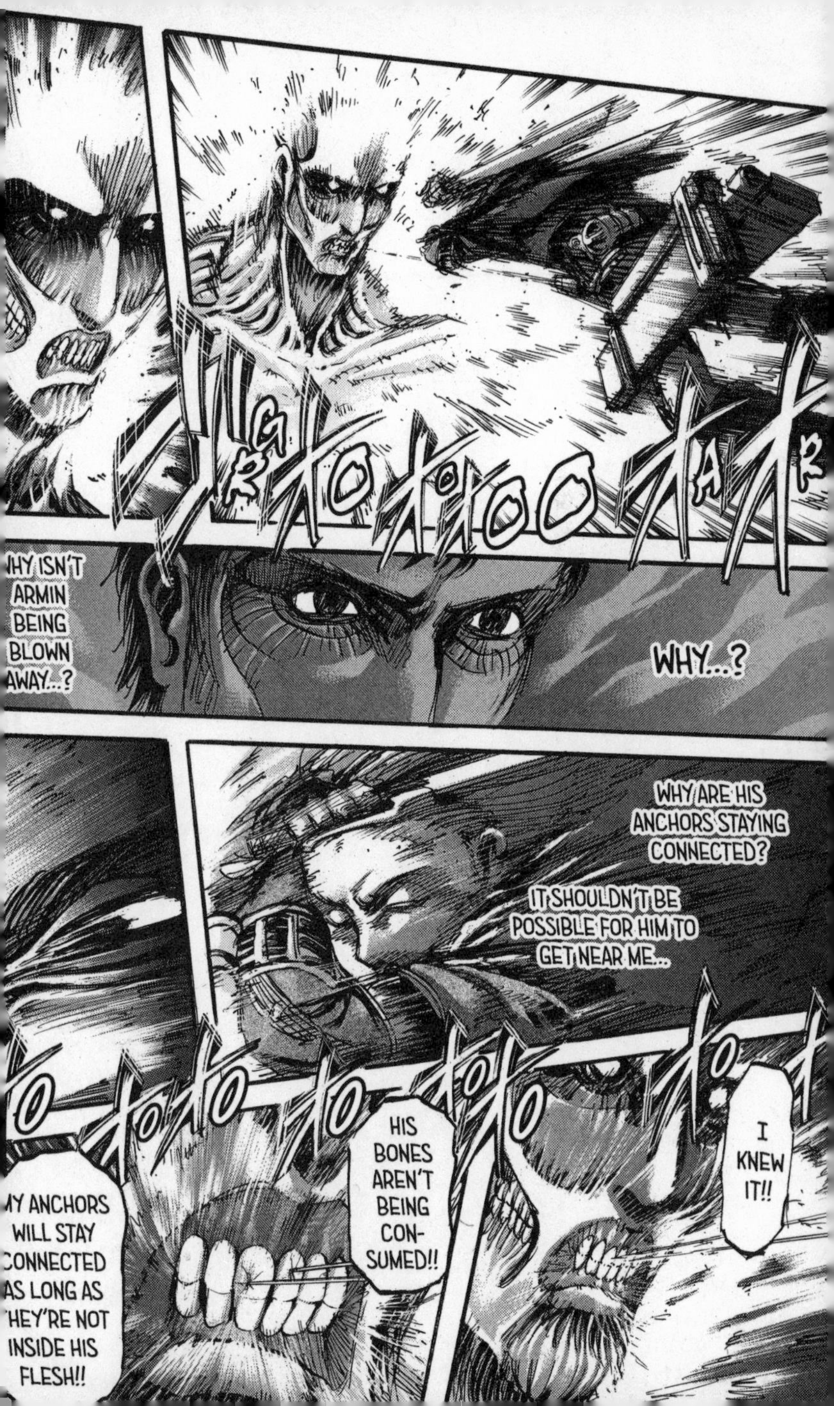
WHY...?
HY ISN'T ARMIN BEING BLOWN AWAY...?
WHY ARE HIS ANCHORS STAYING CONNECTED?
IT SHOULDN'T BE POSSIBLE FOR HIM TO GET NEAR ME...
I KNEW IT!!
HIS BONES AREN'T BEING CON-SUMED!!
MY ANCHORS WILL STAY CONNECTED AS LONG AS THEY'RE NOT INSIDE HIS FLESH!!

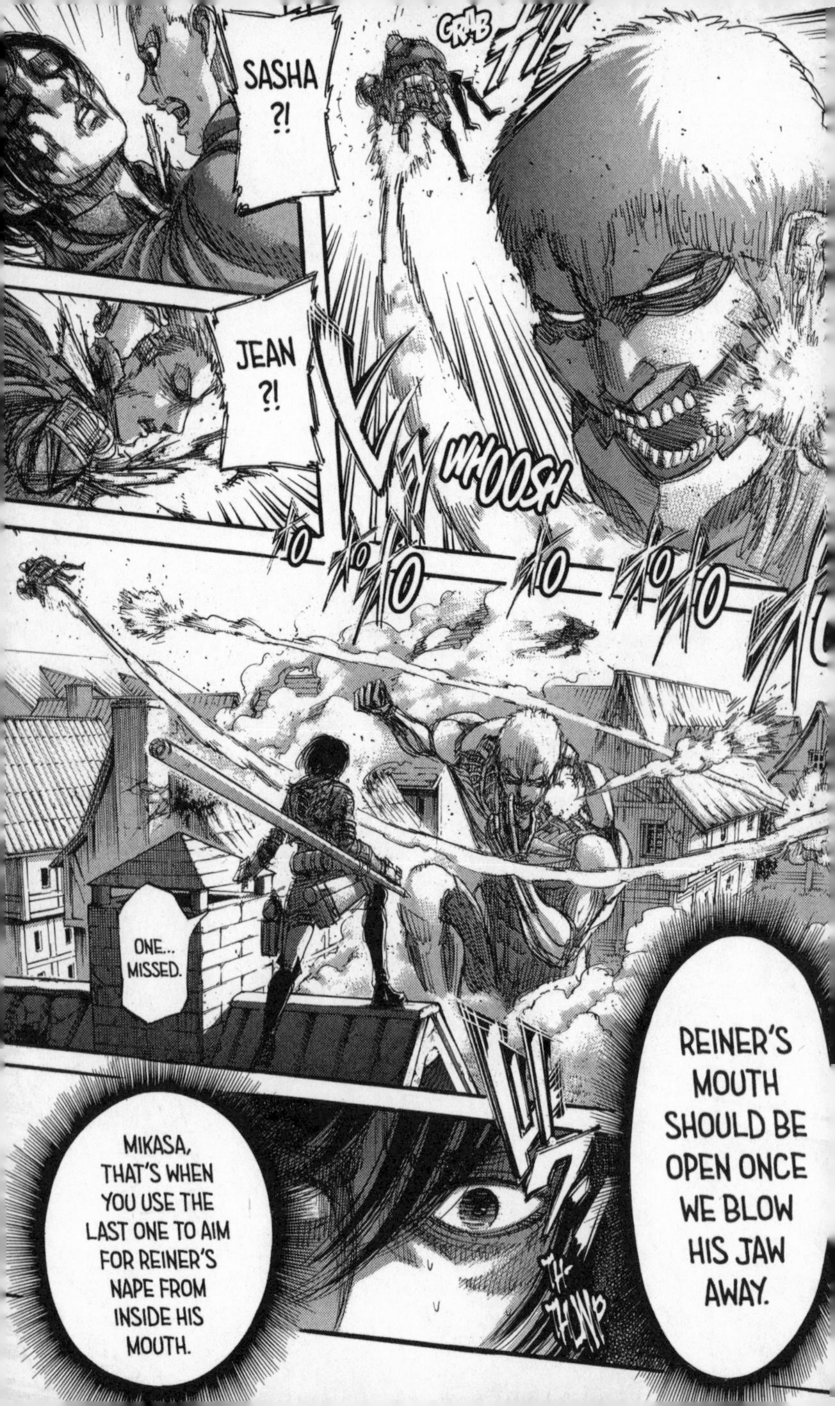
SASHA ?!
GRAB
JEAN ?!
WHOOSH
FOOM
ONE... MISSED.
REINER'S MOUTH SHOULD BE OPEN ONCE WE BLOW HIS JAW AWAY.
MIKASA, THAT'S WHEN YOU USE THE LAST ONE TO AIM FOR REINER'S NAPE FROM INSIDE HIS MOUTH.
TH-THUMP

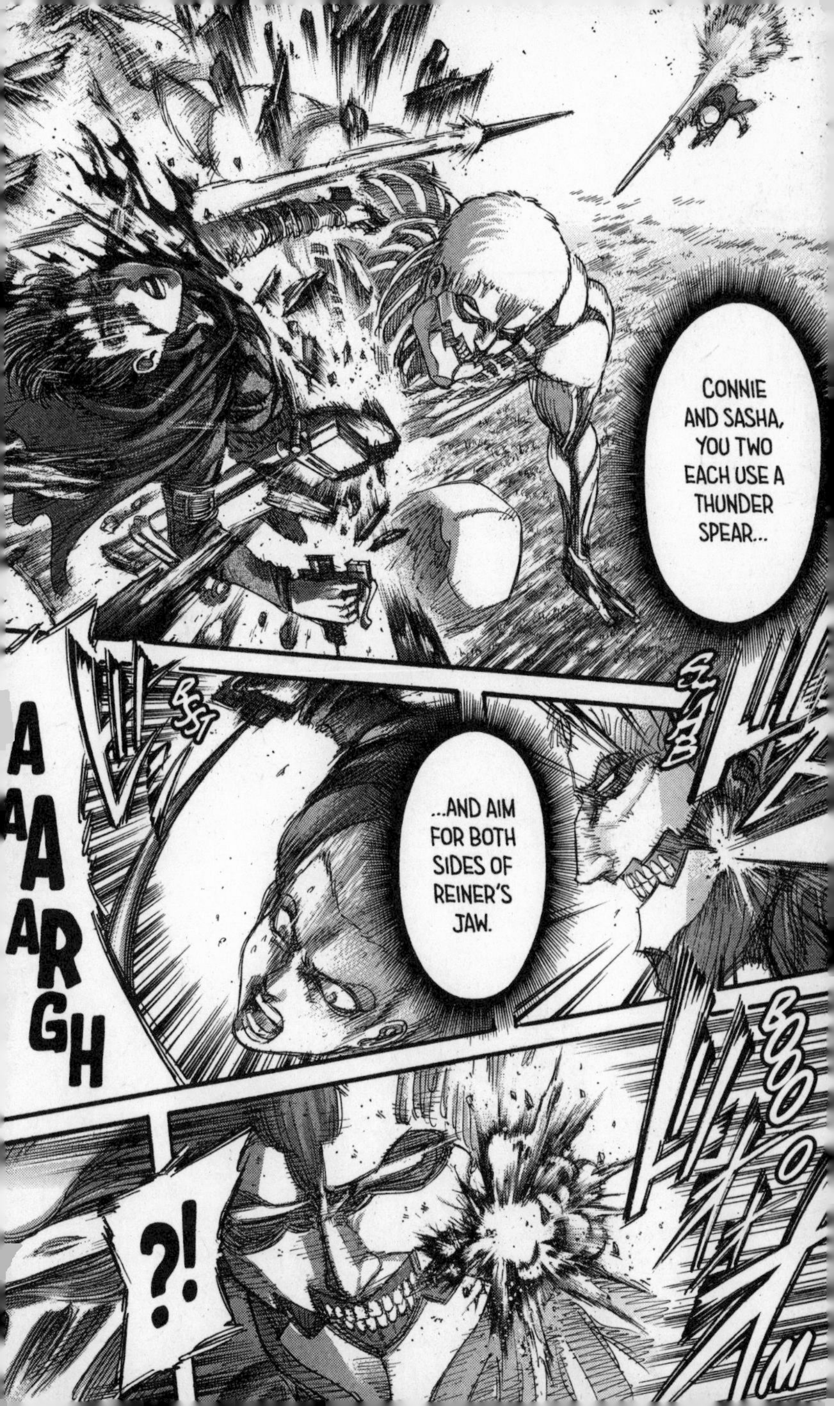
CONNIE AND SASHA, YOU TWO EACH USE A THUNDER SPEAR...
...AND AIM FOR BOTH SIDES OF REINER'S JAW.
AAAARGH
BOOOOM
?!

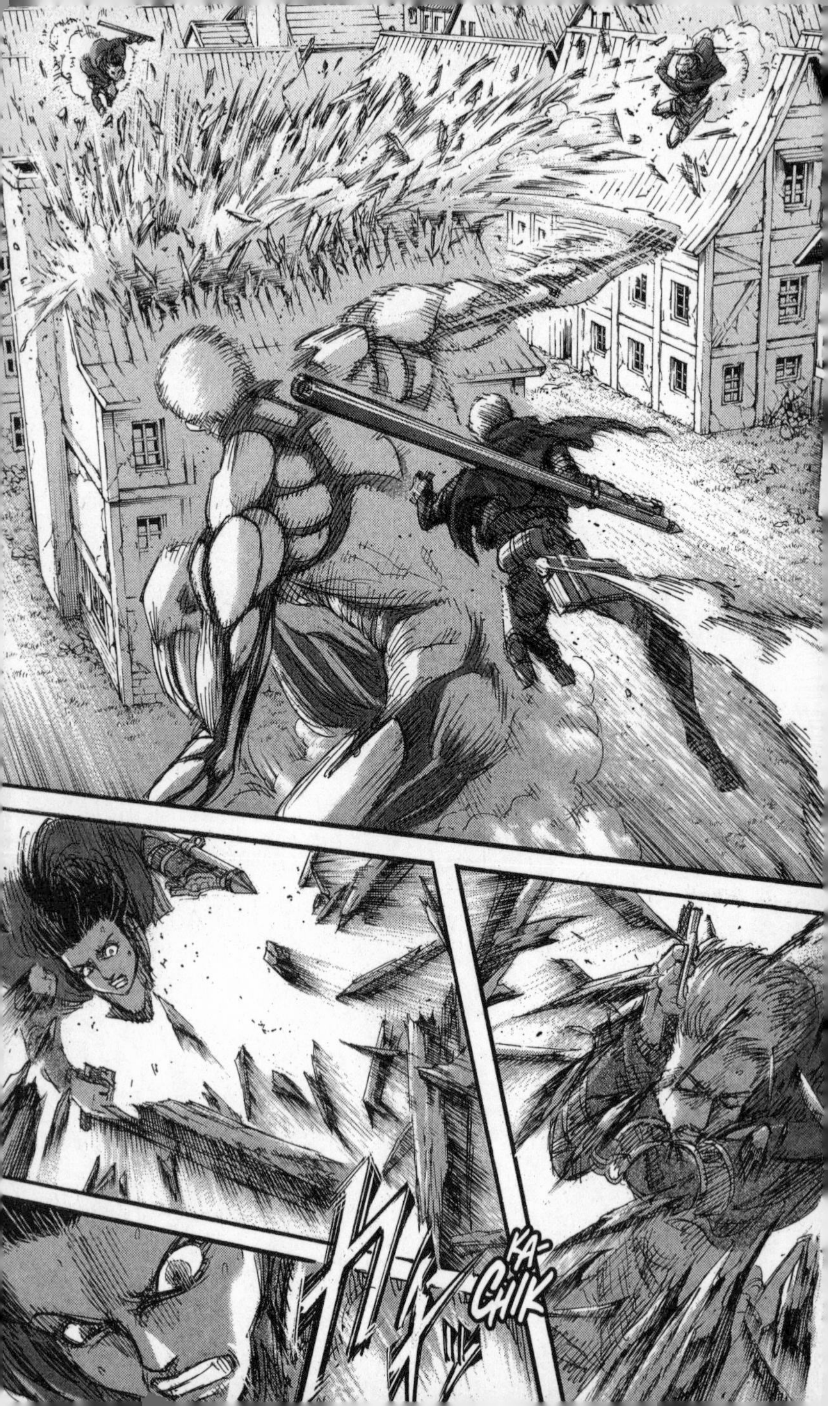
KA-
CHIK

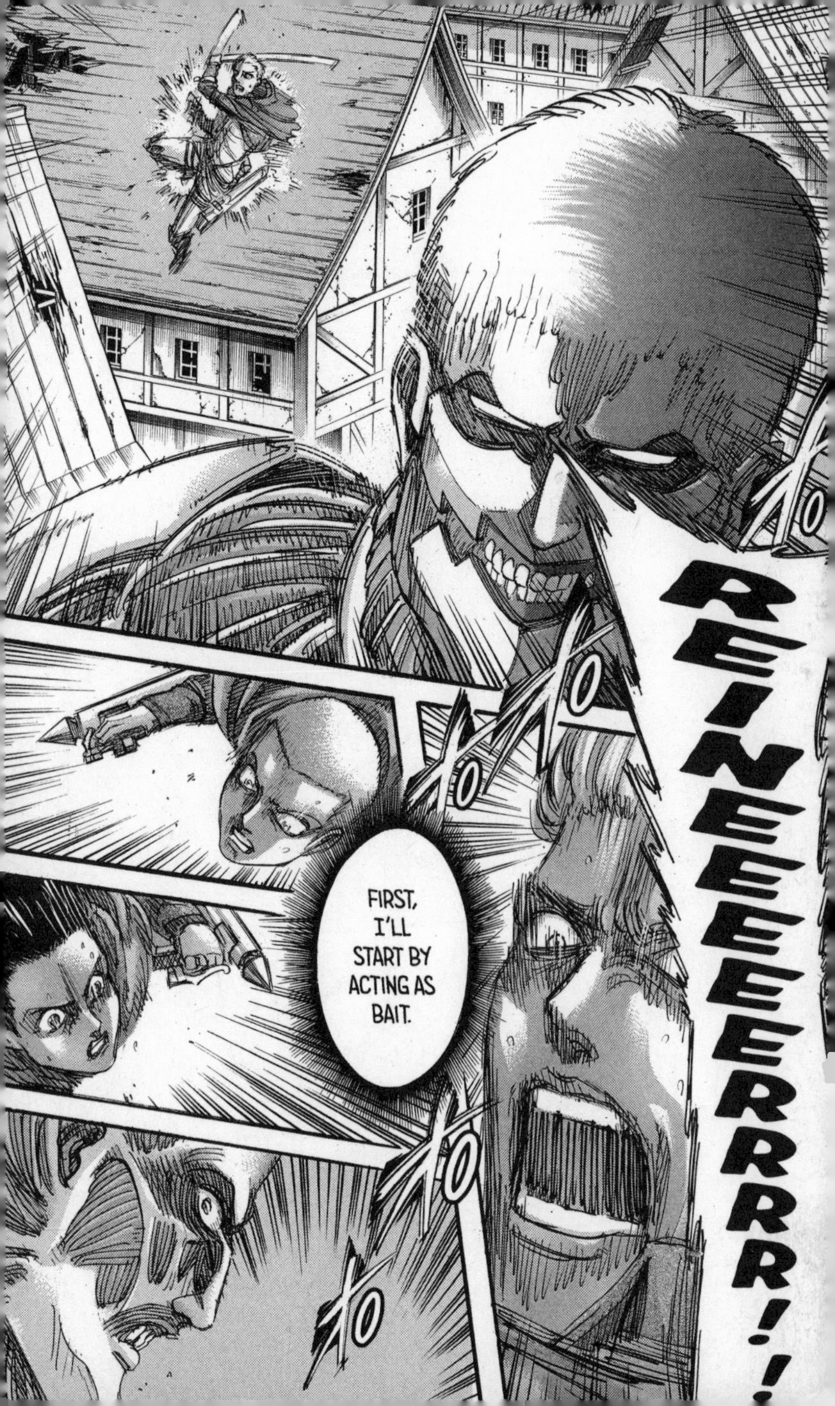

REINEEEERRRR!!
FIRST, I'LL START BY ACTING AS BAIT.

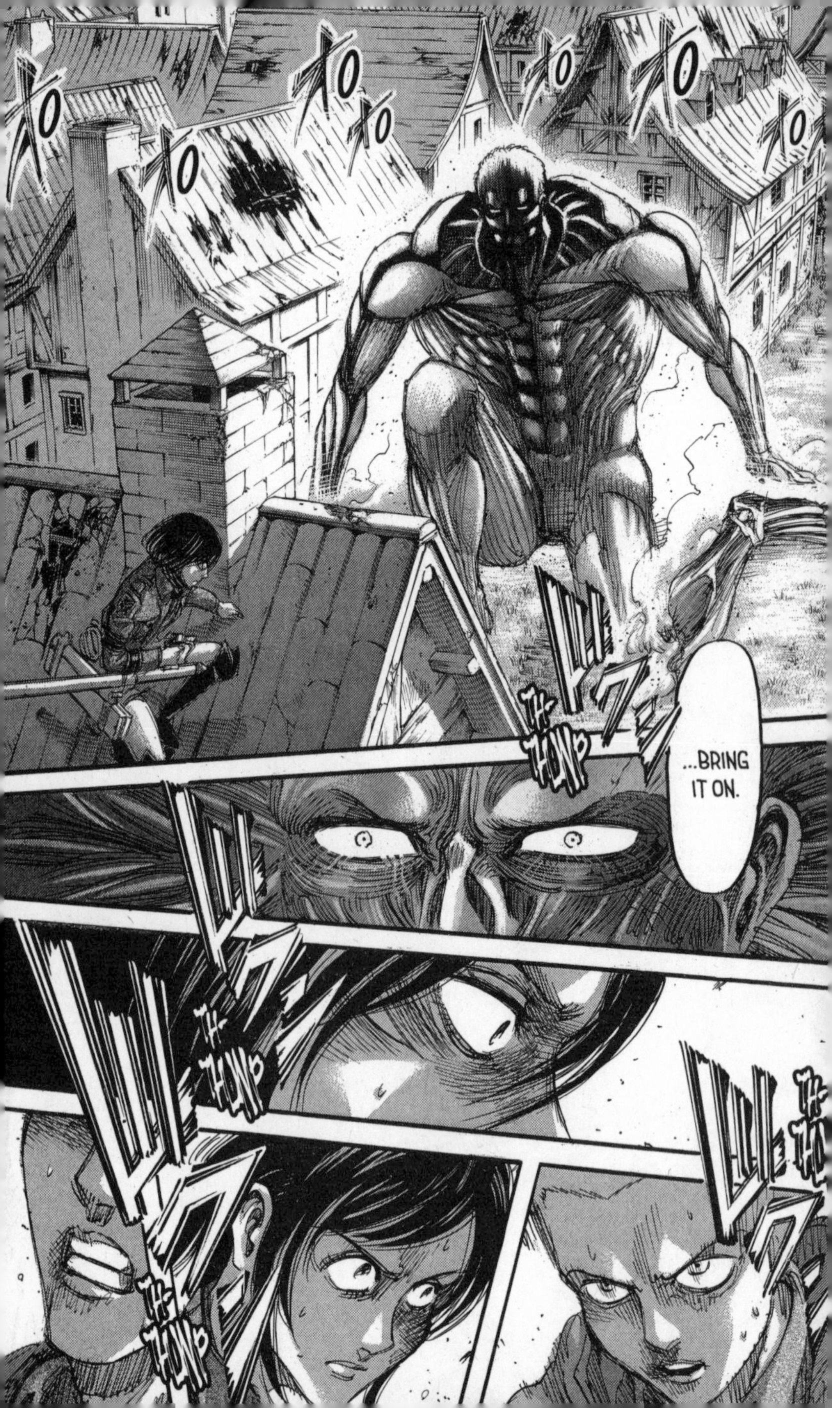
...BRING IT ON.
TH-THOMP
TH-THOMP
TH-THOMP
TH-THOMP

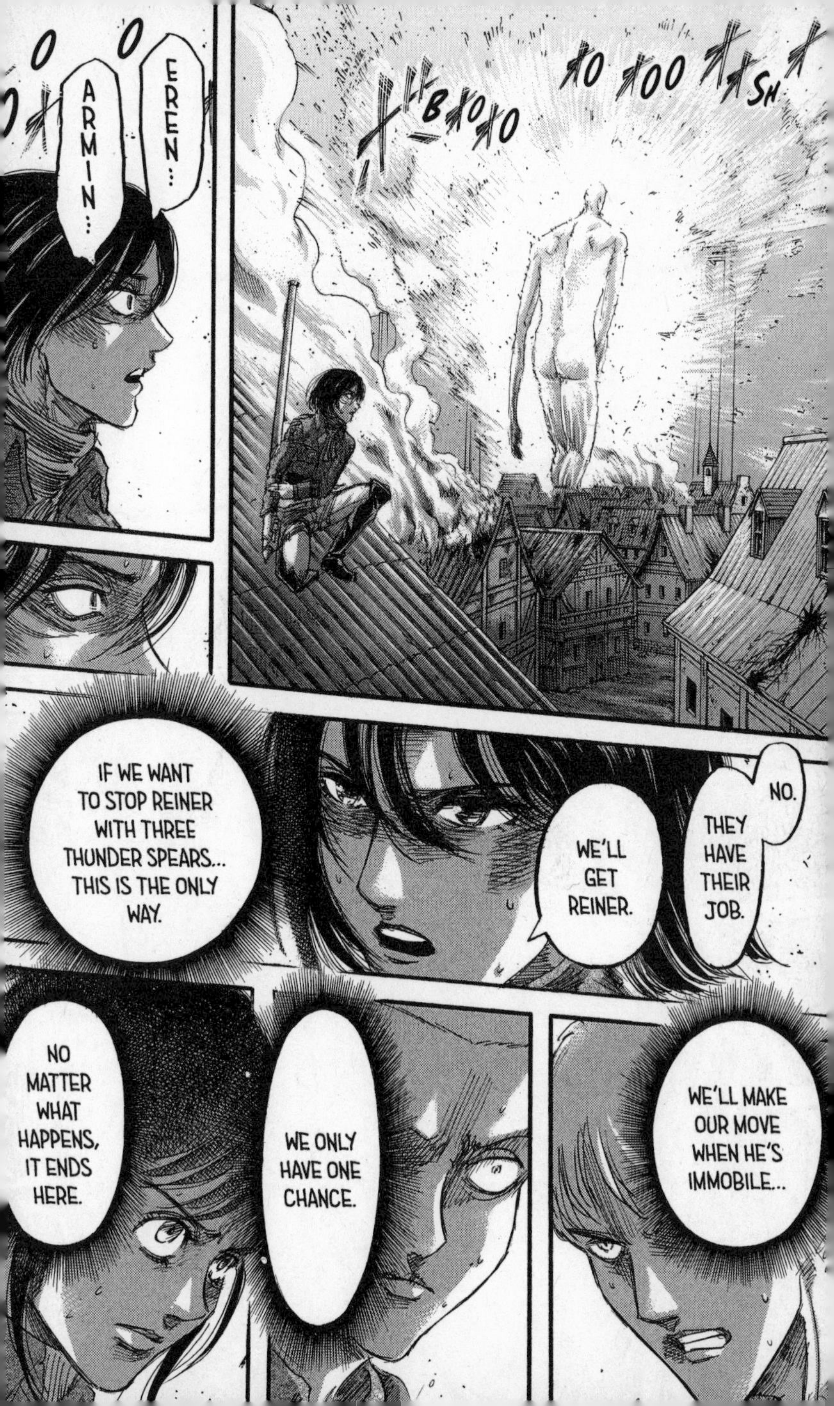
EREN...
ARMIN...
NO.
THEY HAVE THEIR JOB.
WE'LL GET REINER.
IF WE WANT TO STOP REINER WITH THREE THUNDER SPEARS... THIS IS THE ONLY WAY.
WE'LL MAKE OUR MOVE WHEN HE'S IMMOBILE...
WE ONLY HAVE ONE CHANCE.
NO MATTER WHAT HAPPENS, IT ENDS HERE.

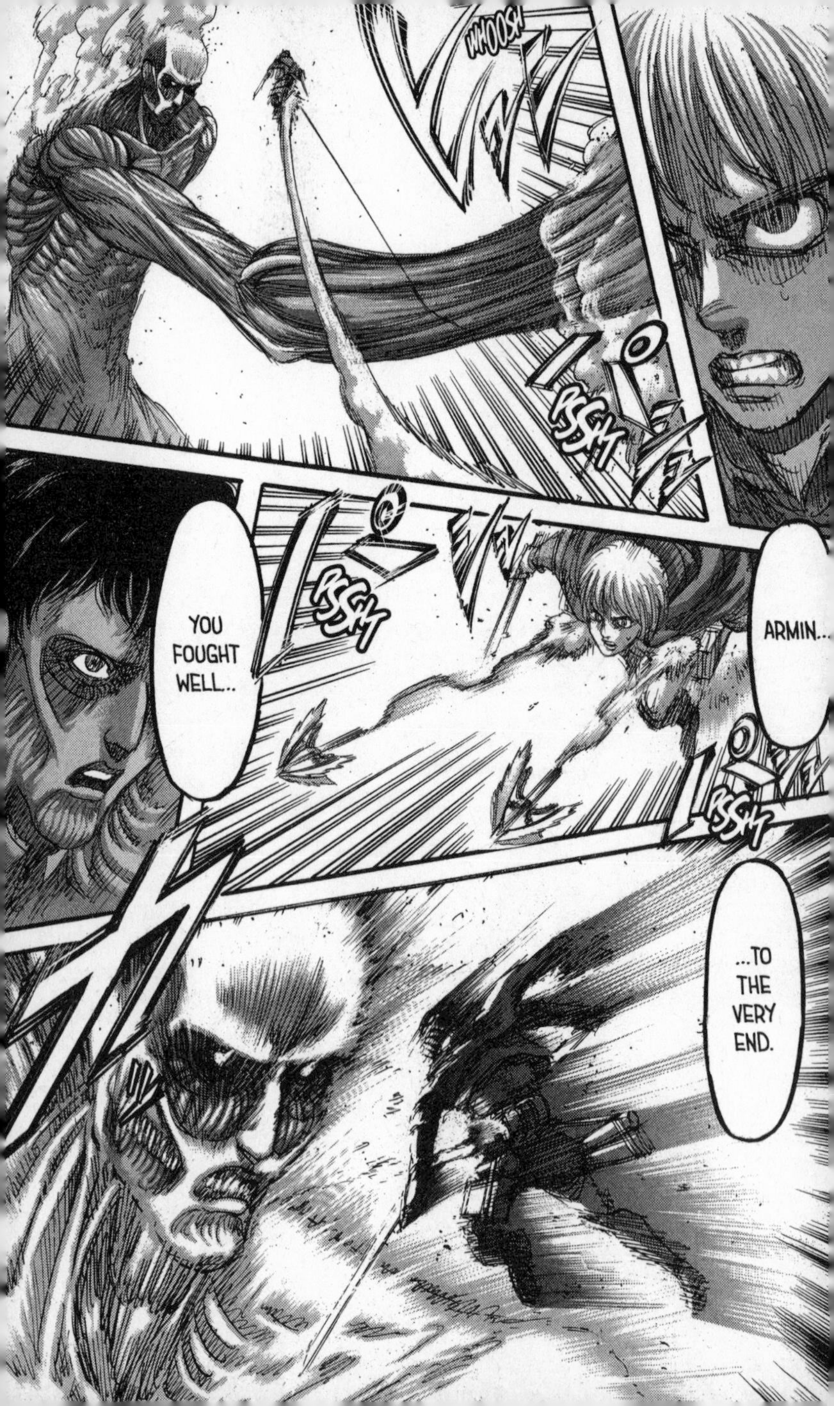
WHOOSH
PSSH
ARMIN...
PSSH
PSSH
YOU FOUGHT WELL..
...TO THE VERY END.

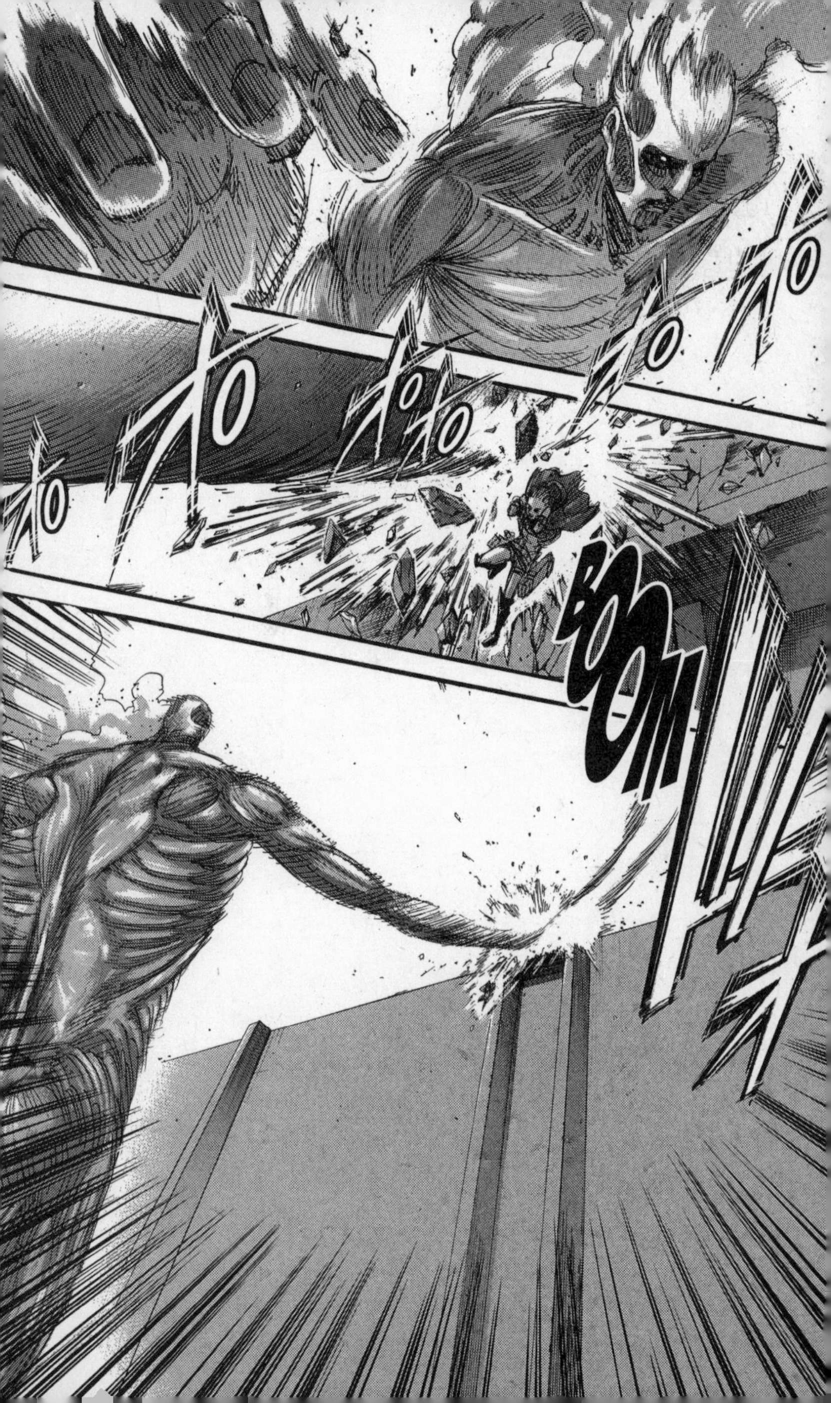
BOOM

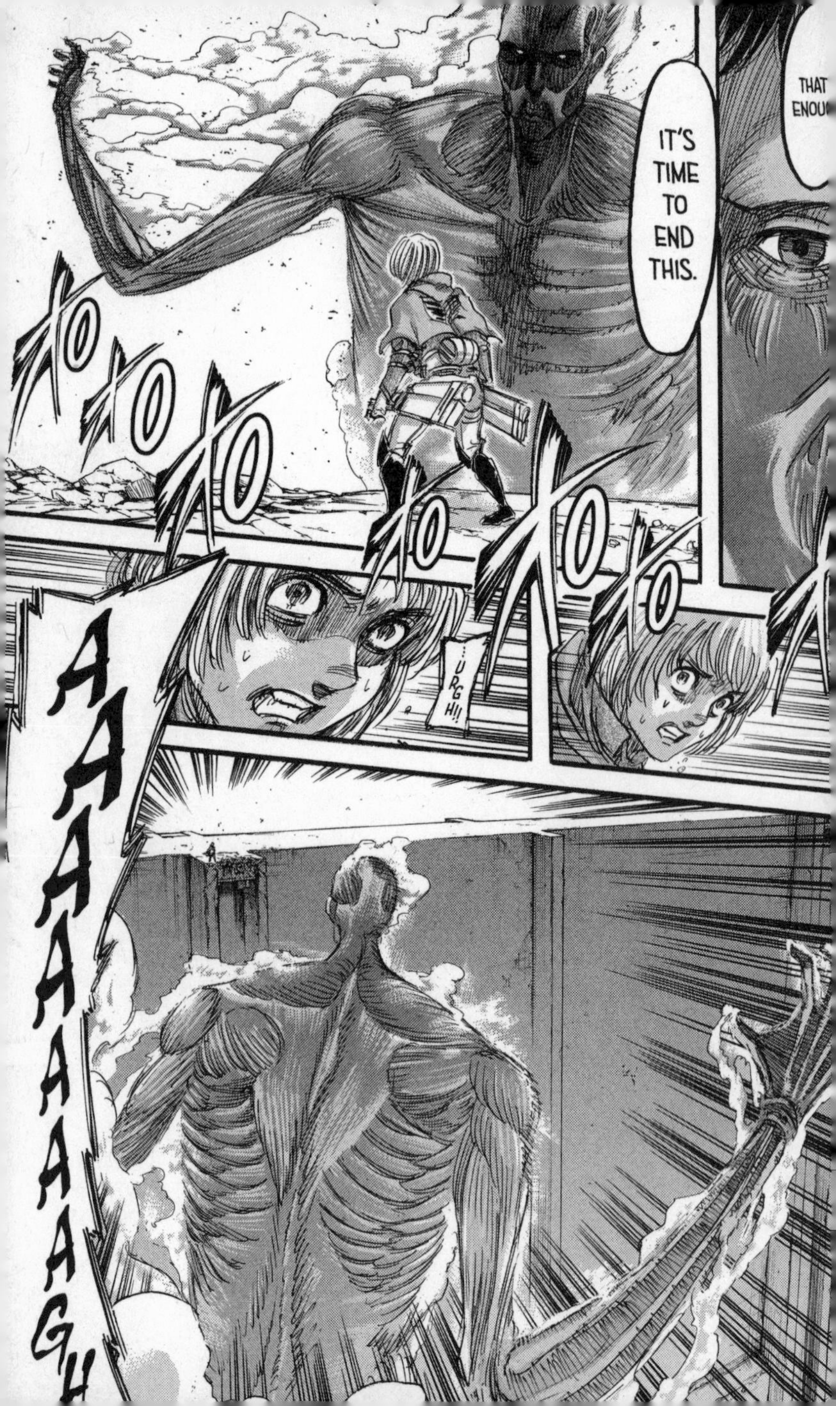
THAT ENOU
IT'S TIME TO END THIS.
...URGH!!
AAAAAAAGH

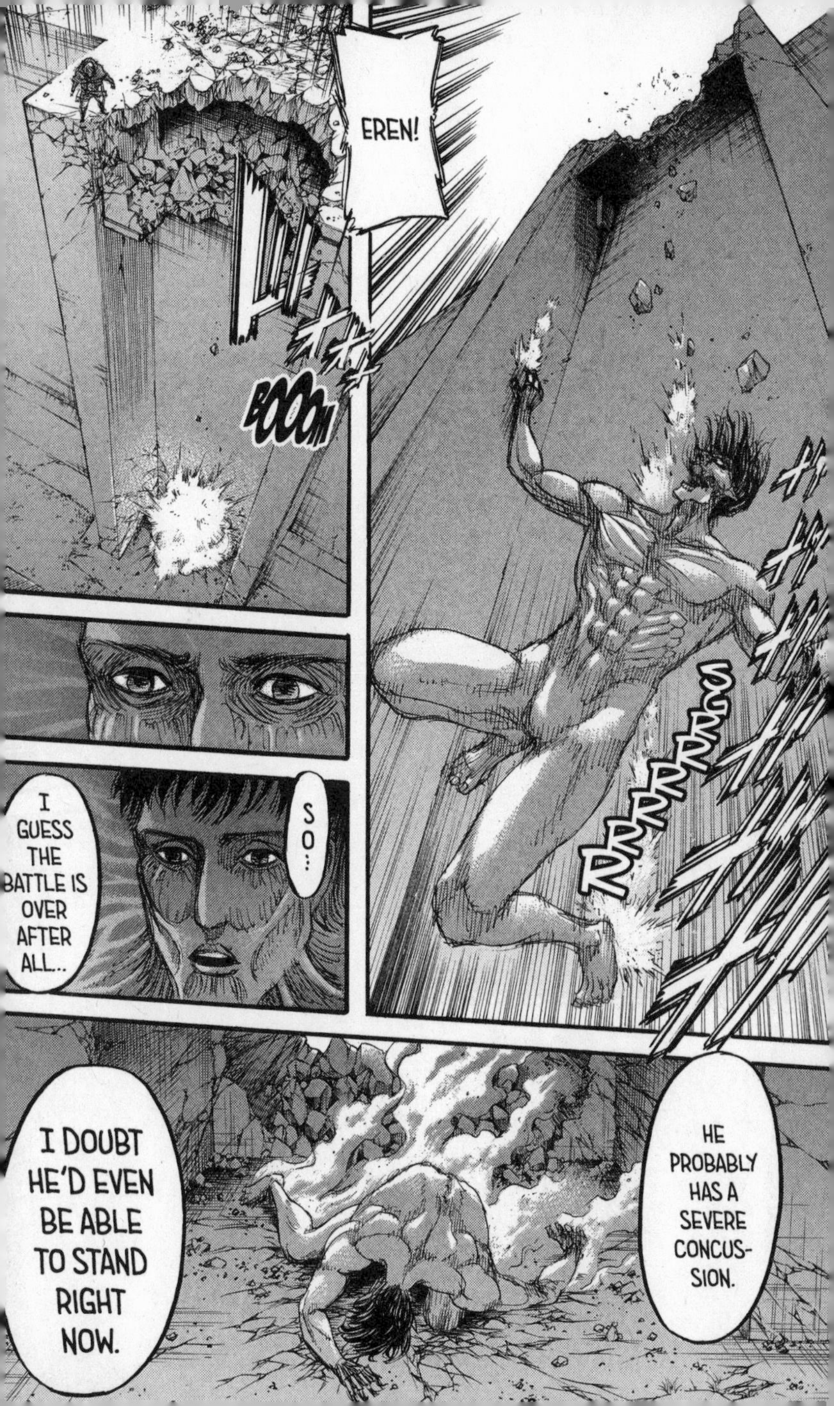
EREN!
BOOOM
SO...
I GUESS THE BATTLE IS OVER AFTER ALL...
HE PROBABLY HAS A SEVERE CONCUS-SION.
I DOUBT HE'D EVEN BE ABLE TO STAND RIGHT NOW.

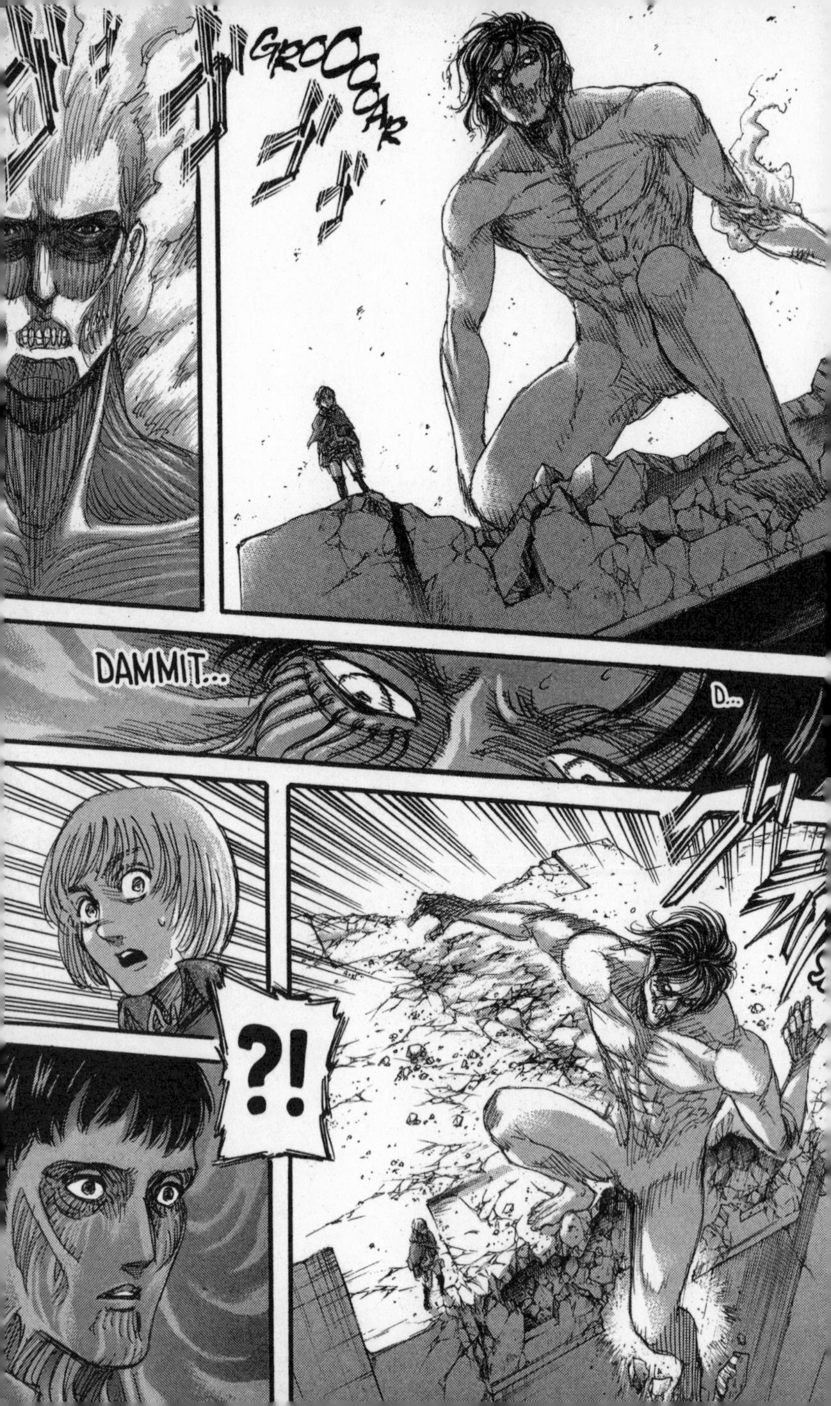
GROOOOOAR
D...
DAMMIT...
?!

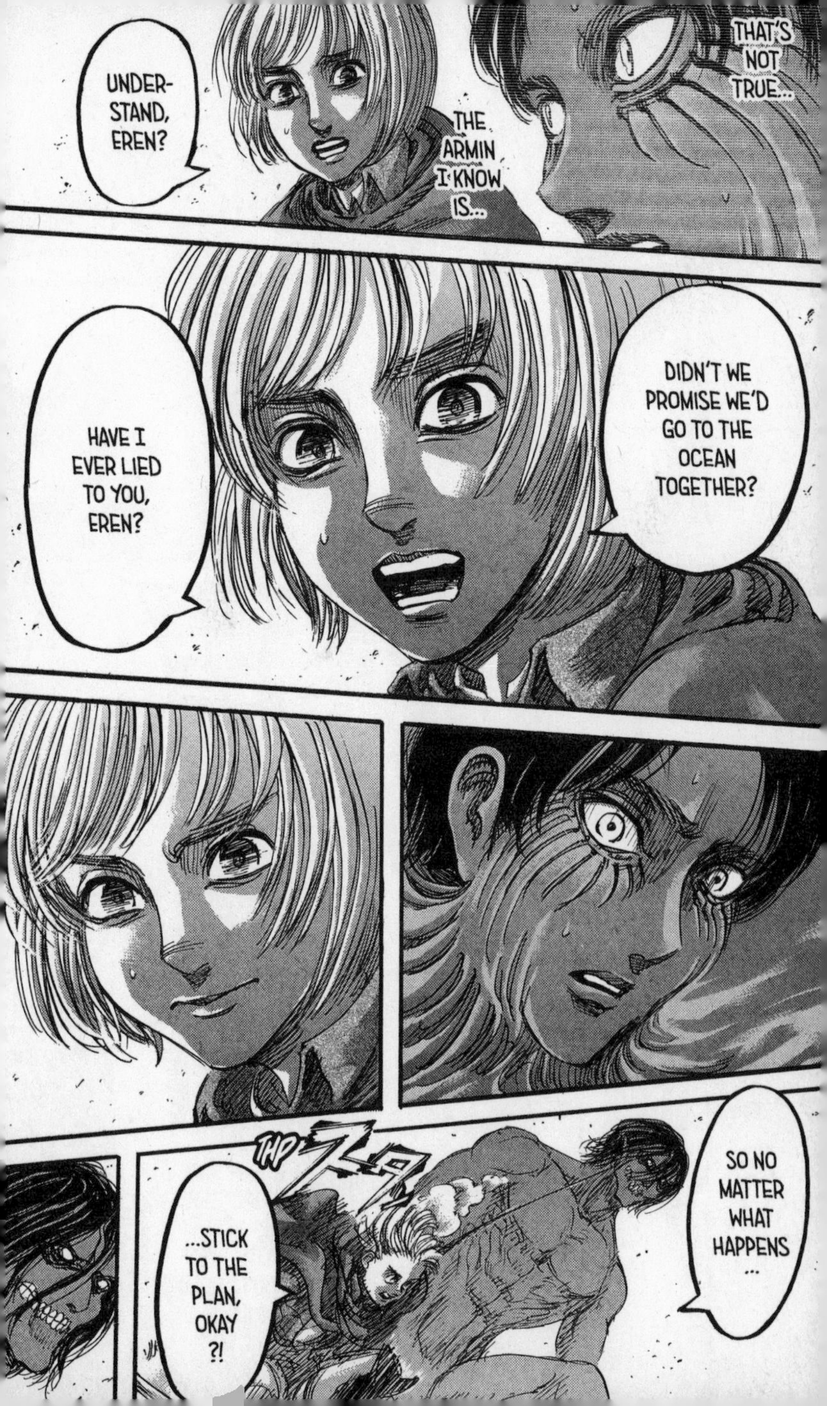
THAT'S NOT TRUE...
THE ARMIN I KNOW IS...
UNDER-STAND, EREN?
DIDN'T WE PROMISE WE'D GO TO THE OCEAN TOGETHER?
HAVE I EVER LIED TO YOU, EREN?
SO NO MATTER WHAT HAPPENS ...
THP
...STICK TO THE PLAN, OKAY ?!

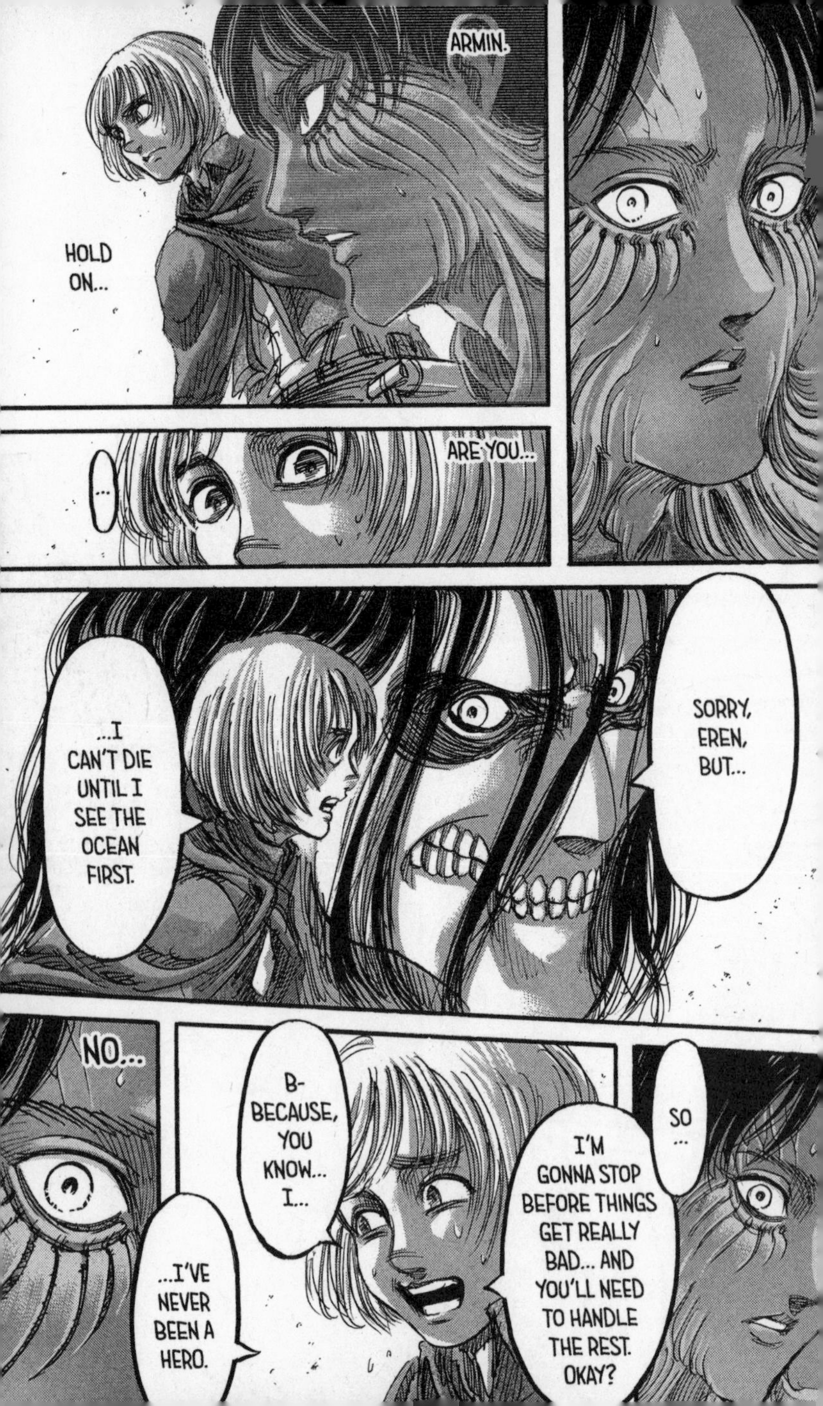
ARMIN.
HOLD ON...
ARE YOU...
...
SORRY, EREN, BUT...
...I CAN'T DIE UNTIL I SEE THE OCEAN FIRST.
SO...
B- BECAUSE, YOU KNOW... I...
I'M GONNA STOP BEFORE THINGS GET REALLY BAD... AND YOU'LL NEED TO HANDLE THE REST. OKAY?
NO...
...I'VE NEVER BEEN A HERO.

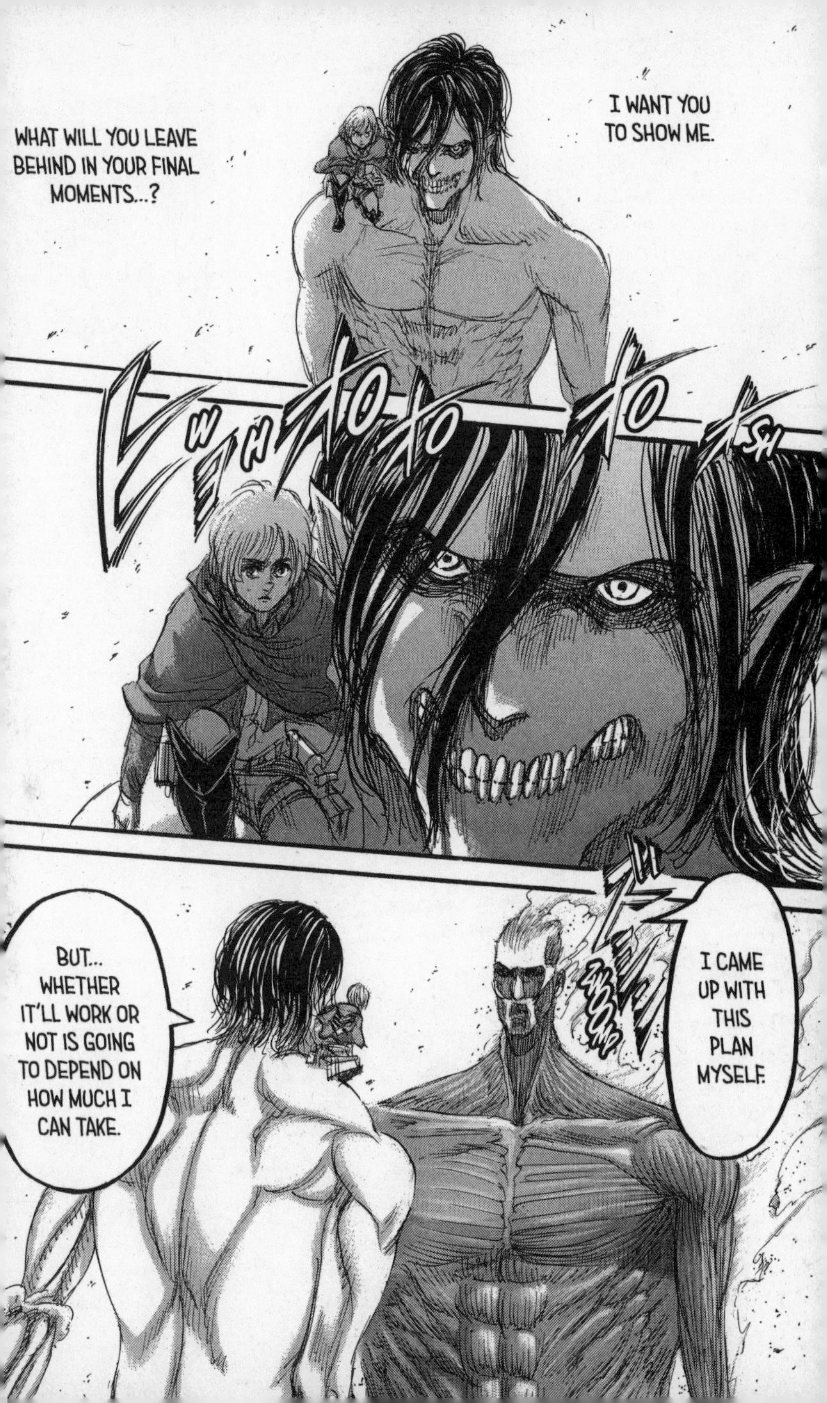
I WANT YOU TO SHOW ME.
WHAT WILL YOU LEAVE BEHIND IN YOUR FINAL MOMENTS...?
I CAME UP WITH THIS PLAN MYSELF.
BUT... WHETHER IT'LL WORK OR NOT IS GOING TO DEPEND ON HOW MUCH I CAN TAKE.

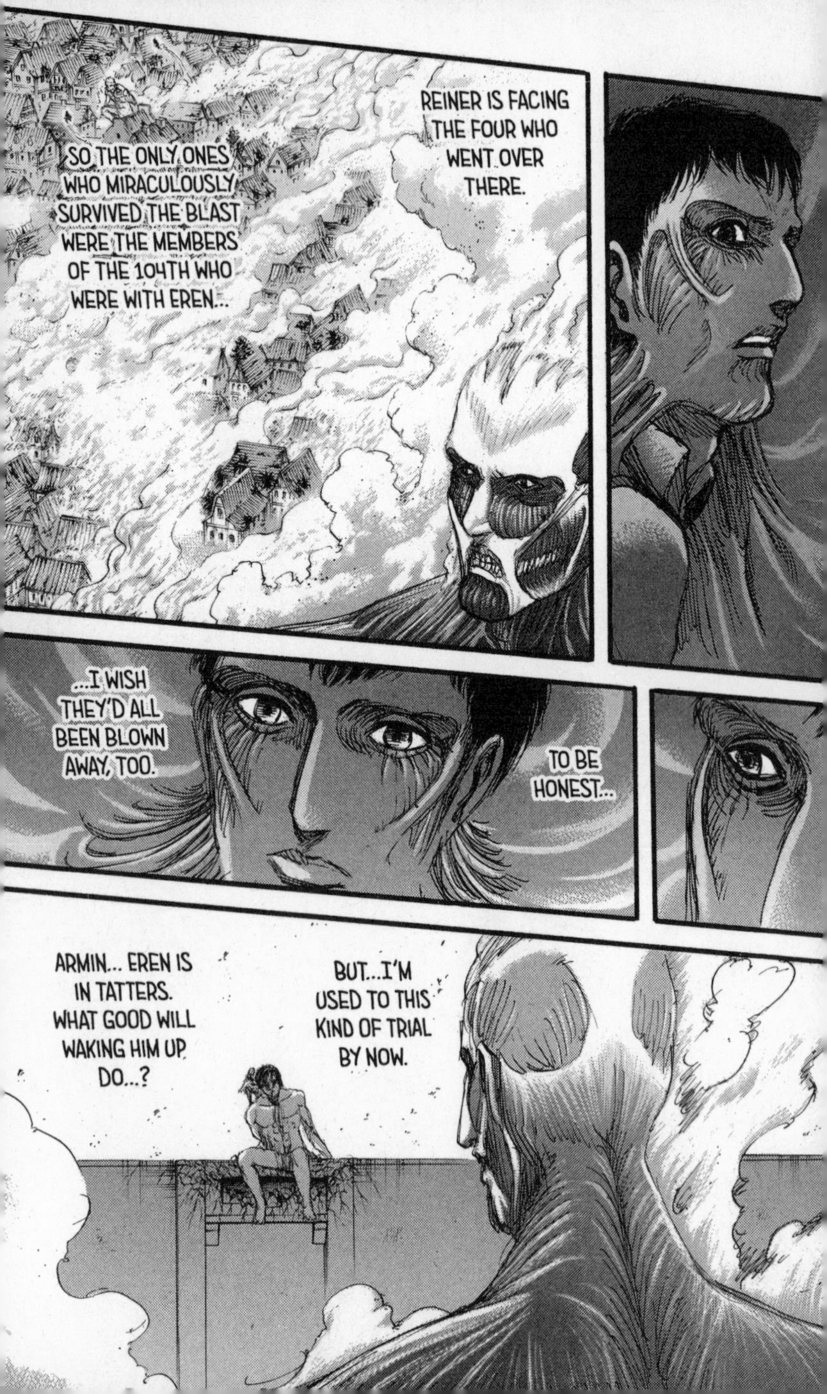
REINER IS FACING THE FOUR WHO WENT OVER THERE.
SO THE ONLY ONES WHO MIRACULOUSLY SURVIVED THE BLAST WERE THE MEMBERS OF THE 104TH WHO WERE WITH EREN...
TO BE HONEST...
...I WISH THEY'D ALL BEEN BLOWN AWAY, TOO.
BUT...I'M USED TO THIS KIND OF TRIAL BY NOW.
ARMIN... EREN IS IN TATTERS. WHAT GOOD WILL WAKING HIM UP DO...?

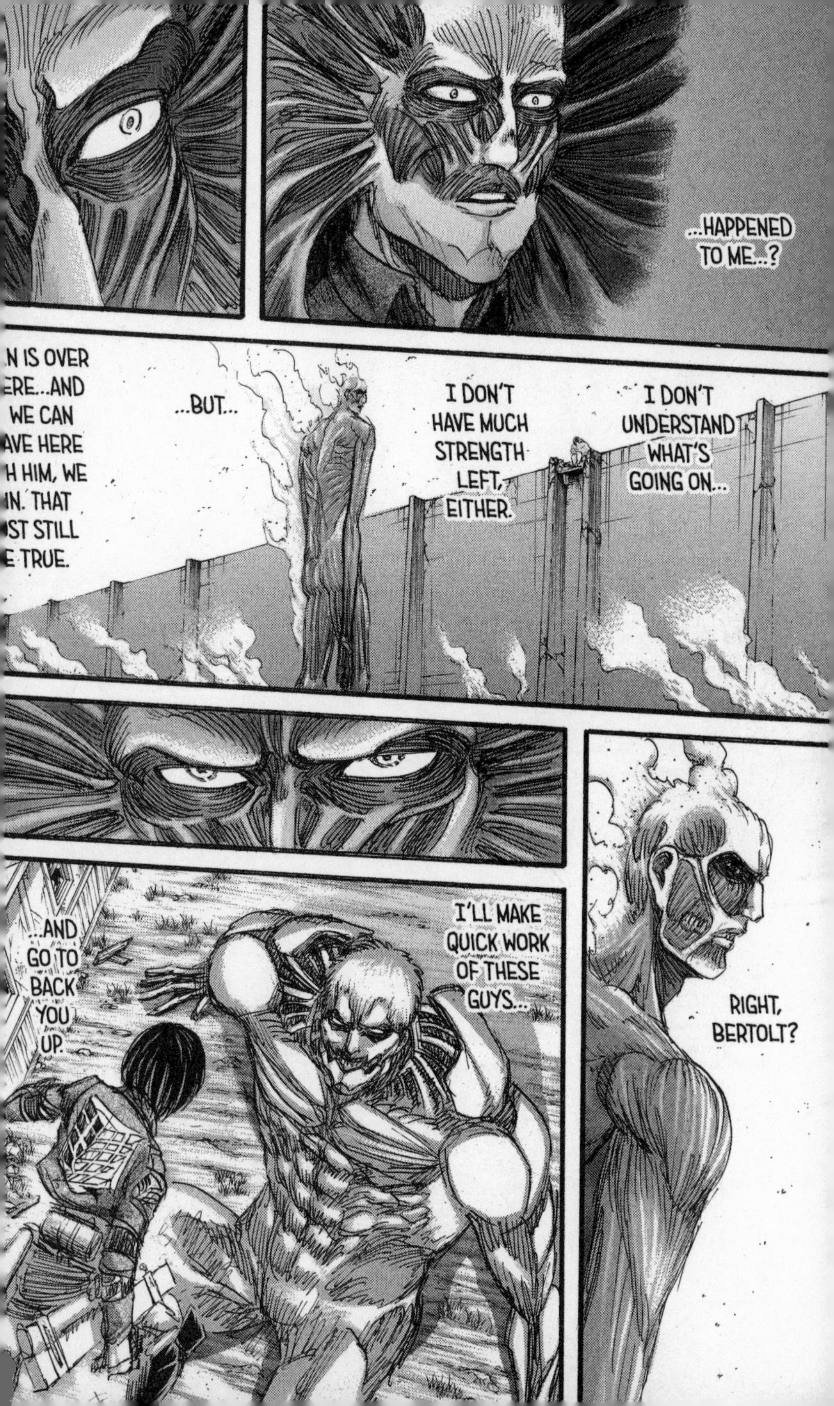
...HAPPENED TO ME...?
I DON'T UNDERSTAND WHAT'S GOING ON...
I DON'T HAVE MUCH STRENGTH LEFT, EITHER.
...BUT...
N IS OVER ERE...AND WE CAN AVE HERE H HIM, WE N. THAT ST STILL E TRUE.
RIGHT, BERTOLT?
I'LL MAKE QUICK WORK OF THESE GUYS...
...AND GO TO BACK YOU UP.

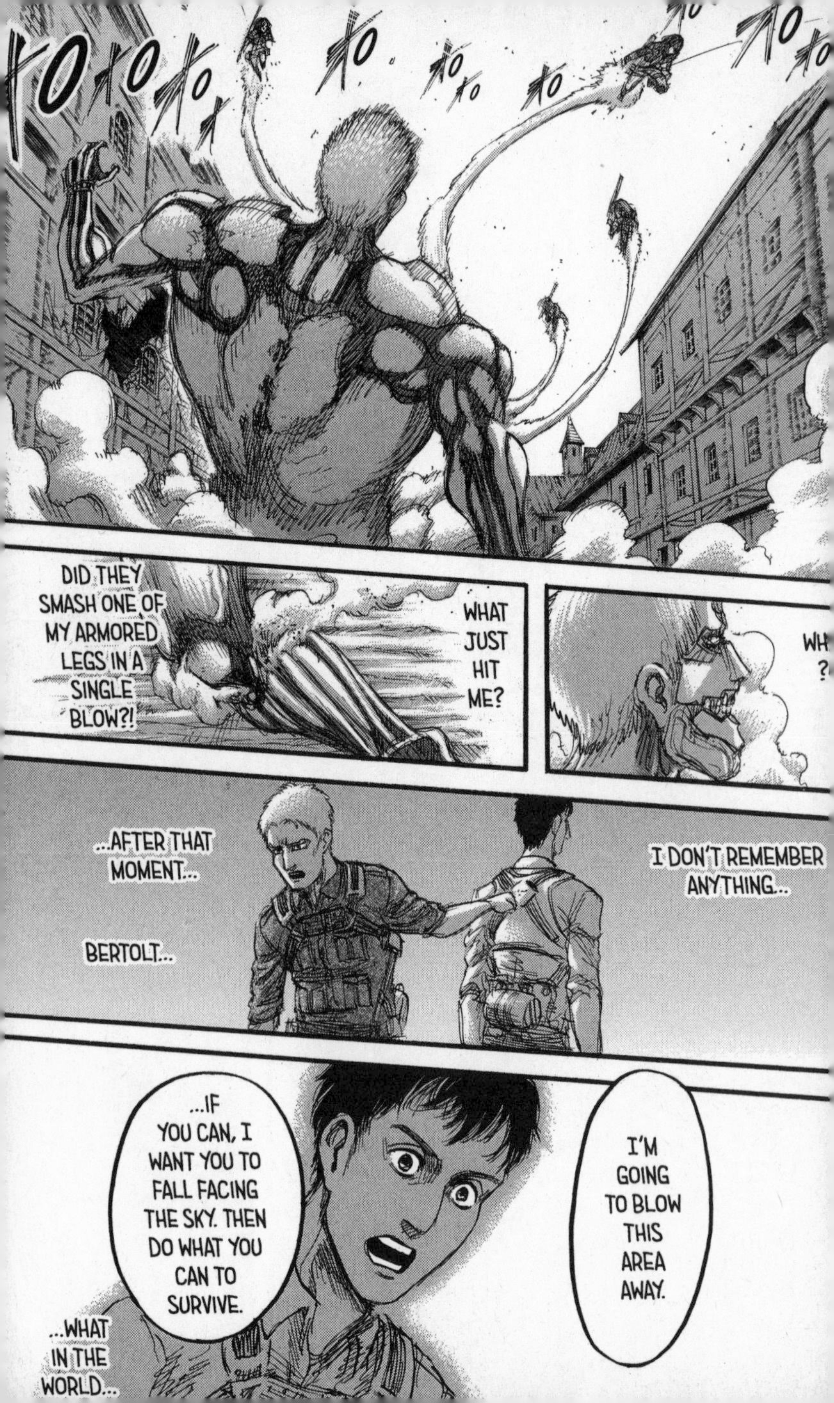
WH ?
WHAT JUST HIT ME?
DID THEY SMASH ONE OF MY ARMORED LEGS IN A SINGLE BLOW?!
I DON'T REMEMBER ANYTHING...
...AFTER THAT MOMENT...
BERTOLT...
I'M GOING TO BLOW THIS AREA AWAY.
...IF YOU CAN, I WANT YOU TO FALL FACING THE SKY. THEN DO WHAT YOU CAN TO SURVIVE.
...WHAT IN THE WORLD...

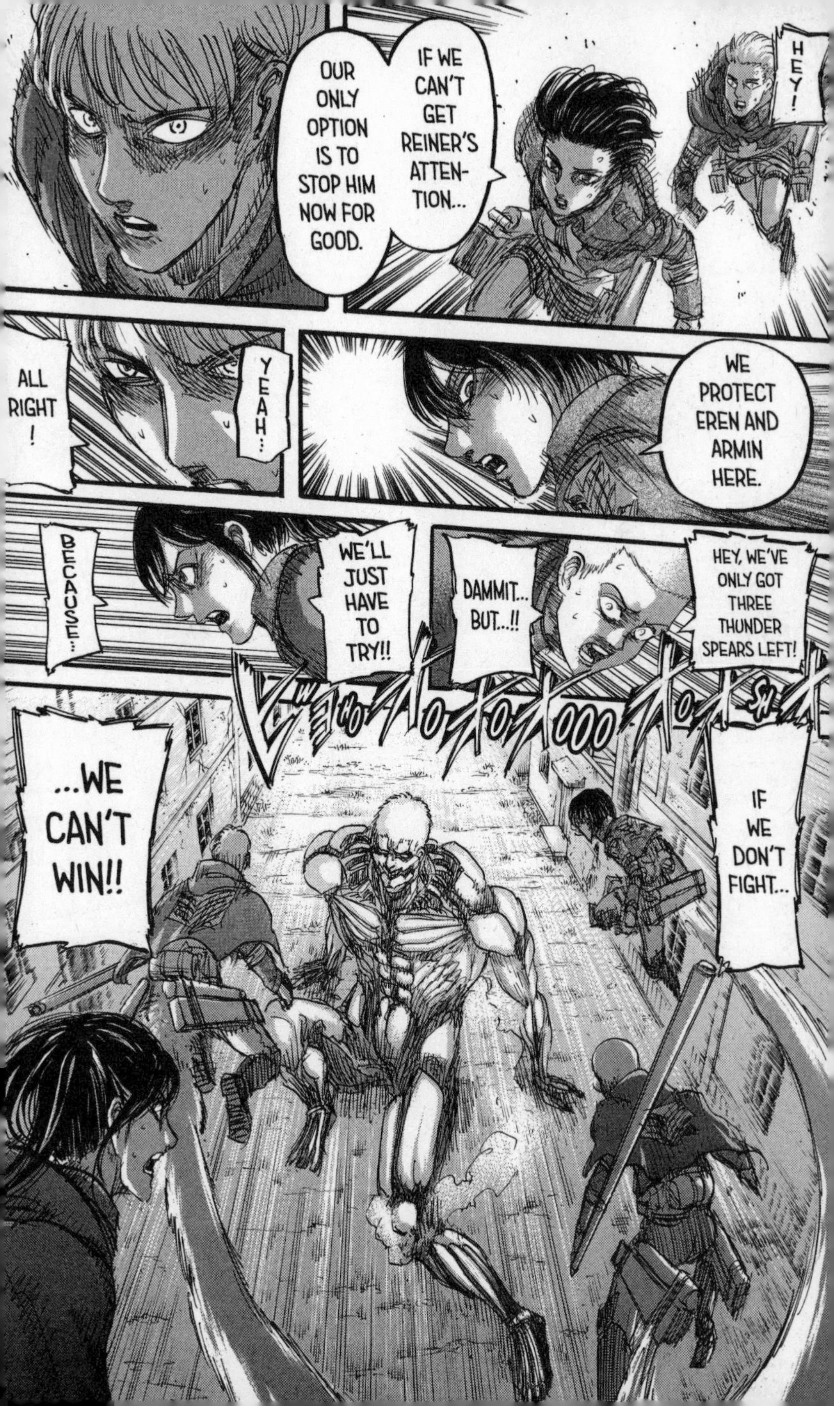
HEY!
IF WE CAN'T GET REINER'S ATTENTION...
OUR ONLY OPTION IS TO STOP HIM NOW FOR GOOD.
WE PROTECT EREN AND ARMIN HERE.
YEAH...
ALL RIGHT!
HEY, WE'VE ONLY GOT THREE THUNDER SPEARS LEFT!
DAMMIT... BUT...!!
WE'LL JUST HAVE TO TRY!!
BECAUSE...
IF WE DON'T FIGHT...
...WE CAN'T WIN!!

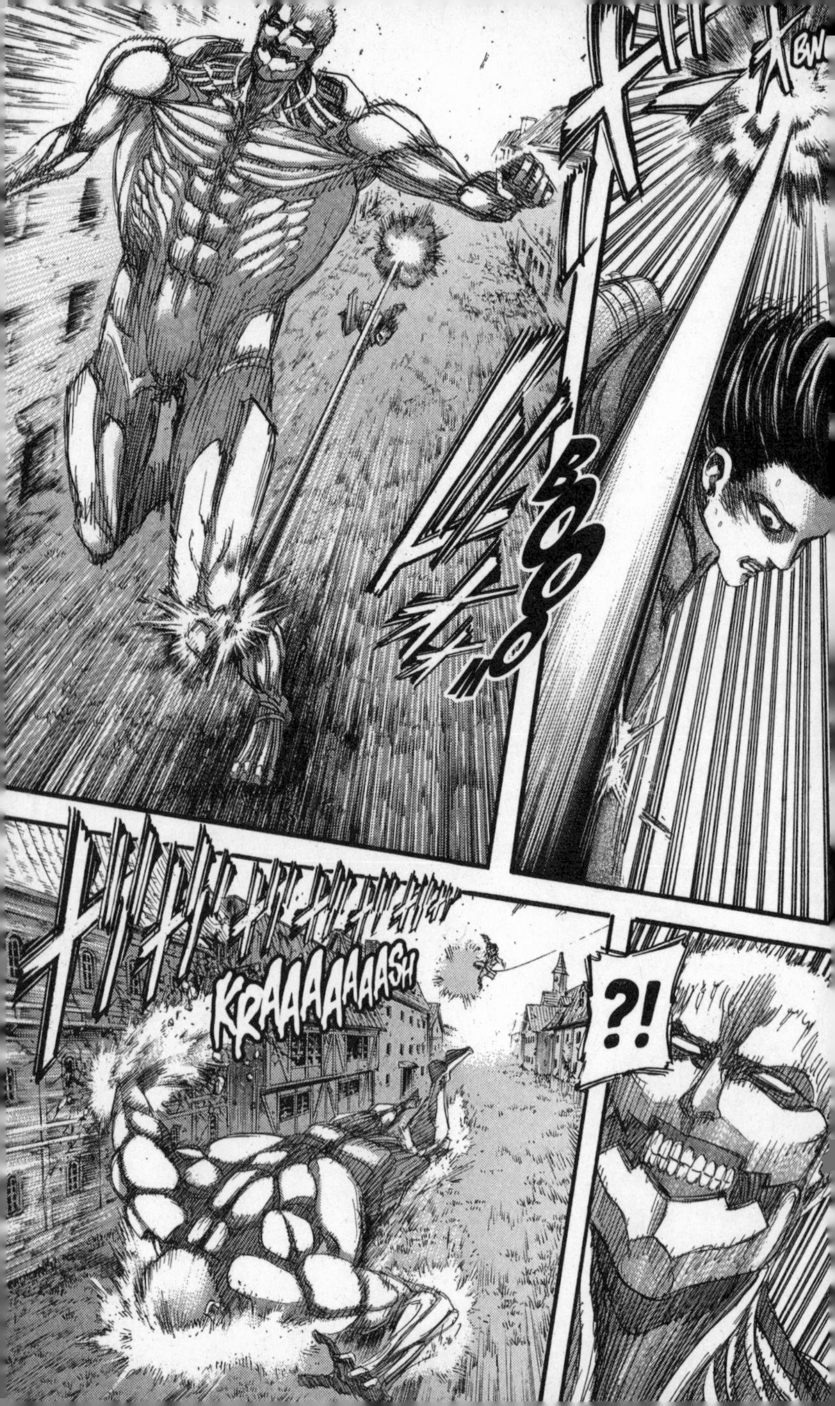
BW
BOOOOM
?!
KRAAAAAAASH

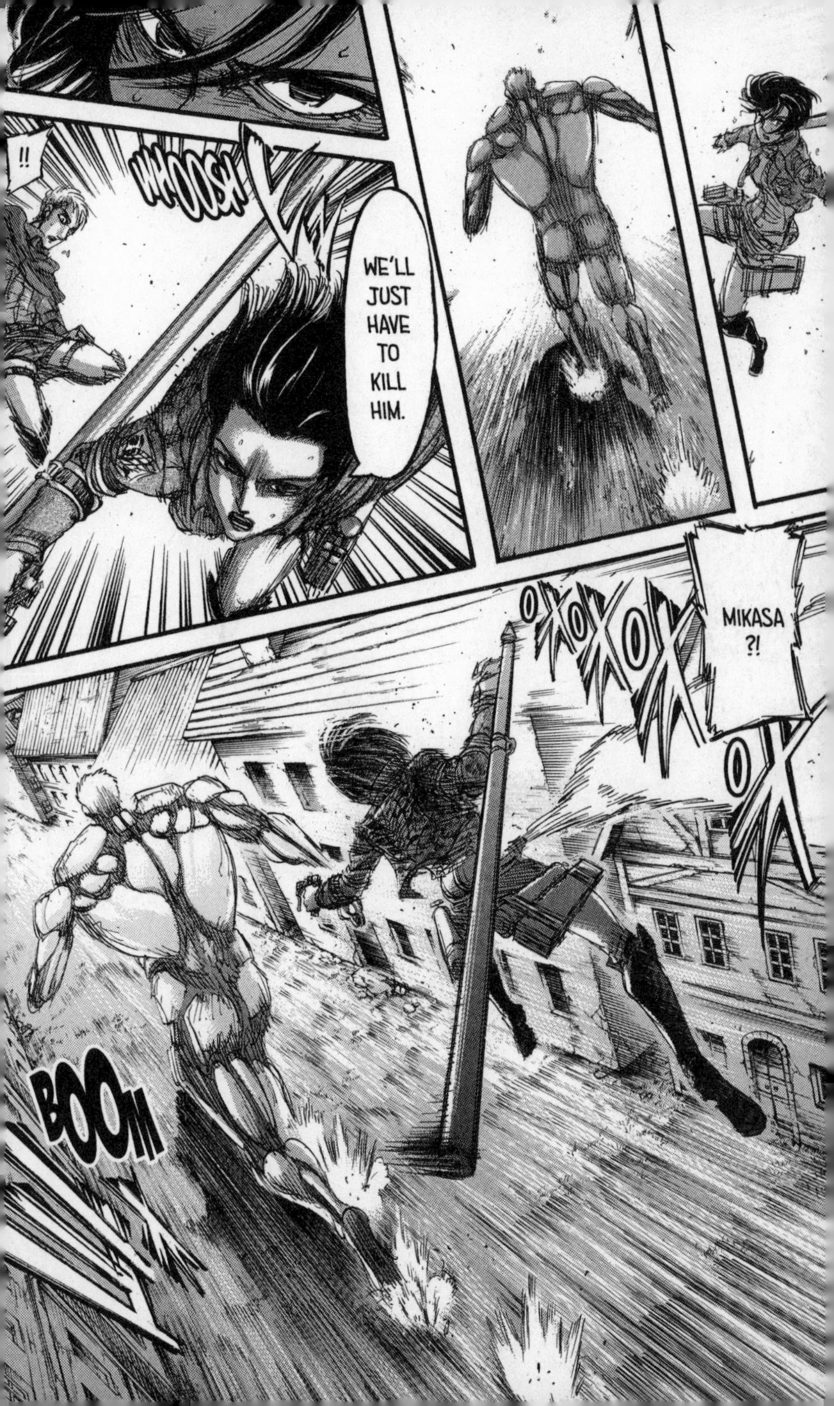

WE'LL JUST HAVE TO KILL HIM.
WHOOSH
!!
MIKASA ?!
OXOXOX
OX
BOOM

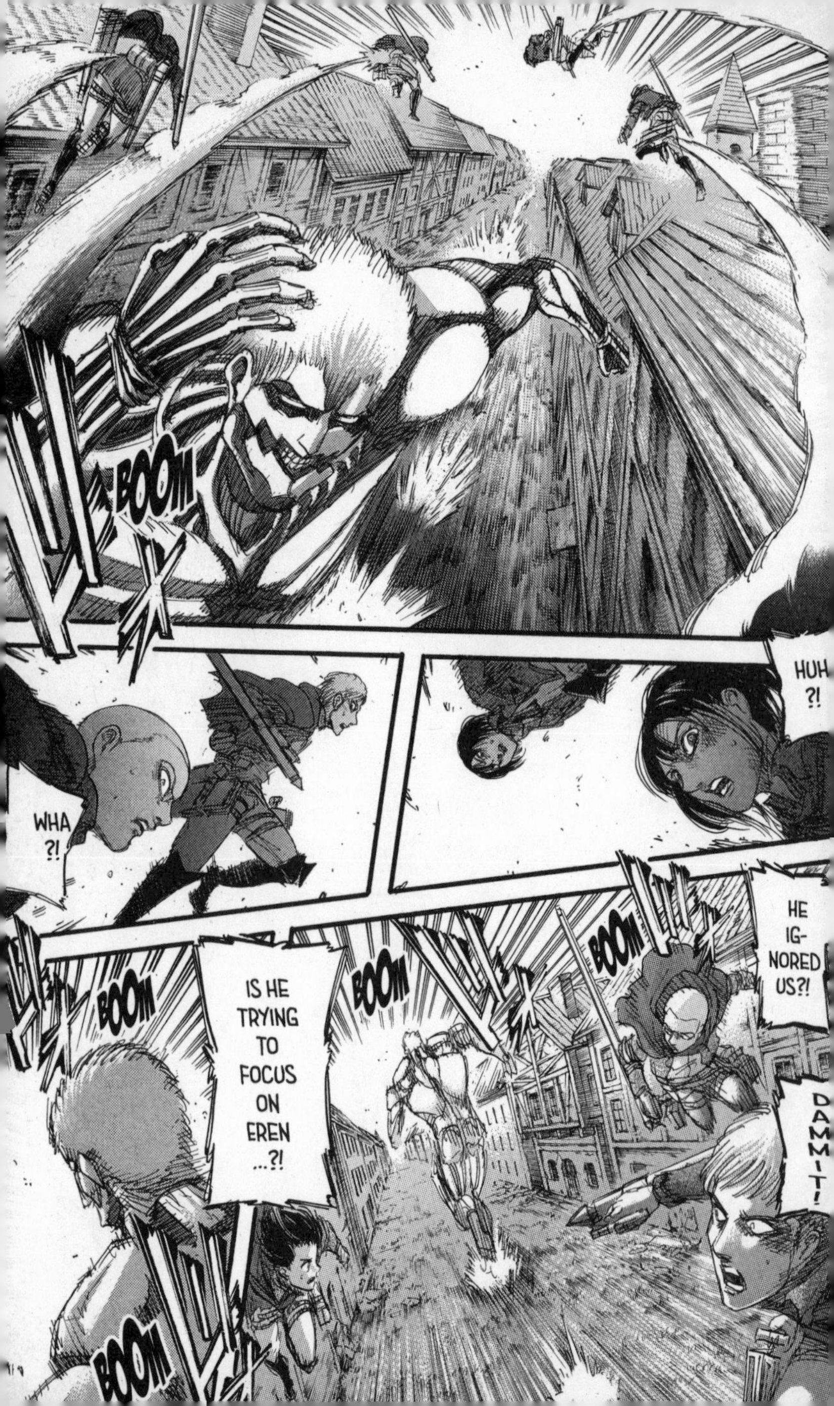
BOOM
HUH ?!
WHA ?!
HE IG-NORED US?!
BOOM
DAMMIT!
BOOM
IS HE TRYING TO FOCUS ON EREN ...?!
BOOM
BOOM

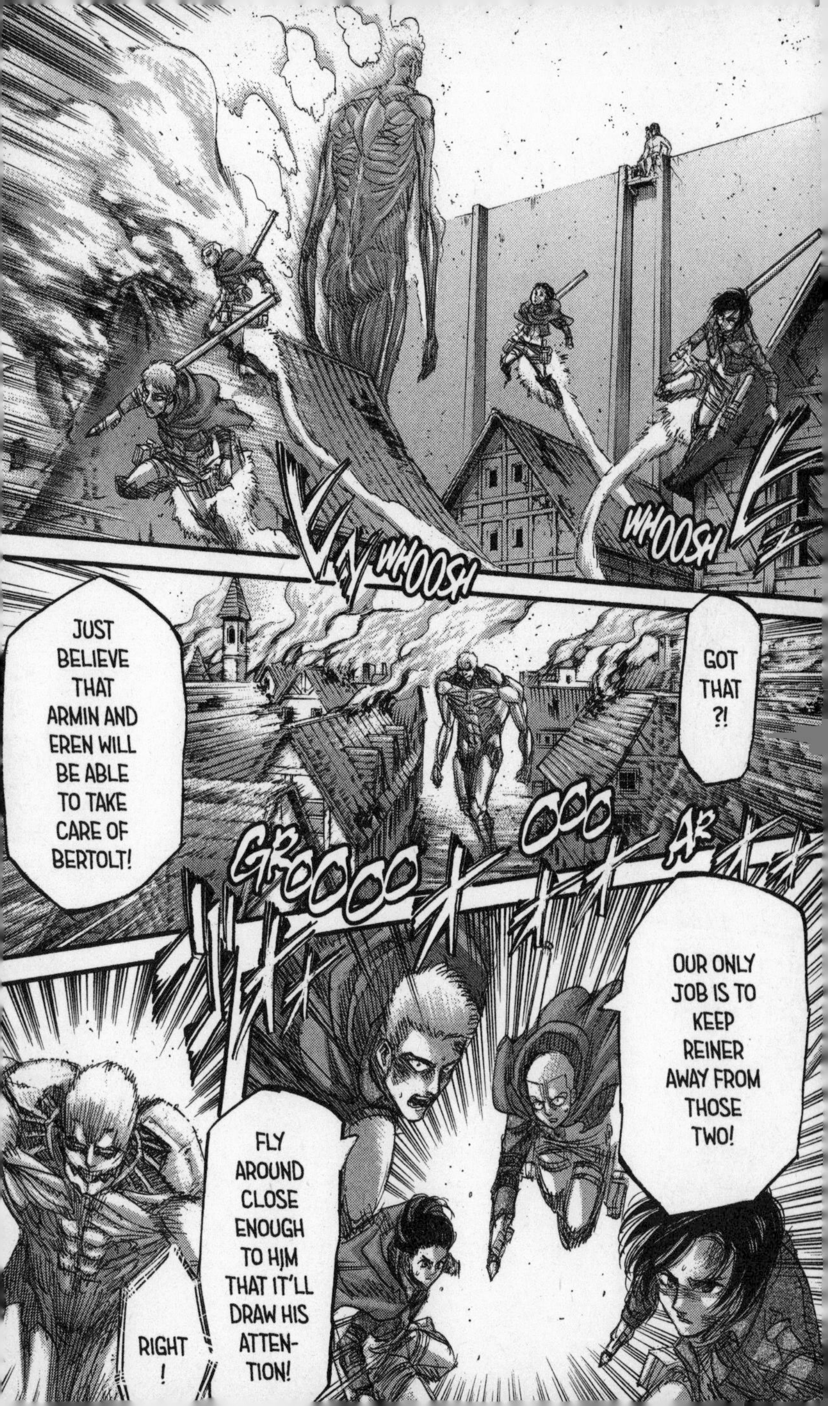

WHOOSH
WHOOSH
JUST BELIEVE THAT ARMIN AND EREN WILL BE ABLE TO TAKE CARE OF BERTOLT!
GOT THAT ?!
GROOOOOOOOAR
OUR ONLY JOB IS TO KEEP REINER AWAY FROM THOSE TWO!
FLY AROUND CLOSE ENOUGH TO HIM THAT IT'LL DRAW HIS ATTEN-TION!
RIGHT !

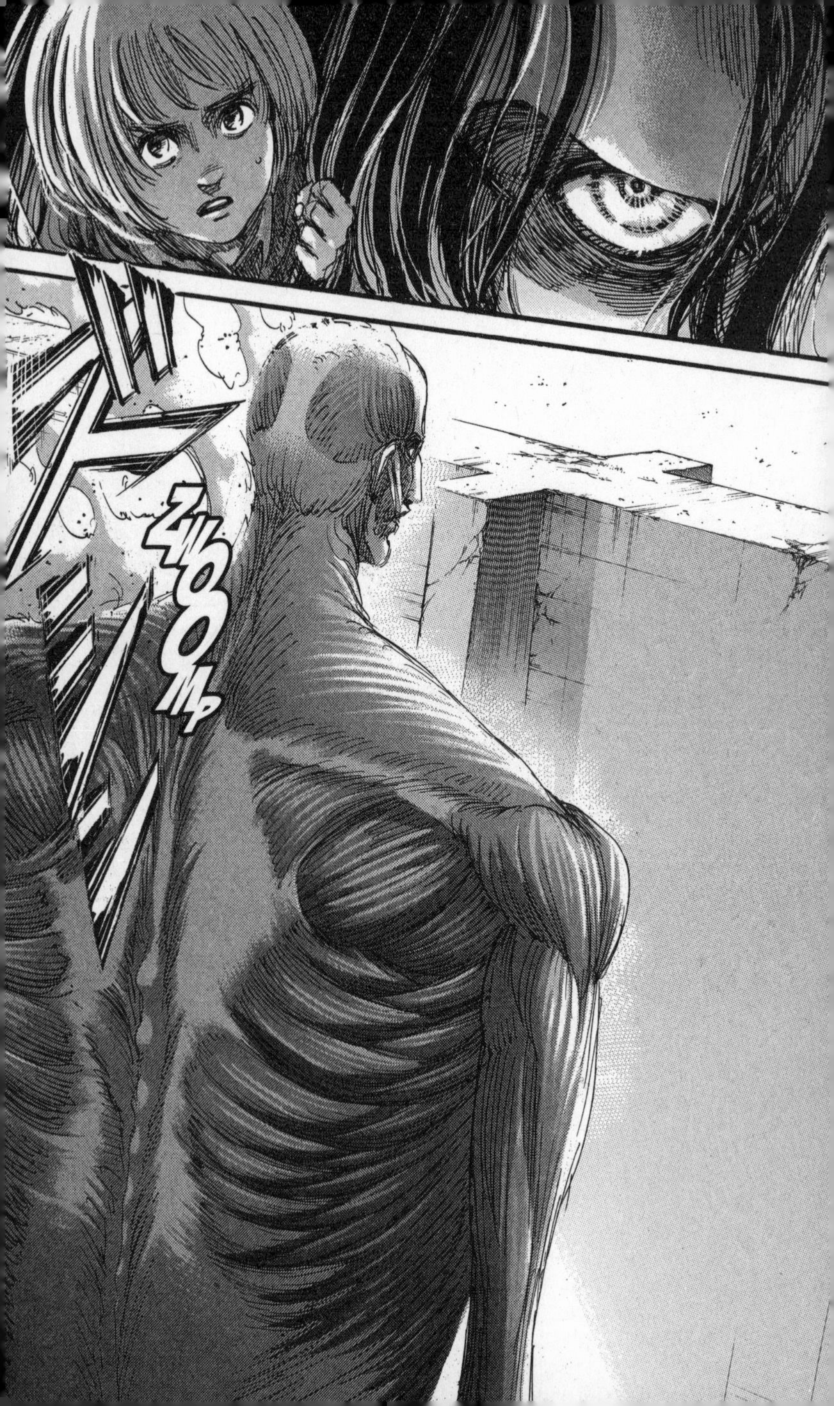
ZWOOOMP

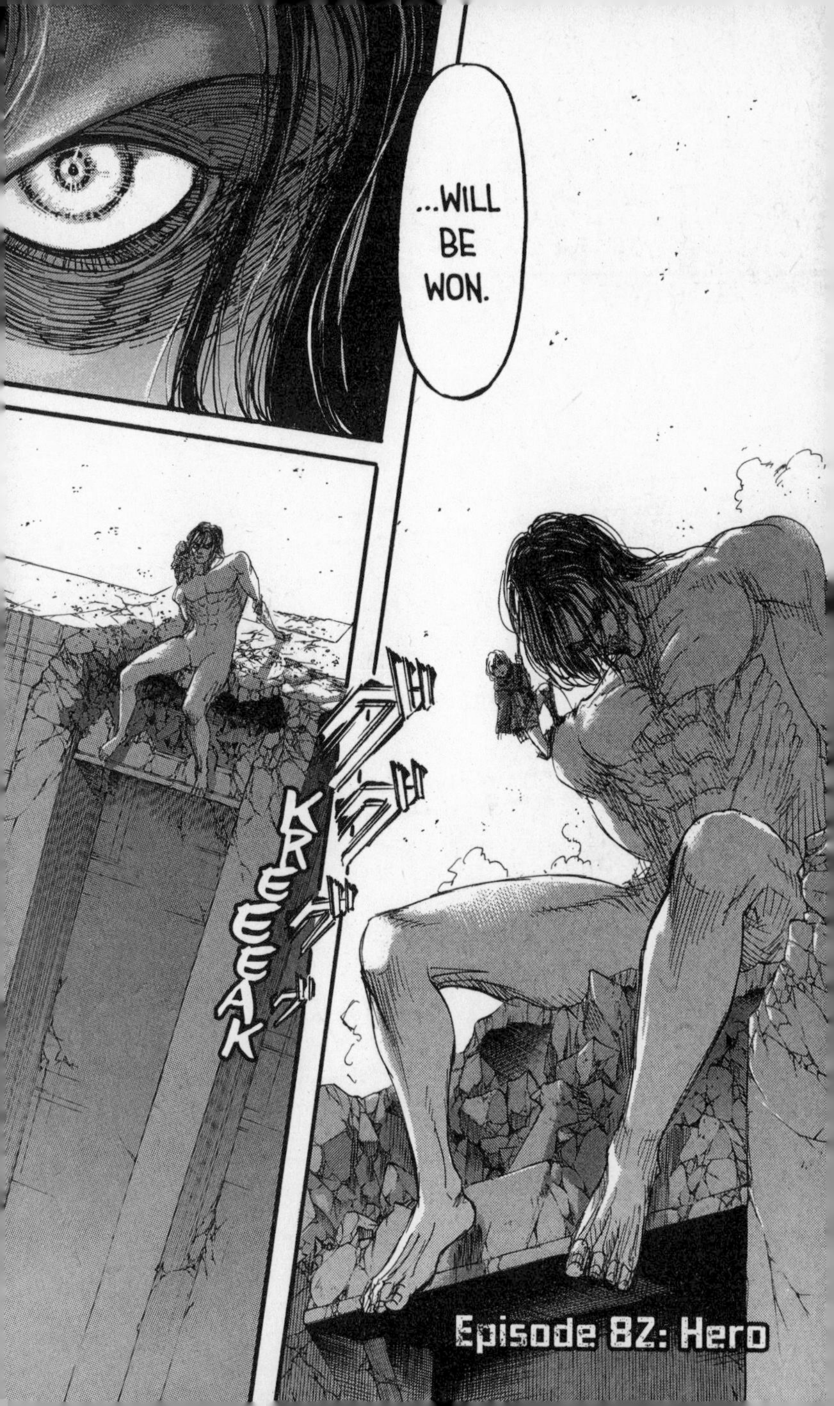
...WILL BE WON.
KREEEEAK
Episode 82: Hero

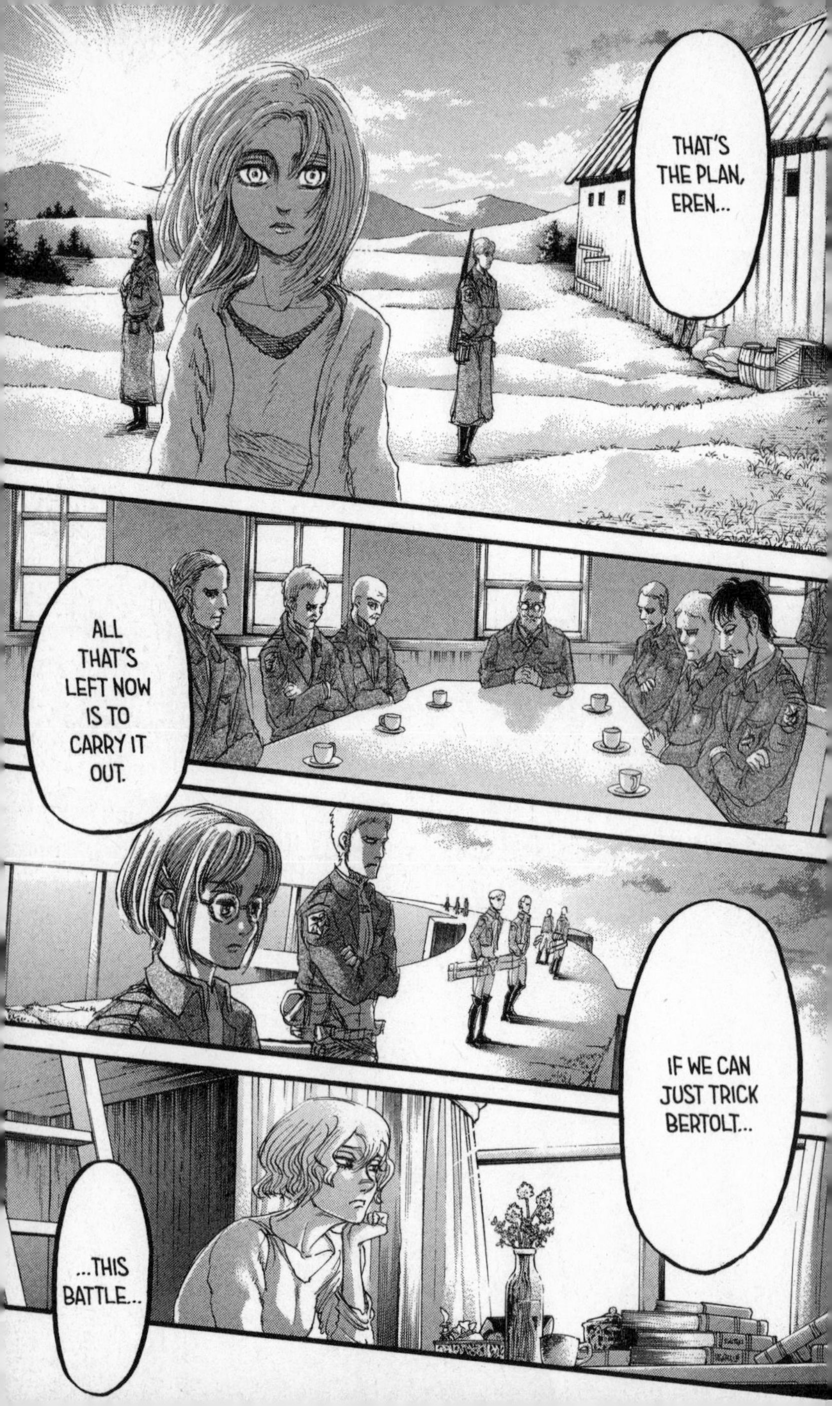
THAT'S THE PLAN, EREN...
ALL THAT'S LEFT NOW IS TO CARRY IT OUT.
IF WE CAN JUST TRICK BERTOLT...
...THIS BATTLE...

ATTACK on TITAN

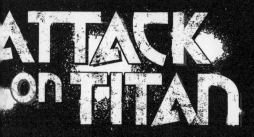

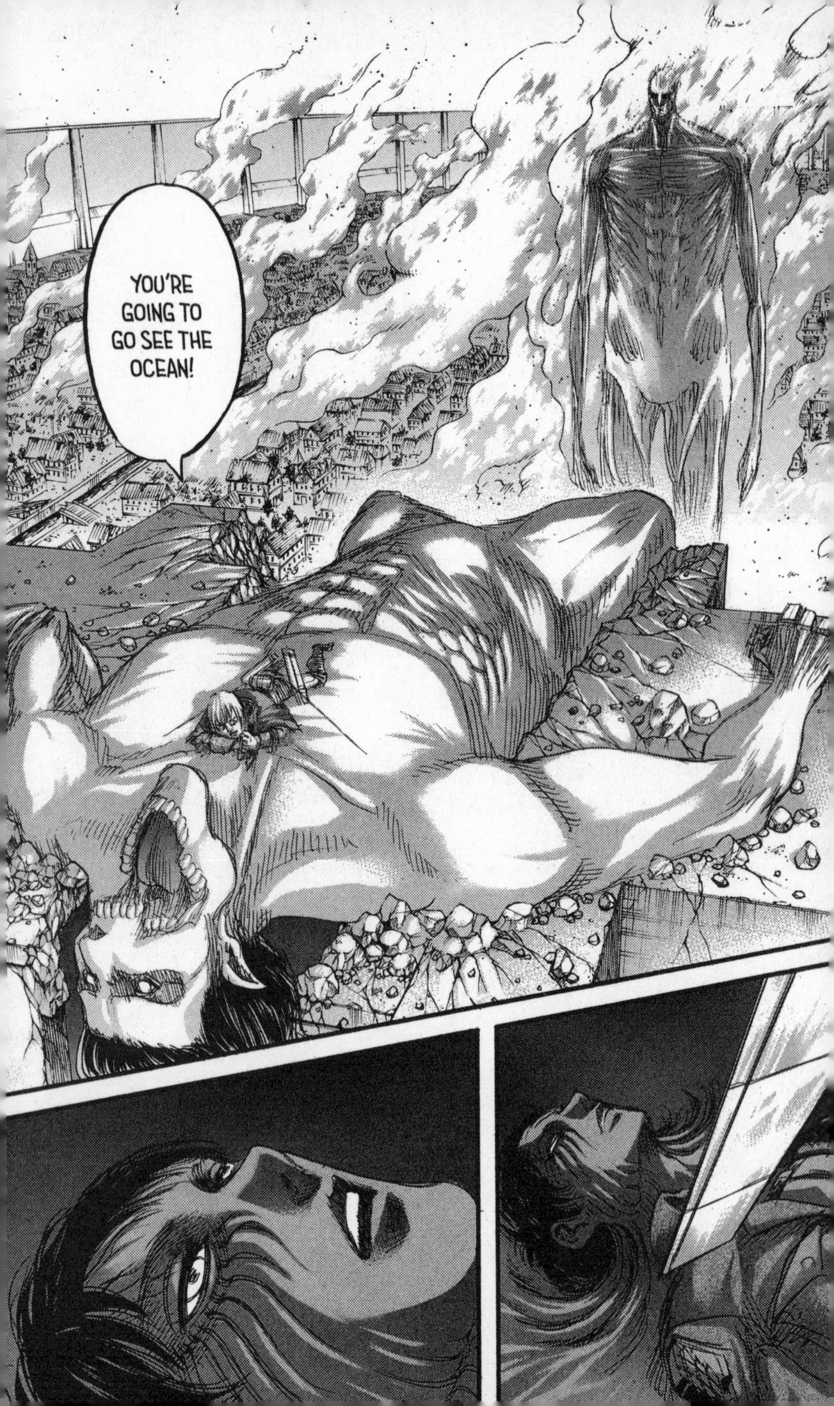
YOU'RE GOING TO GO SEE THE OCEAN!

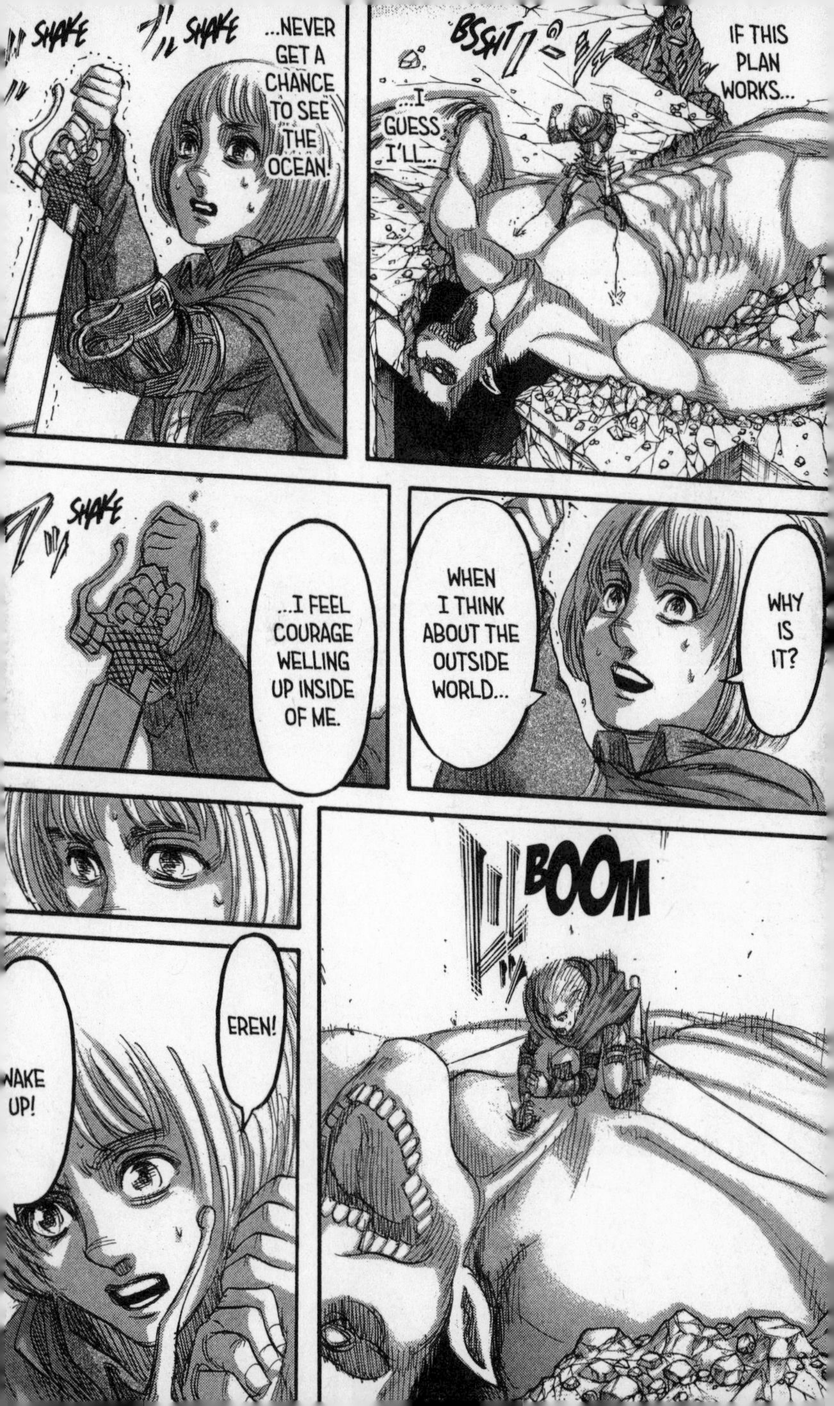
IF THIS PLAN WORKS...
BSSHT
...I GUESS I'LL...
...NEVER GET A CHANCE TO SEE THE OCEAN!
SHAKE
SHAKE
WHY IS IT?
WHEN I THINK ABOUT THE OUTSIDE WORLD...
...I FEEL COURAGE WELLING UP INSIDE OF ME.
SHAKE
BOOM
EREN!
WAKE UP!

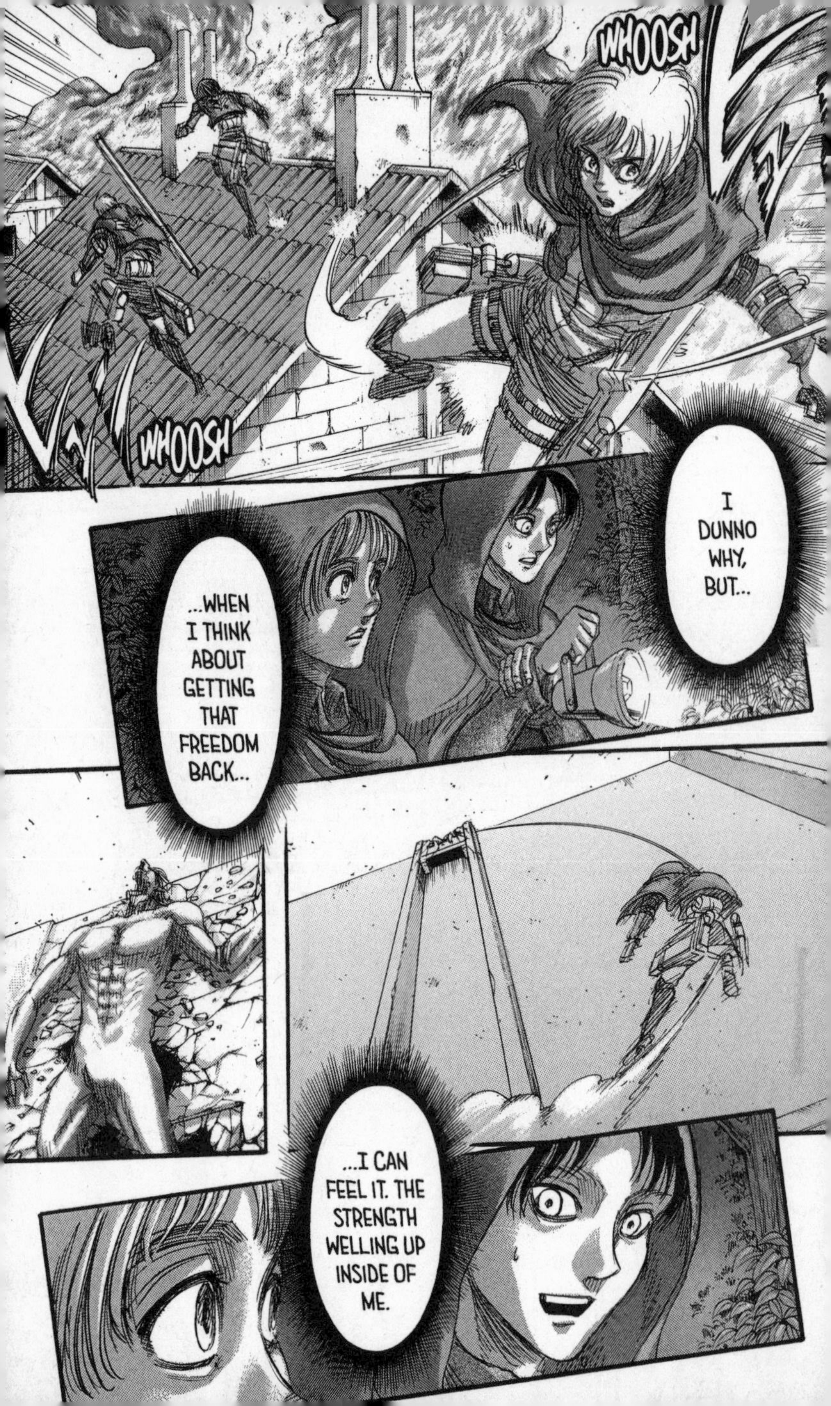
WHOOSH
WHOOSH
I DUNNO WHY, BUT...
...WHEN I THINK ABOUT GETTING THAT FREEDOM BACK...
...I CAN FEEL IT. THE STRENGTH WELLING UP INSIDE OF ME.

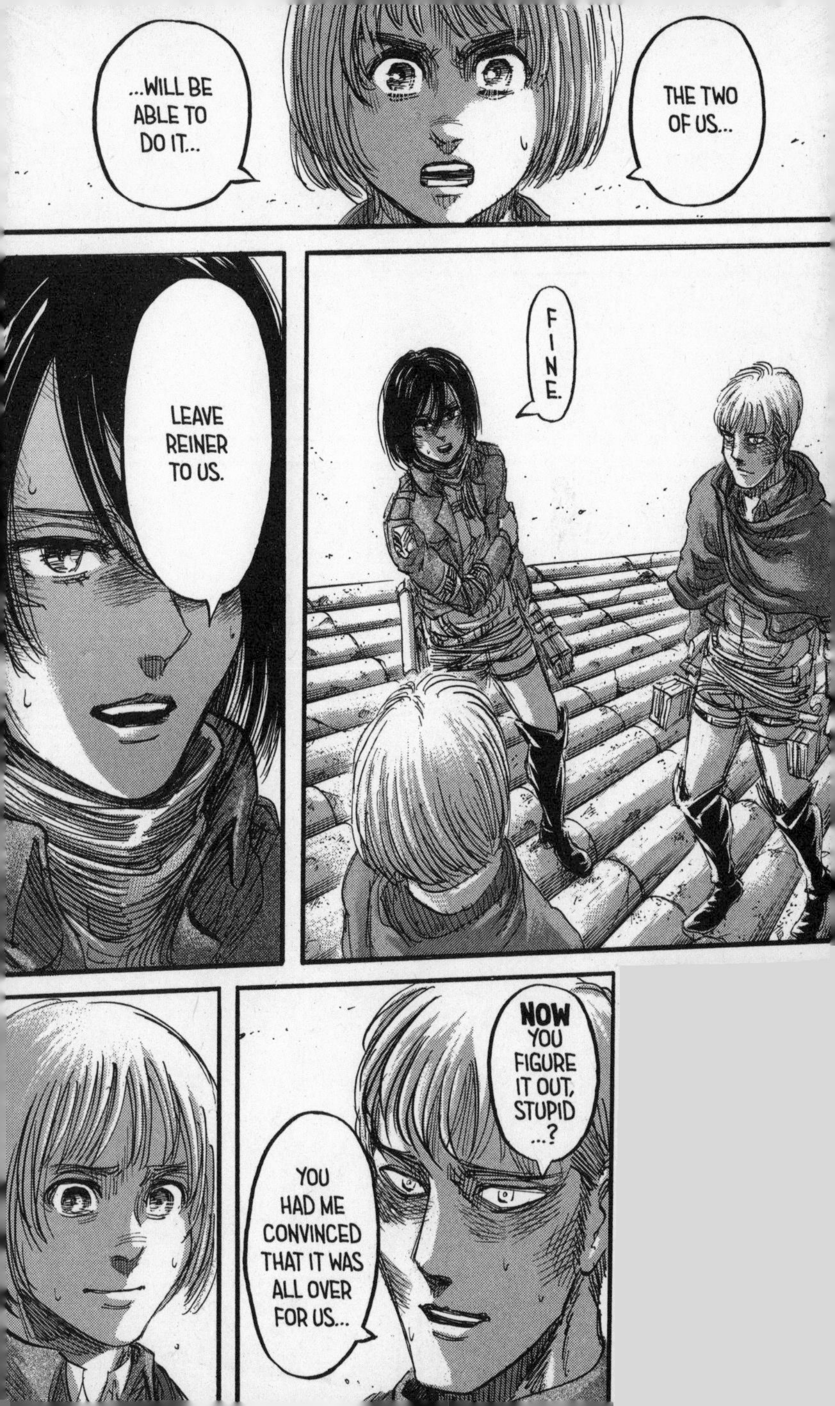
THE TWO OF US...
...WILL BE ABLE TO DO IT...
FINE.
LEAVE REINER TO US.
NOW YOU FIGURE IT OUT, STUPID ...?
YOU HAD ME CONVINCED THAT IT WAS ALL OVER FOR US...

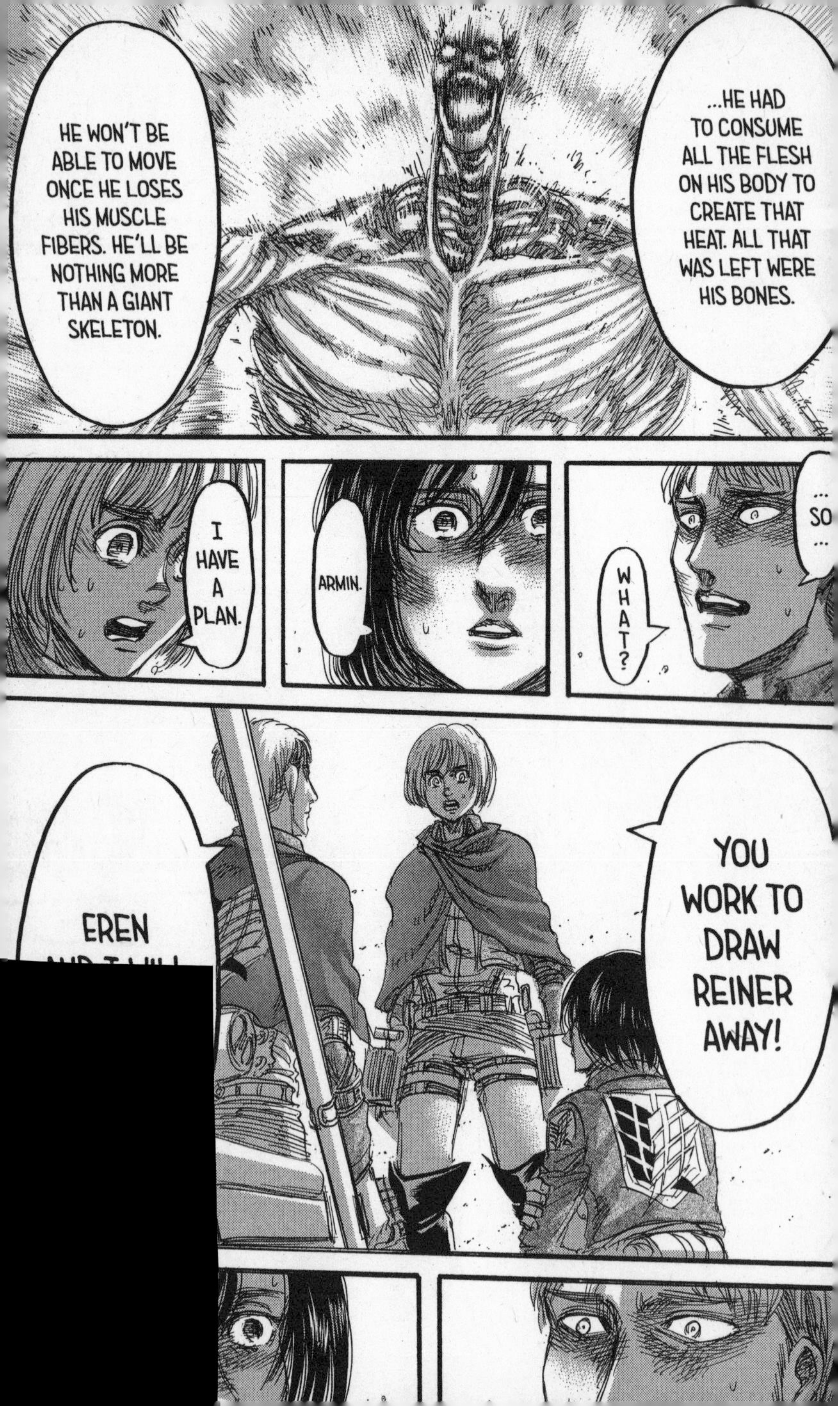
...HE HAD TO CONSUME ALL THE FLESH ON HIS BODY TO CREATE THAT HEAT. ALL THAT WAS LEFT WERE HIS BONES.
HE WON'T BE ABLE TO MOVE ONCE HE LOSES HIS MUSCLE FIBERS. HE'LL BE NOTHING MORE THAN A GIANT SKELETON.
...SO...
WHAT?
ARMIN.
I HAVE A PLAN.
YOU WORK TO DRAW REINER AWAY!
EREN [redacted]

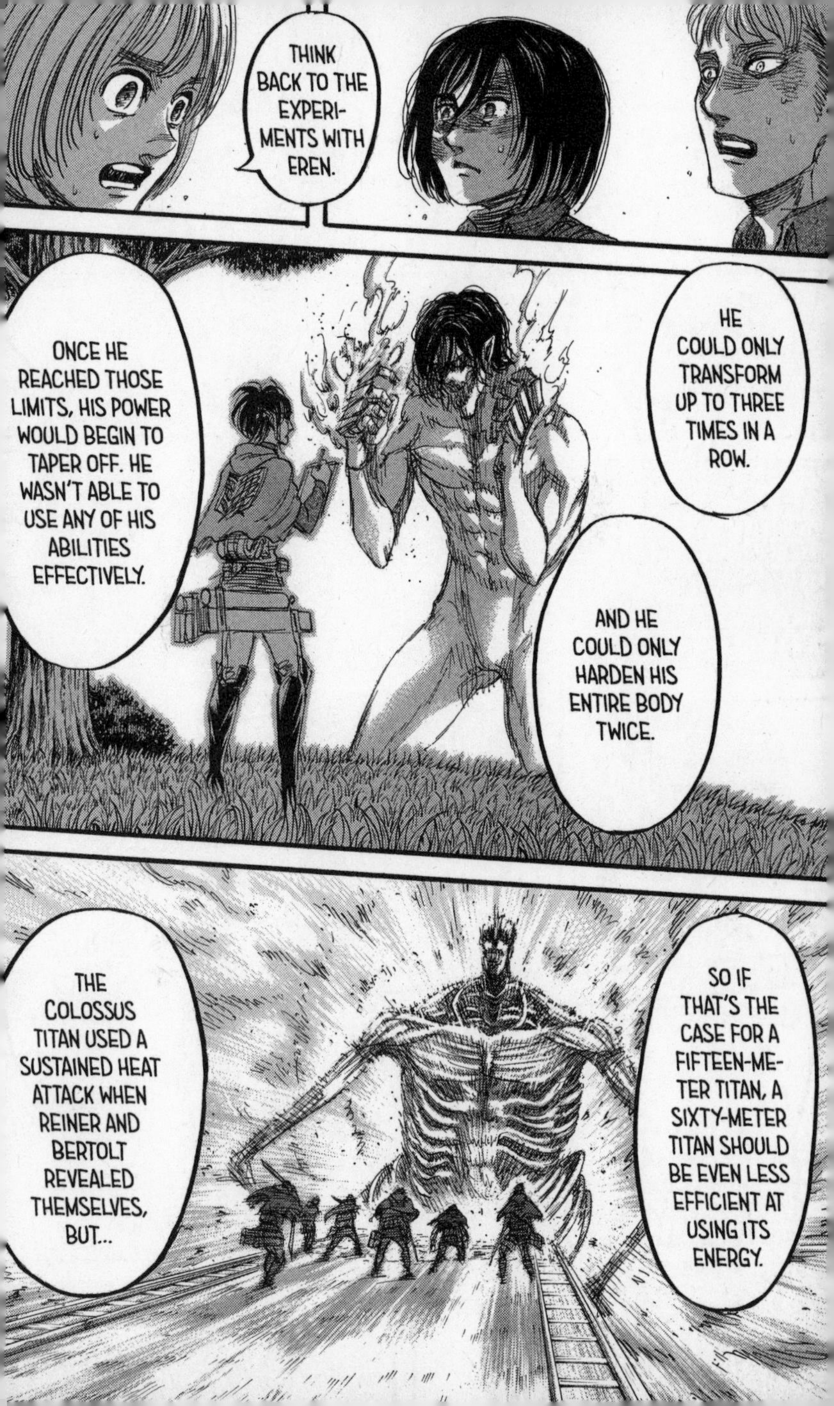
THINK BACK TO THE EXPERI-MENTS WITH EREN.
HE COULD ONLY TRANSFORM UP TO THREE TIMES IN A ROW.
AND HE COULD ONLY HARDEN HIS ENTIRE BODY TWICE.
ONCE HE REACHED THOSE LIMITS, HIS POWER WOULD BEGIN TO TAPER OFF. HE WASN'T ABLE TO USE ANY OF HIS ABILITIES EFFECTIVELY.
SO IF THAT'S THE CASE FOR A FIFTEEN-ME-TER TITAN, A SIXTY-METER TITAN SHOULD BE EVEN LESS EFFICIENT AT USING ITS ENERGY.
THE COLOSSUS TITAN USED A SUSTAINED HEAT ATTACK WHEN REINER AND BERTOLT REVEALED THEMSELVES, BUT...

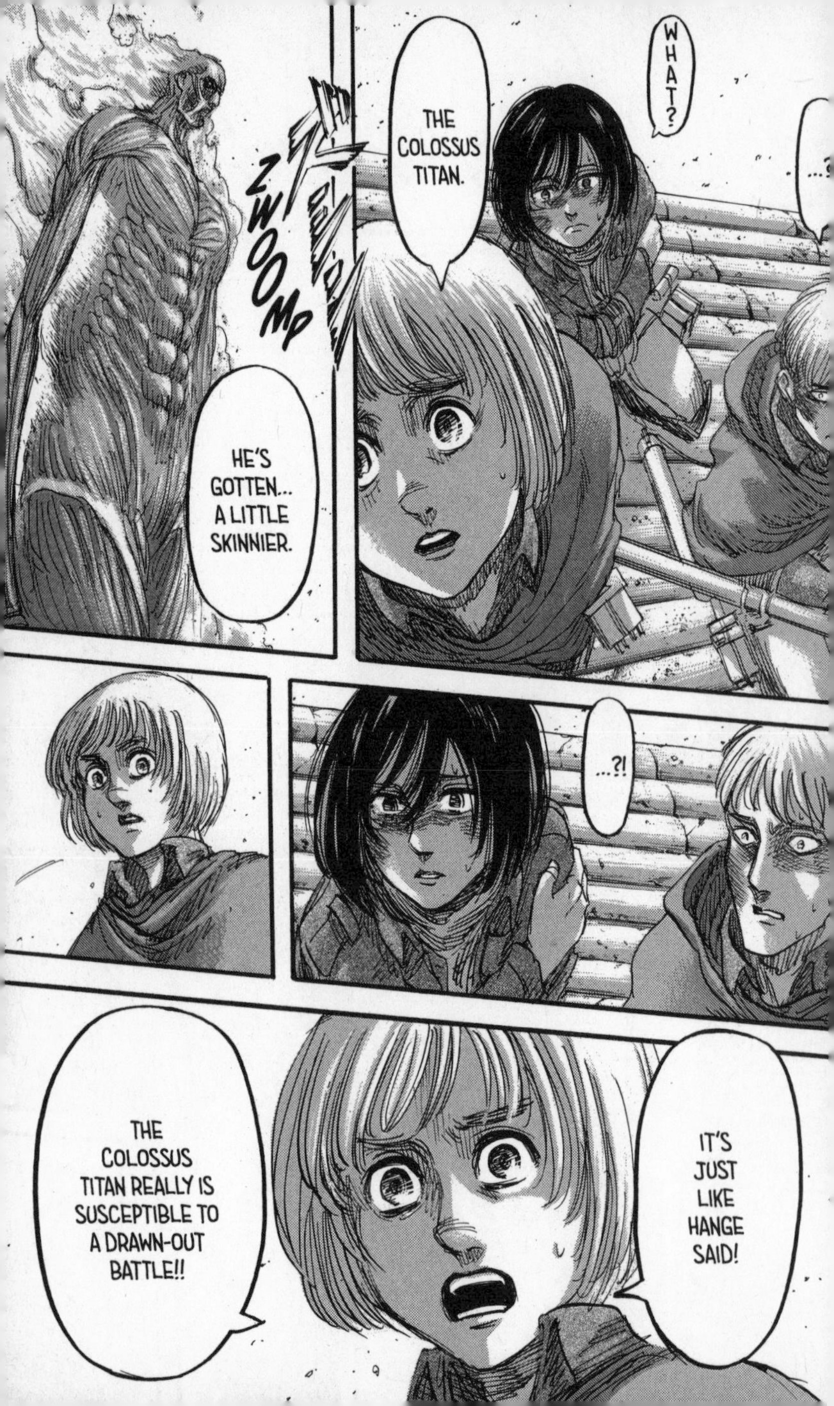
WHAT?
...?
THE COLOSSUS TITAN.
ZWOOM
HE'S GOTTEN... A LITTLE SKINNIER.
...?!
IT'S JUST LIKE HANGE SAID!
THE COLOSSUS TITAN REALLY IS SUSCEPTIBLE TO A DRAWN-OUT BATTLE!!

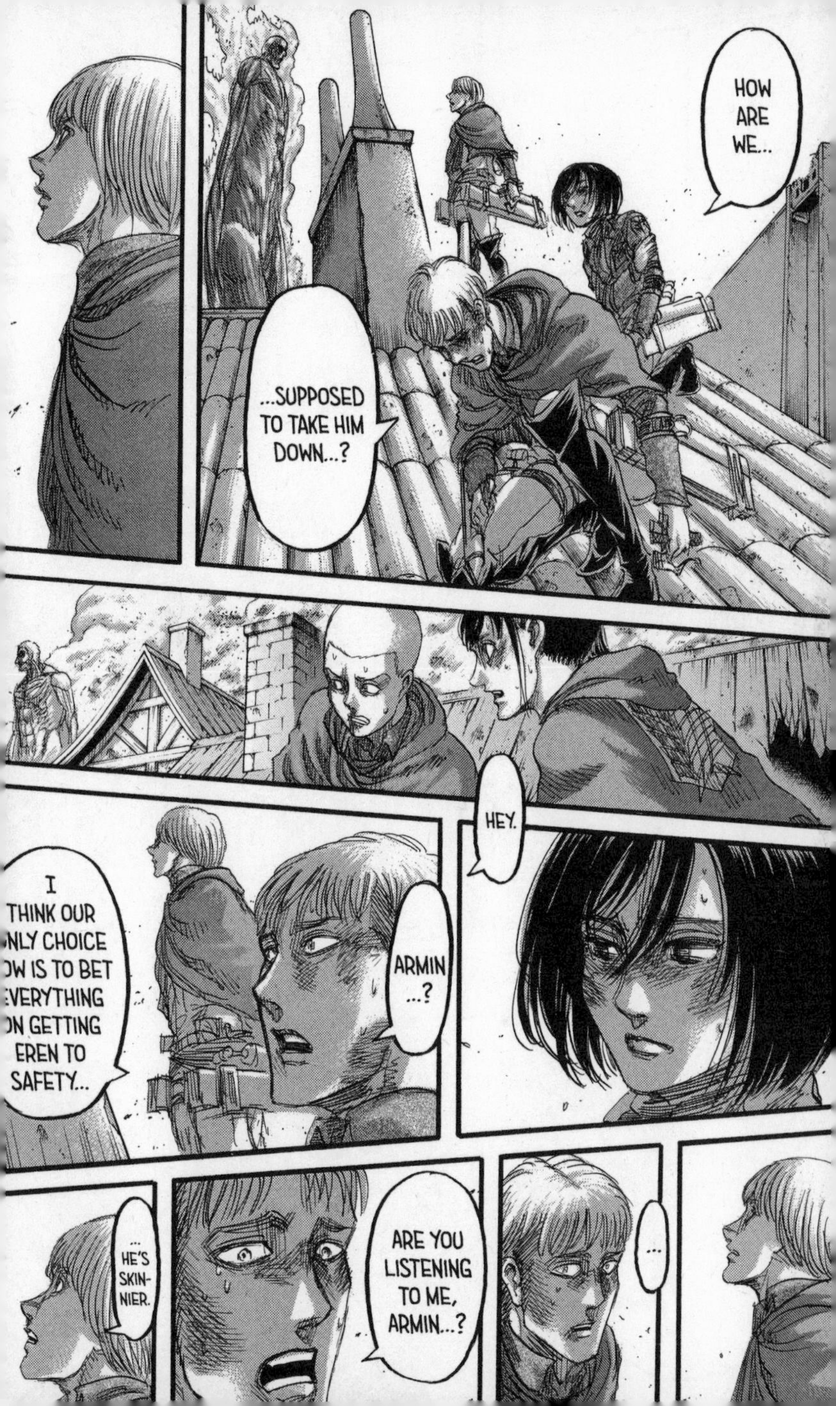
HOW ARE WE...
...SUPPOSED TO TAKE HIM DOWN...?
HEY.
ARMIN ...?
I THINK OUR NLY CHOICE OW IS TO BET VERYTHING ON GETTING EREN TO SAFETY...
...
ARE YOU LISTENING TO ME, ARMIN...?
... HE'S SKIN-NIER.

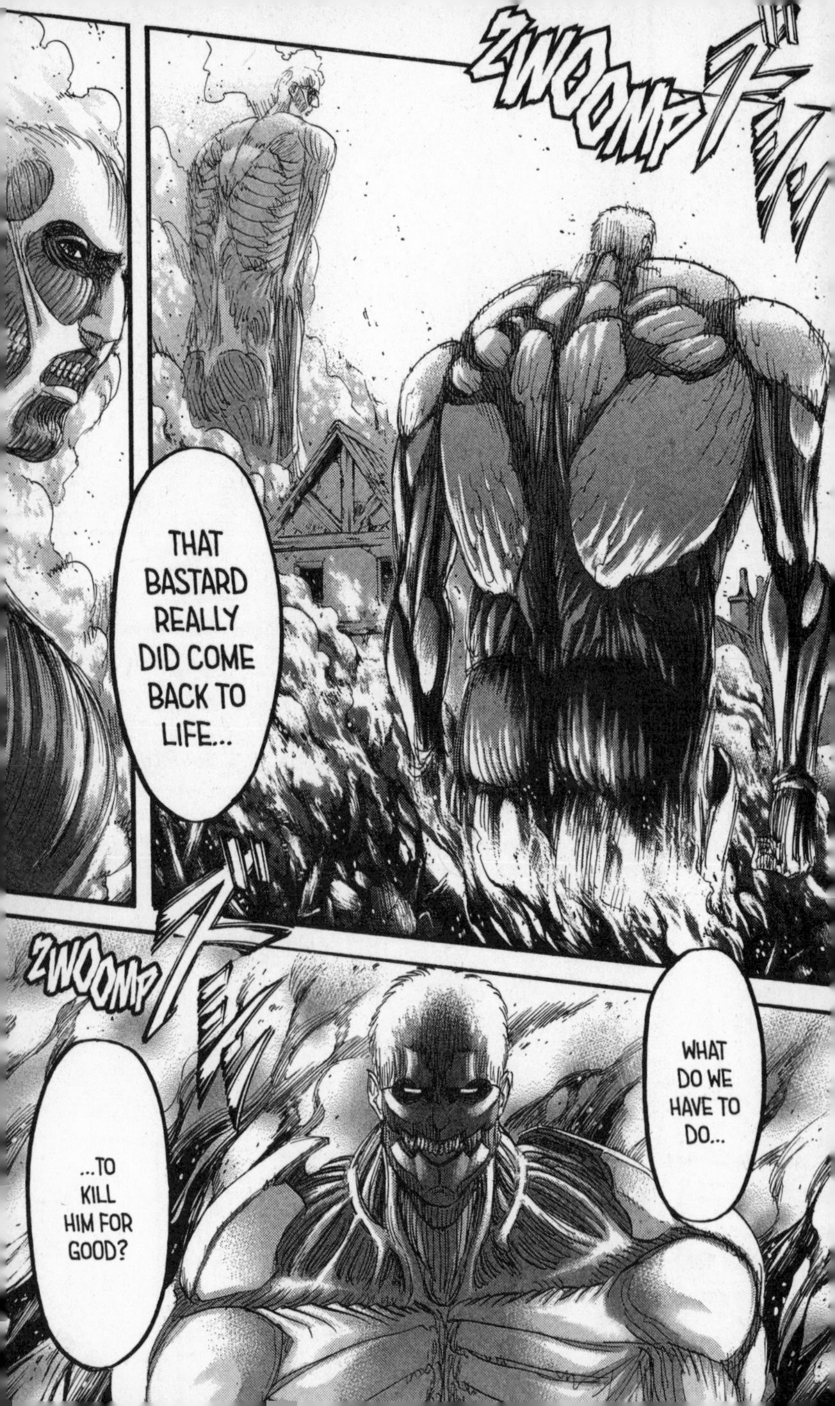
ZWOOMP
THAT BASTARD REALLY DID COME BACK TO LIFE...
ZWOOMP
WHAT DO WE HAVE TO DO...
...TO KILL HIM FOR GOOD?

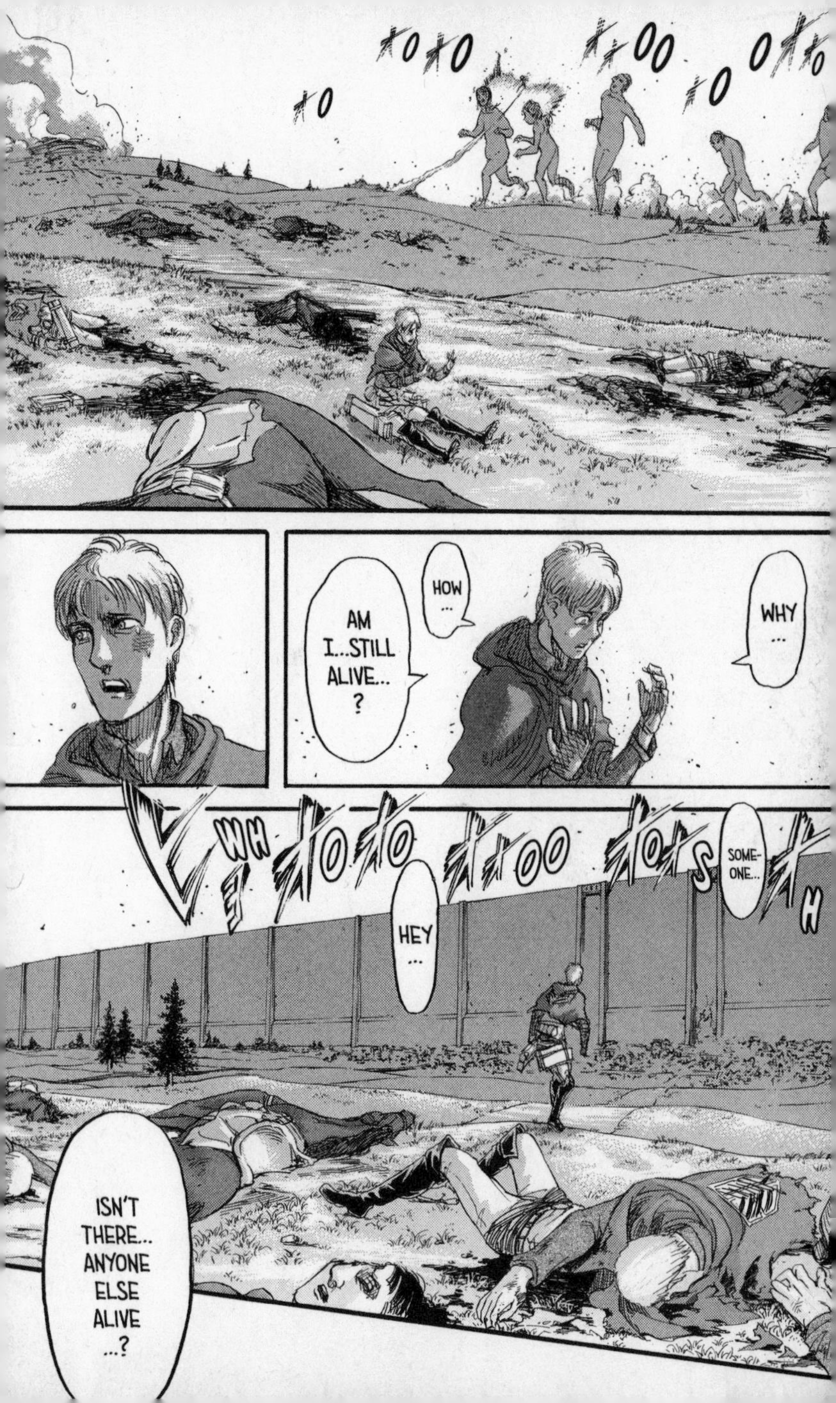
WHY ...
HOW ...
AM I...STILL ALIVE... ?
SOME-ONE...
HEY ...
ISN'T THERE... ANYONE ELSE ALIVE ...?

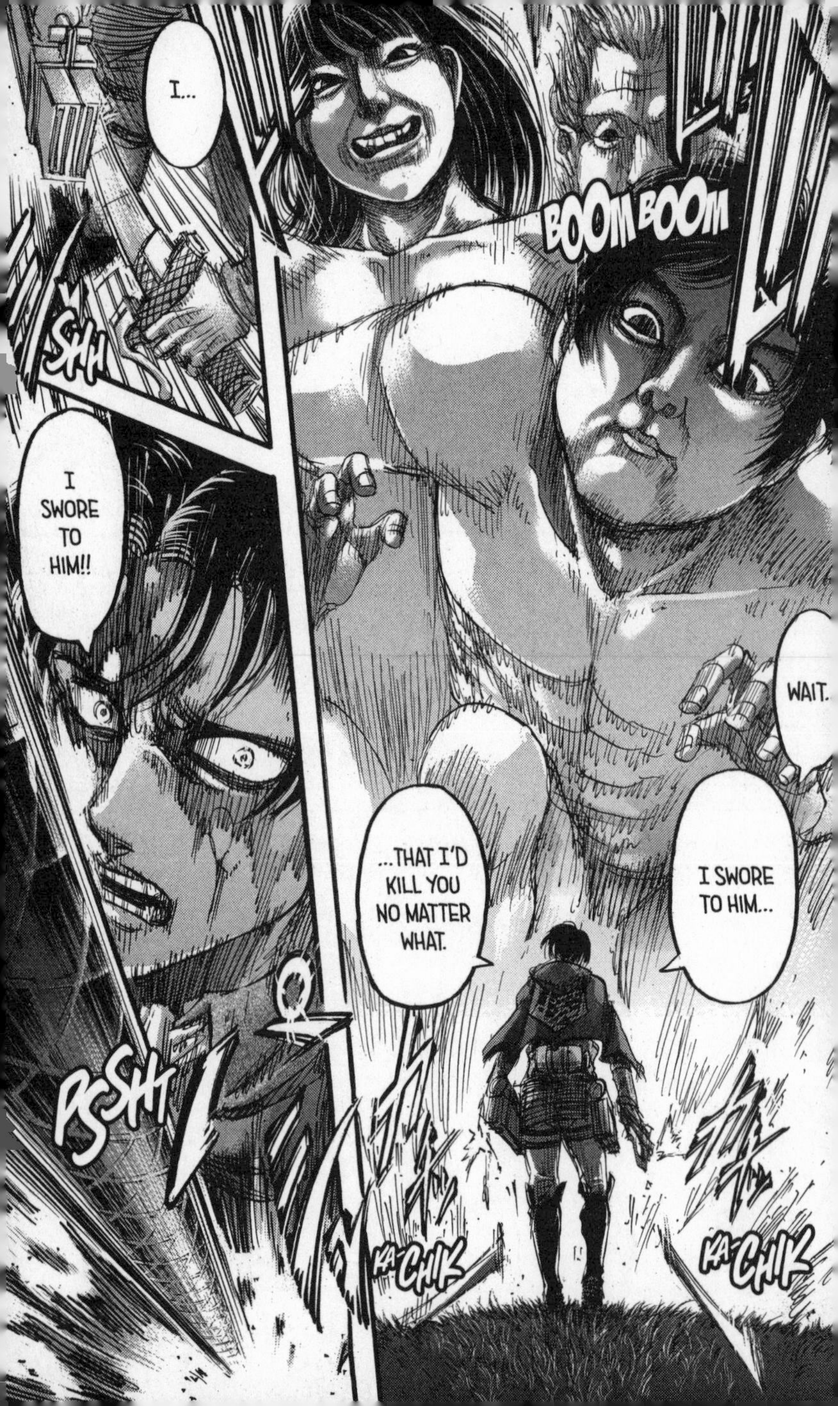
BOOM BOOM
WAIT.
I SWORE TO HIM...
...THAT I'D KILL YOU NO MATTER WHAT.
KA-CHIK
KA-CHIK
I...
SHH
I SWORE TO HIM!!
PSSHT

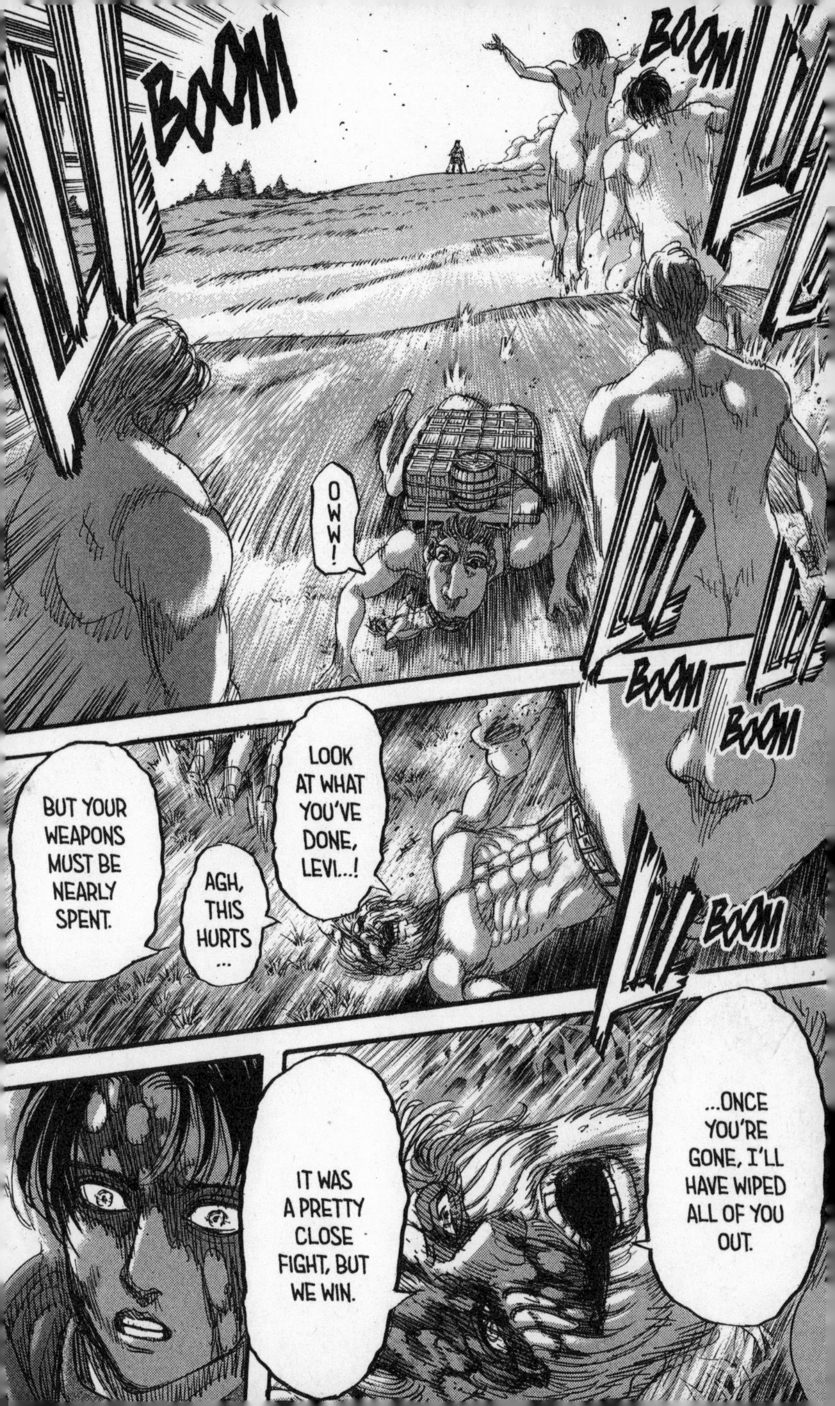

BOOM
BOOM
OWW!
BOOM
BOOM
LOOK AT WHAT YOU'VE DONE, LEVI...!
AGH, THIS HURTS...
BUT YOUR WEAPONS MUST BE NEARLY SPENT.
BOOM
...ONCE YOU'RE GONE, I'LL HAVE WIPED ALL OF YOU OUT.
IT WAS A PRETTY CLOSE FIGHT, BUT WE WIN.

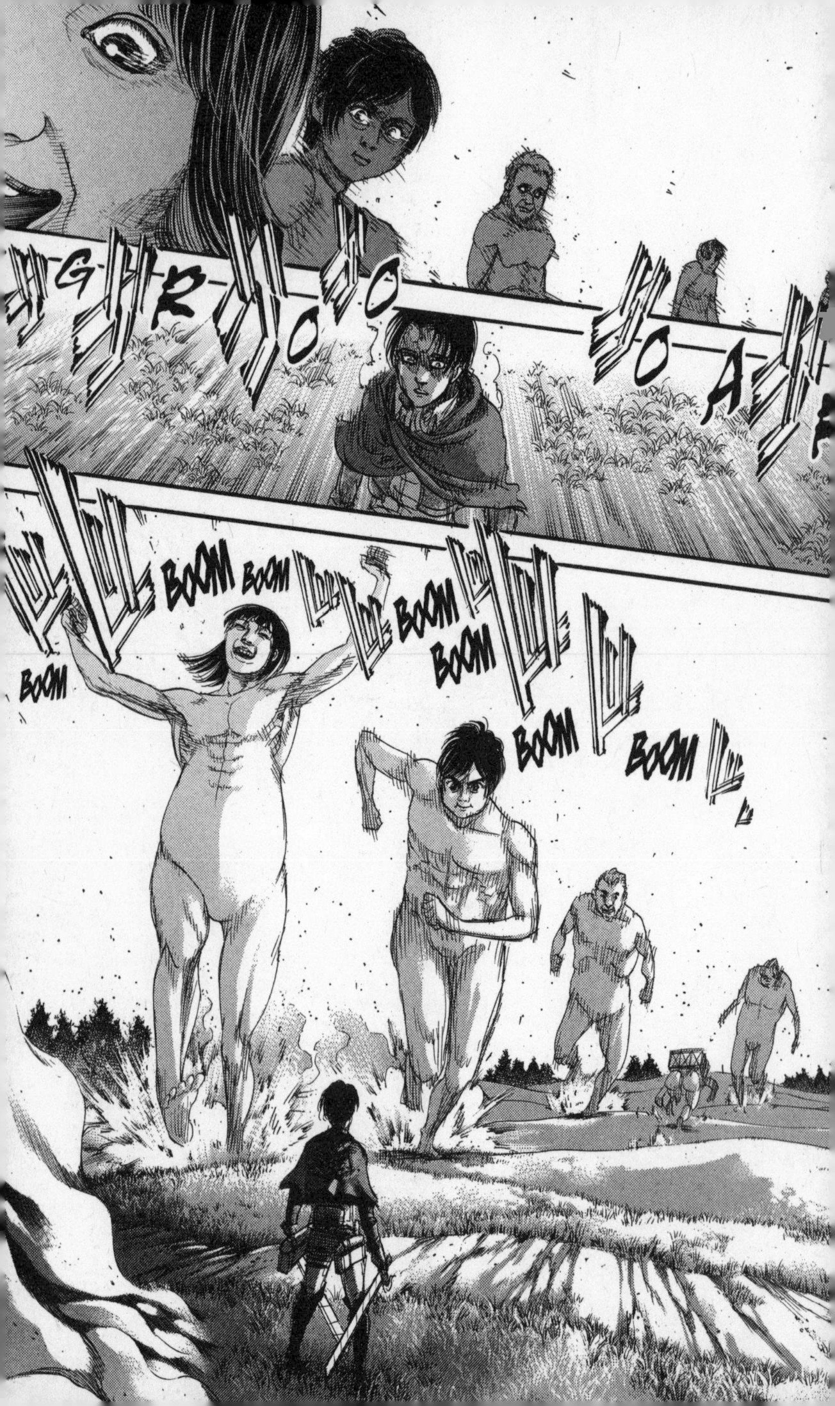
GROOOA
BOOM
BOOM
BOOM
BOOM
BOOM
BOOM BOOM
BOOM

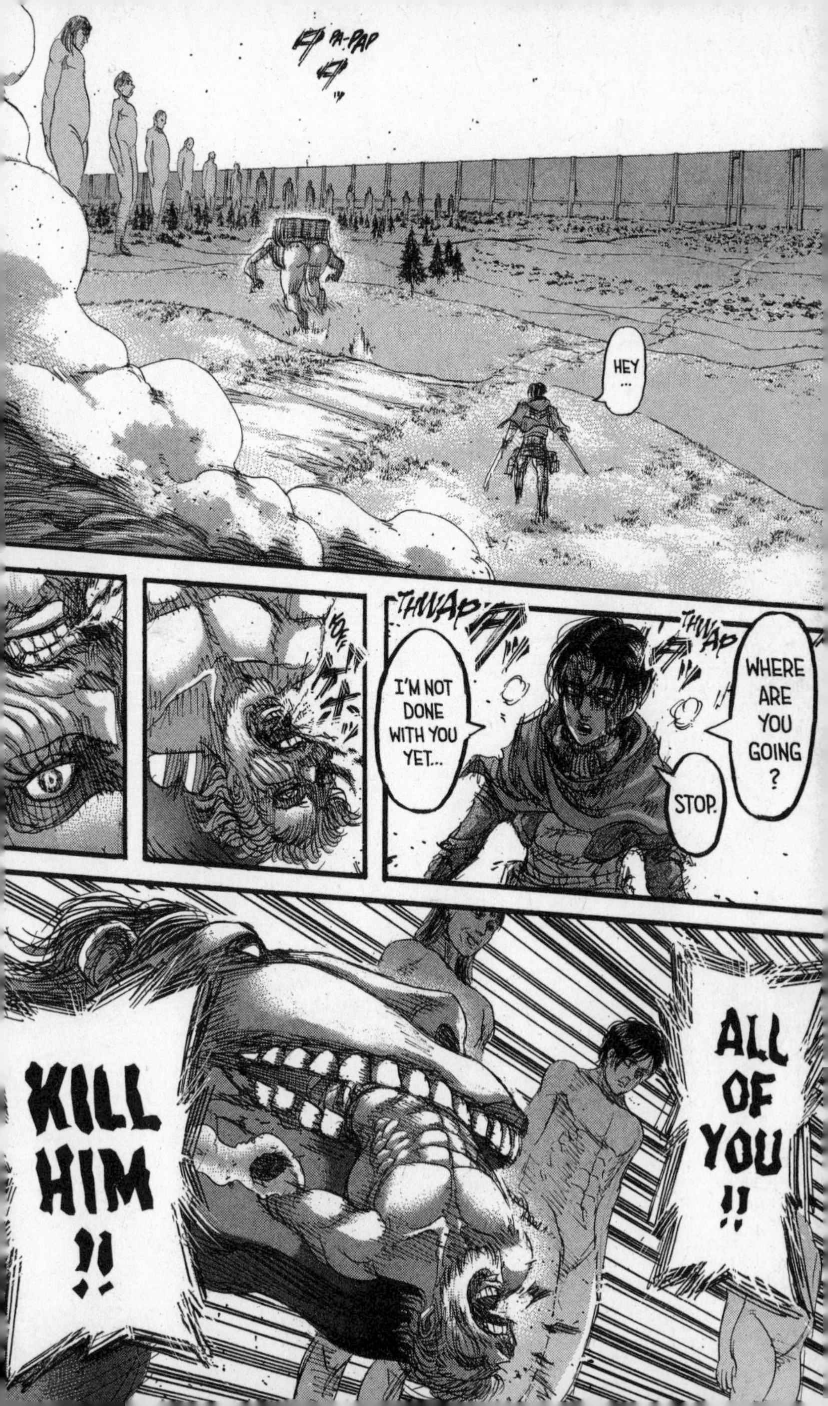
PA-PAP
HEY ...
THWAP
WHERE ARE YOU GOING ?
STOP.
THWAP
I'M NOT DONE WITH YOU YET...
ALL OF YOU !!
KILL HIM !!

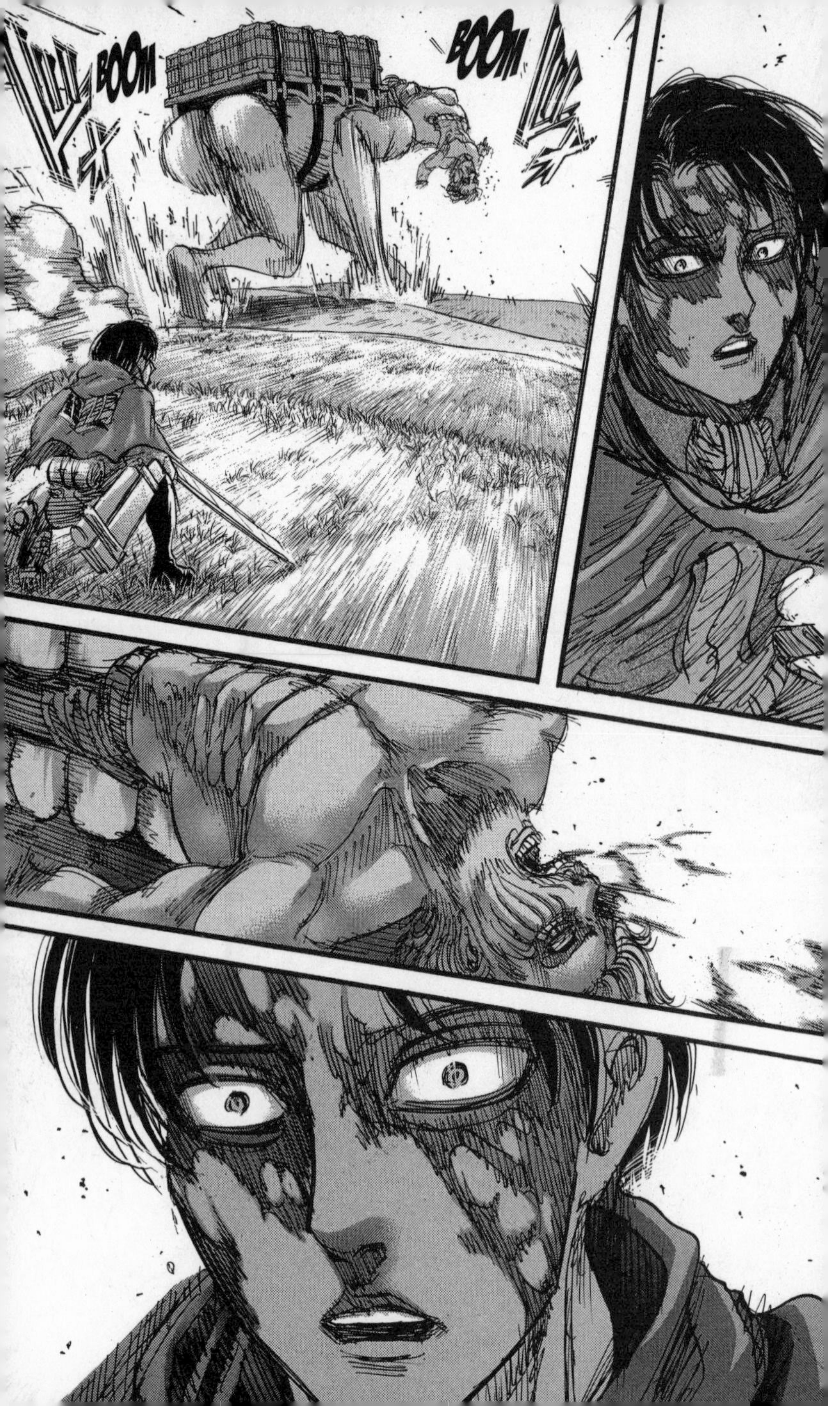
BOOM
BOOM

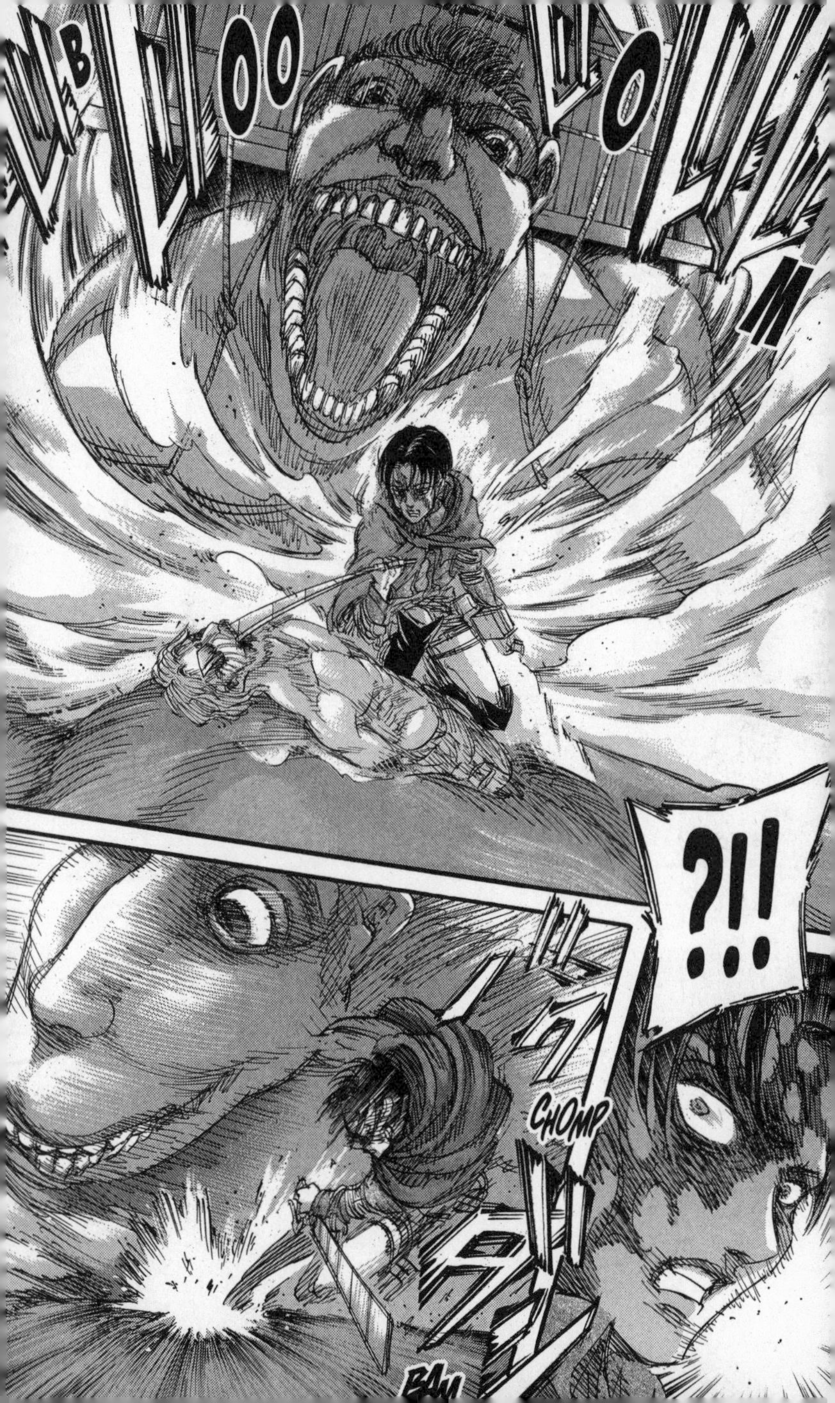
?!!
CHOMP
BAM

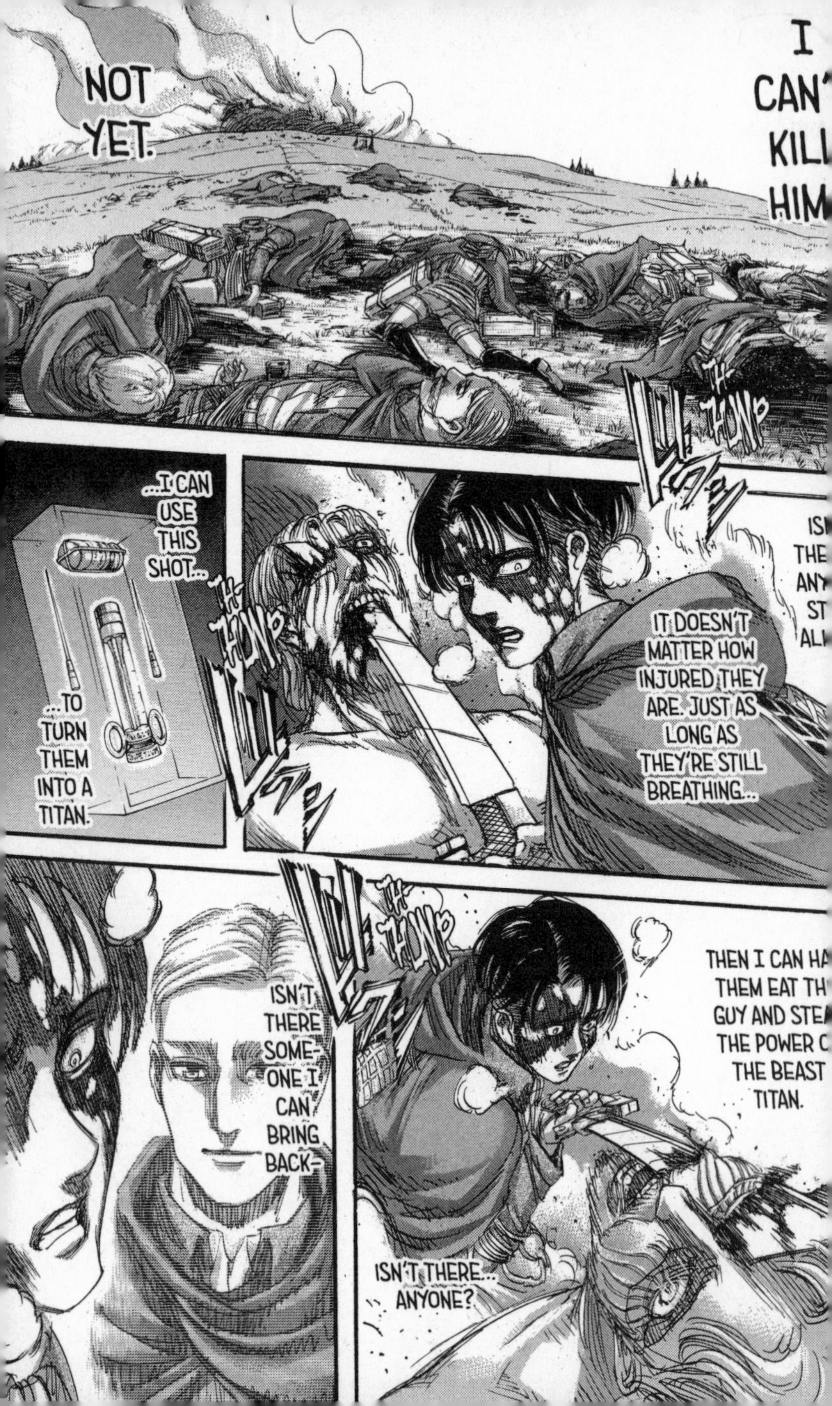
I CAN' KIL HIM
NOT YET.
TH THUMP
IS THE ANY ST ALI
IT DOESN'T MATTER HOW INJURED THEY ARE. JUST AS LONG AS THEY'RE STILL BREATHING...
TH THUMP
...I CAN USE THIS SHOT...
...TO TURN THEM INTO A TITAN.
TH THUMP
THEN I CAN HA THEM EAT TH GUY AND STE THE POWER O THE BEAST TITAN.
ISN'T THERE... ANYONE?
ISN'T THERE SOME-ONE I CAN BRING BACK-

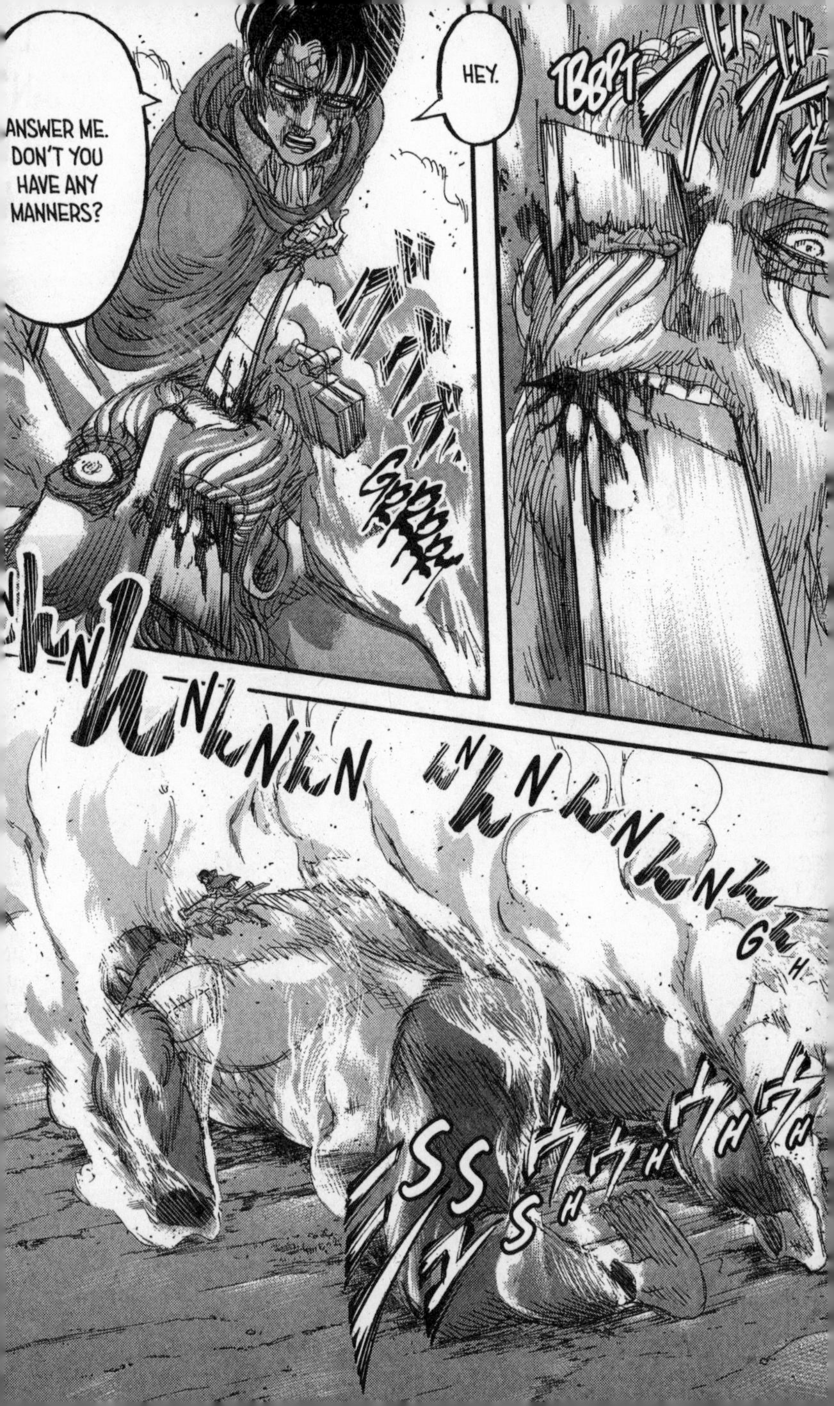
TBBPT
HEY.
ANSWER ME. DON'T YOU HAVE ANY MANNERS?

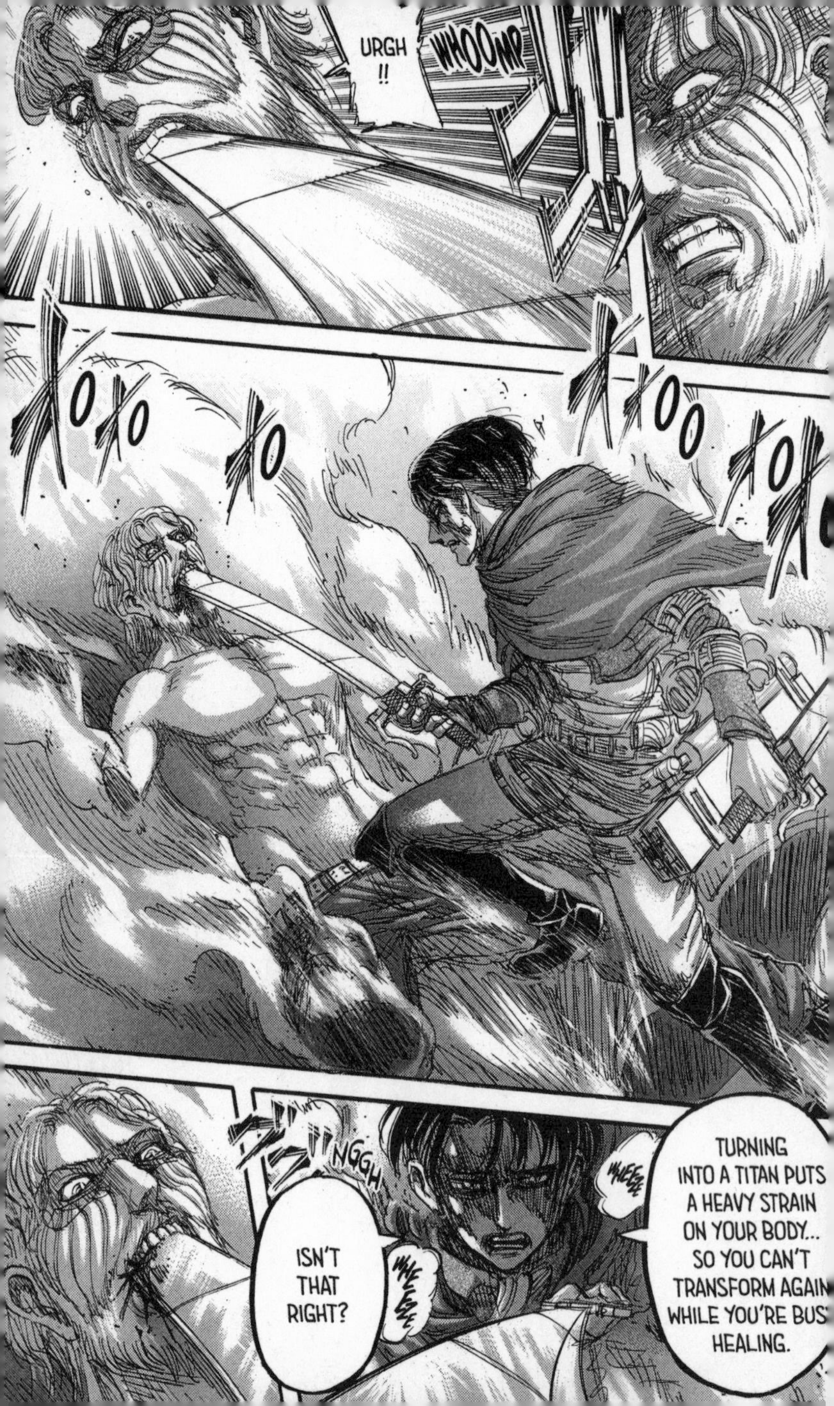
URGH !!
WHOOMP
TURNING INTO A TITAN PUTS A HEAVY STRAIN ON YOUR BODY... SO YOU CAN'T TRANSFORM AGAIN WHILE YOU'RE BUSY HEALING.
WHEEZE
ISN'T THAT RIGHT?
WHEEZE
NGGH

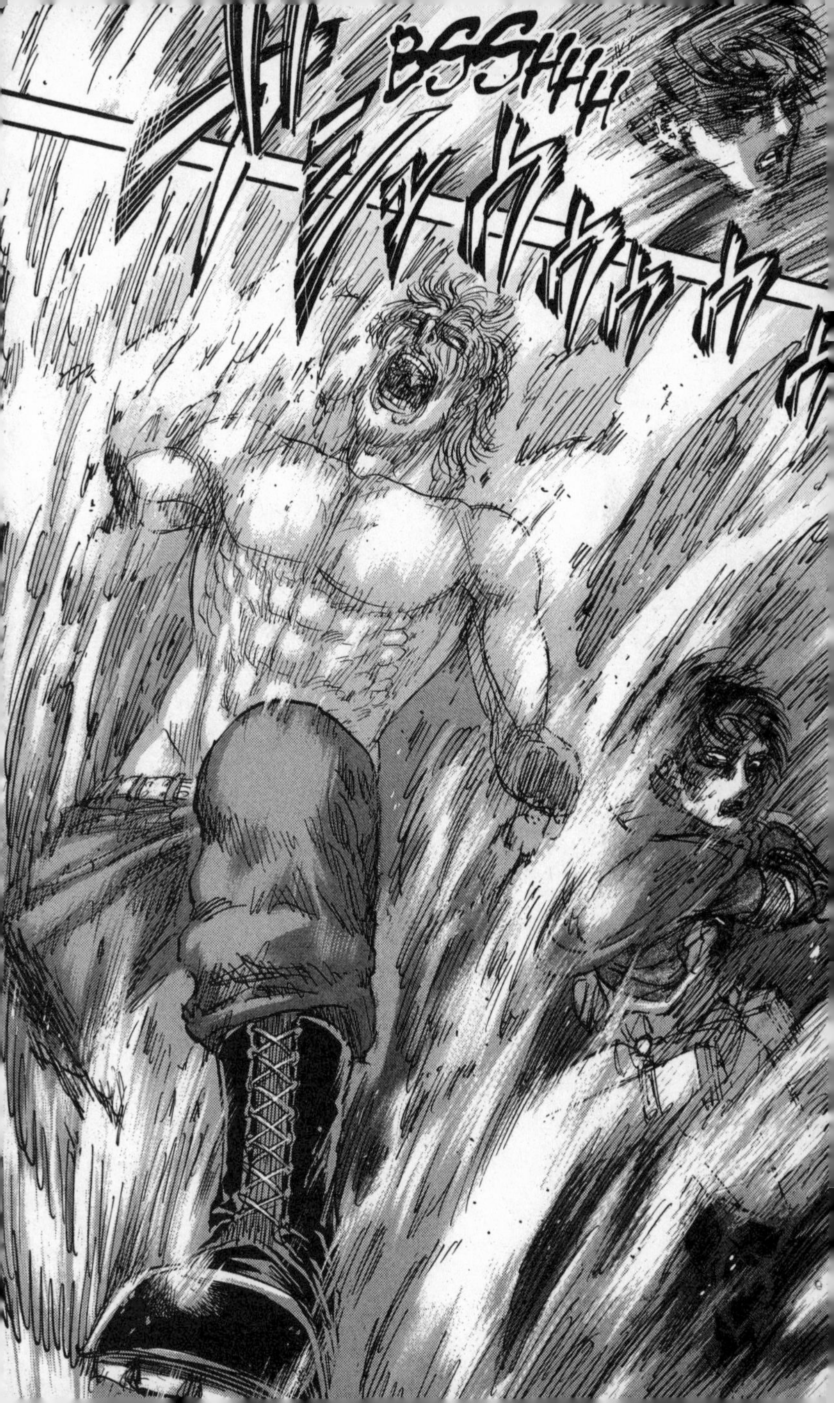
BSSHHH

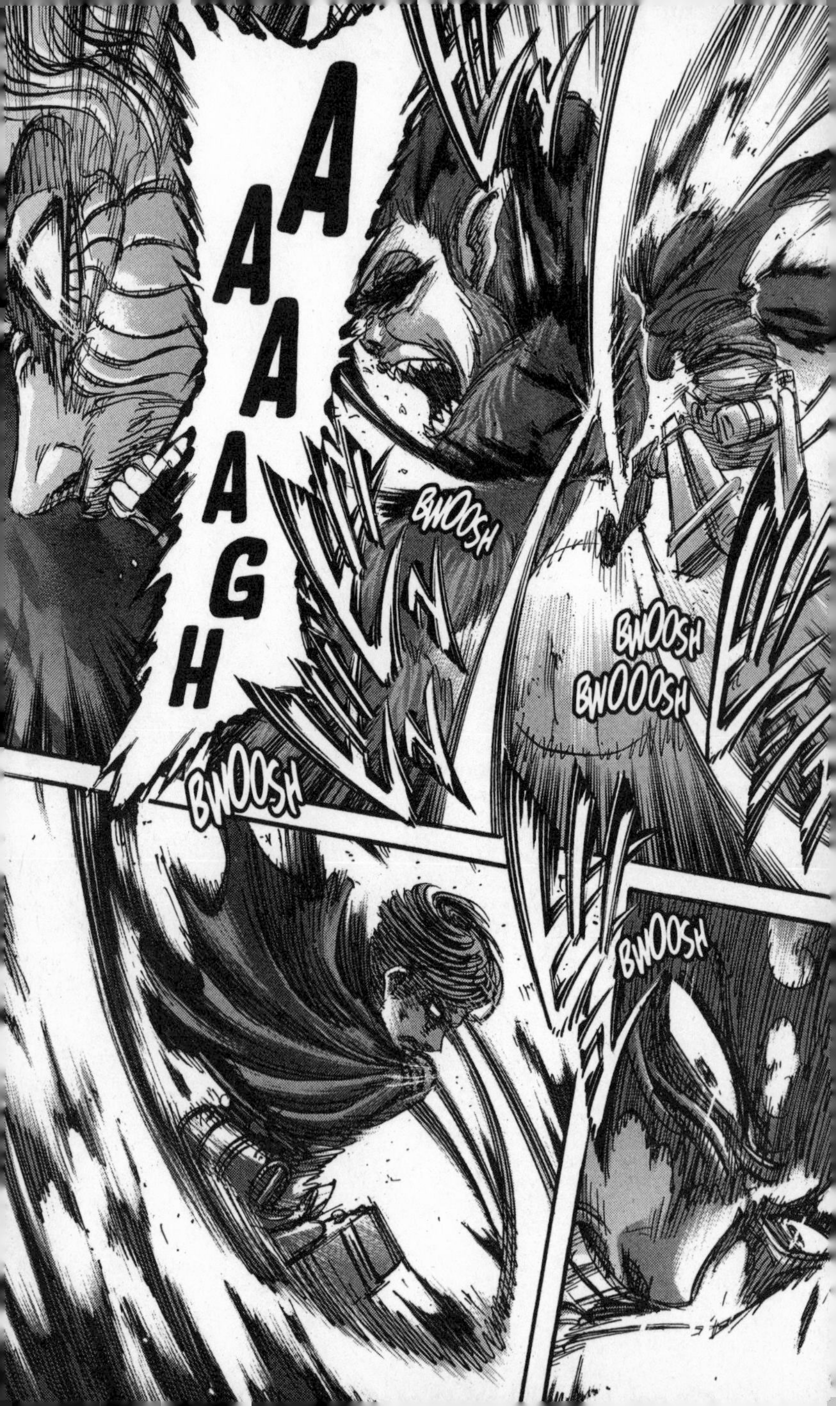
BWOOSH
BWOOOSH
AAAAAGH
BWOOSH
BWOOSH
BWOOSH

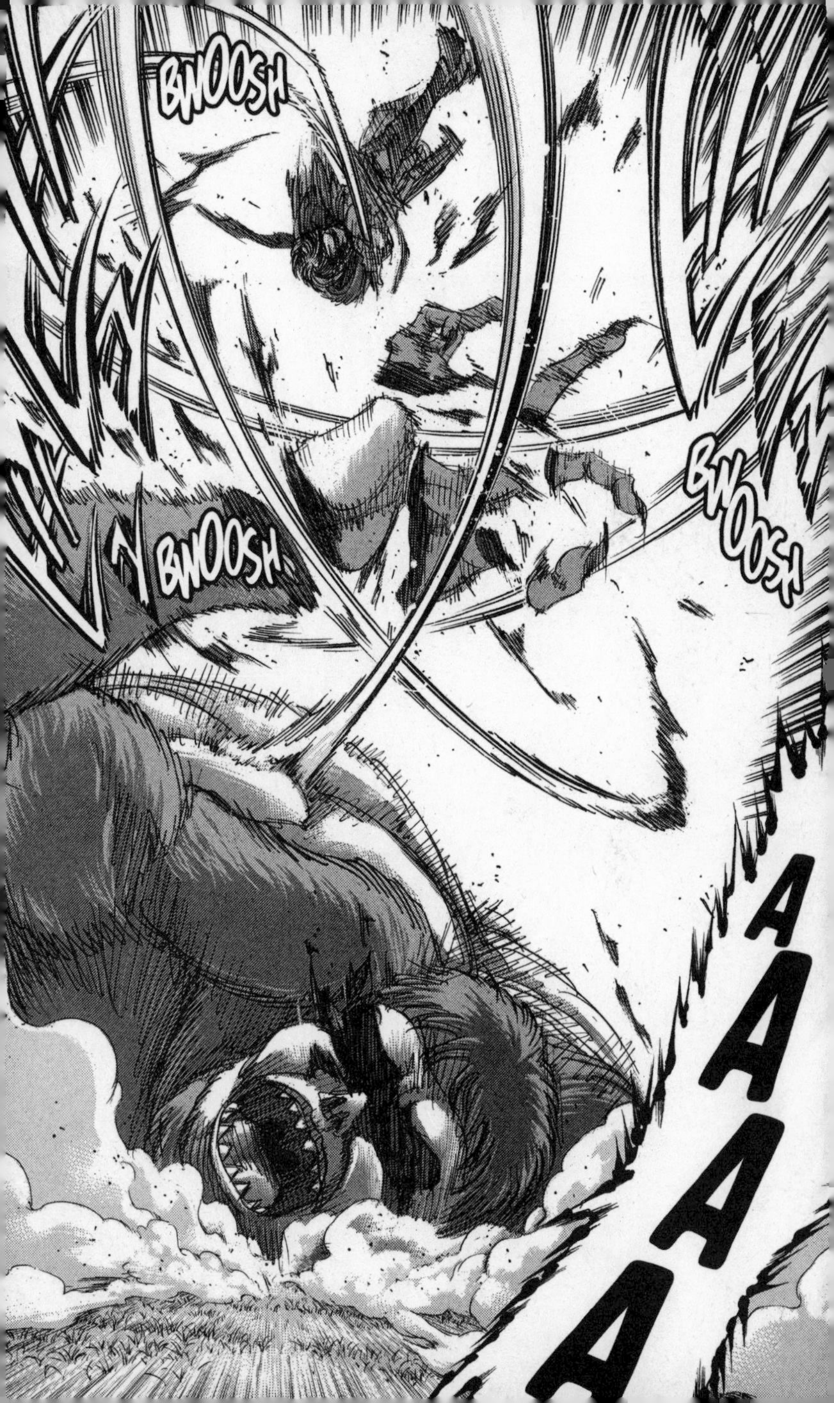
BWOOSH
BWOOSH
BWOOSH
AAAAA

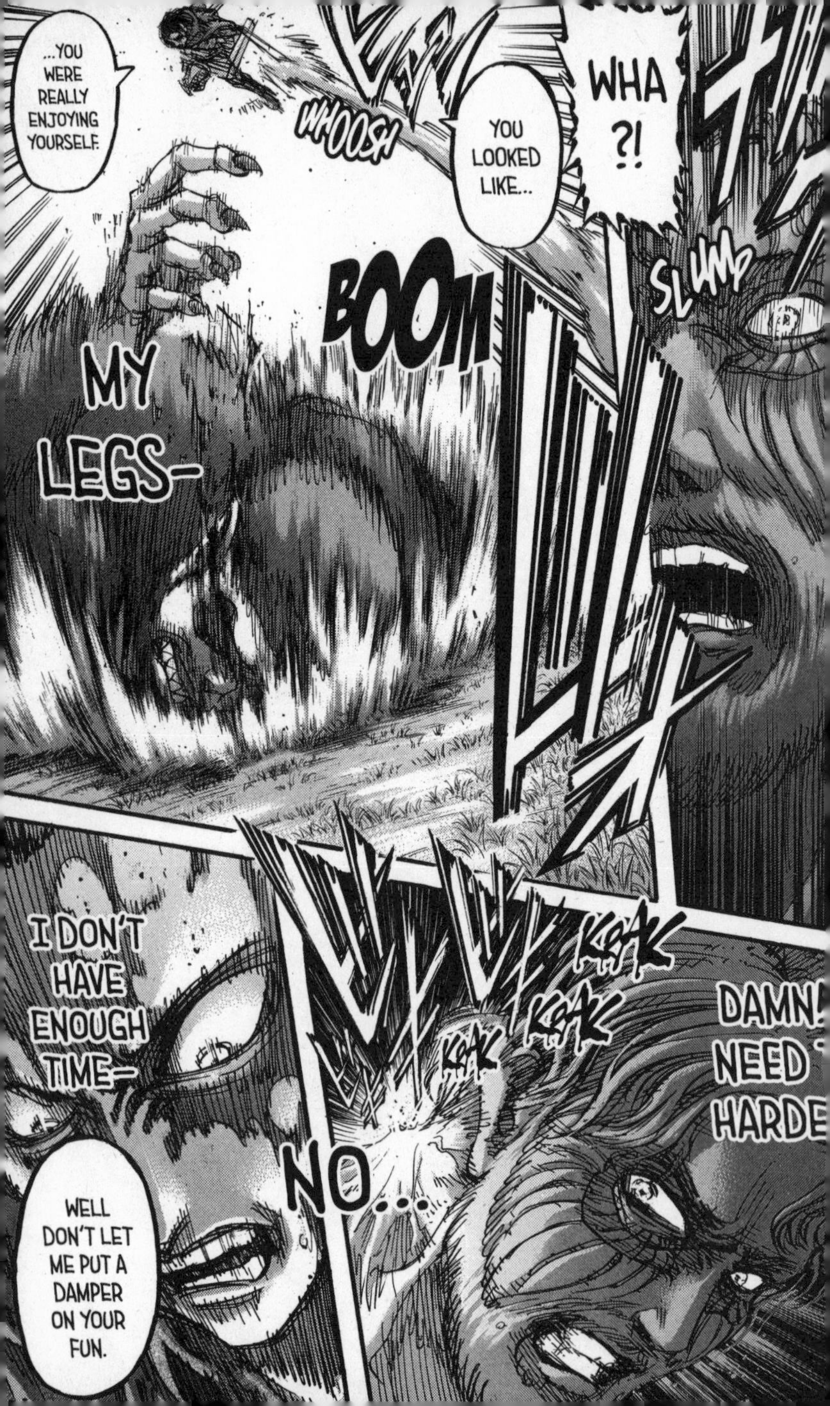
WHA ?!
SLUMP
YOU LOOKED LIKE...
WHOOSH
...YOU WERE REALLY ENJOYING YOURSELF.
BOOM
MY LEGS-
DAMN! NEED HARDE
KRAK KRAK KRAK
NO...
I DON'T HAVE ENOUGH TIME-
WELL DON'T LET ME PUT A DAMPER ON YOUR FUN.

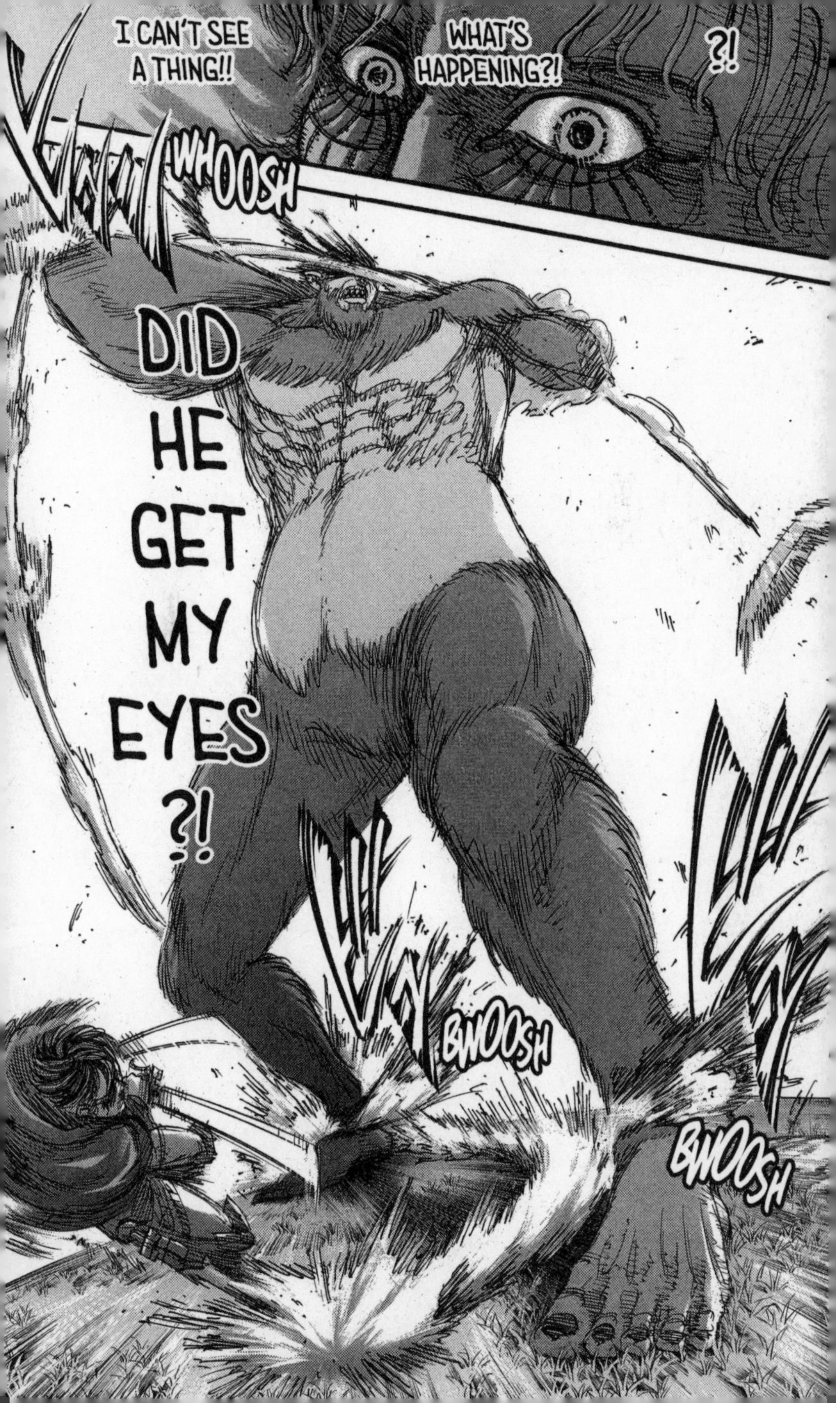
?!
WHAT'S HAPPENING?!
I CAN'T SEE A THING!!
WHOOSH
DID HE GET MY EYES ?!
BWOOSH
BWOOSH

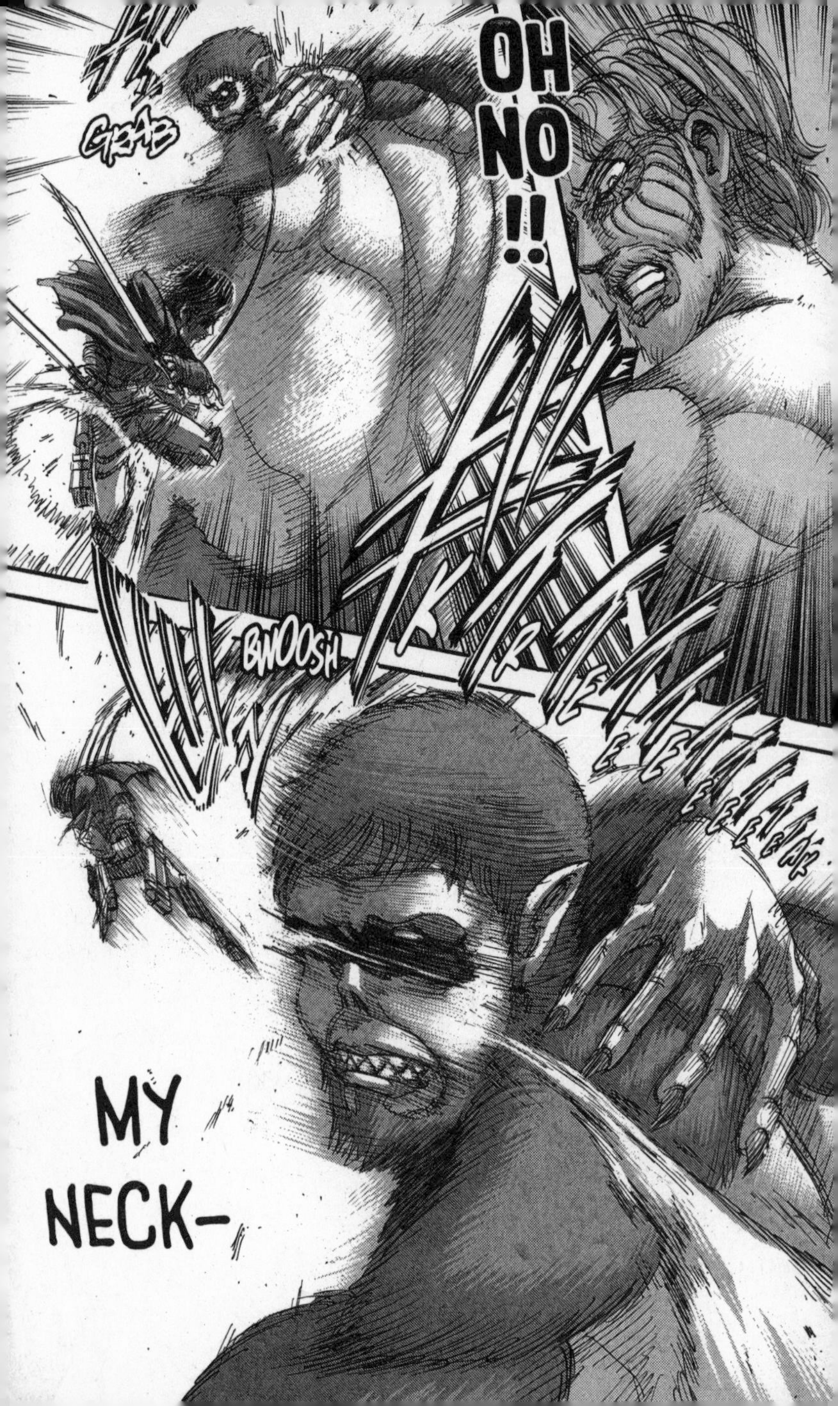
GRAB
OH NO!!
BWOOSH
MY NECK-

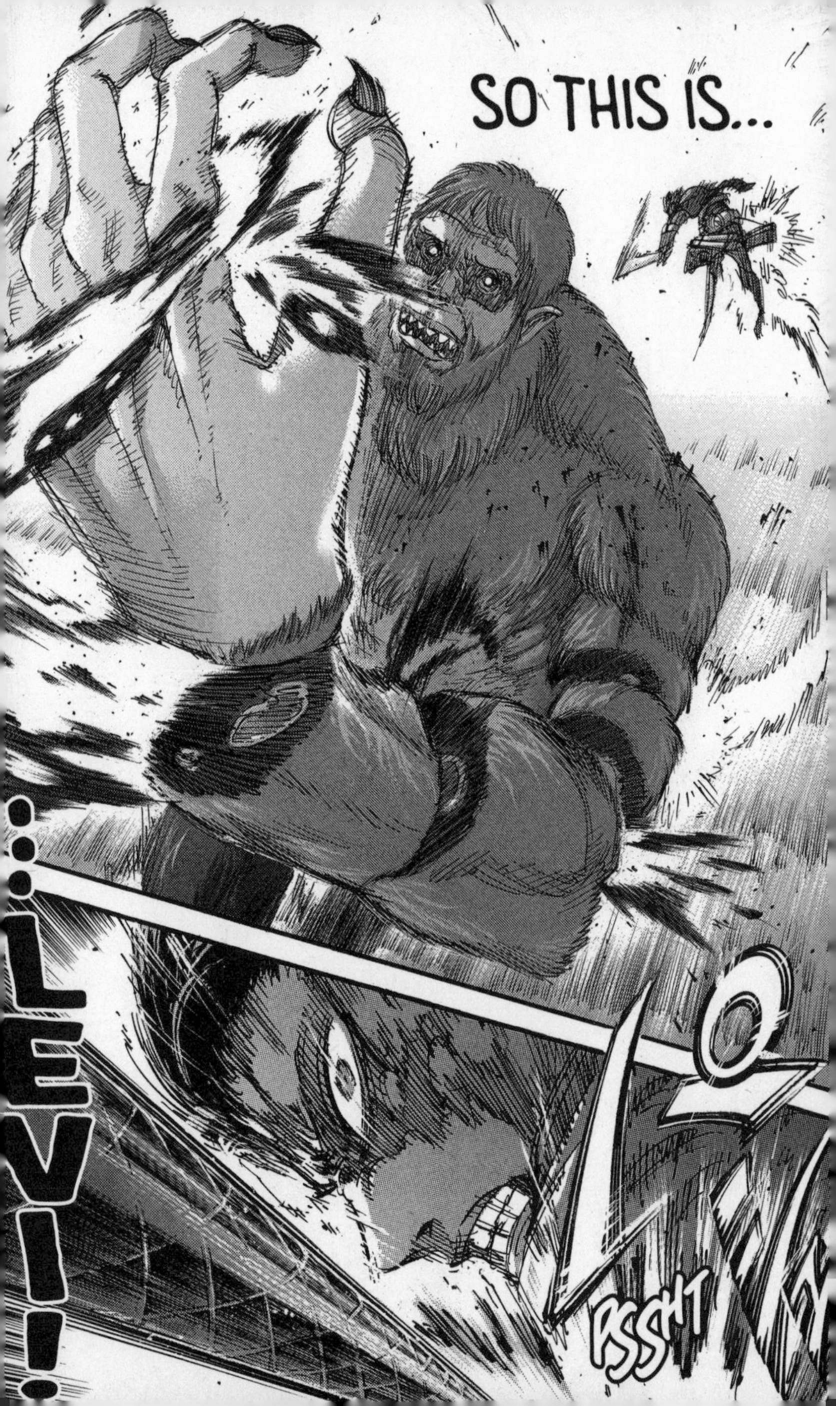
SO THIS IS...
...LEVI!
PSSHT

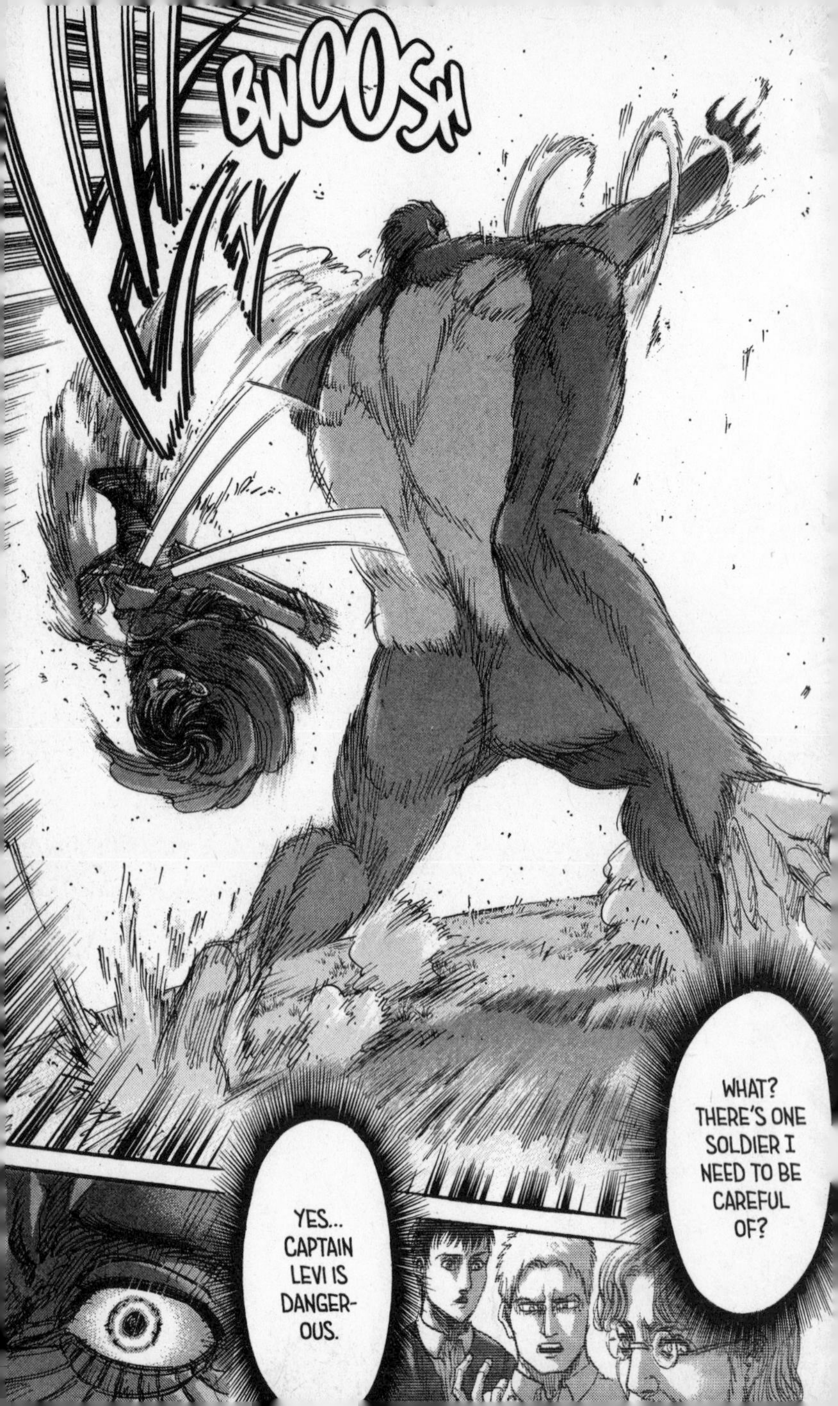
BWOOSH
WHAT? THERE'S ONE SOLDIER I NEED TO BE CAREFUL OF?
YES... CAPTAIN LEVI IS DANGER-OUS.

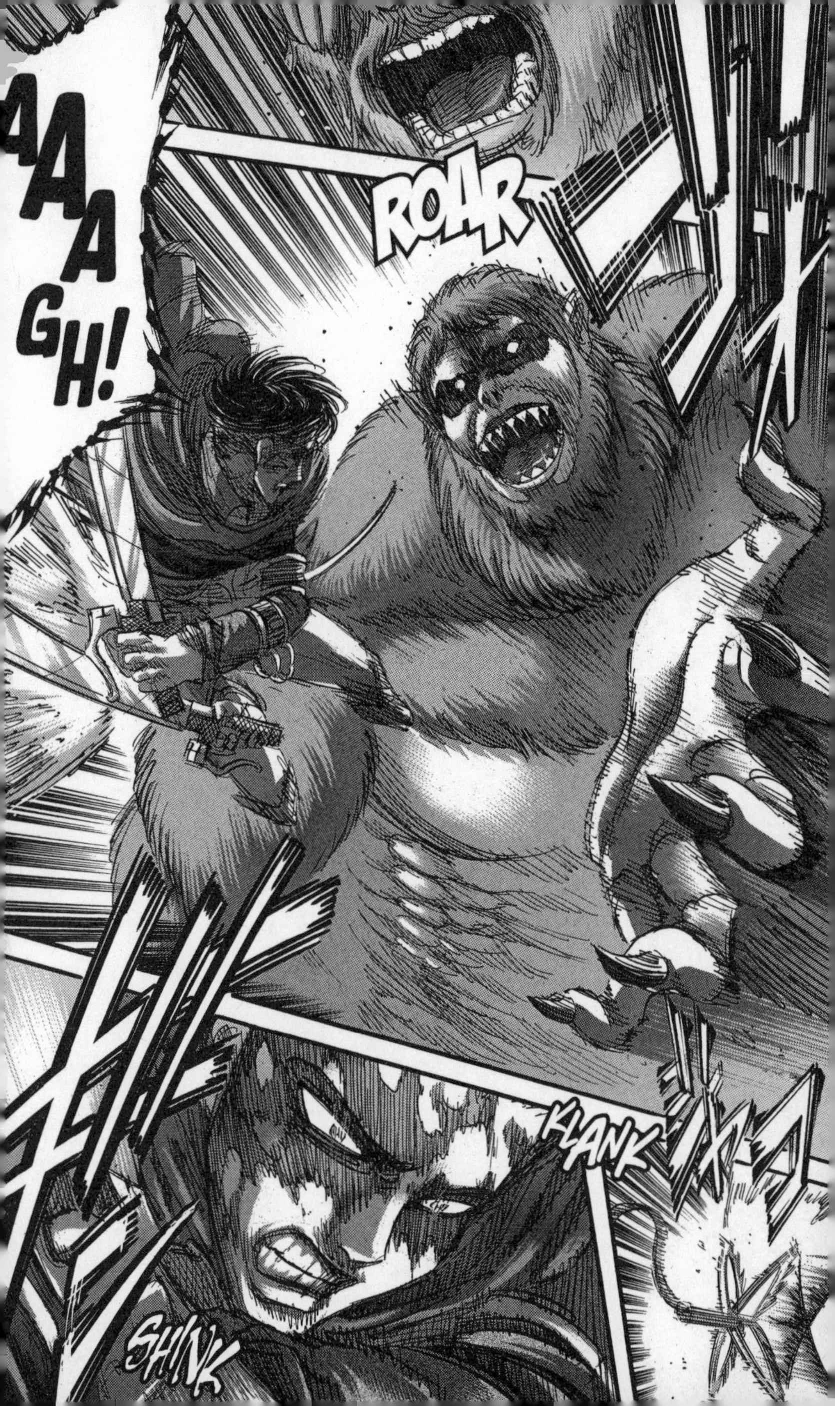

ROAR
AAAAGH!
KLANK
SHINK

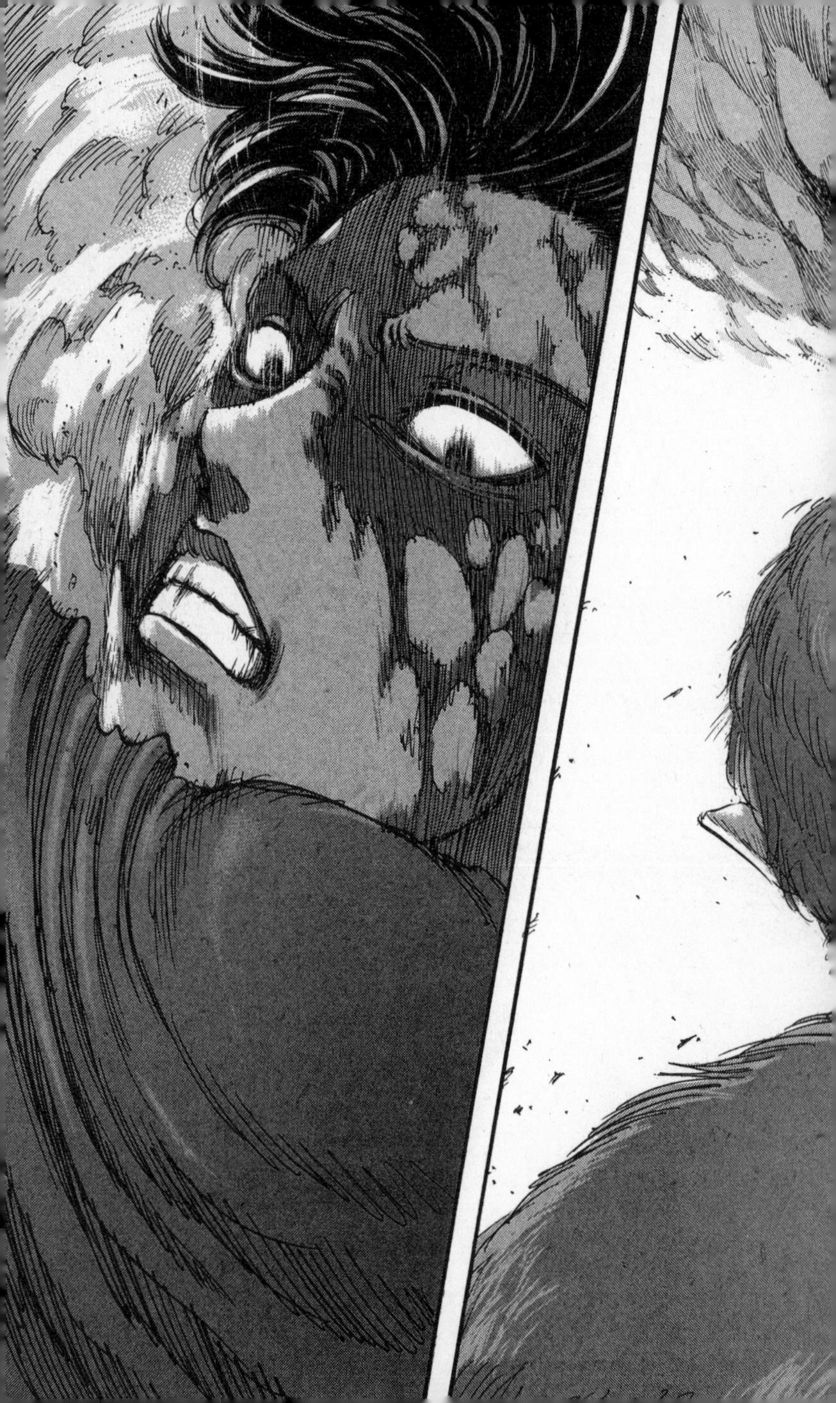

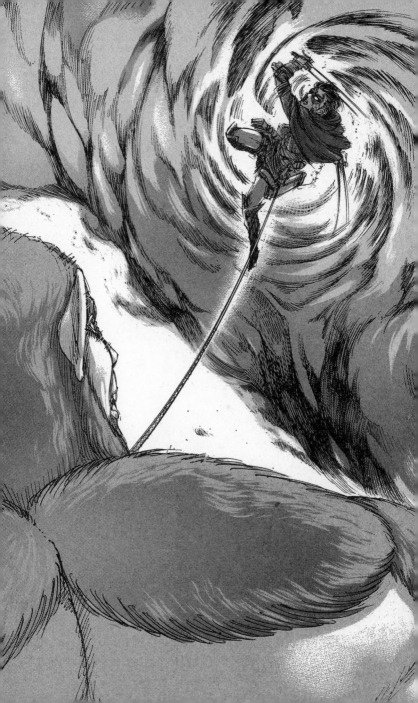

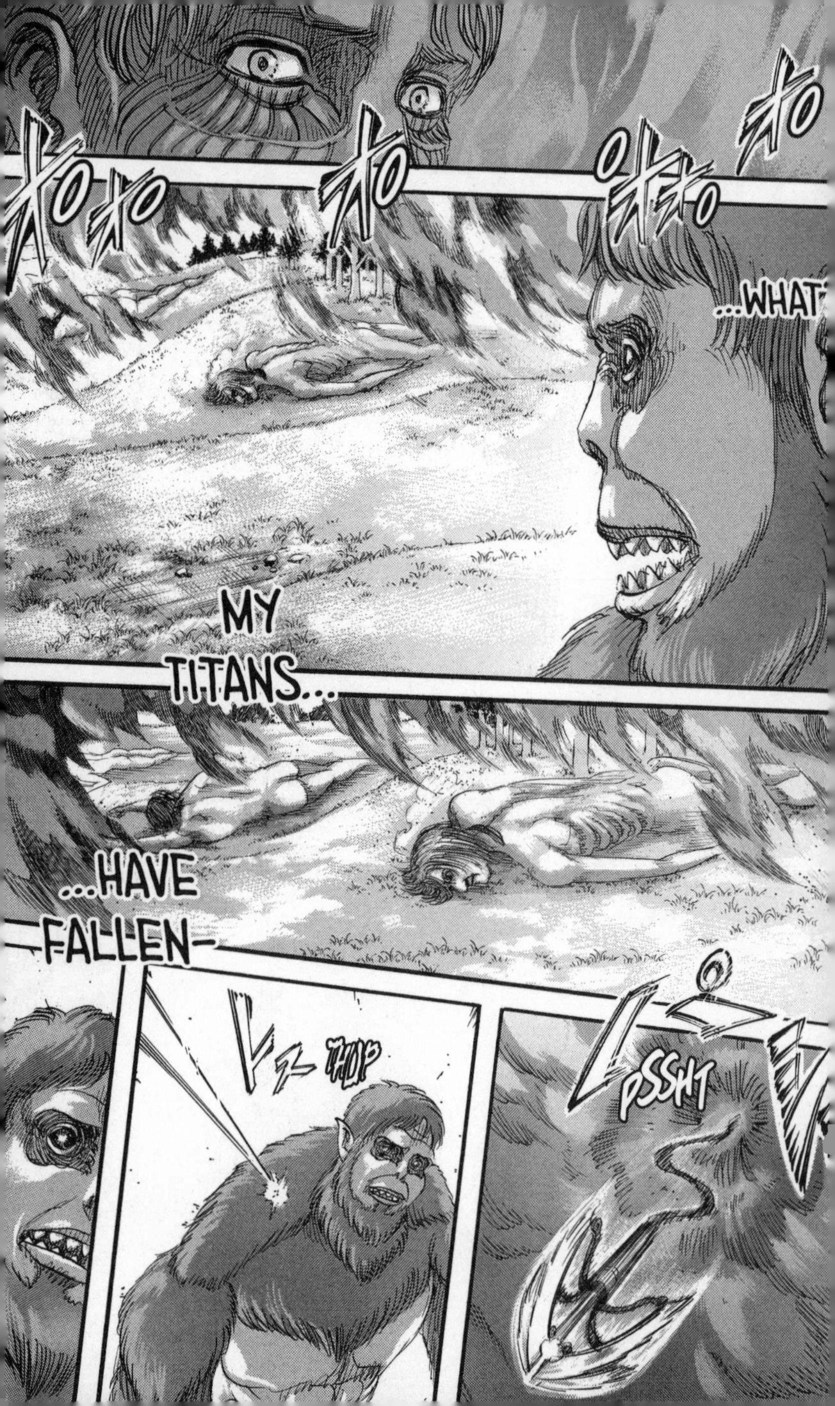
...WHAT
MY TITANS...
...HAVE FALLEN
THUP
PSSHT

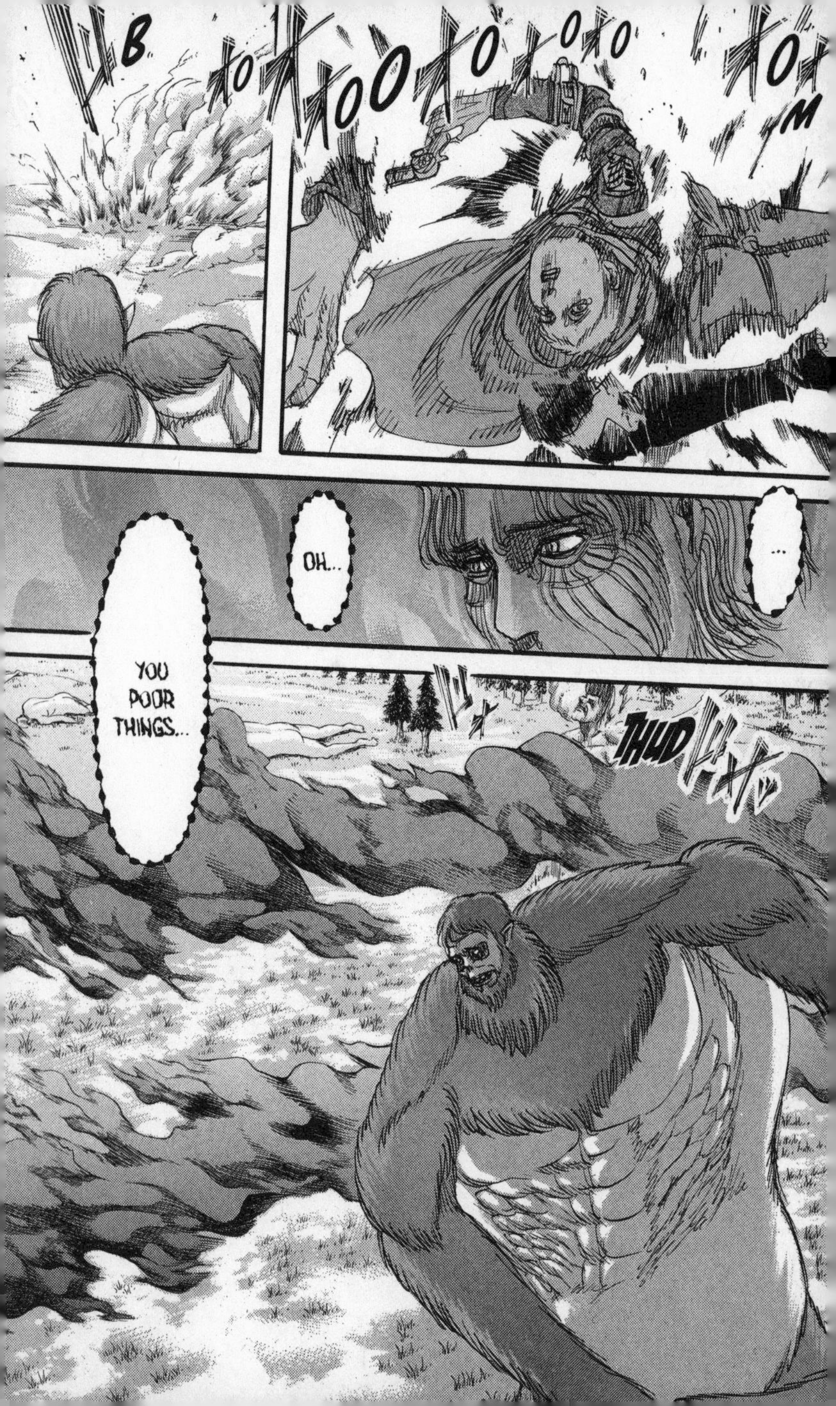
BOOOOOOOOM
...
OH...
YOU POOR THINGS...
THUD

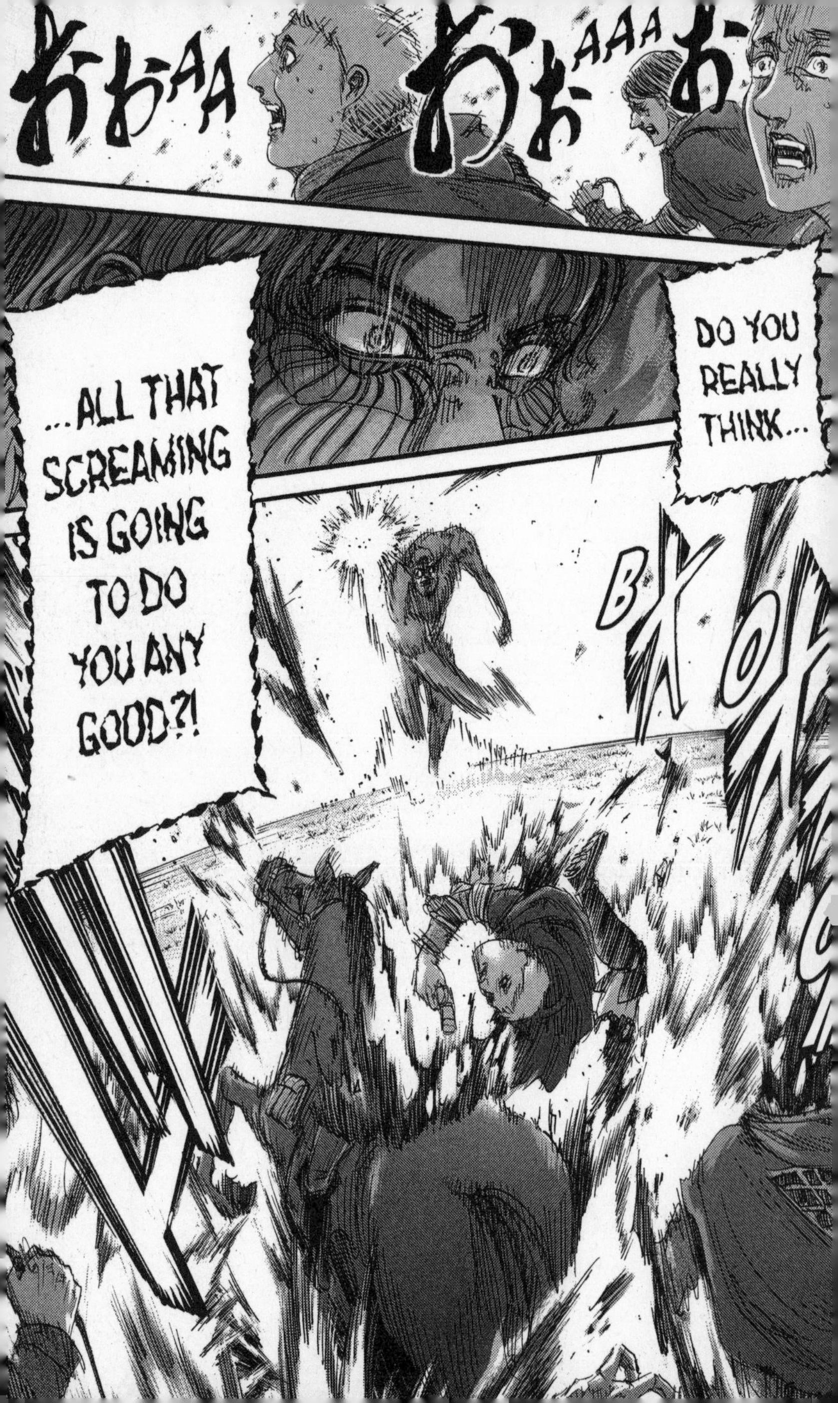
DO YOU REALLY THINK...
...ALL THAT SCREAMING IS GOING TO DO YOU ANY GOOD?!

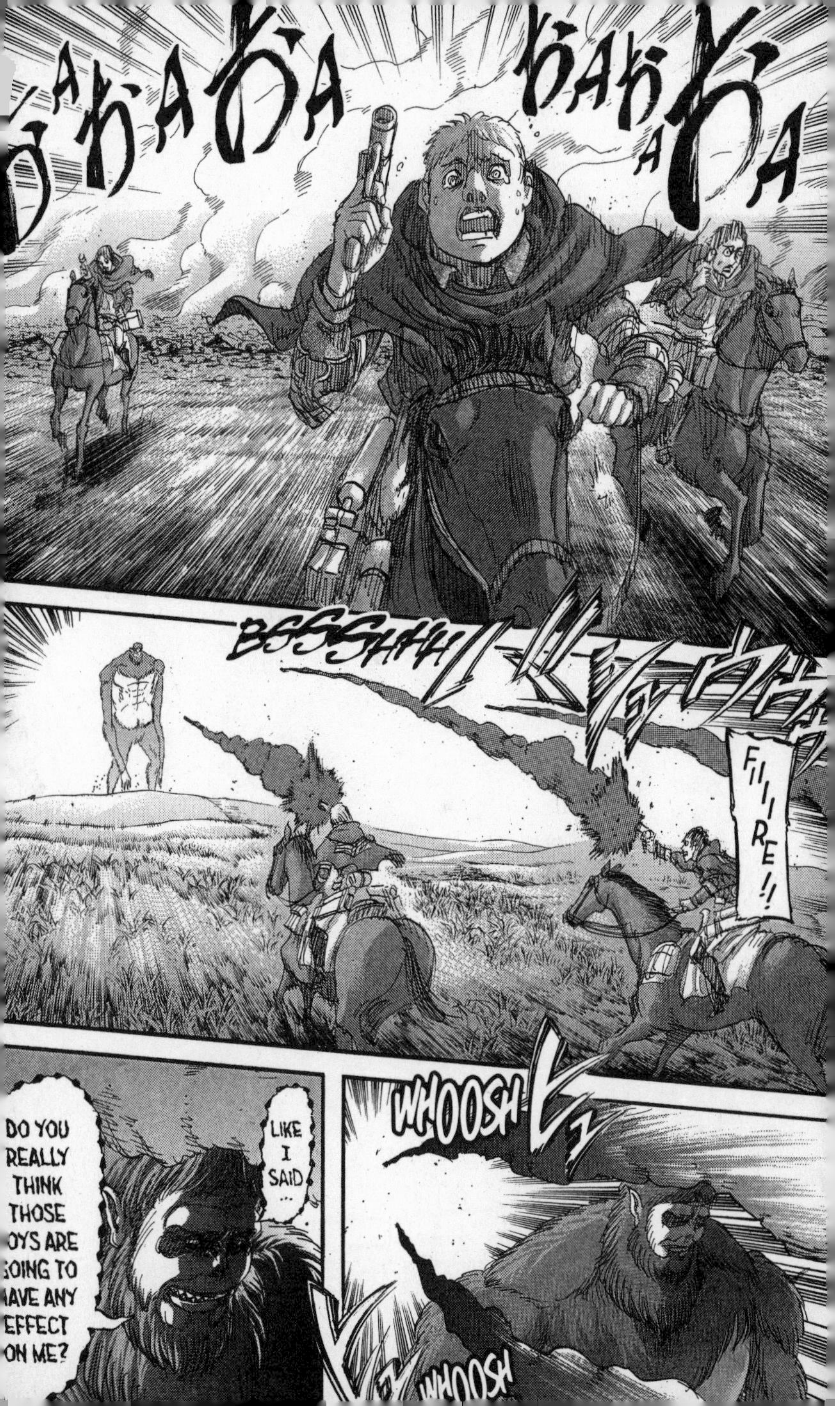
AAAA
AAAA
BSSSHHH
FIIIIIRE!!
WHOOSH
WHOOSH
LIKE I SAID...
DO YOU REALLY THINK THOSE OYS ARE OING TO AVE ANY EFFECT ON ME?

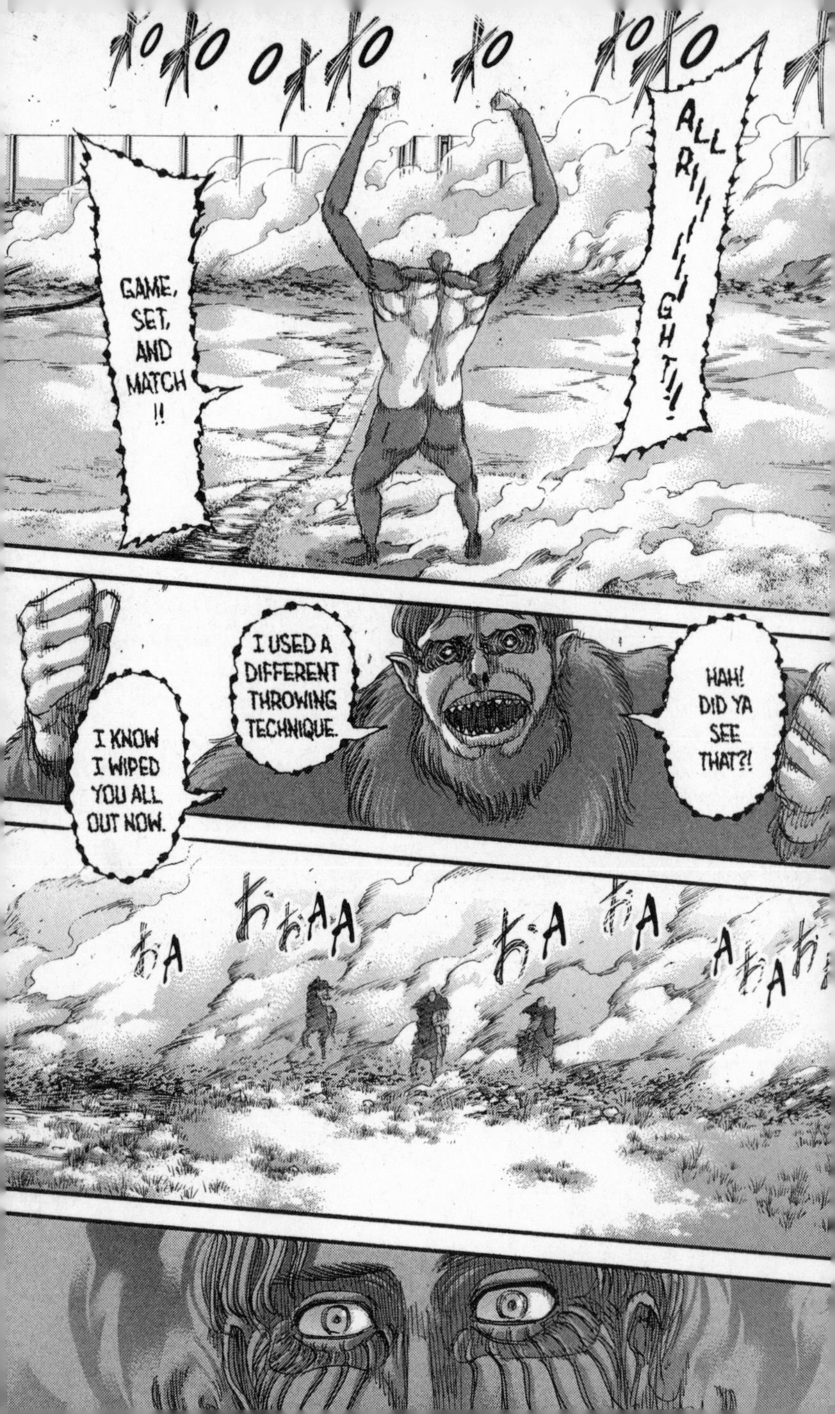
ALL RIIIIIIIIGHT!!
GAME, SET, AND MATCH!!
HAH! DID YA SEE THAT?!
I USED A DIFFERENT THROWING TECHNIQUE.
I KNOW I WIPED YOU ALL OUT NOW.

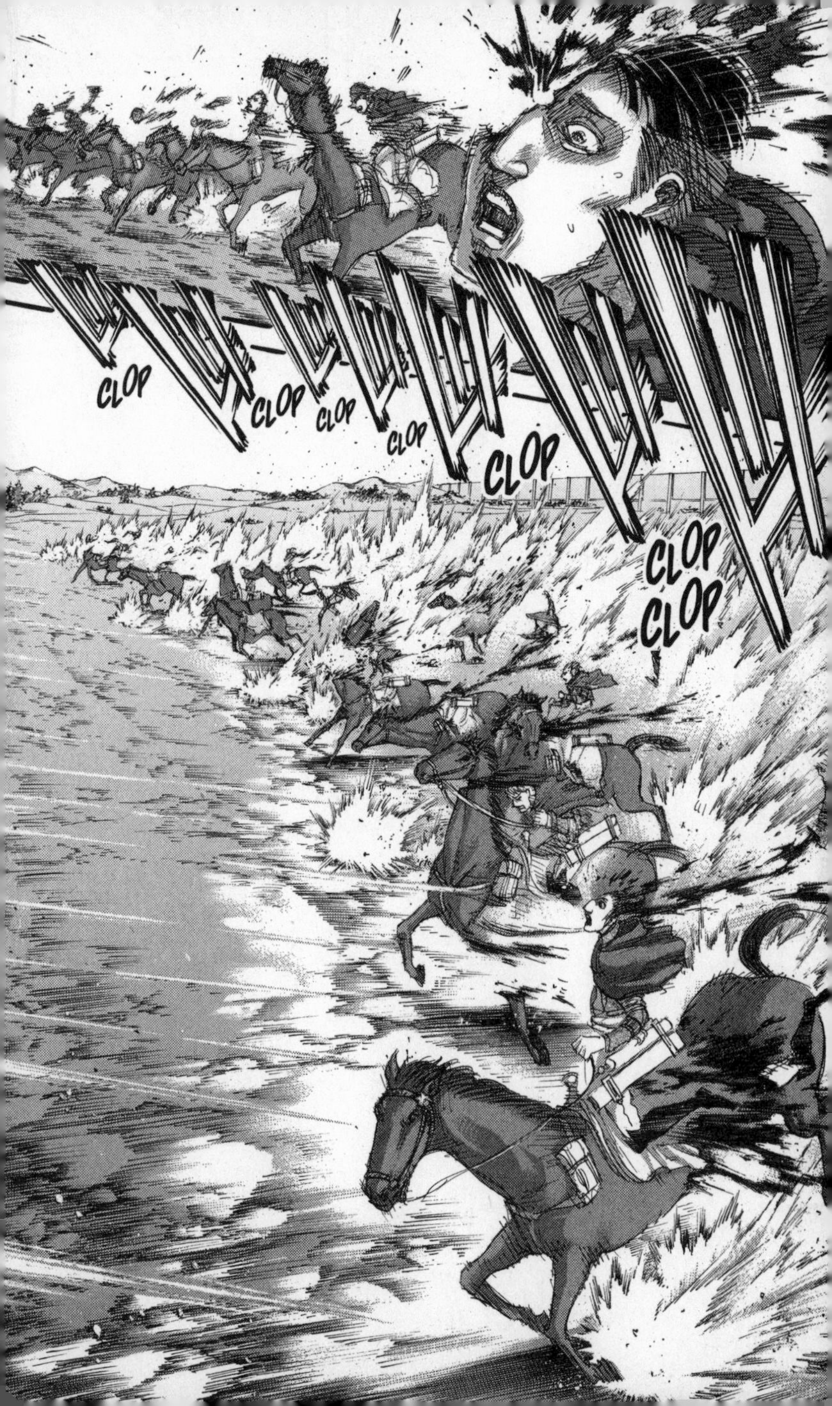
CLOP
CLOP
CLOP
CLOP
CLOP
CLOP
CLOP
CLOP
CLOP

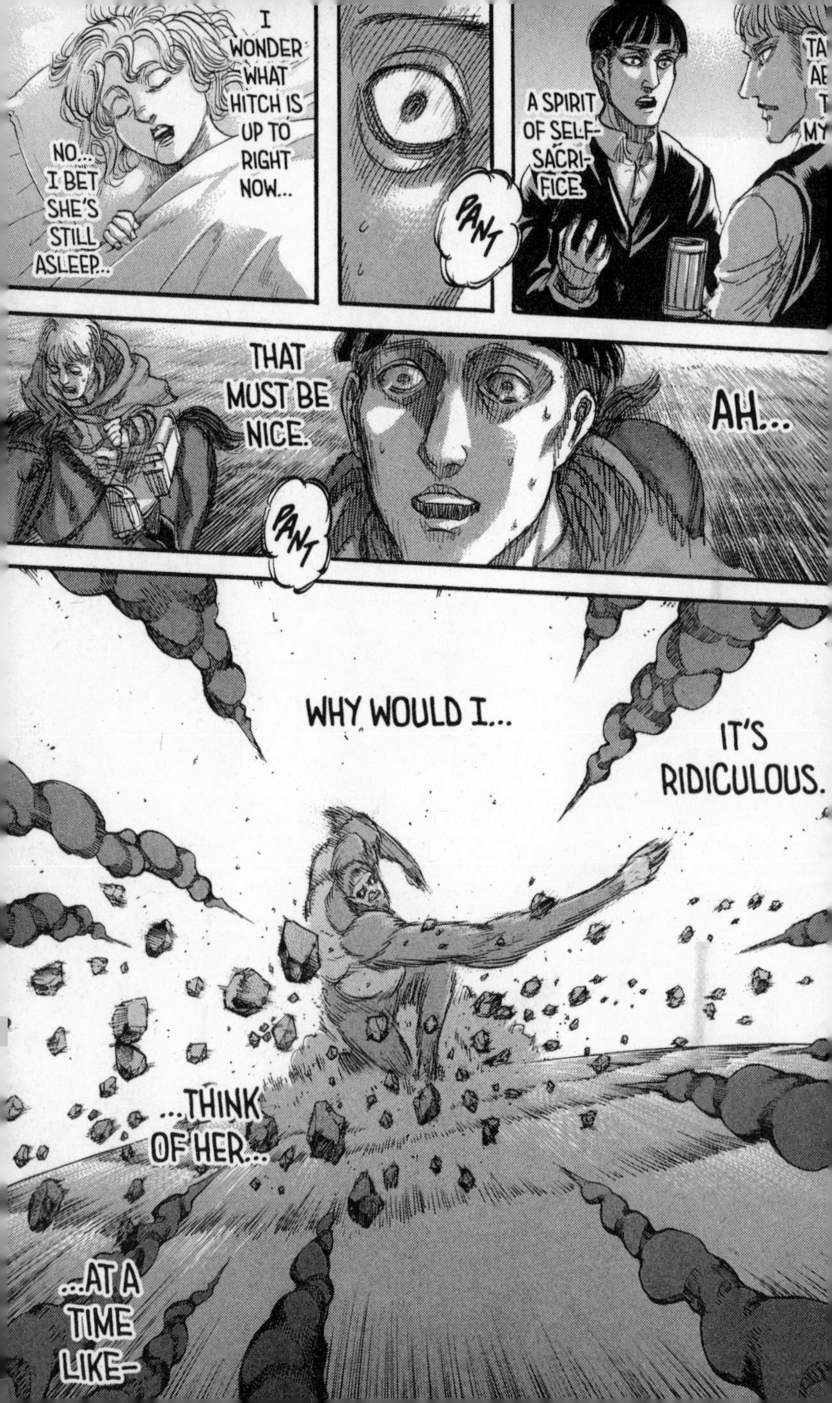
A SPIRIT OF SELF-SACRIFICE.
PANT
I WONDER WHAT HITCH IS UP TO RIGHT NOW...
NO... I BET SHE'S STILL ASLEEP...
AH...
PANT
THAT MUST BE NICE.
IT'S RIDICULOUS.
WHY WOULD I...
...THINK OF HER...
...AT A TIME LIKE-

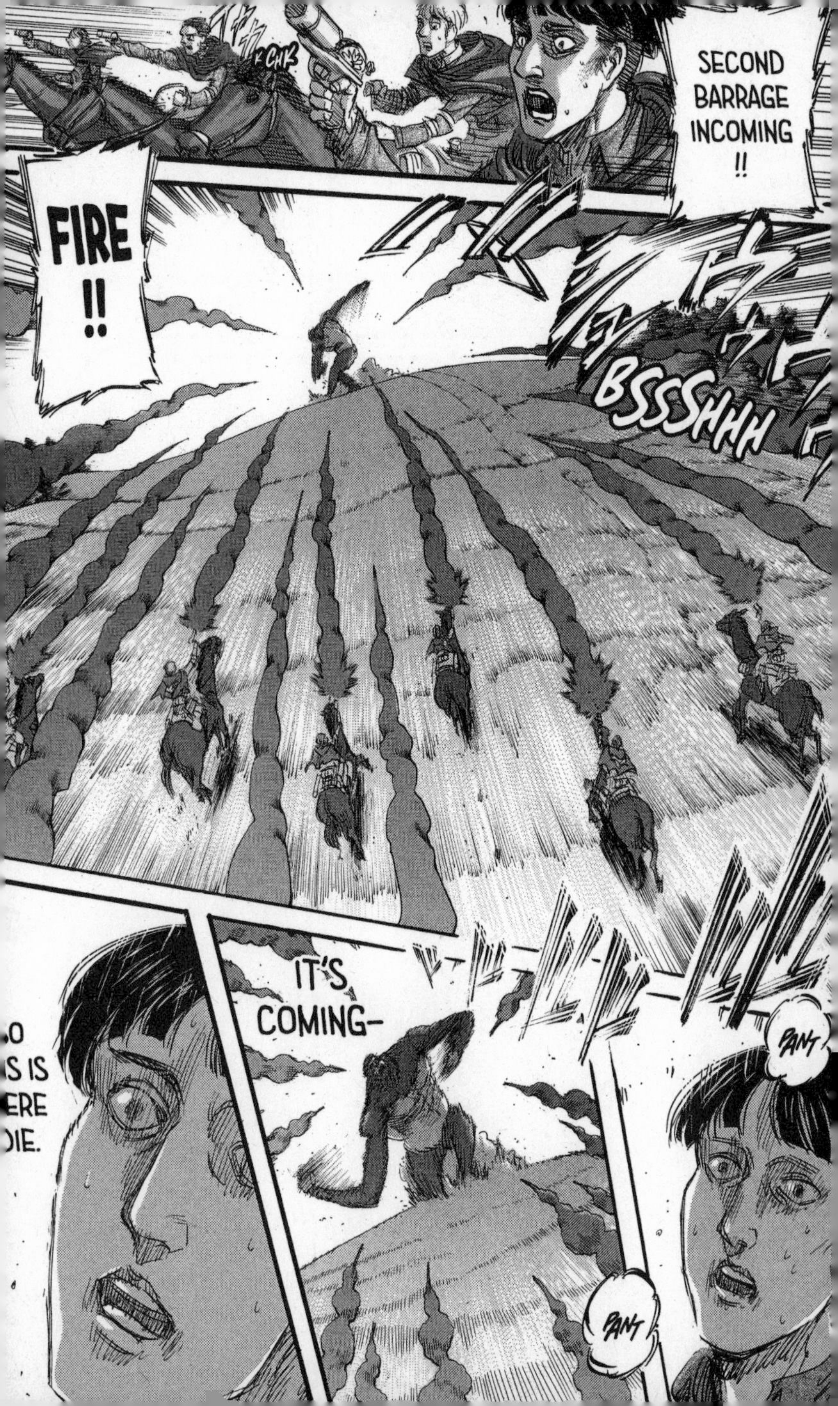
SECOND BARRAGE INCOMING !!
KCHK
FIRE !!
BSSSHHH
PANT
PANT
IT'S COMING-

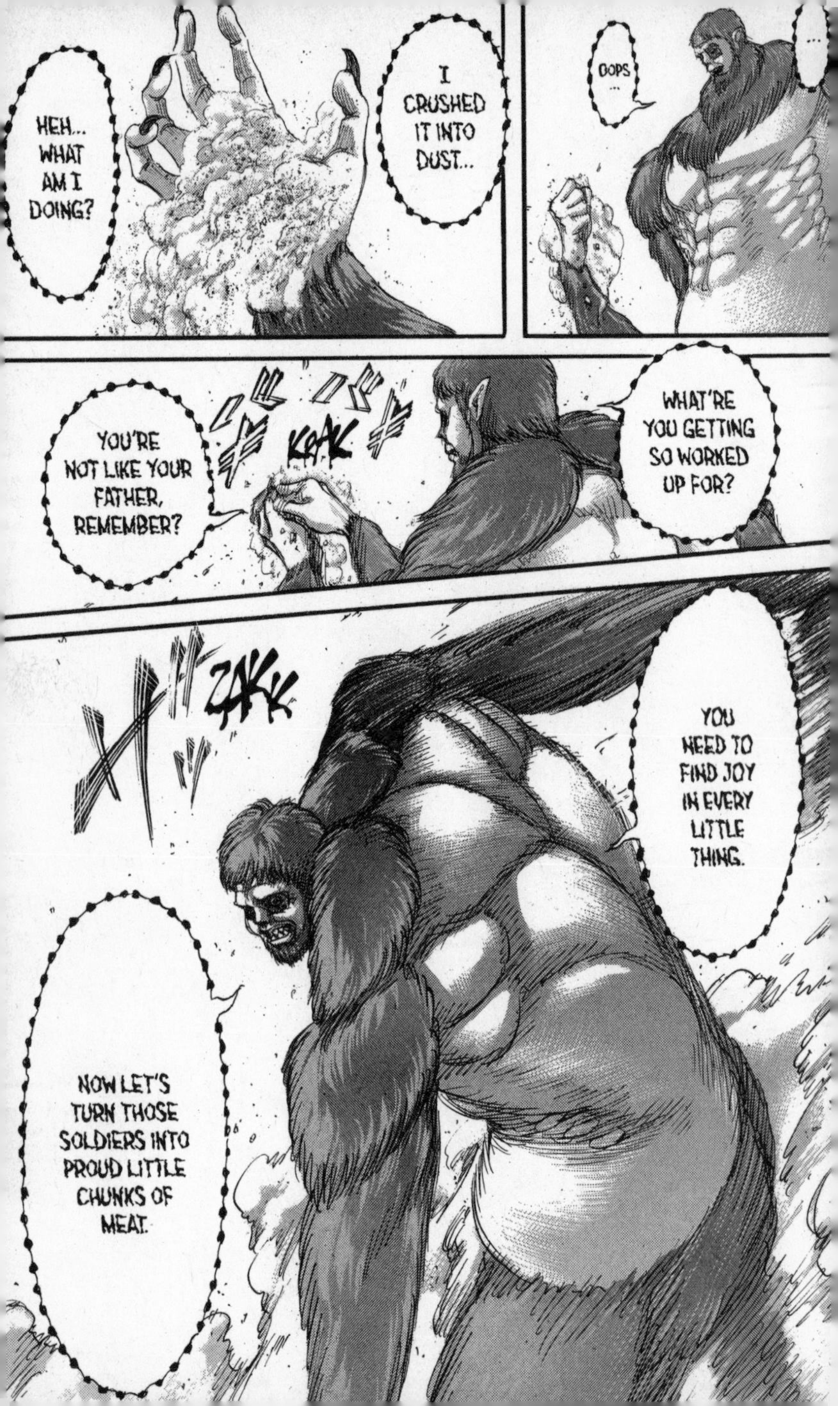
...
OOPS...
I CRUSHED IT INTO DUST...
HEH... WHAT AM I DOING?
WHAT'RE YOU GETTING SO WORKED UP FOR?
KRAK
YOU'RE NOT LIKE YOUR FATHER, REMEMBER?
YOU NEED TO FIND JOY IN EVERY LITTLE THING.
ZAKK
NOW LET'S TURN THOSE SOLDIERS INTO PROUD LITTLE CHUNKS OF MEAT.

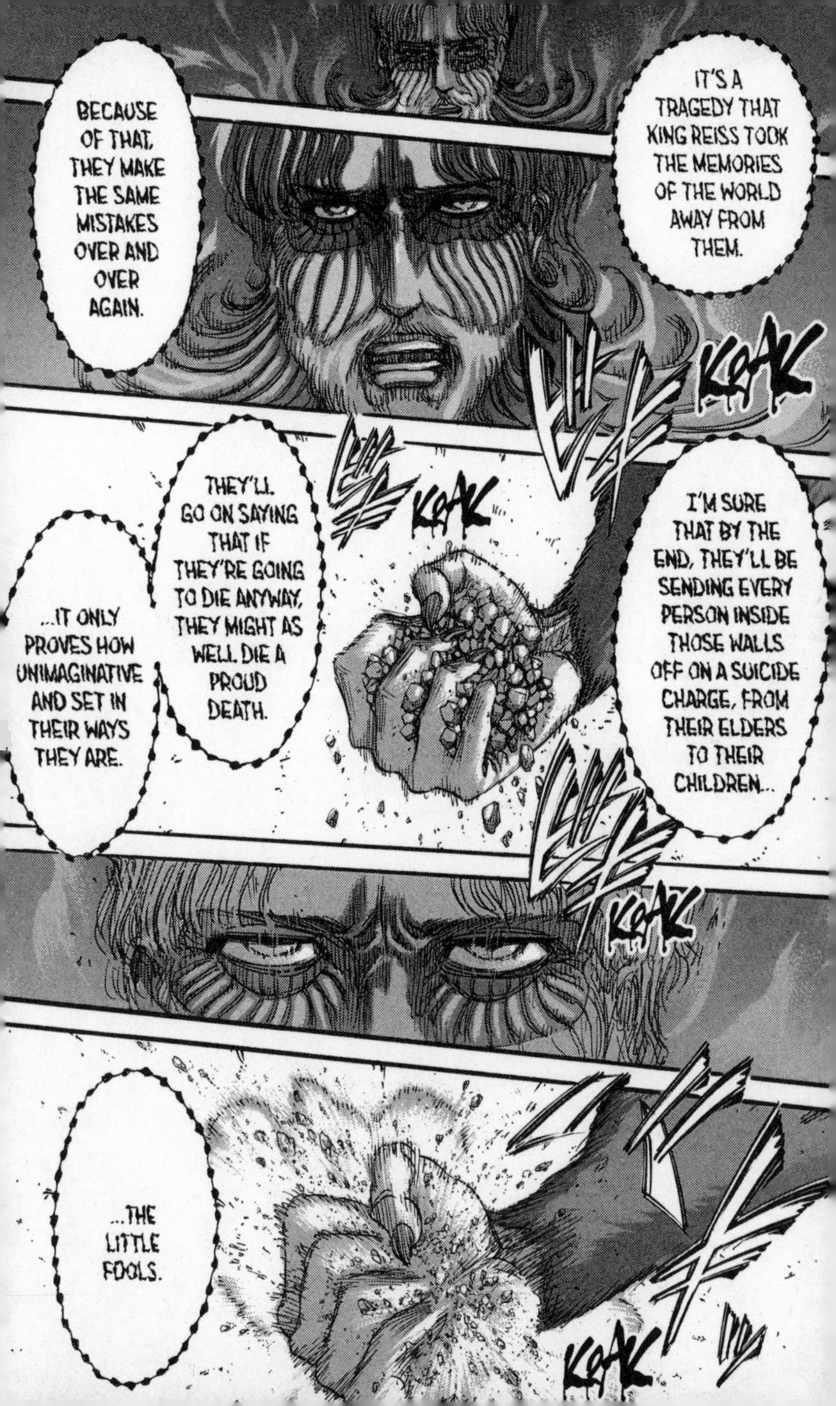
IT'S A TRAGEDY THAT KING REISS TOOK THE MEMORIES OF THE WORLD AWAY FROM THEM.
BECAUSE OF THAT, THEY MAKE THE SAME MISTAKES OVER AND OVER AGAIN.
KRAK
I'M SURE THAT BY THE END, THEY'LL BE SENDING EVERY PERSON INSIDE THOSE WALLS OFF ON A SUICIDE CHARGE, FROM THEIR ELDERS TO THEIR CHILDREN...
KRAK
THEY'LL GO ON SAYING THAT IF THEY'RE GOING TO DIE ANYWAY, THEY MIGHT AS WELL DIE A PROUD DEATH.
...IT ONLY PROVES HOW UNIMAGINATIVE AND SET IN THEIR WAYS THEY ARE.
KRAK
KRAK
...THE LITTLE FOOLS.

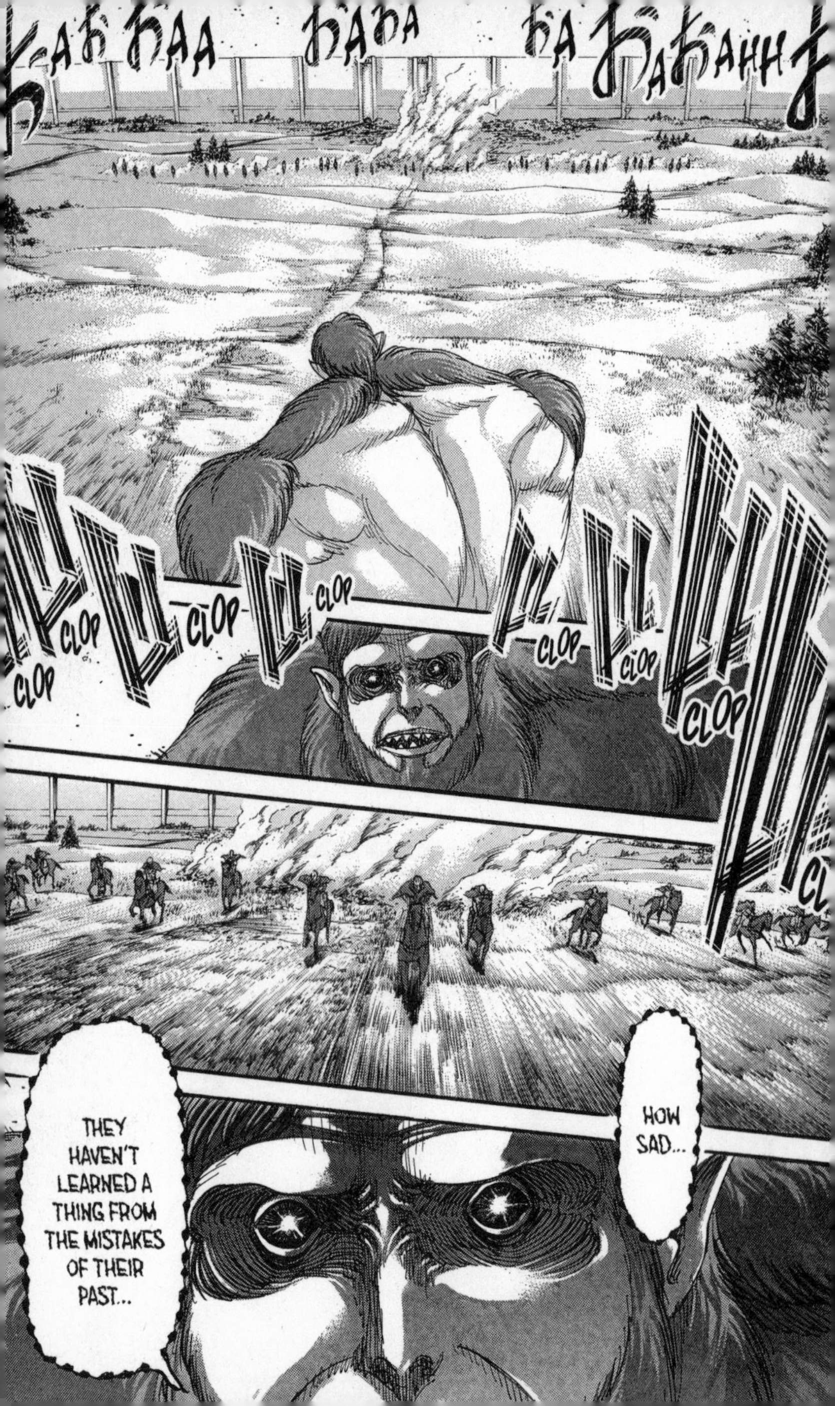
CLOP
CLOP
CLOP
CLOP
CLOP
CLOP
CLOP
THEY HAVEN'T LEARNED A THING FROM THE MISTAKES OF THEIR PAST...
HOW SAD...

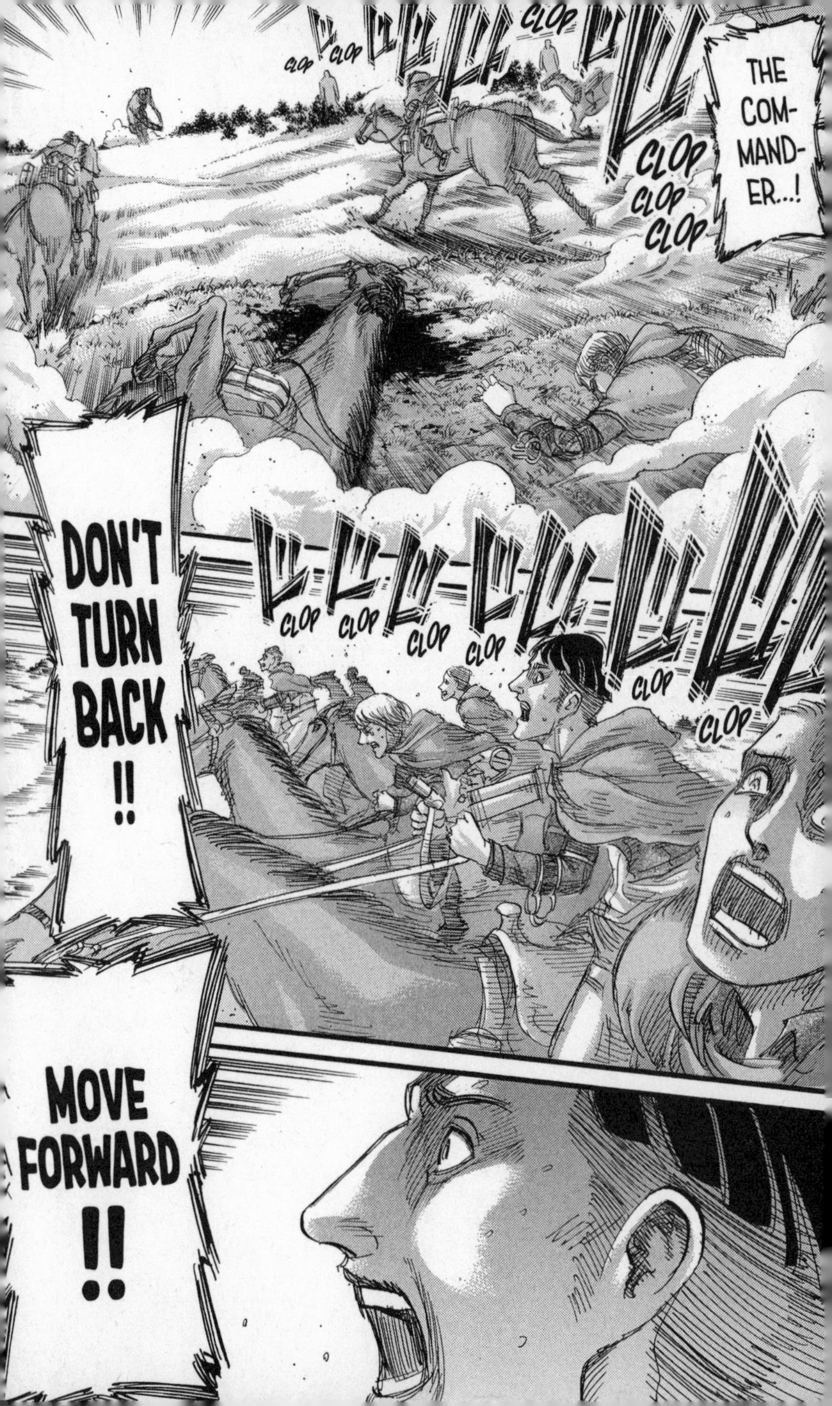

THE COMMANDER...!
CLOP CLOP
CLOP
CLOP CLOP CLOP
DON'T TURN BACK!!
CLOP CLOP CLOP CLOP CLOP CLOP
MOVE FORWARD!!

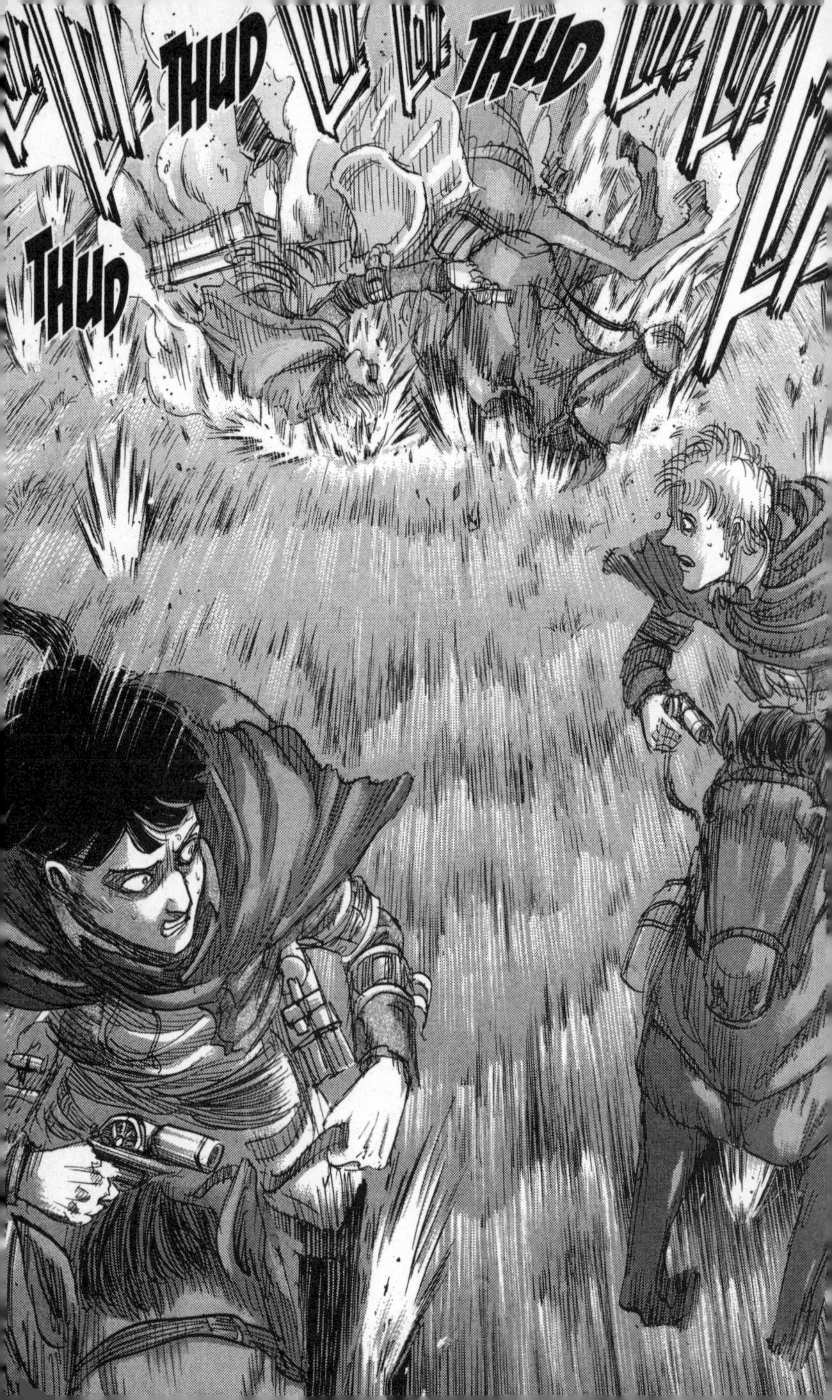
THUD
THUD
THUD

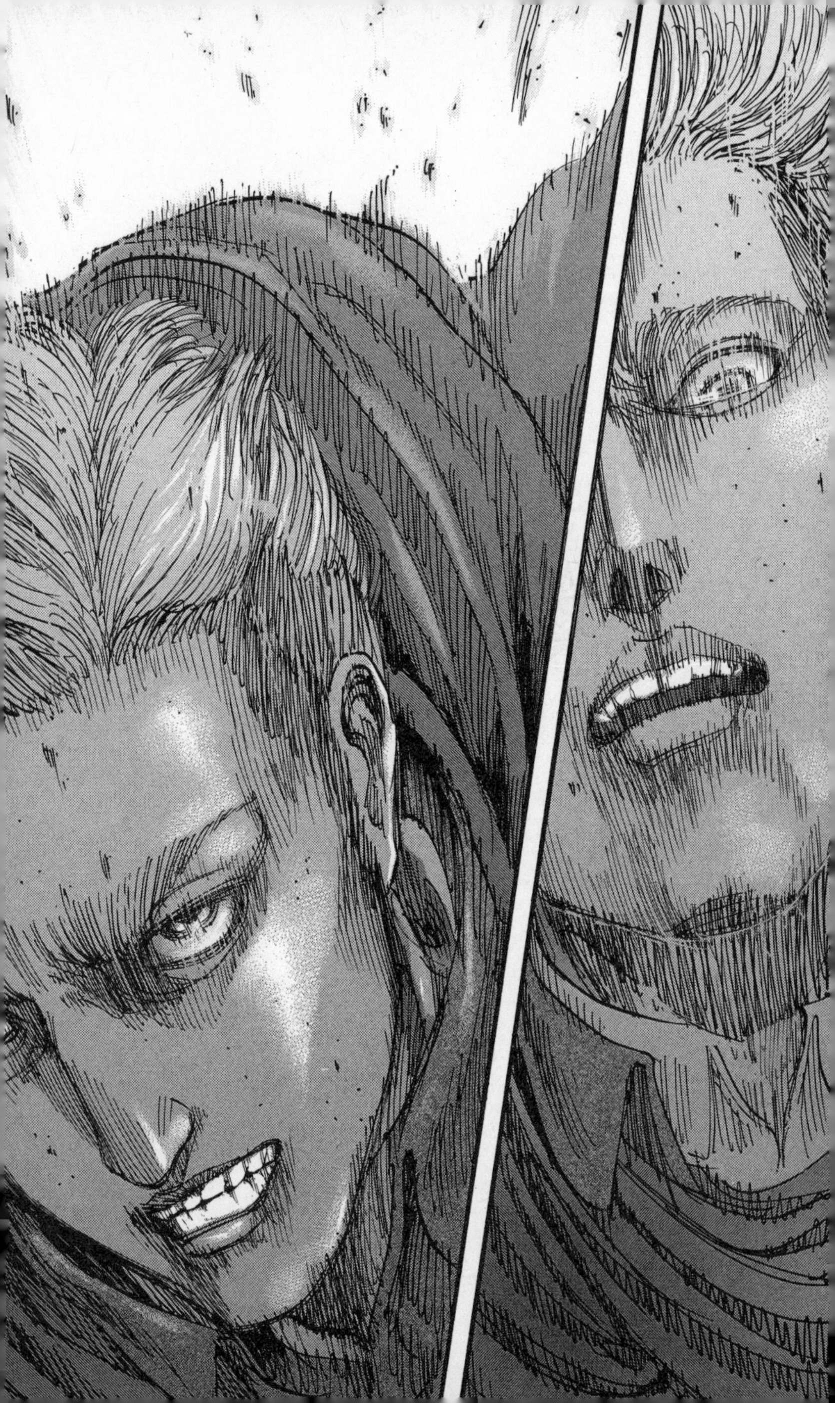

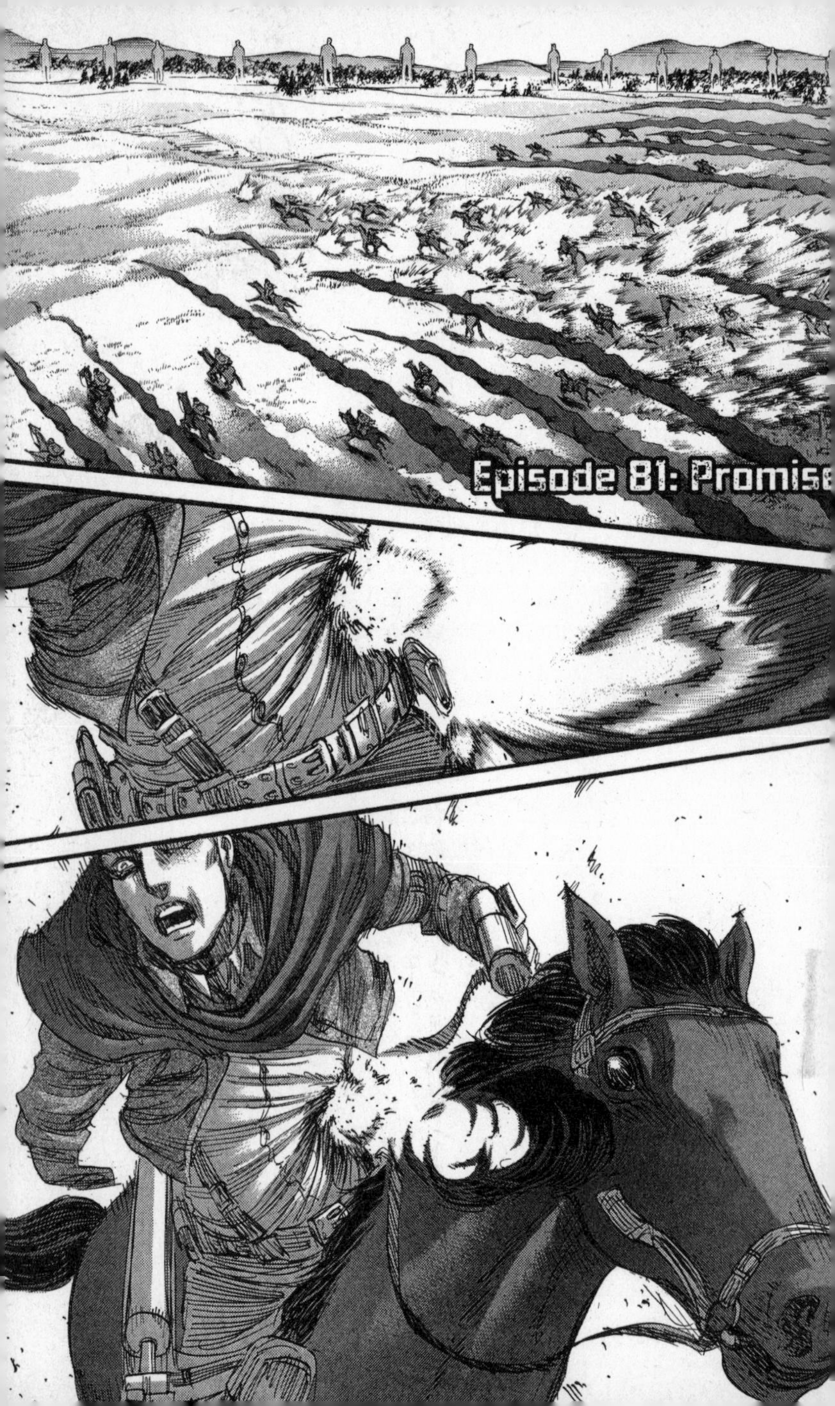
Episode 81: Promise

ATTACK on TITAN

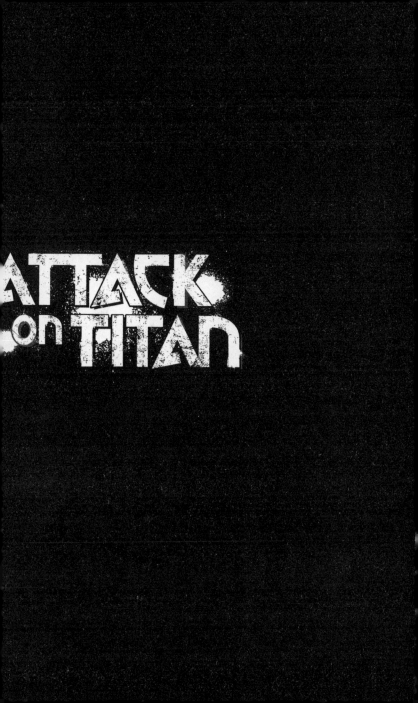

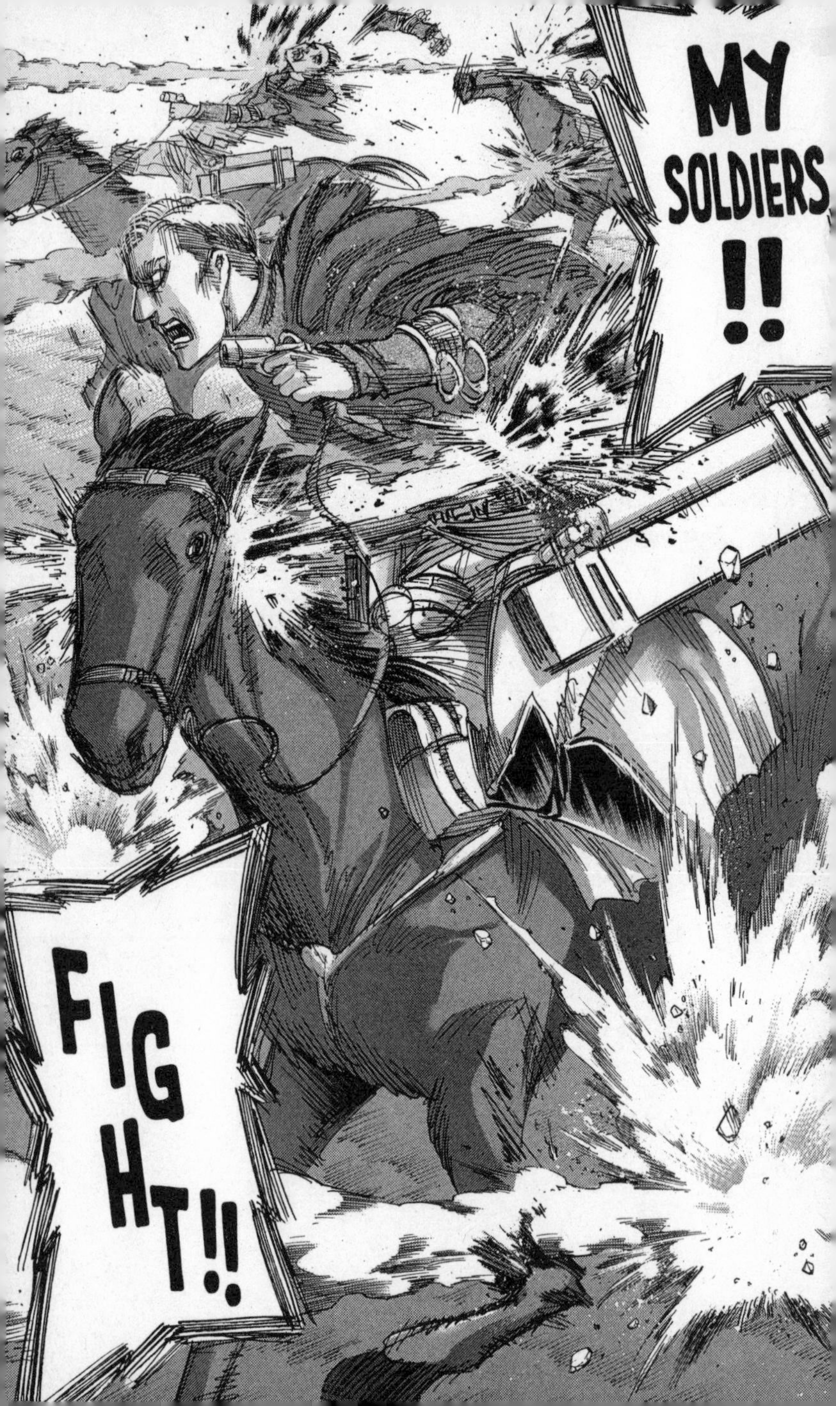
MY SOLDIERS!!
FIGHT!!

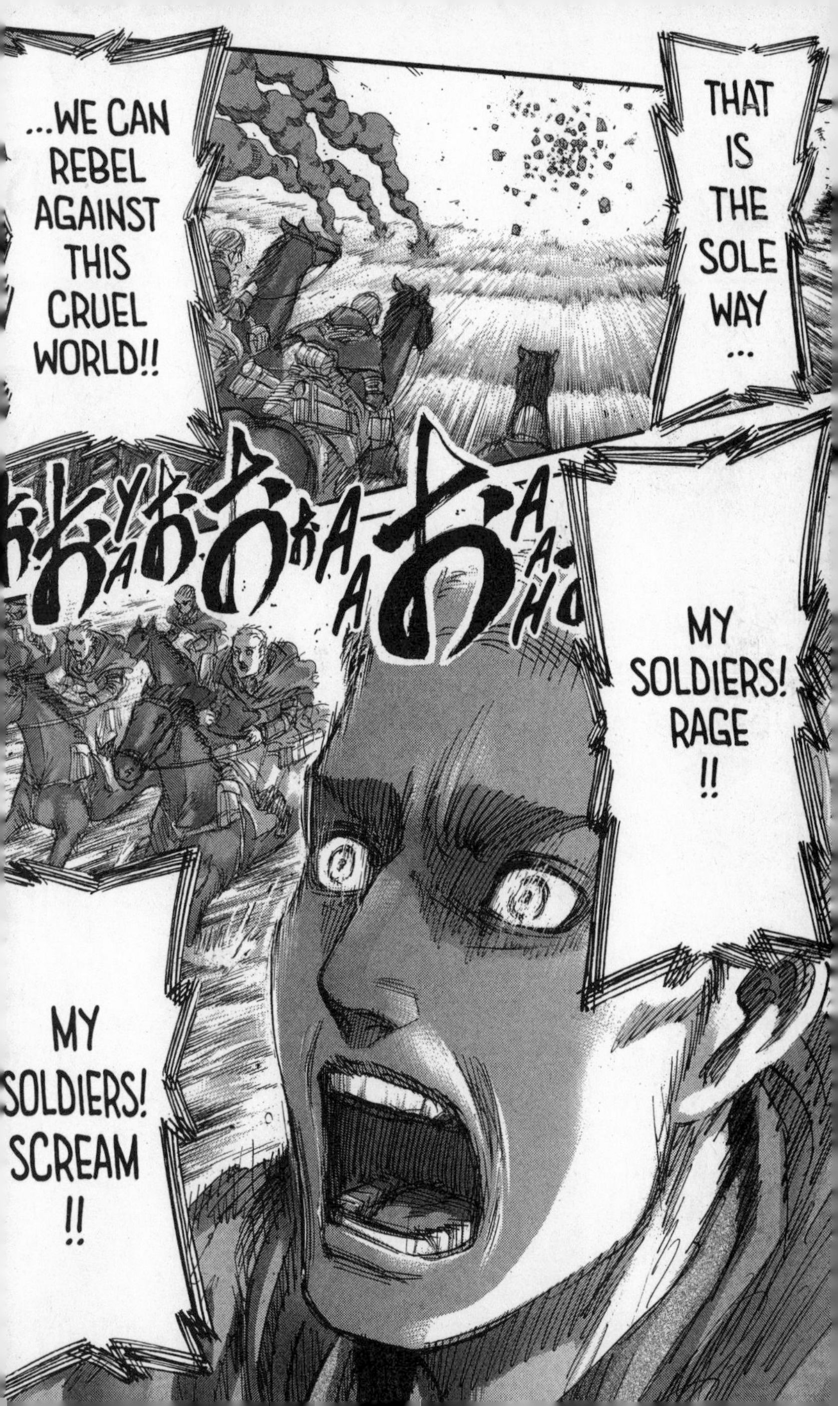
THAT IS THE SOLE WAY ...
...WE CAN REBEL AGAINST THIS CRUEL WORLD!!
MY SOLDIERS! RAGE!!
MY SOLDIERS! SCREAM!!

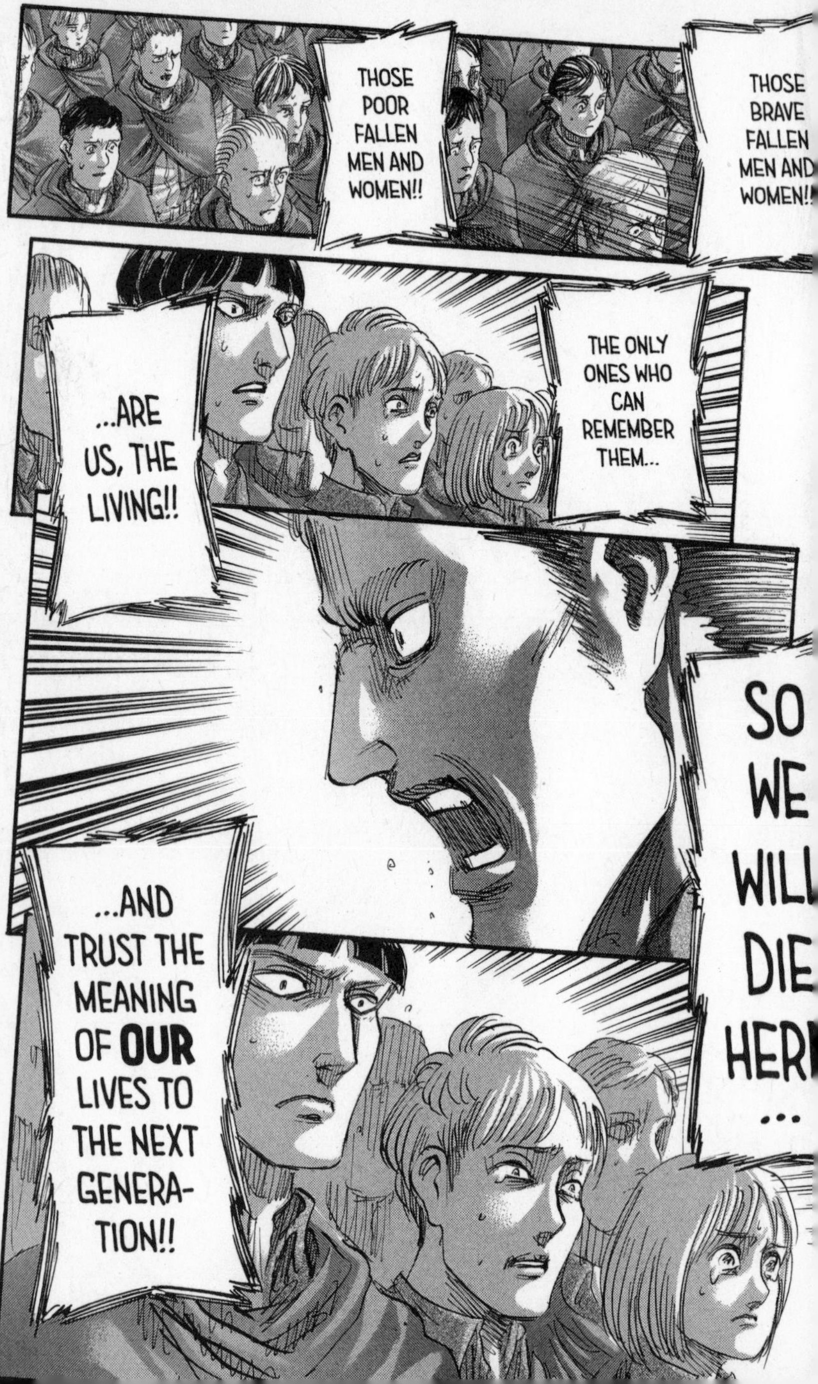
THOSE BRAVE FALLEN MEN AND WOMEN!!
THOSE POOR FALLEN MEN AND WOMEN!!
THE ONLY ONES WHO CAN REMEMBER THEM...
...ARE US, THE LIVING!!
SO WE WILL DIE HERE...
...AND TRUST THE MEANING OF **OUR** LIVES TO THE NEXT GENERATION!!

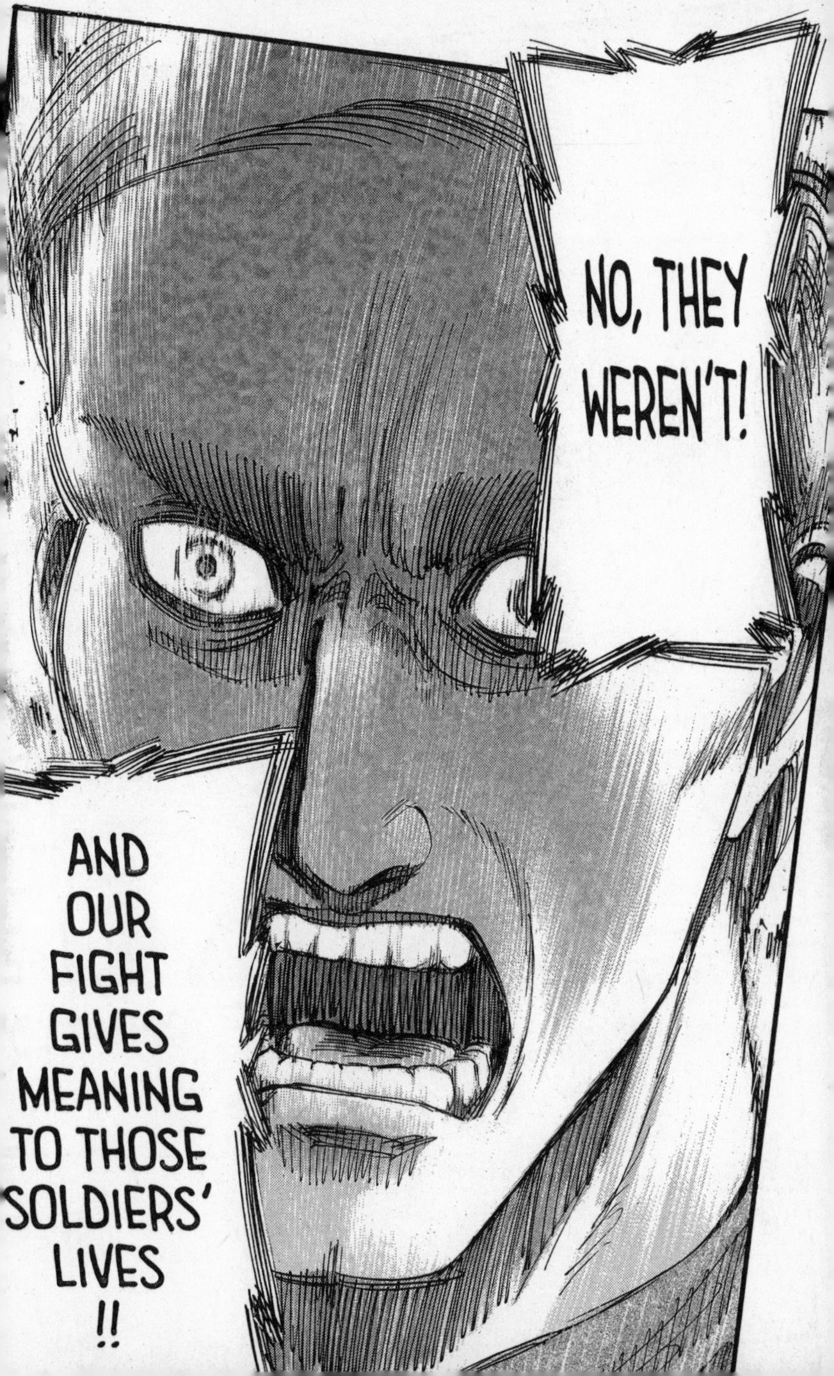
NO, THEY WERE'NT!
AND OUR FIGHT GIVES MEANING TO THOSE SOLDIERS' LIVES !!

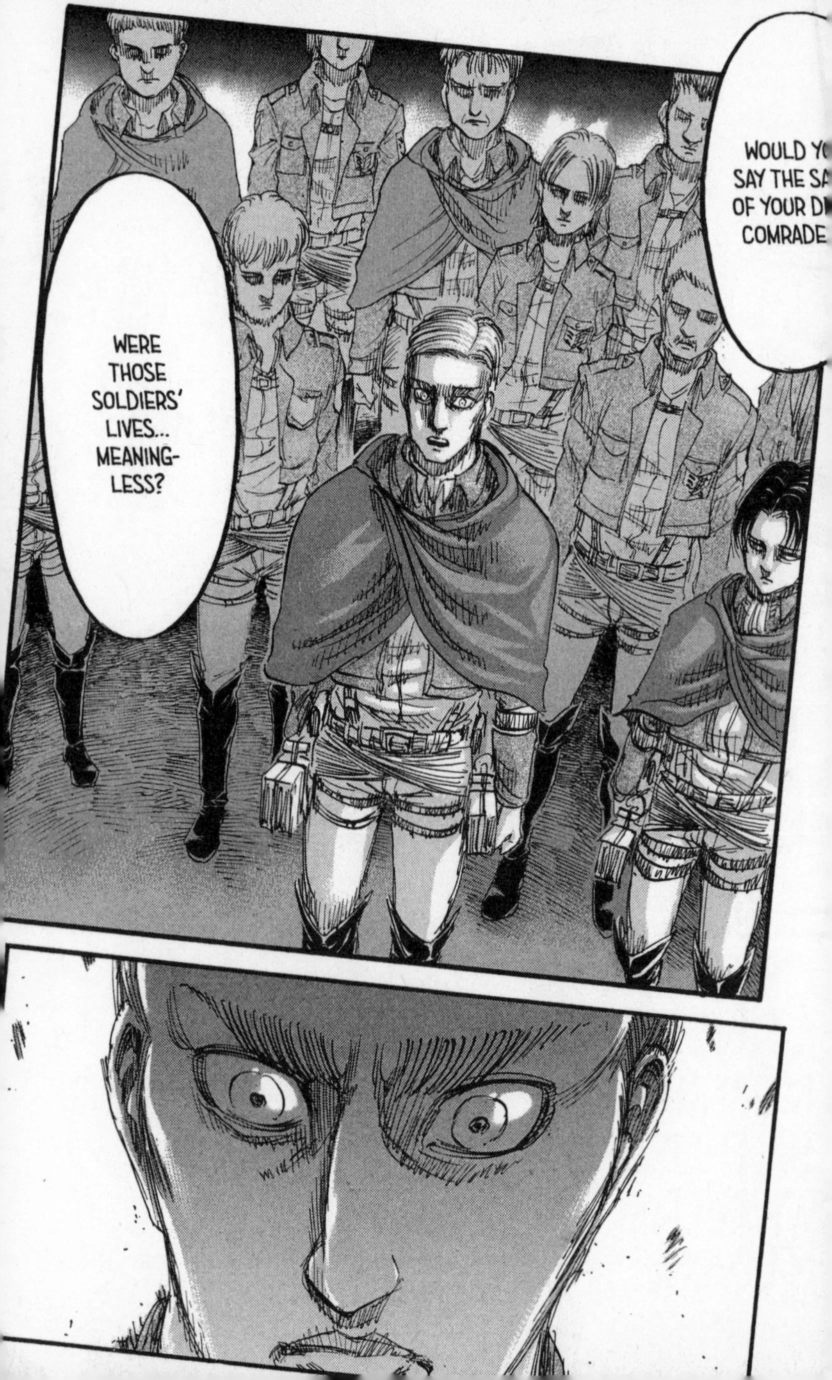
WOULD Y SAY THE SA OF YOUR D COMRADE
WERE THOSE SOLDIERS' LIVES... MEANING-LESS?

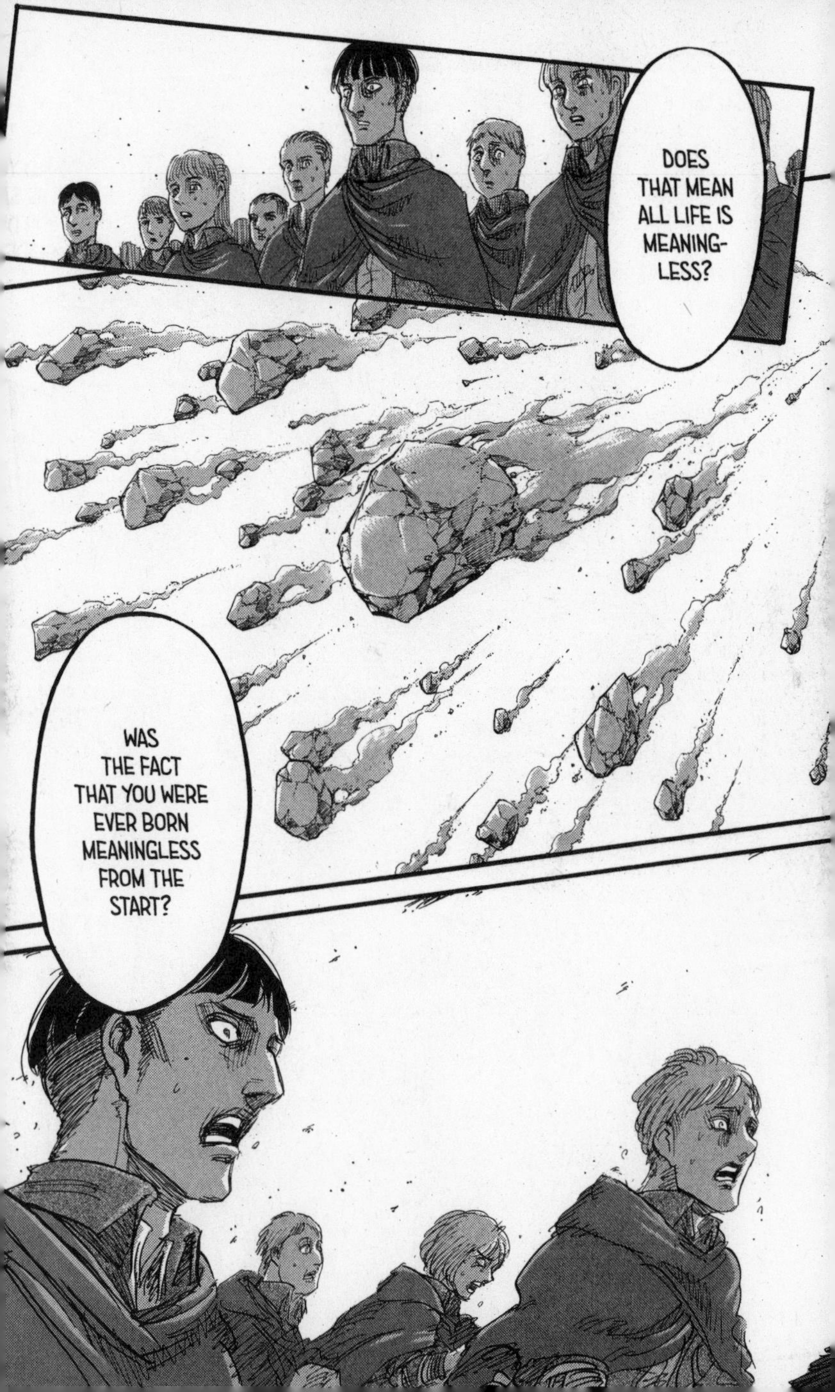
DOES THAT MEAN ALL LIFE IS MEANING-LESS?
WAS THE FACT THAT YOU WERE EVER BORN MEANINGLESS FROM THE START?

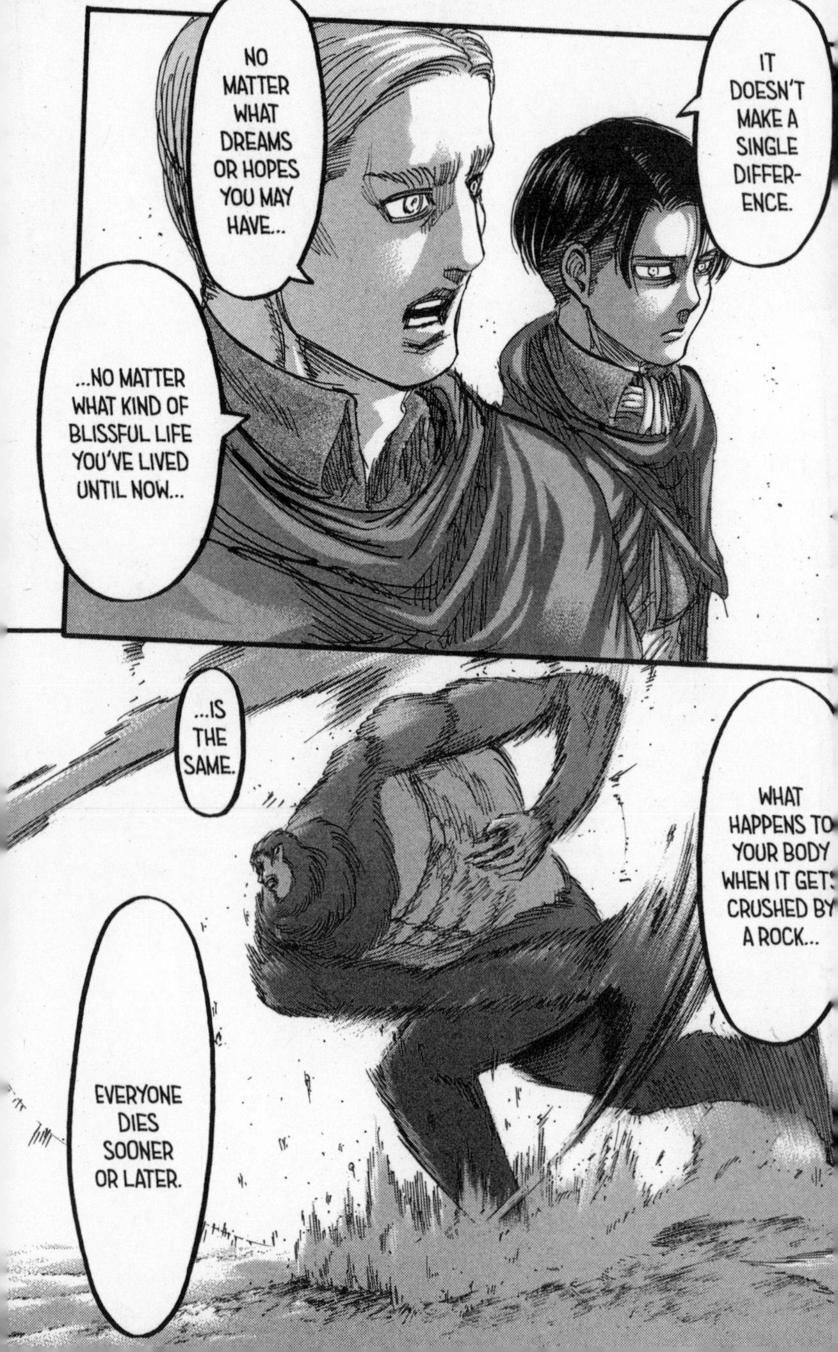
IT DOESN'T MAKE A SINGLE DIFFER-ENCE.
NO MATTER WHAT DREAMS OR HOPES YOU MAY HAVE...
...NO MATTER WHAT KIND OF BLISSFUL LIFE YOU'VE LIVED UNTIL NOW...
WHAT HAPPENS TO YOUR BODY WHEN IT GETS CRUSHED BY A ROCK...
...IS THE SAME.
EVERYONE DIES SOONER OR LATER.

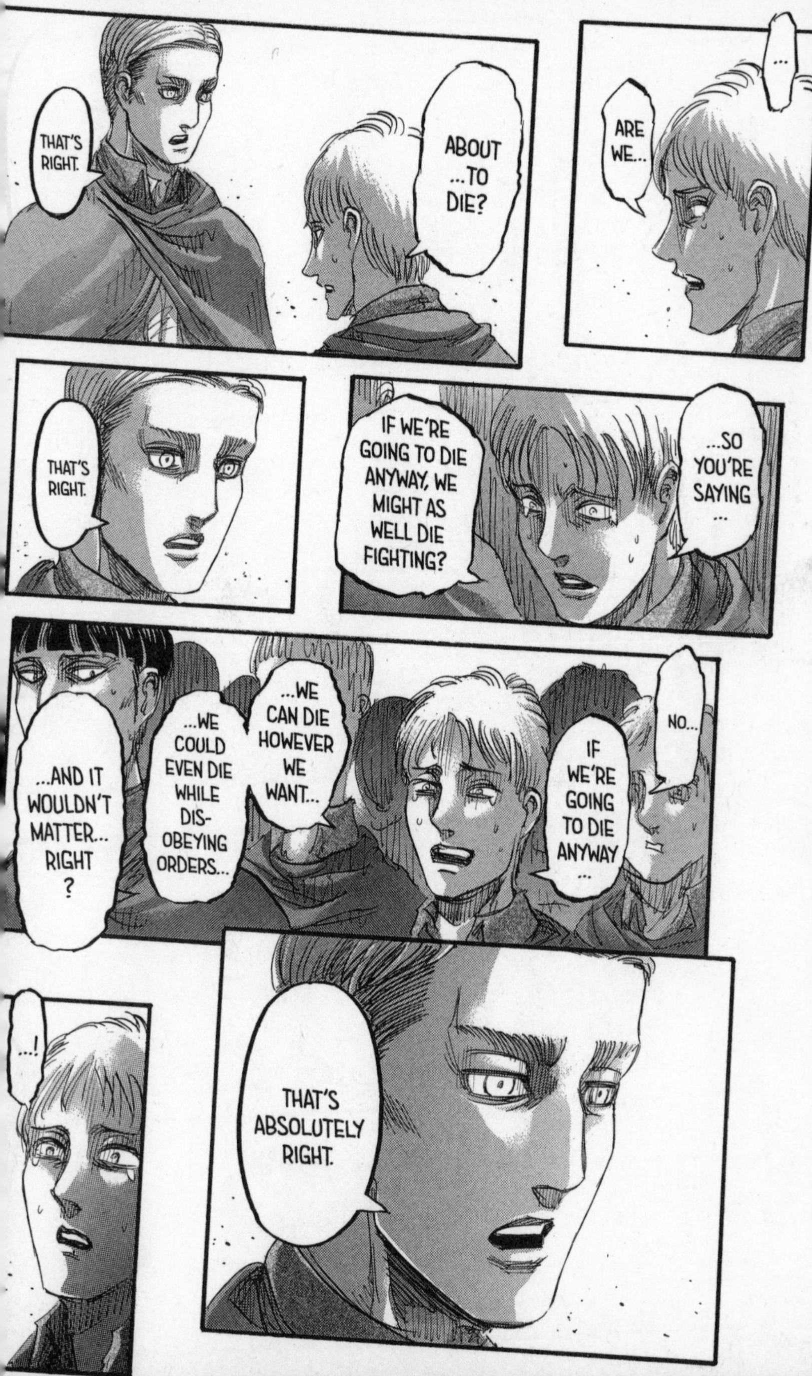
...
ARE WE...
ABOUT ...TO DIE?
THAT'S RIGHT.
...SO YOU'RE SAYING ...
IF WE'RE GOING TO DIE ANYWAY, WE MIGHT AS WELL DIE FIGHTING?
THAT'S RIGHT.
NO...
IF WE'RE GOING TO DIE ANYWAY ...
...WE CAN DIE HOWEVER WE WANT...
...WE COULD EVEN DIE WHILE DIS-OBEYING ORDERS...
...AND IT WOULDN'T MATTER... RIGHT ?
THAT'S ABSOLUTELY RIGHT.
...!

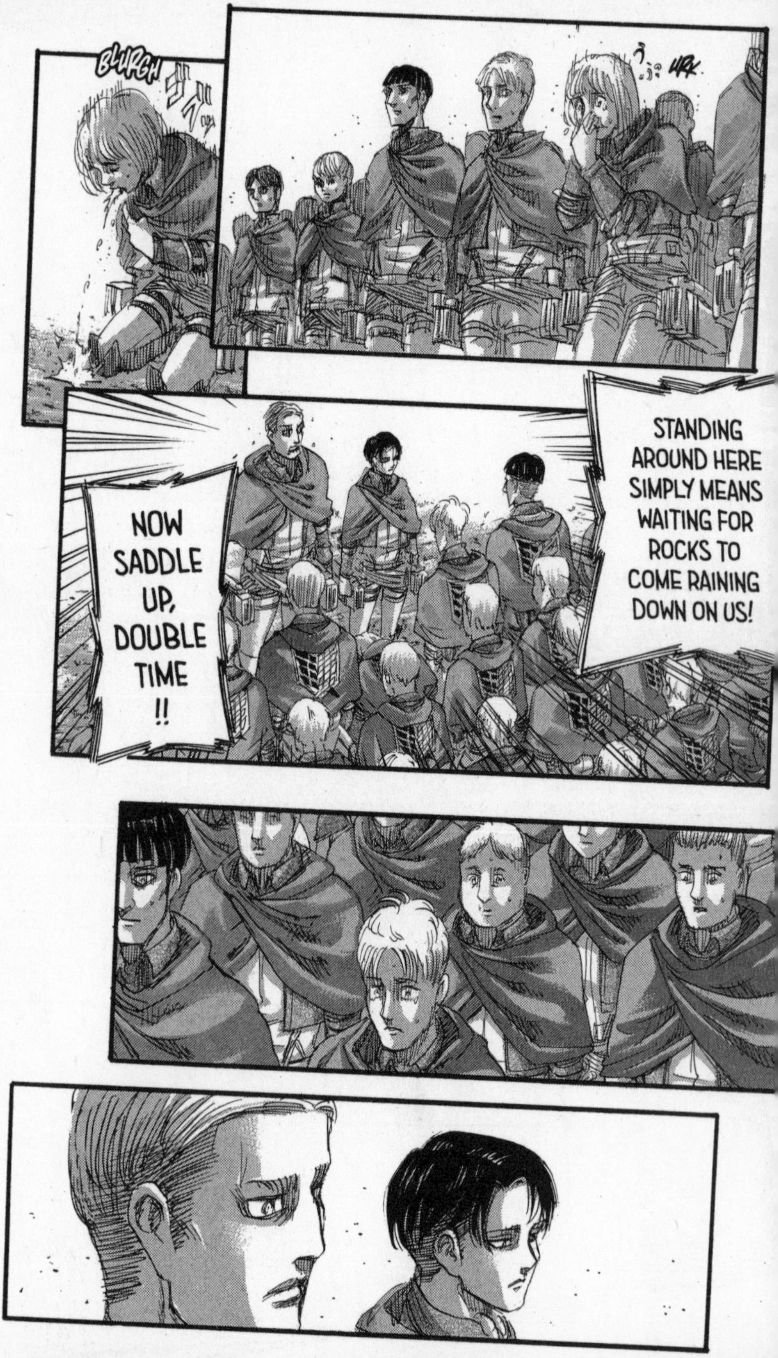
URK
BLURGH
STANDING AROUND HERE SIMPLY MEANS WAITING FOR ROCKS TO COME RAINING DOWN ON US!
NOW SADDLE UP, DOUBLE TIME !!

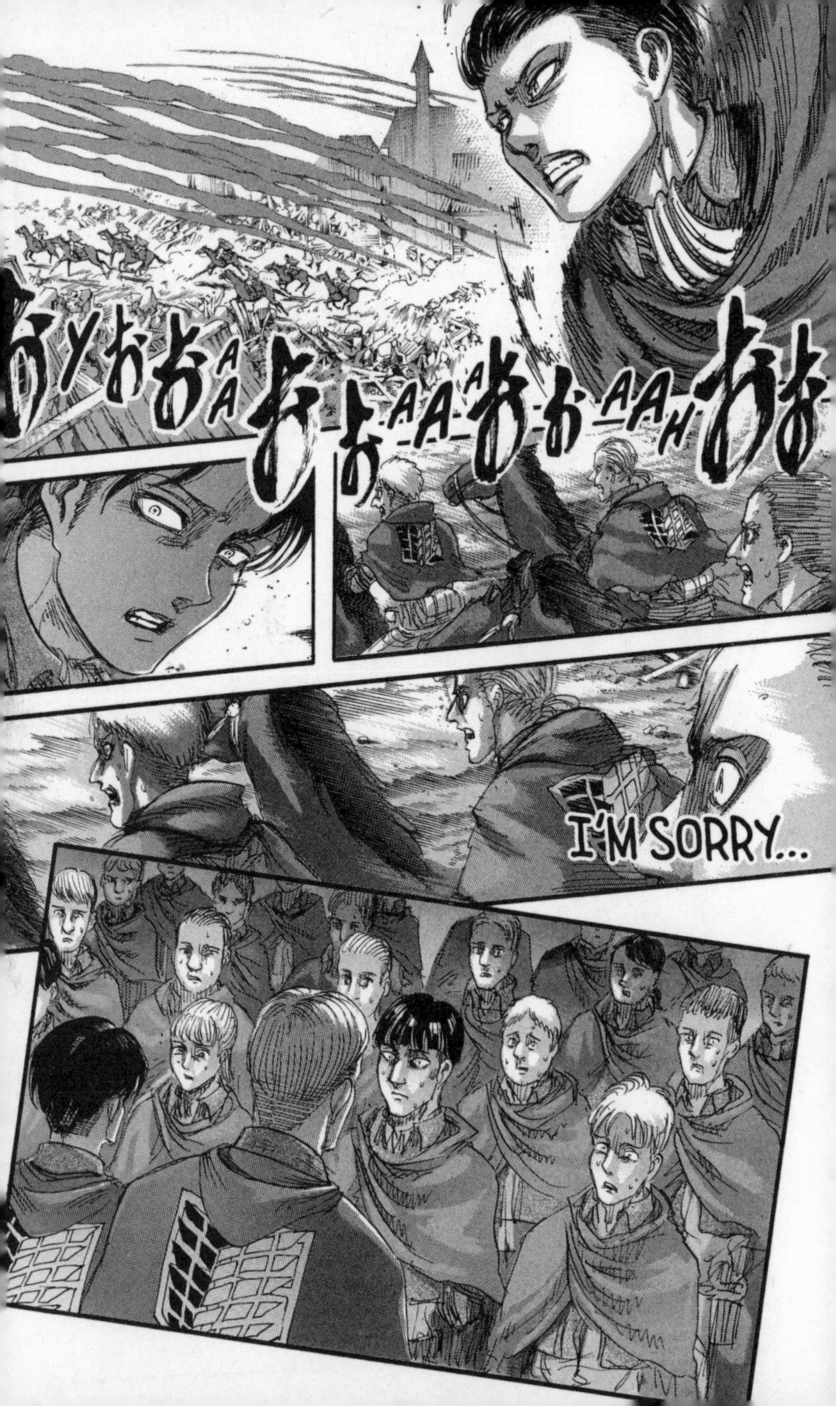
AAAAAAAH
I'M SORRY...

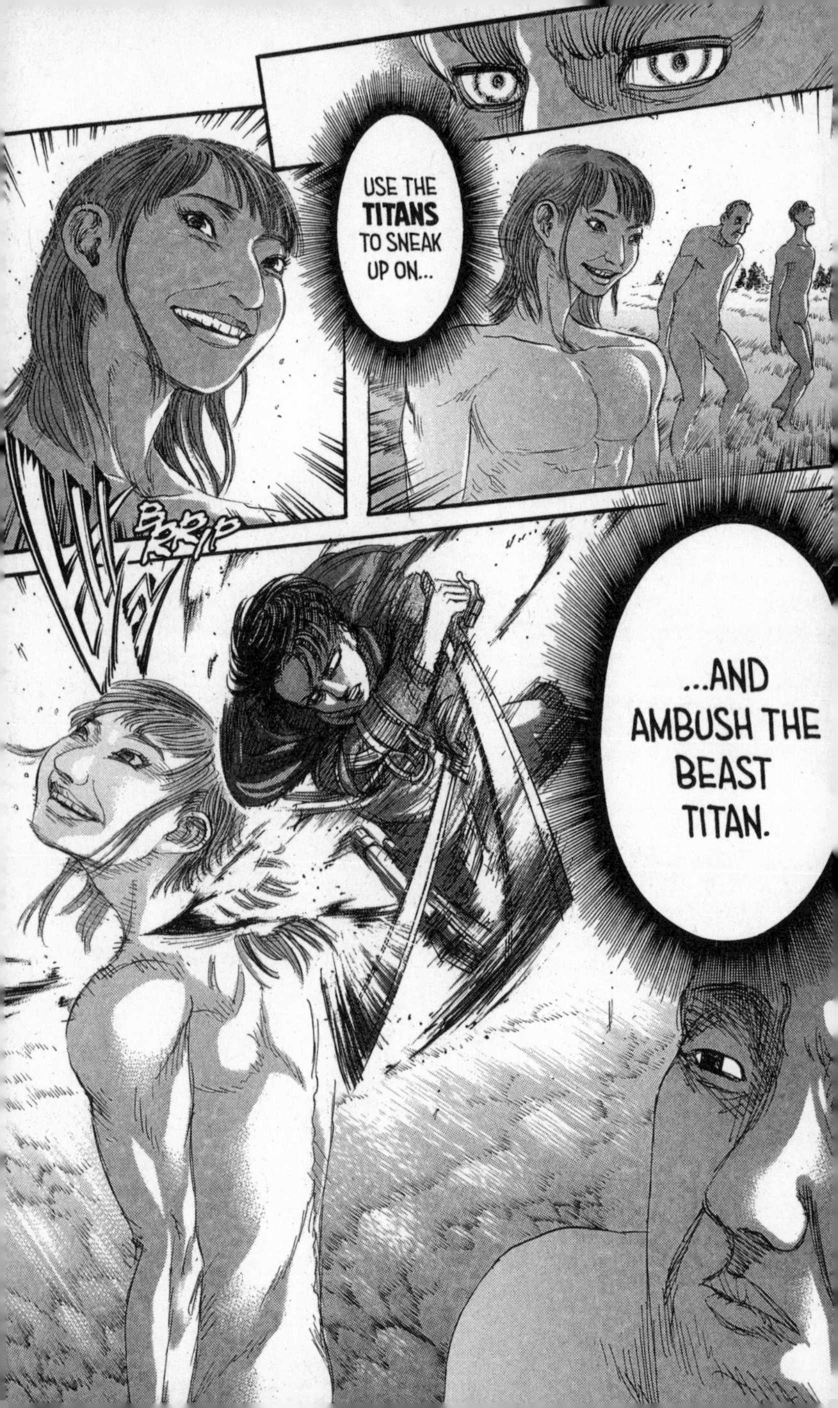
USE THE TITANS TO SNEAK UP ON...
...AND AMBUSH THE BEAST TITAN.

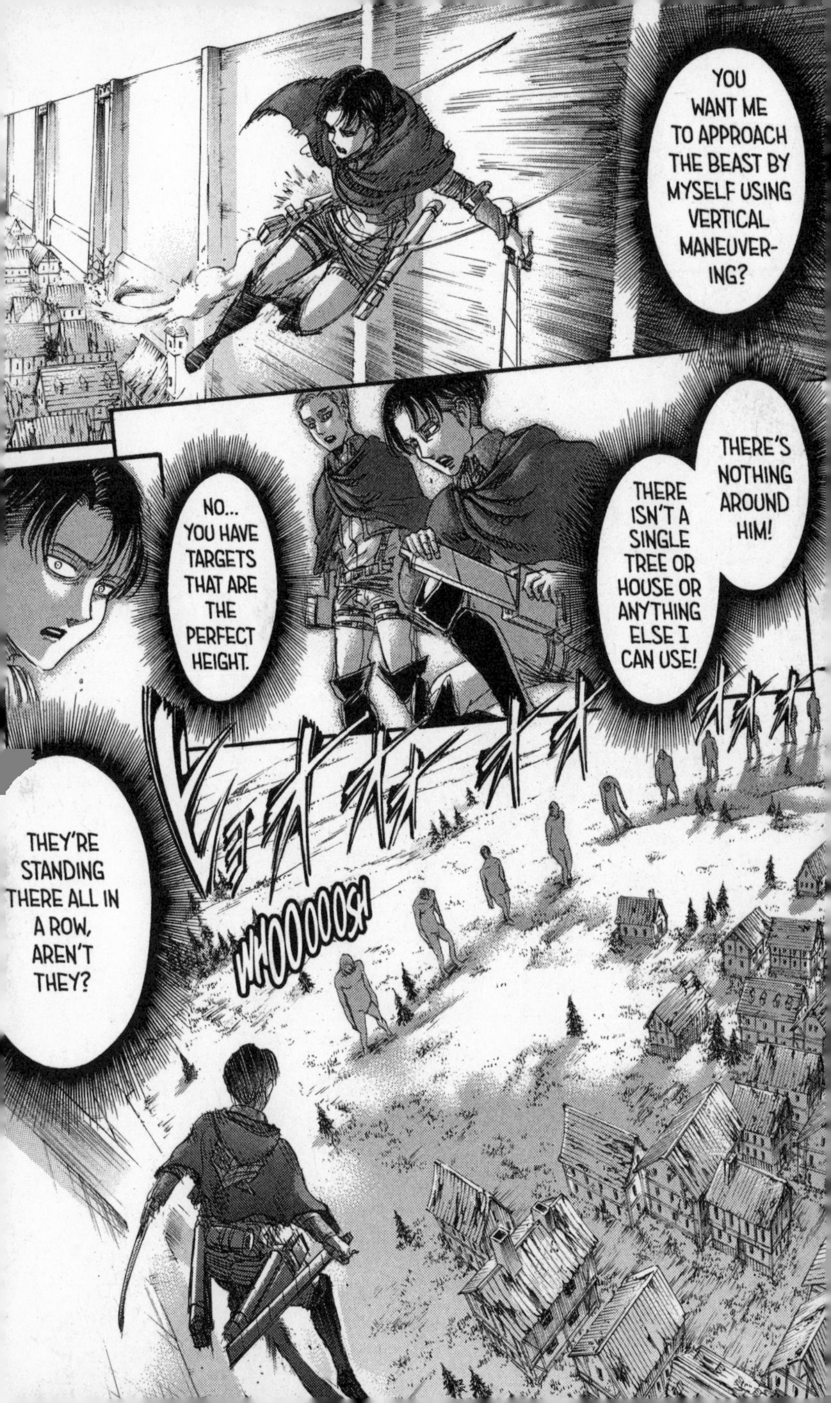
YOU WANT ME TO APPROACH THE BEAST BY MYSELF USING VERTICAL MANEUVERING?
THERE'S NOTHING AROUND HIM!
THERE ISN'T A SINGLE TREE OR HOUSE OR ANYTHING ELSE I CAN USE!
NO... YOU HAVE TARGETS THAT ARE THE PERFECT HEIGHT.
WHOOOOOSH!
THEY'RE STANDING THERE ALL IN A ROW, AREN'T THEY?

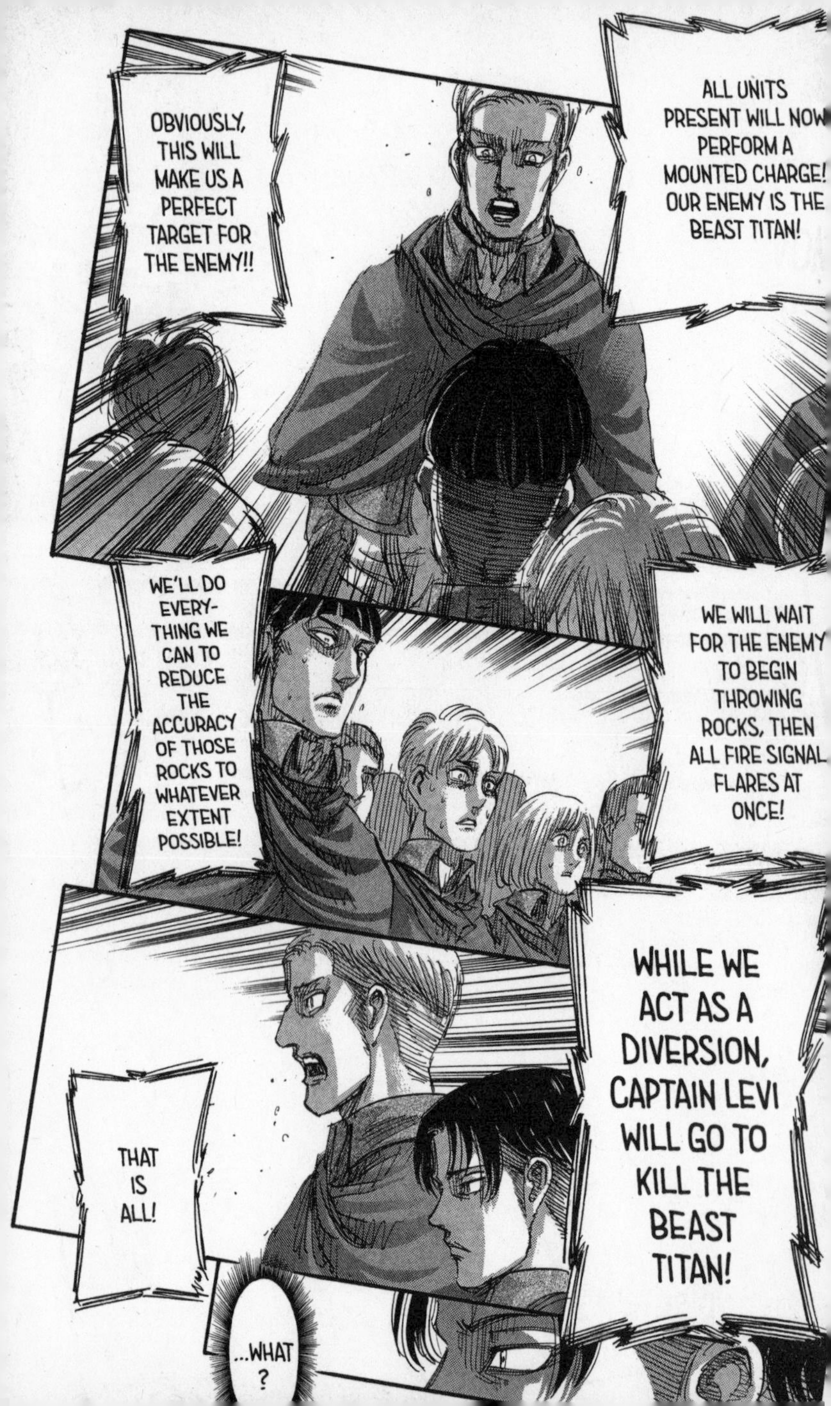
ALL UNITS PRESENT WILL NOW PERFORM A MOUNTED CHARGE! OUR ENEMY IS THE BEAST TITAN!
OBVIOUSLY, THIS WILL MAKE US A PERFECT TARGET FOR THE ENEMY!!
WE WILL WAIT FOR THE ENEMY TO BEGIN THROWING ROCKS, THEN ALL FIRE SIGNAL FLARES AT ONCE!
WE'LL DO EVERY-THING WE CAN TO REDUCE THE ACCURACY OF THOSE ROCKS TO WHATEVER EXTENT POSSIBLE!
WHILE WE ACT AS A DIVERSION, CAPTAIN LEVI WILL GO TO KILL THE BEAST TITAN!
THAT IS ALL!
...WHAT?

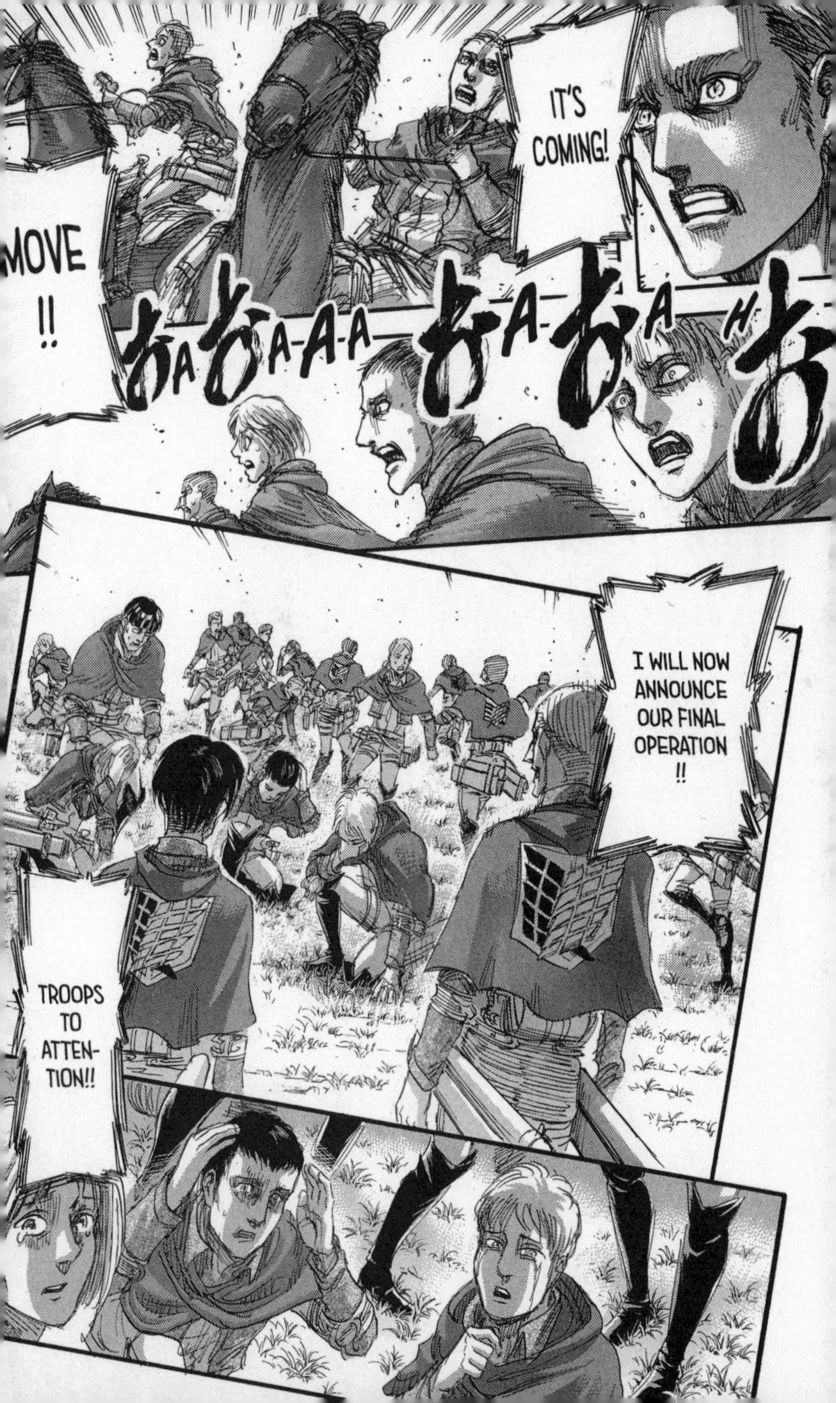
IT'S COMING!
MOVE !!
あAあA-A-A-あAあAHあ
I WILL NOW ANNOUNCE OUR FINAL OPERATION !!
TROOPS TO ATTEN-TION!!

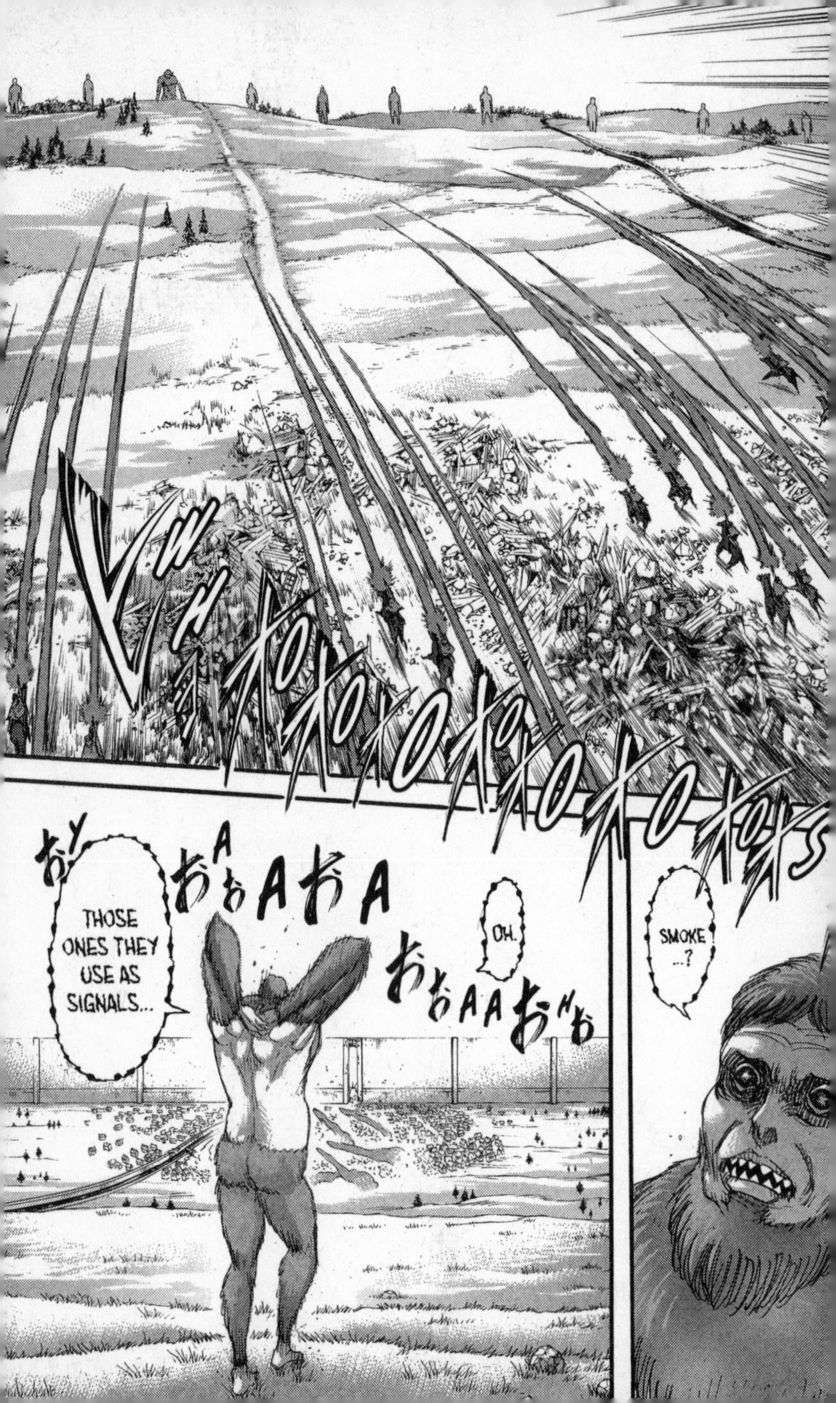
SMOKE ...?
OH.
THOSE ONES THEY USE AS SIGNALS...

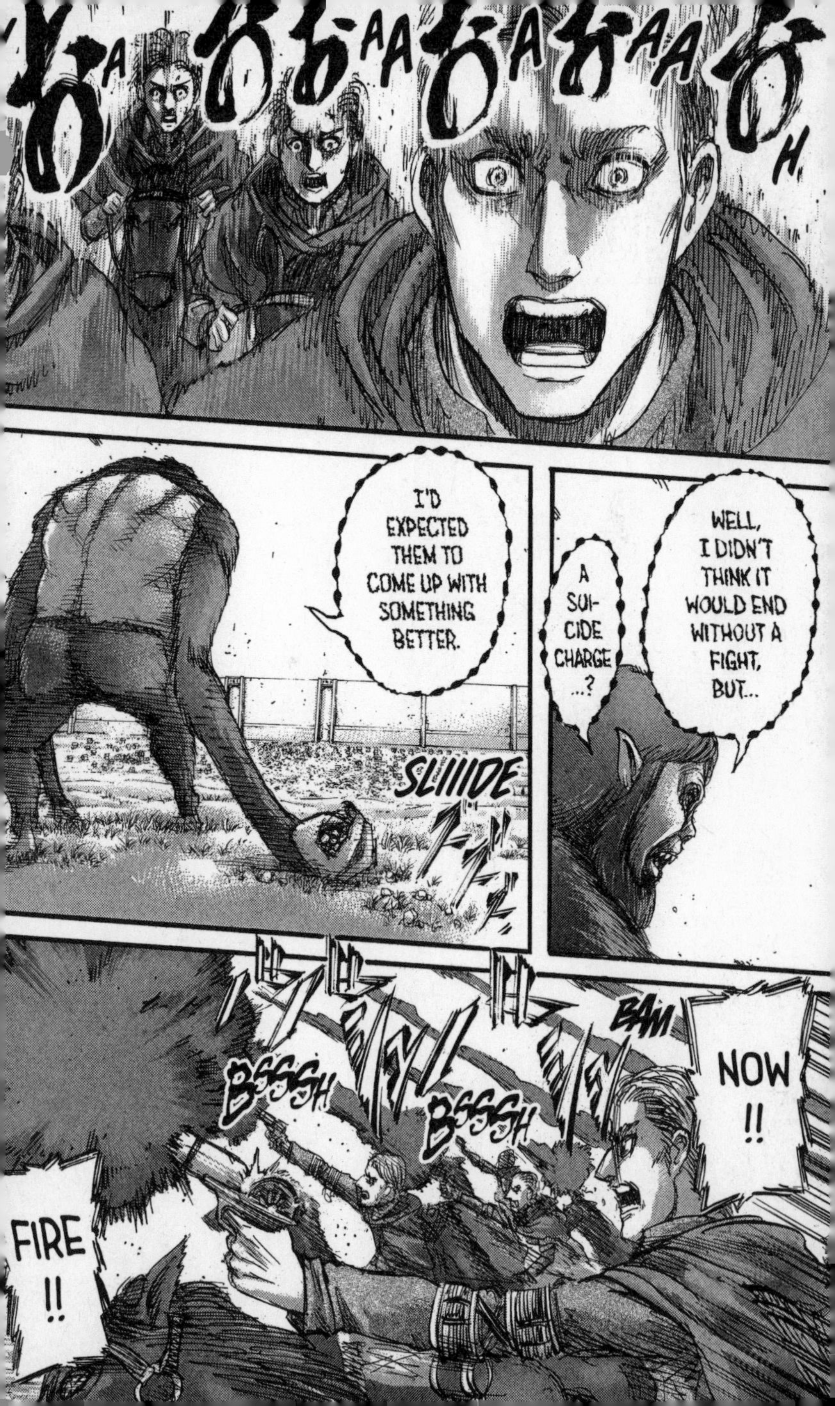
WELL, I DIDN'T THINK IT WOULD END WITHOUT A FIGHT, BUT...
A SUI-CIDE CHARGE ...?
I'D EXPECTED THEM TO COME UP WITH SOMETHING BETTER.
SLIIIDE
NOW !!
BAM
BSSSH
BSSSH
FIRE !!

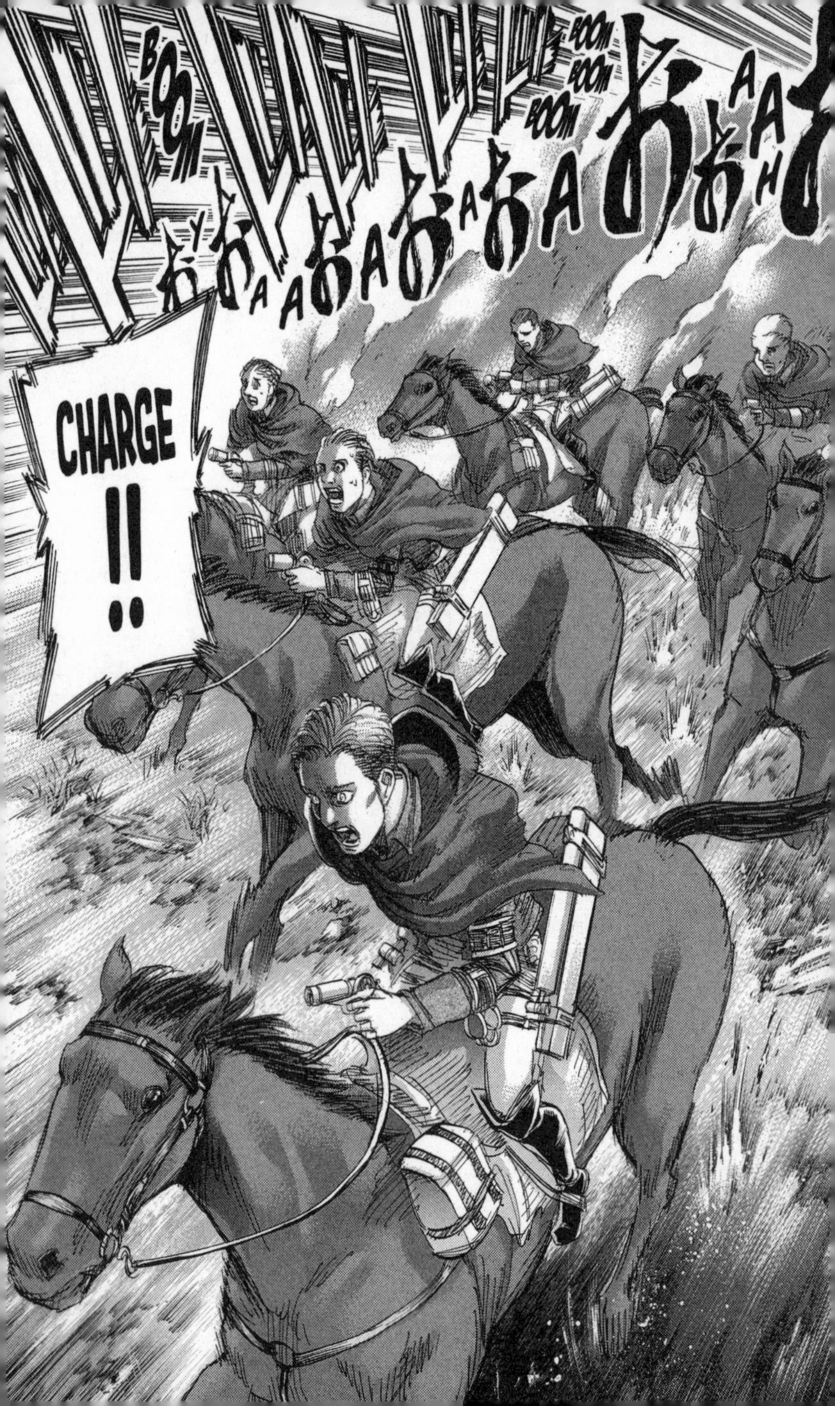
BOOM
BOOM BOOM BOOM
YAAAAAAAH
CHARGE!!

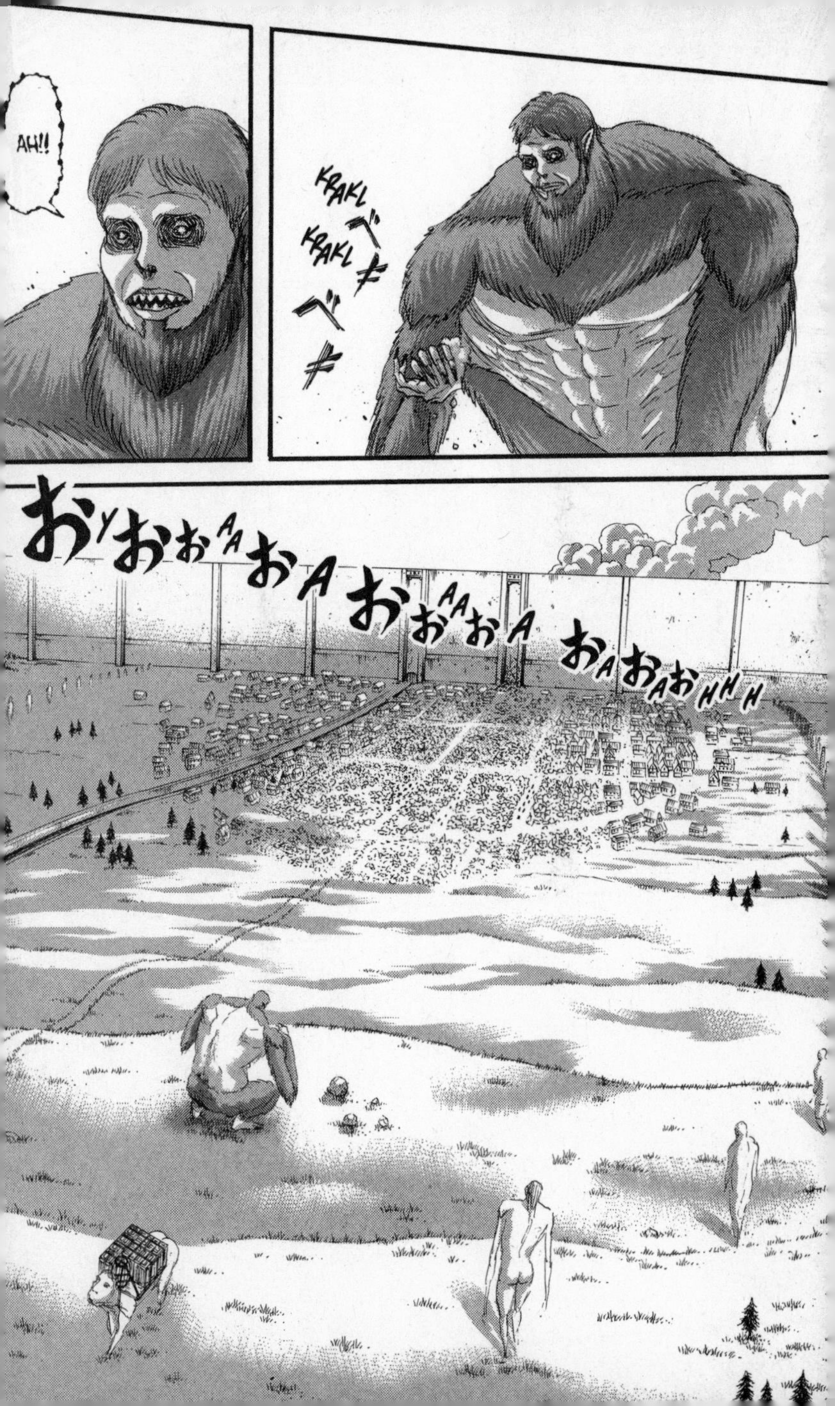

KRAKL べキ
KRAKL べキ
AH!!
おYおおAAおAおAAおおAおAおAおHHH

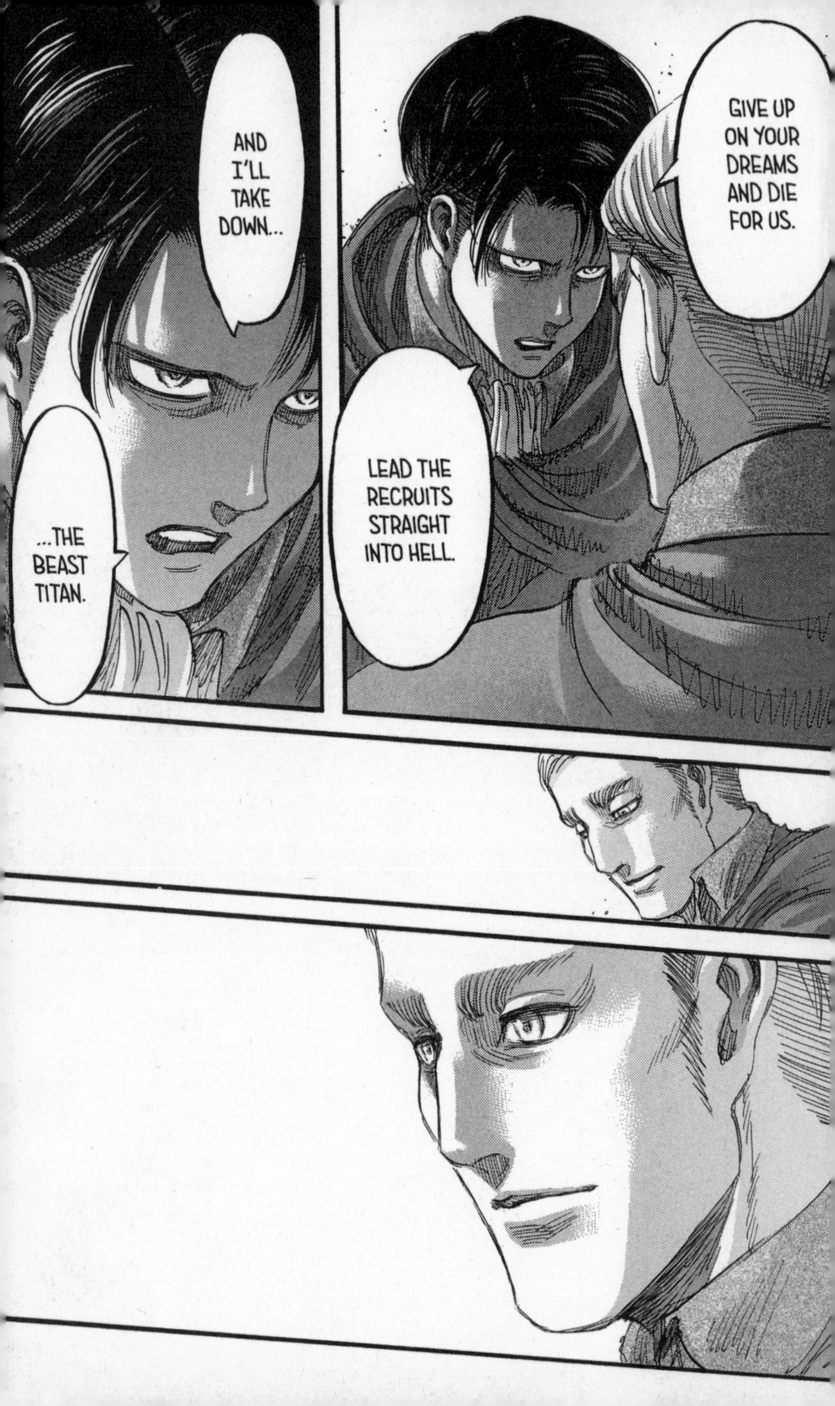
GIVE UP ON YOUR DREAMS AND DIE FOR US.
LEAD THE RECRUITS STRAIGHT INTO HELL.
AND I'LL TAKE DOWN...
...THE BEAST TITAN.

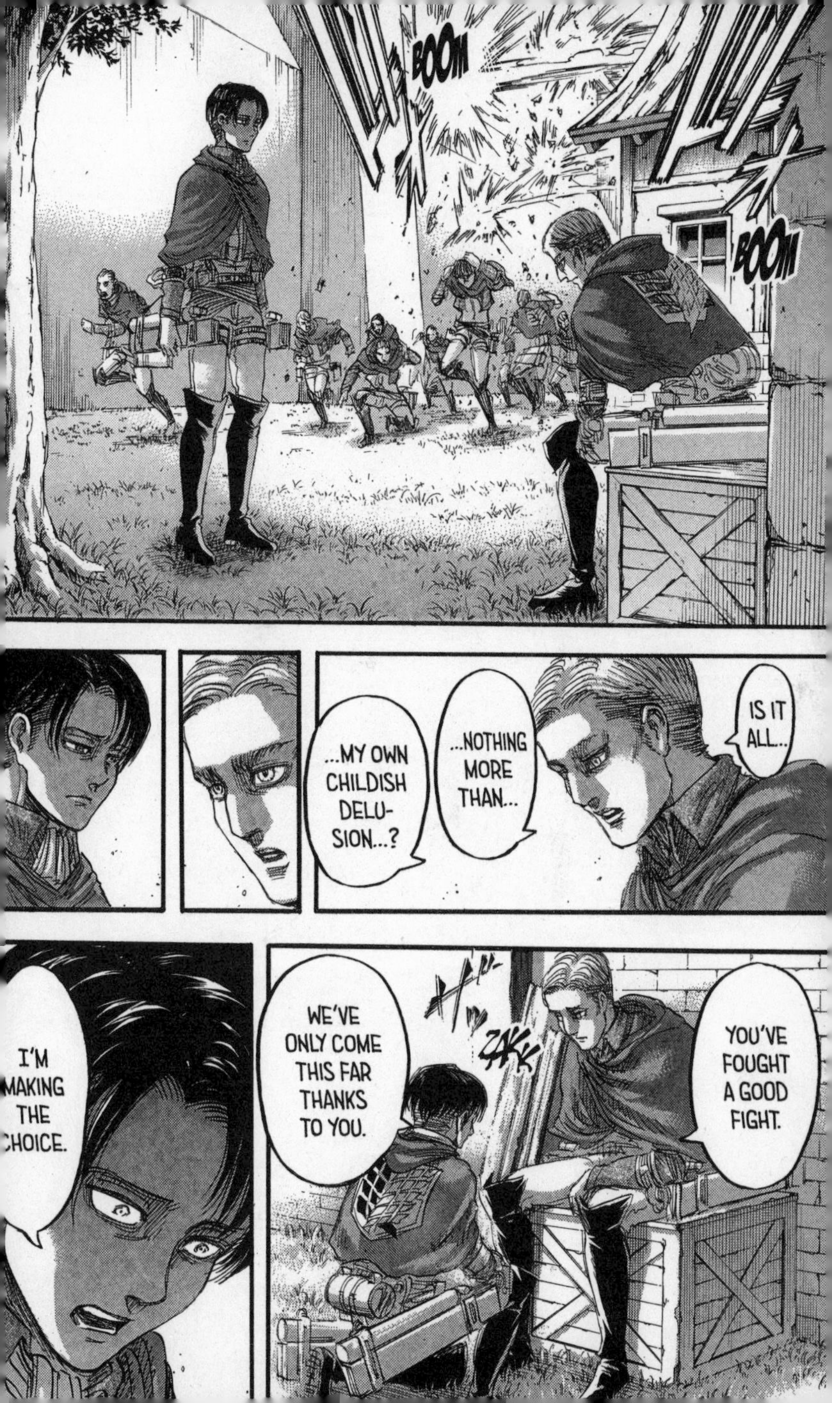
BOOM
BOOM
IS IT ALL...
...NOTHING MORE THAN...
...MY OWN CHILDISH DELU-SION...?
YOU'VE FOUGHT A GOOD FIGHT.
ZAKK
WE'VE ONLY COME THIS FAR THANKS TO YOU.
I'M MAKING THE CHOICE.

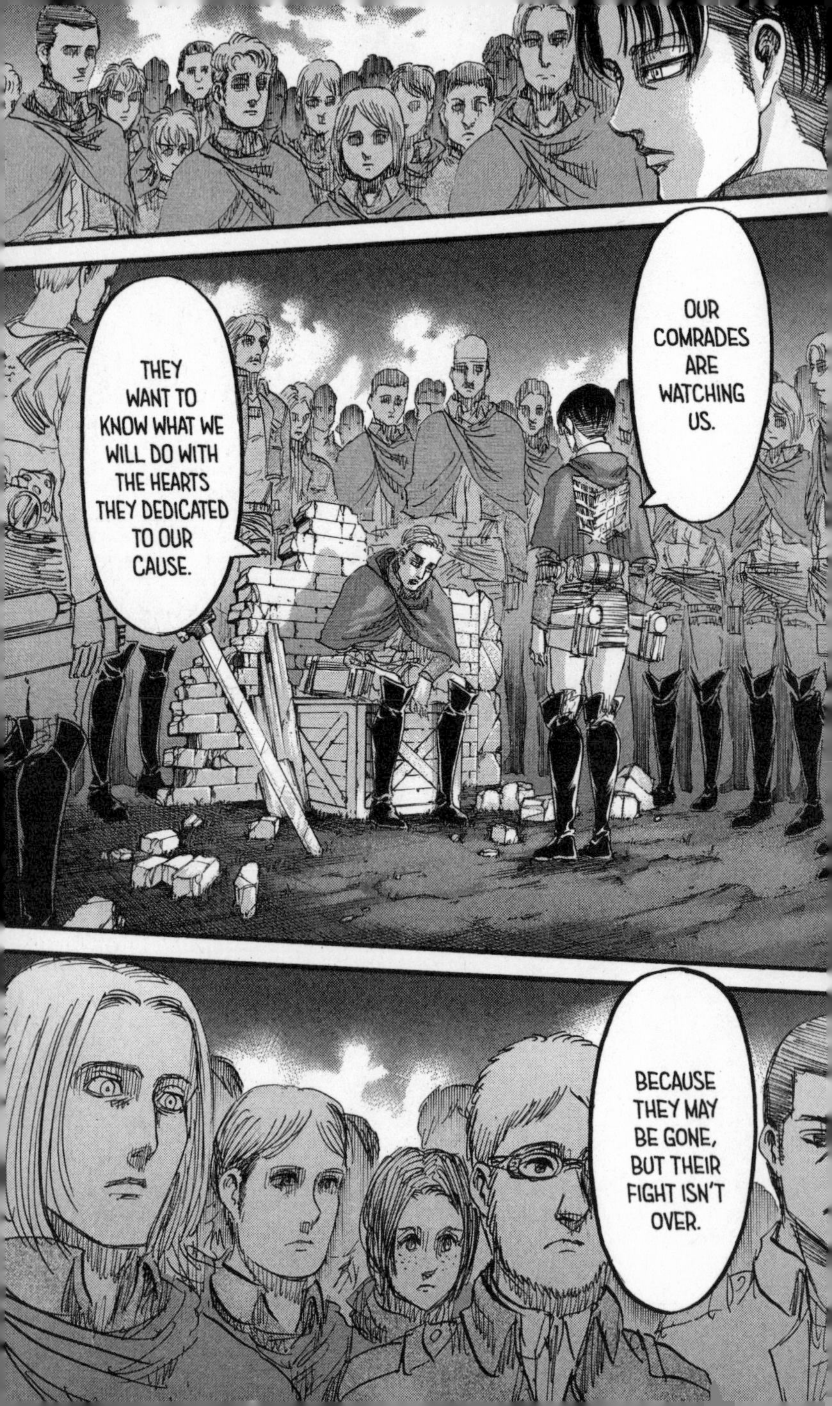
OUR COMRADES ARE WATCHING US.
THEY WANT TO KNOW WHAT WE WILL DO WITH THE HEARTS THEY DEDICATED TO OUR CAUSE.
BECAUSE THEY MAY BE GONE, BUT THEIR FIGHT ISN'T OVER.

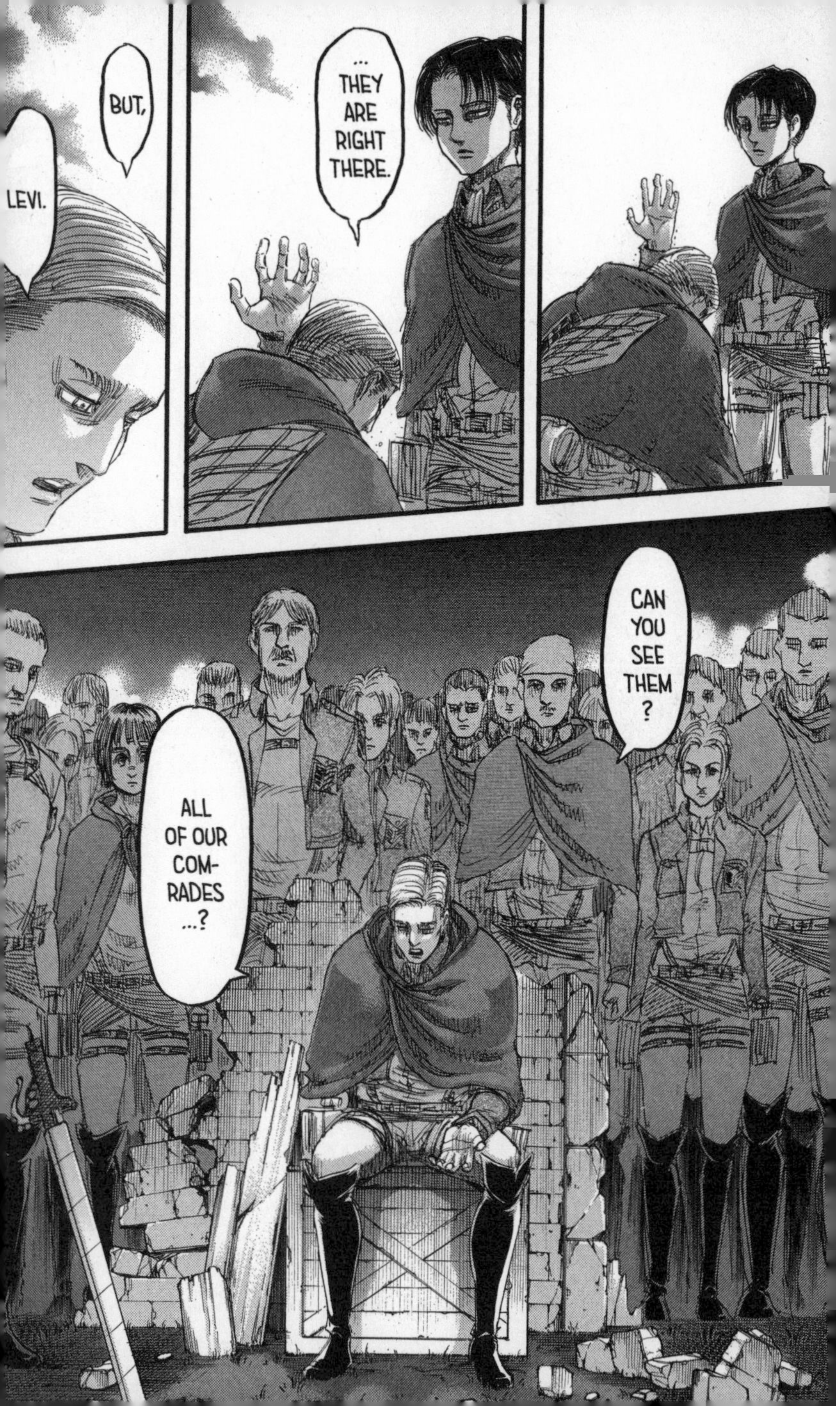
... THEY ARE RIGHT THERE.
BUT,
LEVI.
CAN YOU SEE THEM?
ALL OF OUR COM-RADES ...?

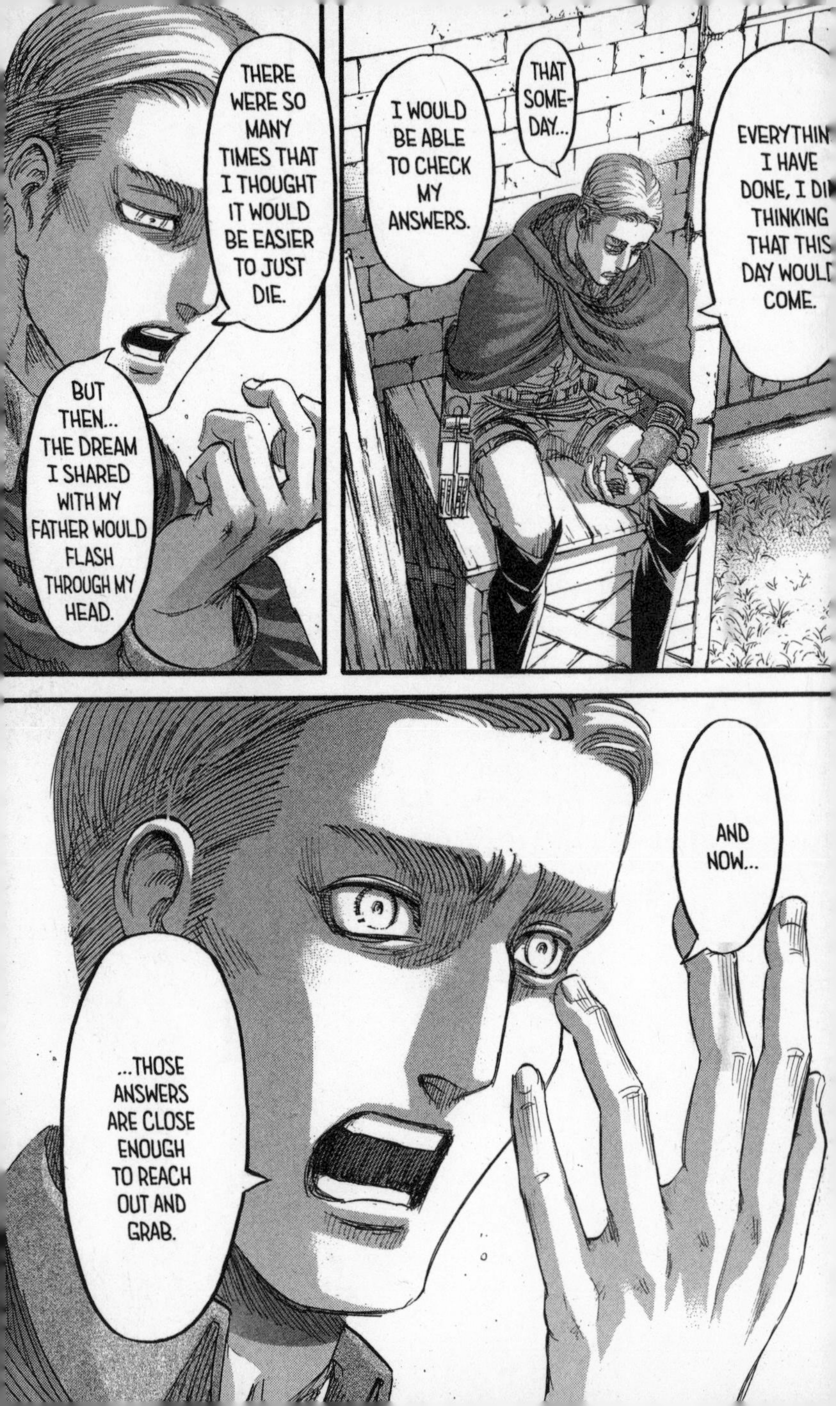
EVERYTHIN I HAVE DONE, I DI THINKING THAT THIS DAY WOUL COME.
THAT SOME-DAY...
I WOULD BE ABLE TO CHECK MY ANSWERS.
THERE WERE SO MANY TIMES THAT I THOUGHT IT WOULD BE EASIER TO JUST DIE.
BUT THEN... THE DREAM I SHARED WITH MY FATHER WOULD FLASH THROUGH MY HEAD.
AND NOW...
...THOSE ANSWERS ARE CLOSE ENOUGH TO REACH OUT AND GRAB.

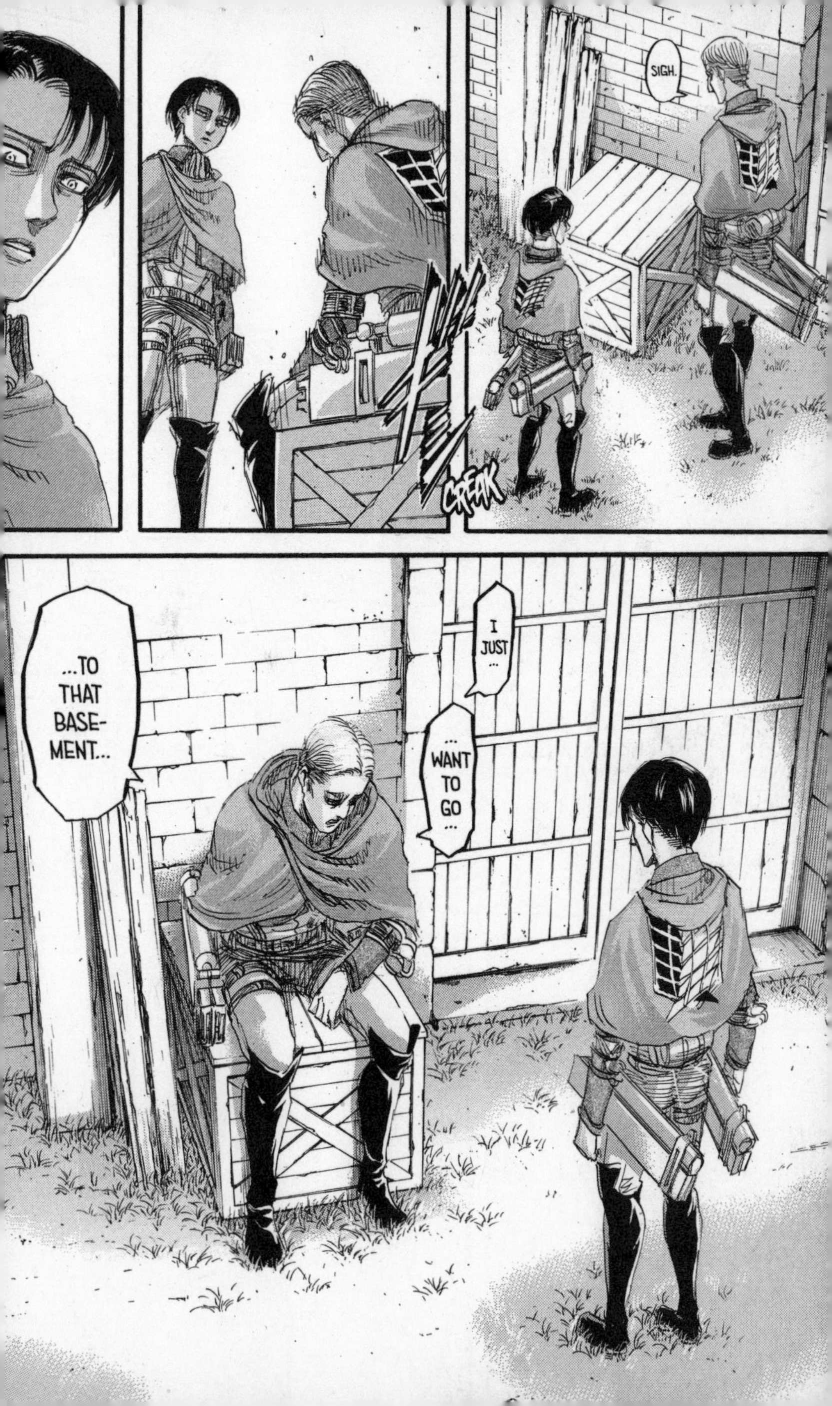
SIGH.
CREAK
I JUST ...
... WANT TO GO ...
...TO THAT BASE-MENT...

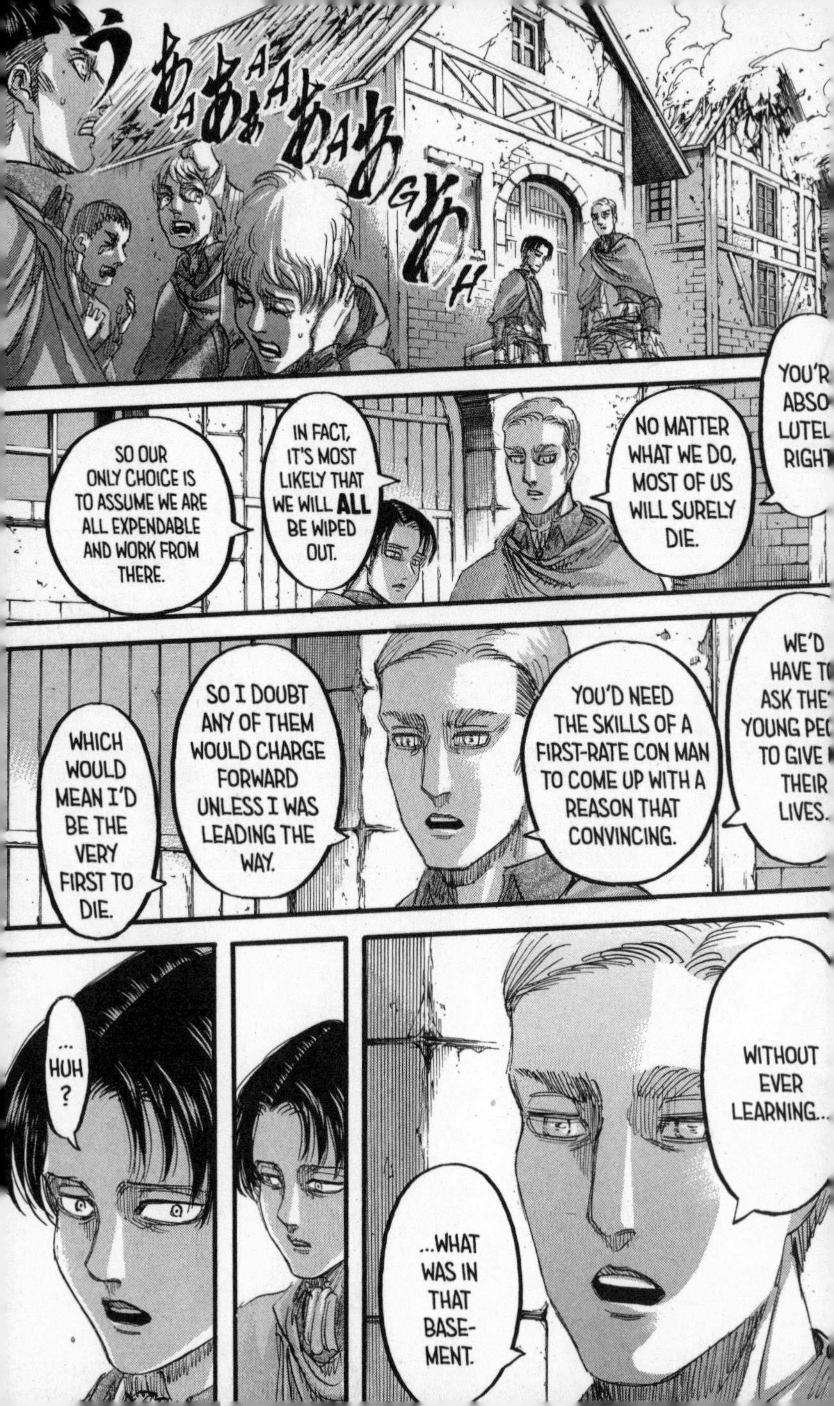
AAAAGH
YOU'R ABSO LUTEL RIGHT
NO MATTER WHAT WE DO, MOST OF US WILL SURELY DIE.
IN FACT, IT'S MOST LIKELY THAT WE WILL **ALL** BE WIPED OUT.
SO OUR ONLY CHOICE IS TO ASSUME WE ARE ALL EXPENDABLE AND WORK FROM THERE.
WE'D HAVE T ASK THE YOUNG PE TO GIVE THEIR LIVES.
YOU'D NEED THE SKILLS OF A FIRST-RATE CON MAN TO COME UP WITH A REASON THAT CONVINCING.
SO I DOUBT ANY OF THEM WOULD CHARGE FORWARD UNLESS I WAS LEADING THE WAY.
WHICH WOULD MEAN I'D BE THE VERY FIRST TO DIE.
WITHOUT EVER LEARNING...
...WHAT WAS IN THAT BASE-MENT.
... HUH?

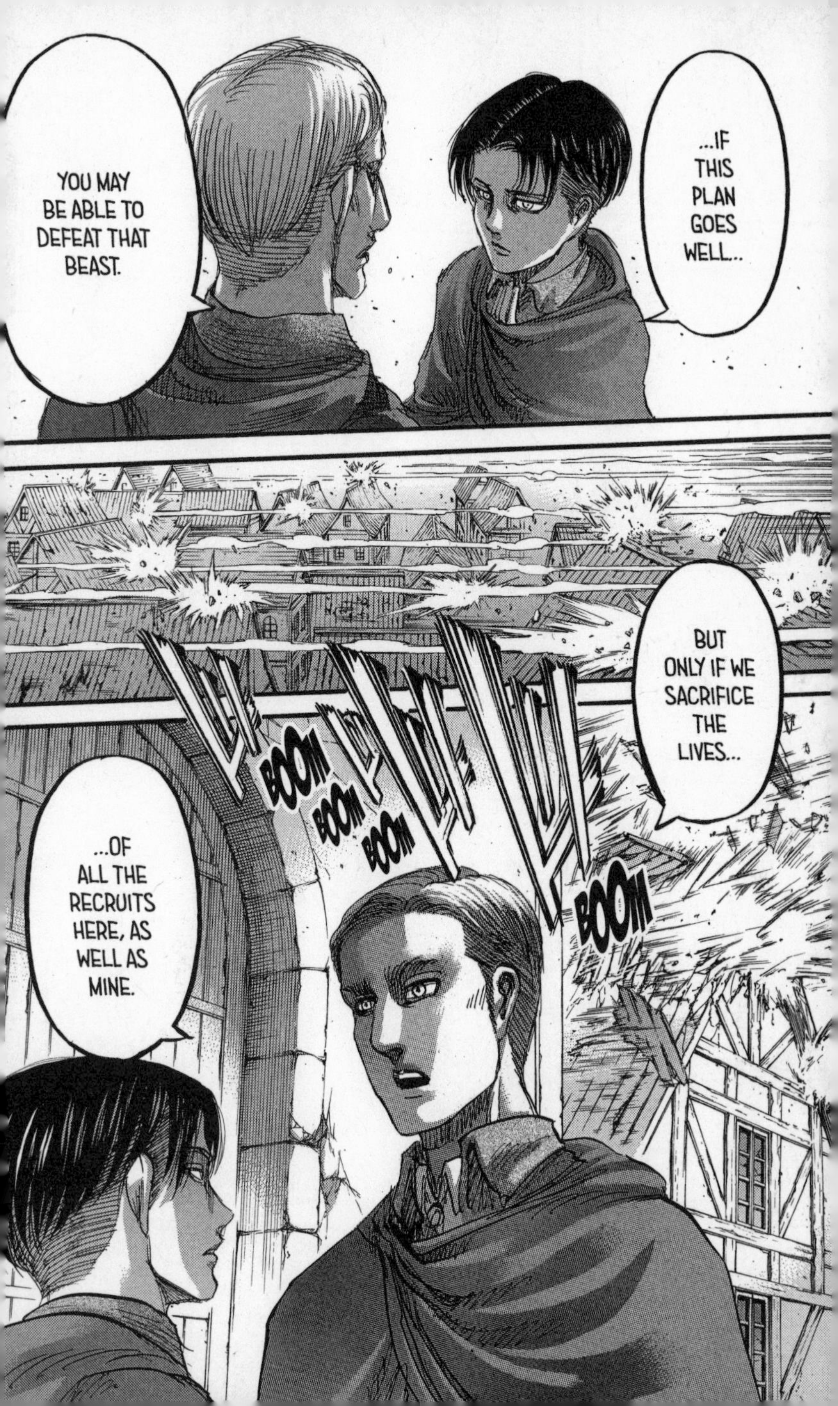
...IF THIS PLAN GOES WELL...
YOU MAY BE ABLE TO DEFEAT THAT BEAST.
BUT ONLY IF WE SACRIFICE THE LIVES...
BOOM
BOOM
BOOM
BOOM
...OF ALL THE RECRUITS HERE, AS WELL AS MINE.

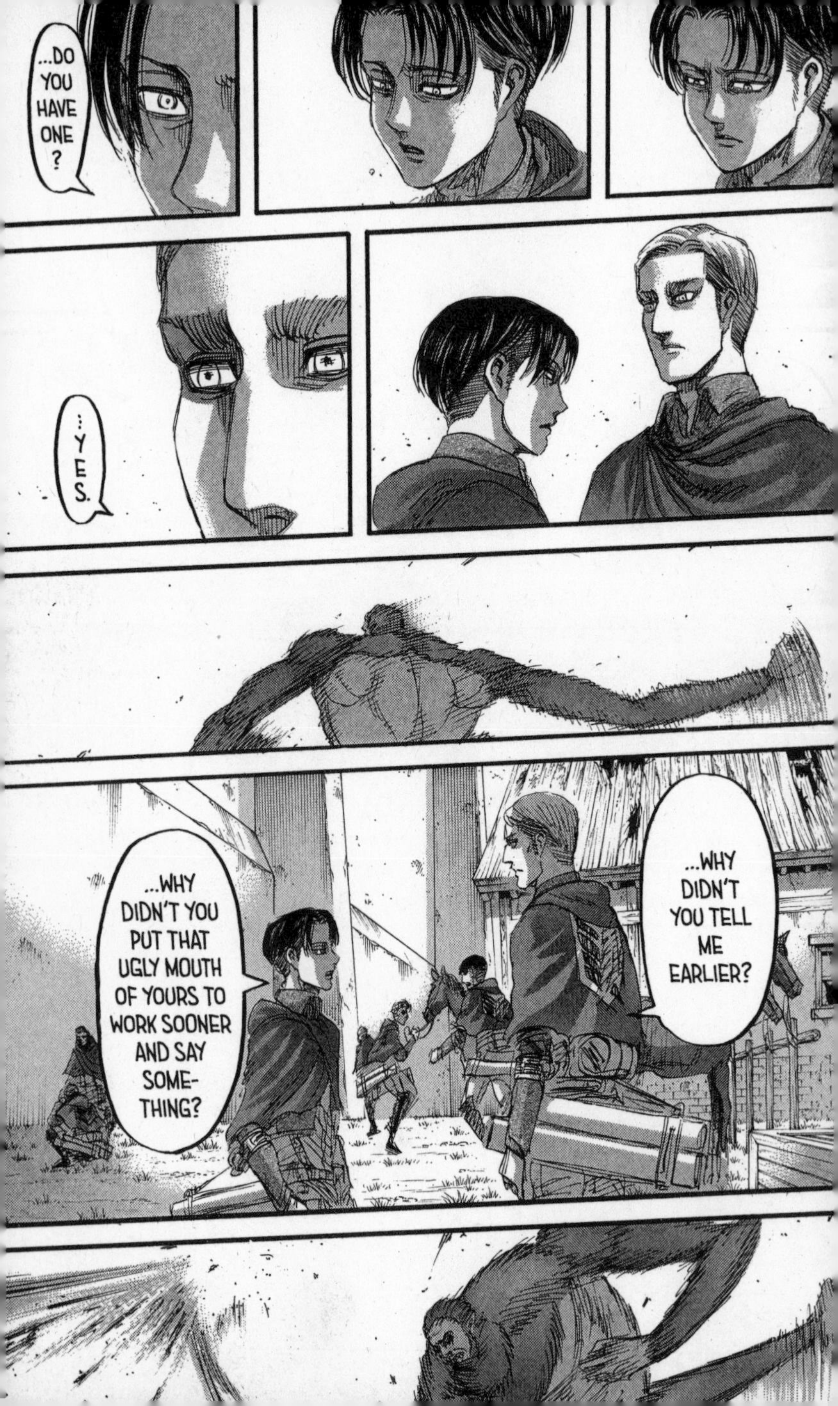
...DO YOU HAVE ONE?
...YES.
...WHY DIDN'T YOU TELL ME EARLIER?
...WHY DIDN'T YOU PUT THAT UGLY MOUTH OF YOURS TO WORK SOONER AND SAY SOMETHING?

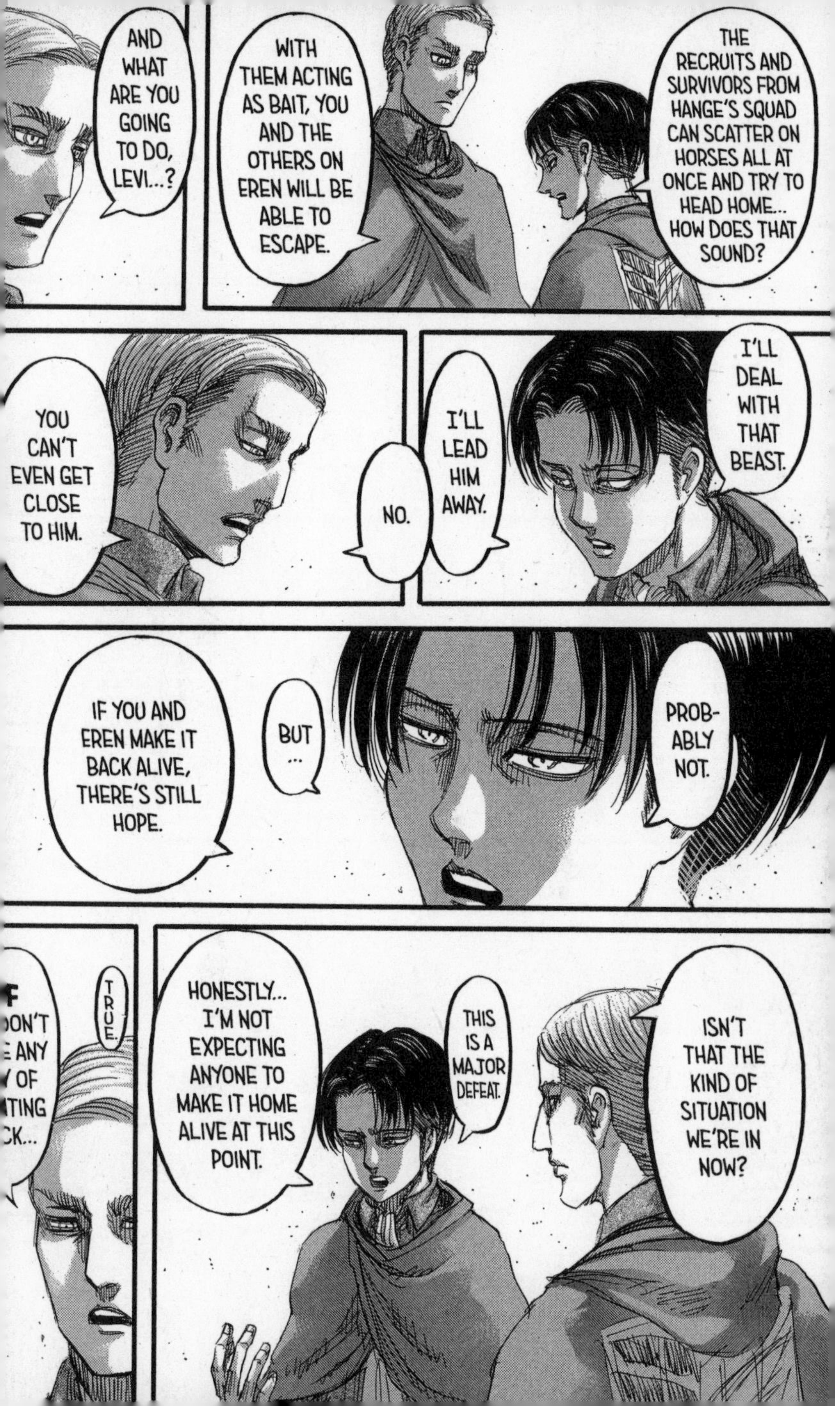
THE RECRUITS AND SURVIVORS FROM HANGE'S SQUAD CAN SCATTER ON HORSES ALL AT ONCE AND TRY TO HEAD HOME... HOW DOES THAT SOUND?
WITH THEM ACTING AS BAIT, YOU AND THE OTHERS ON EREN WILL BE ABLE TO ESCAPE.
AND WHAT ARE YOU GOING TO DO, LEVI...?
I'LL DEAL WITH THAT BEAST.
I'LL LEAD HIM AWAY.
NO.
YOU CAN'T EVEN GET CLOSE TO HIM.
PROB-ABLY NOT.
BUT ...
IF YOU AND EREN MAKE IT BACK ALIVE, THERE'S STILL HOPE.
ISN'T THAT THE KIND OF SITUATION WE'RE IN NOW?
THIS IS A MAJOR DEFEAT.
HONESTLY... I'M NOT EXPECTING ANYONE TO MAKE IT HOME ALIVE AT THIS POINT.
TRUE.

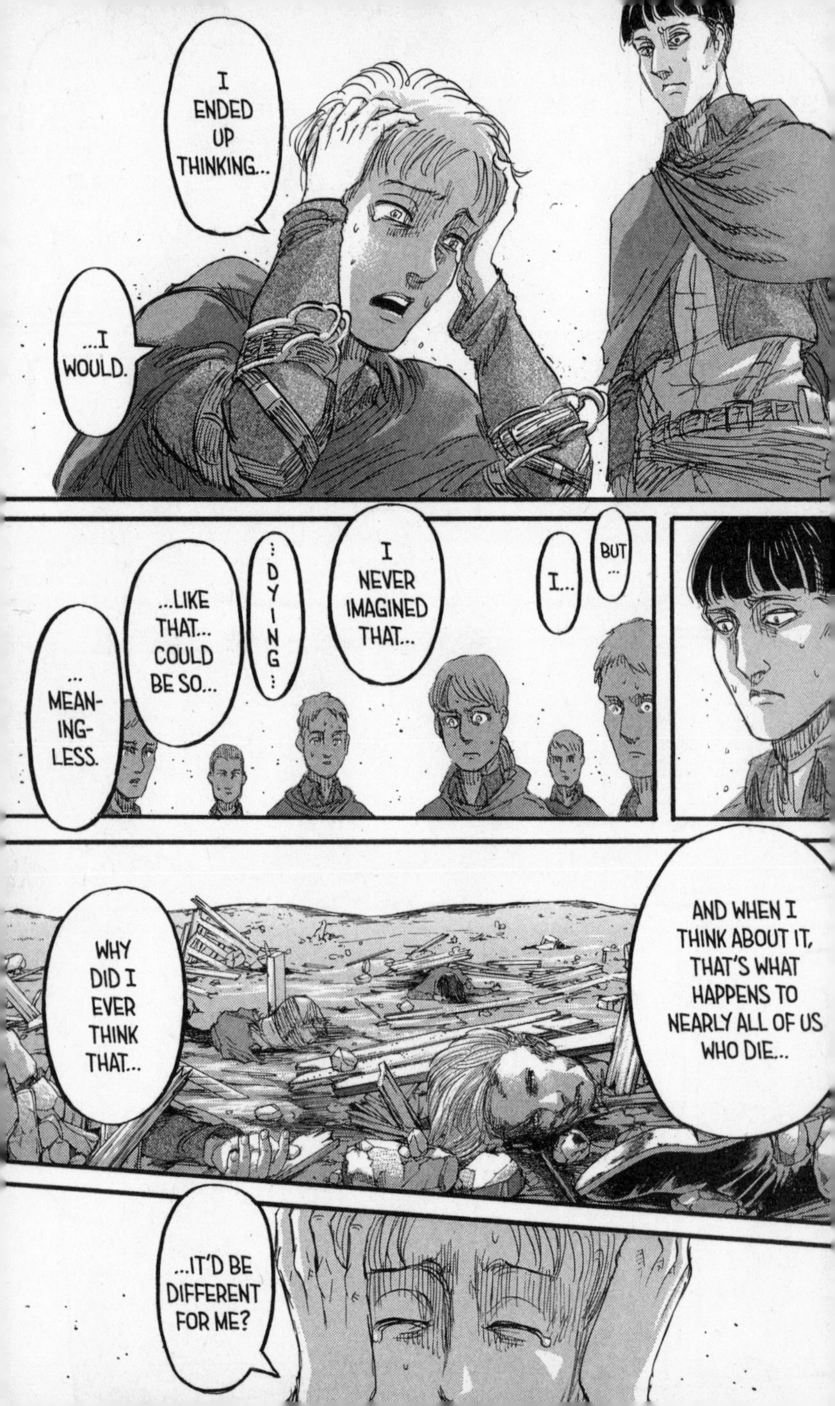
I ENDED UP THINKING...
...I WOULD.
BUT...
I...
I NEVER IMAGINED THAT...
...DYING...
...LIKE THAT... COULD BE SO...
...MEANINGLESS.
AND WHEN I THINK ABOUT IT, THAT'S WHAT HAPPENS TO NEARLY ALL OF US WHO DIE...
WHY DID I EVER THINK THAT...
...IT'D BE DIFFERENT FOR ME?

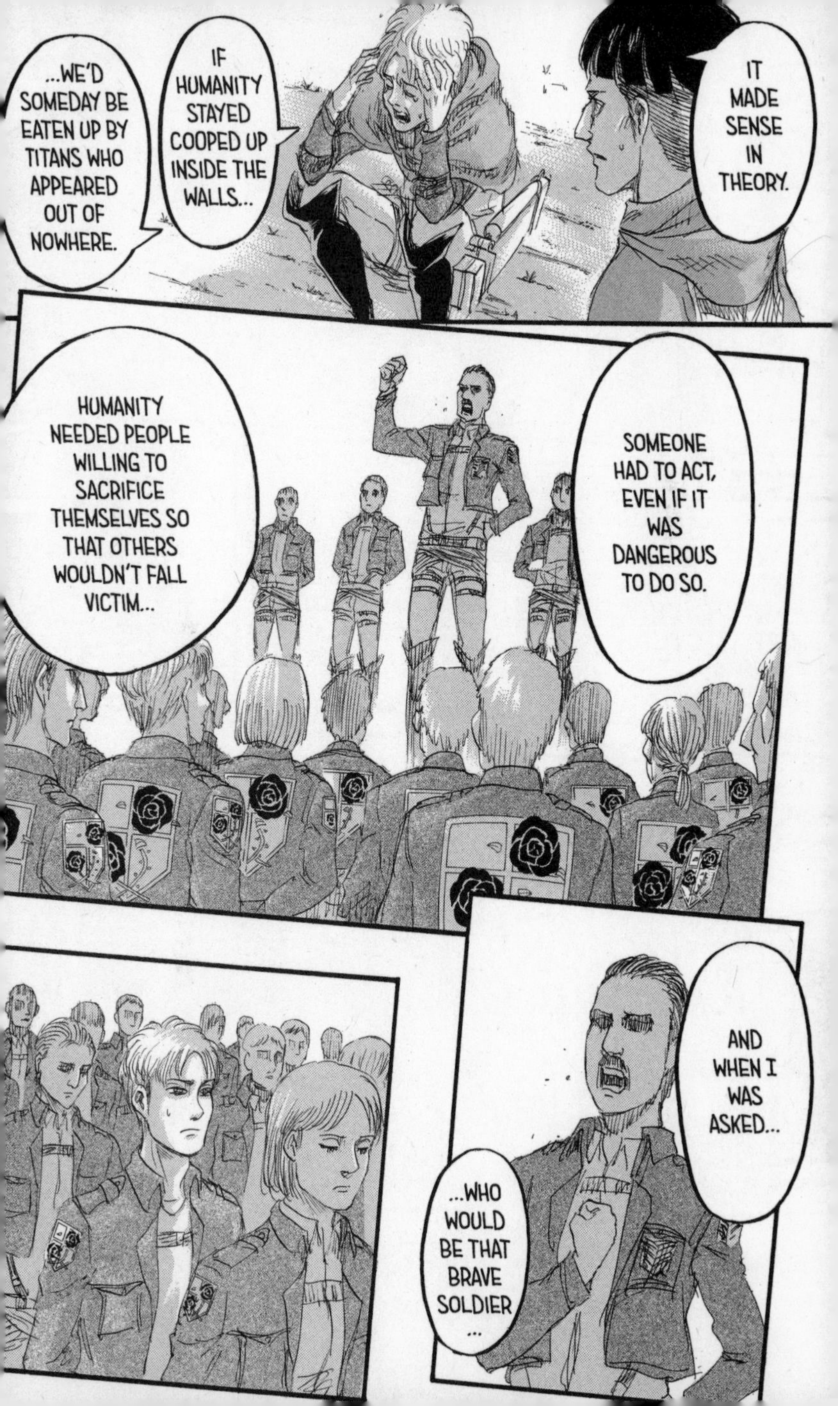
IT MADE SENSE IN THEORY.
IF HUMANITY STAYED COOPED UP INSIDE THE WALLS...
...WE'D SOMEDAY BE EATEN UP BY TITANS WHO APPEARED OUT OF NOWHERE.
SOMEONE HAD TO ACT, EVEN IF IT WAS DANGEROUS TO DO SO.
HUMANITY NEEDED PEOPLE WILLING TO SACRIFICE THEMSELVES SO THAT OTHERS WOULDN'T FALL VICTIM...
AND WHEN I WAS ASKED...
...WHO WOULD BE THAT BRAVE SOLDIER ...

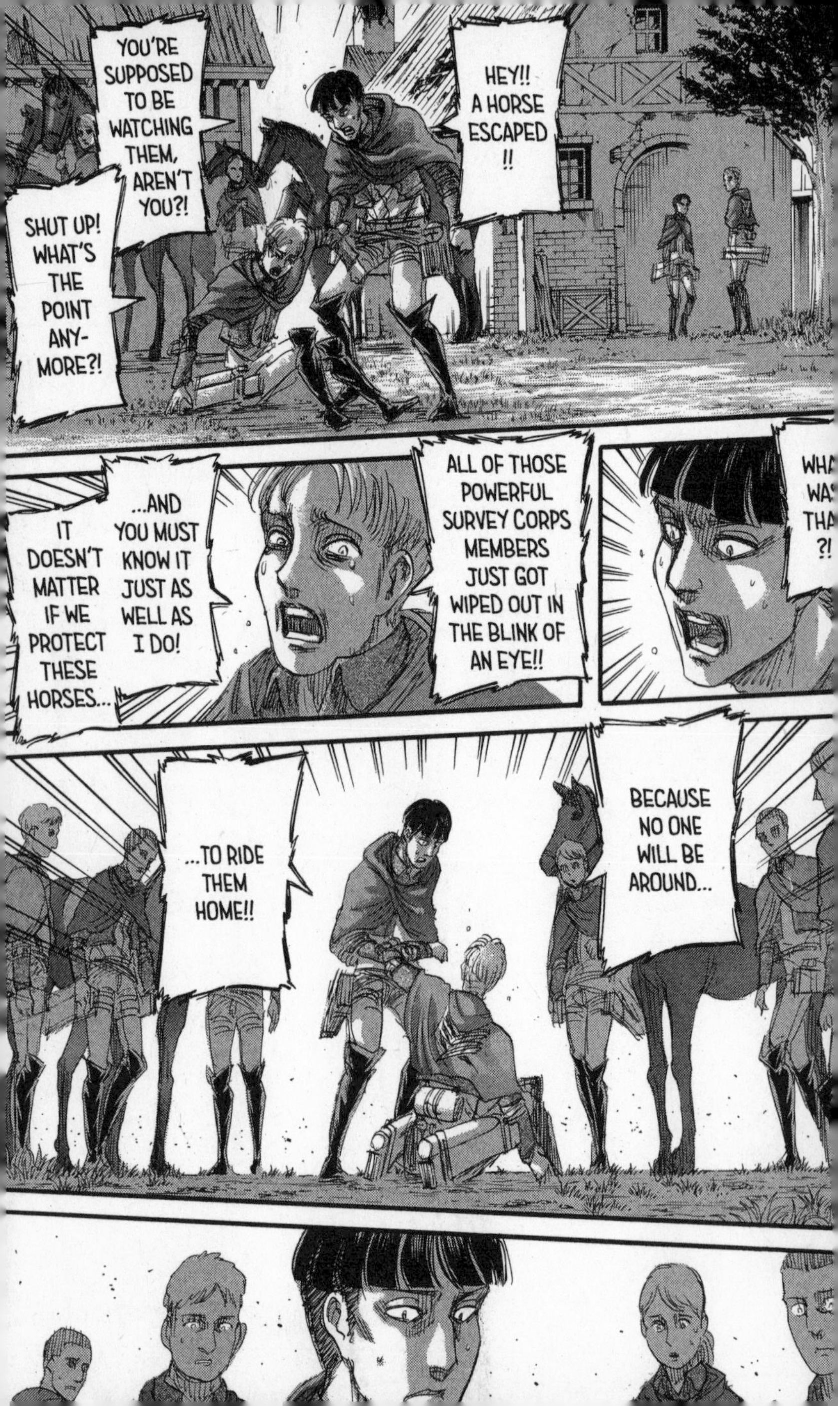
HEY!! A HORSE ESCAPED!!
YOU'RE SUPPOSED TO BE WATCHING THEM, AREN'T YOU?!
SHUT UP! WHAT'S THE POINT ANY-MORE?!
WHA WAS THA ?!
ALL OF THOSE POWERFUL SURVEY CORPS MEMBERS JUST GOT WIPED OUT IN THE BLINK OF AN EYE!!
...AND YOU MUST KNOW IT JUST AS WELL AS I DO!
IT DOESN'T MATTER IF WE PROTECT THESE HORSES...
BECAUSE NO ONE WILL BE AROUND...
...TO RIDE THEM HOME!!

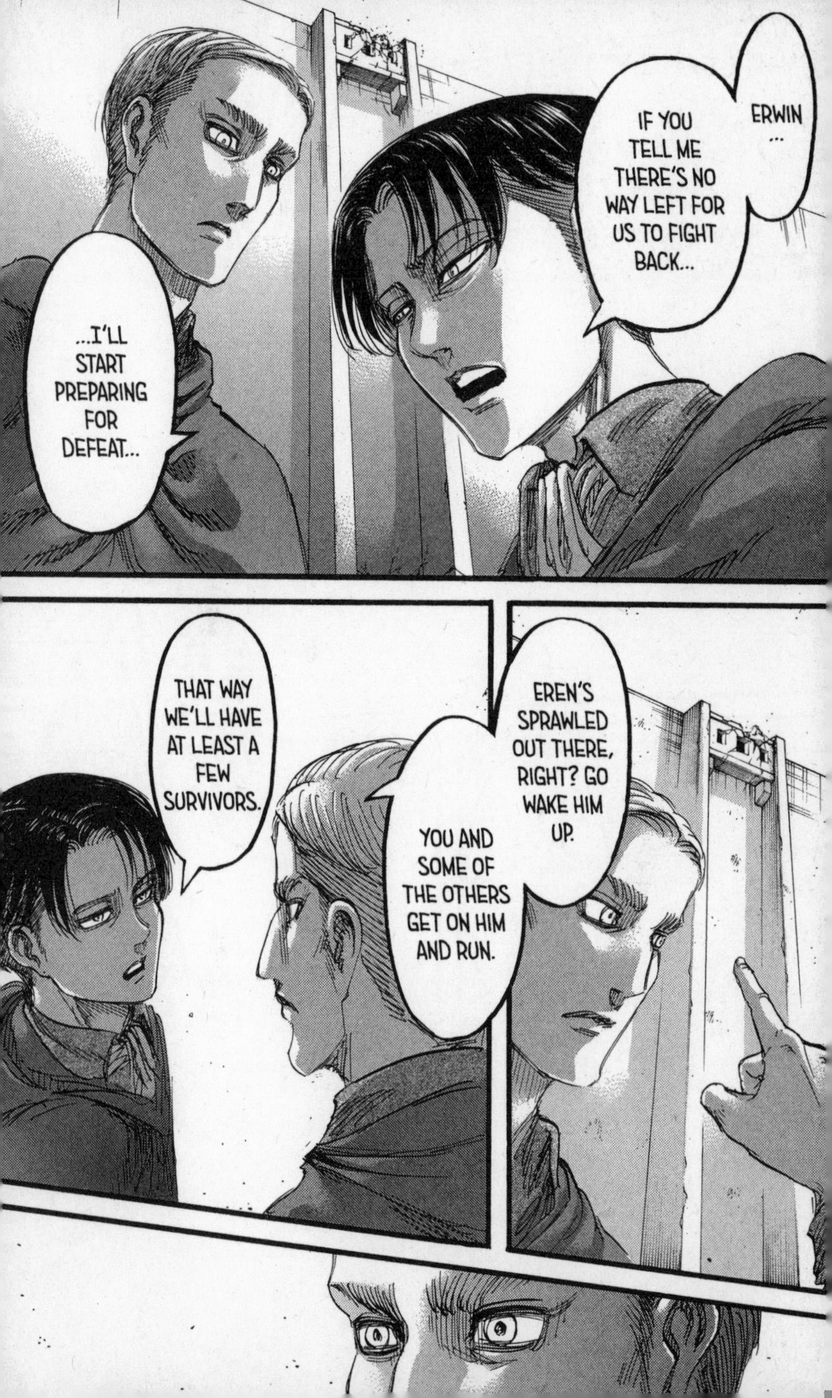
ERWIN ...
IF YOU TELL ME THERE'S NO WAY LEFT FOR US TO FIGHT BACK...
...I'LL START PREPARING FOR DEFEAT...
EREN'S SPRAWLED OUT THERE, RIGHT? GO WAKE HIM UP.
YOU AND SOME OF THE OTHERS GET ON HIM AND RUN.
THAT WAY WE'LL HAVE AT LEAST A FEW SURVIVORS.

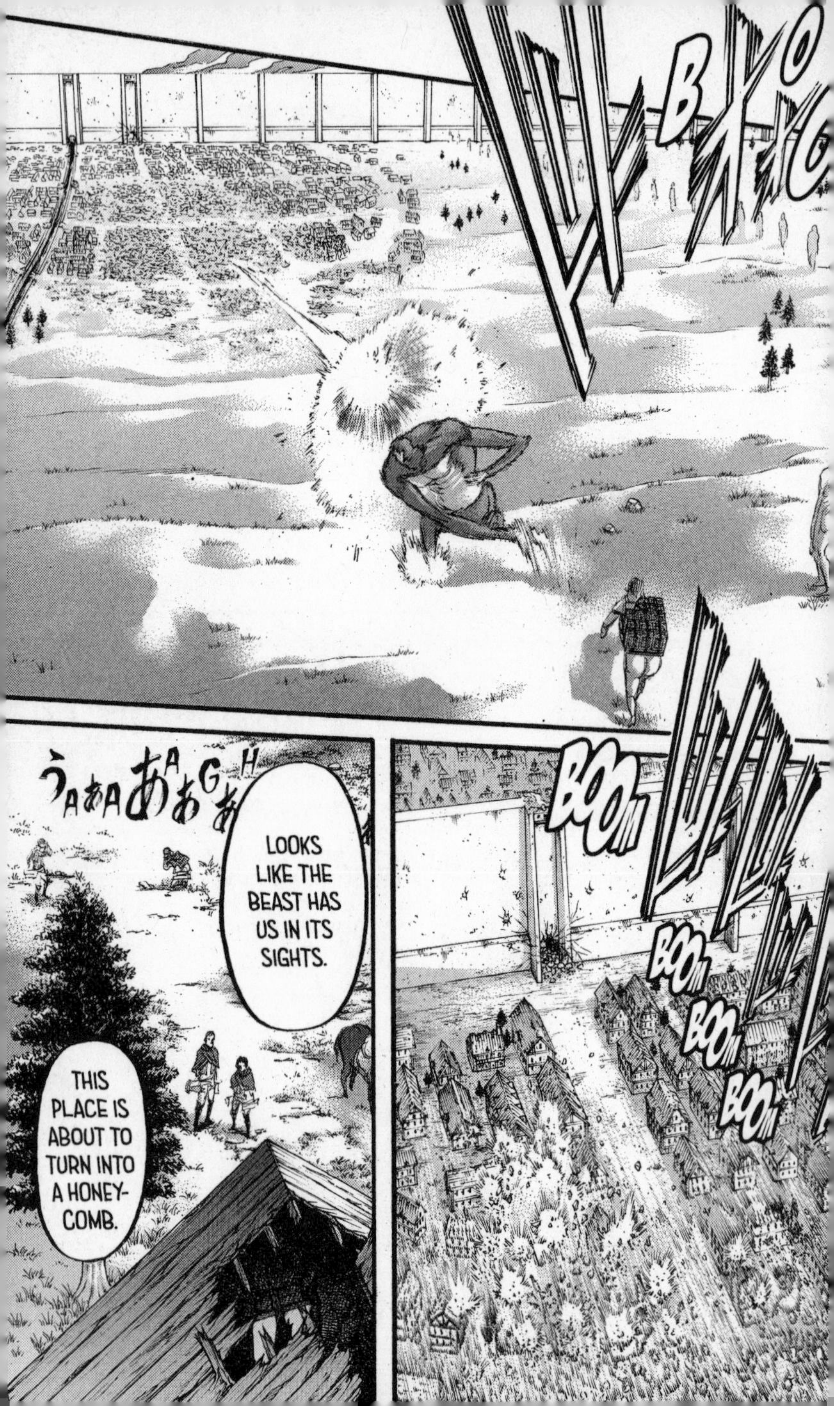
BOOM
BOOM
BOOM
BOOM
LOOKS LIKE THE BEAST HAS US IN ITS SIGHTS.
THIS PLACE IS ABOUT TO TURN INTO A HONEY-COMB.

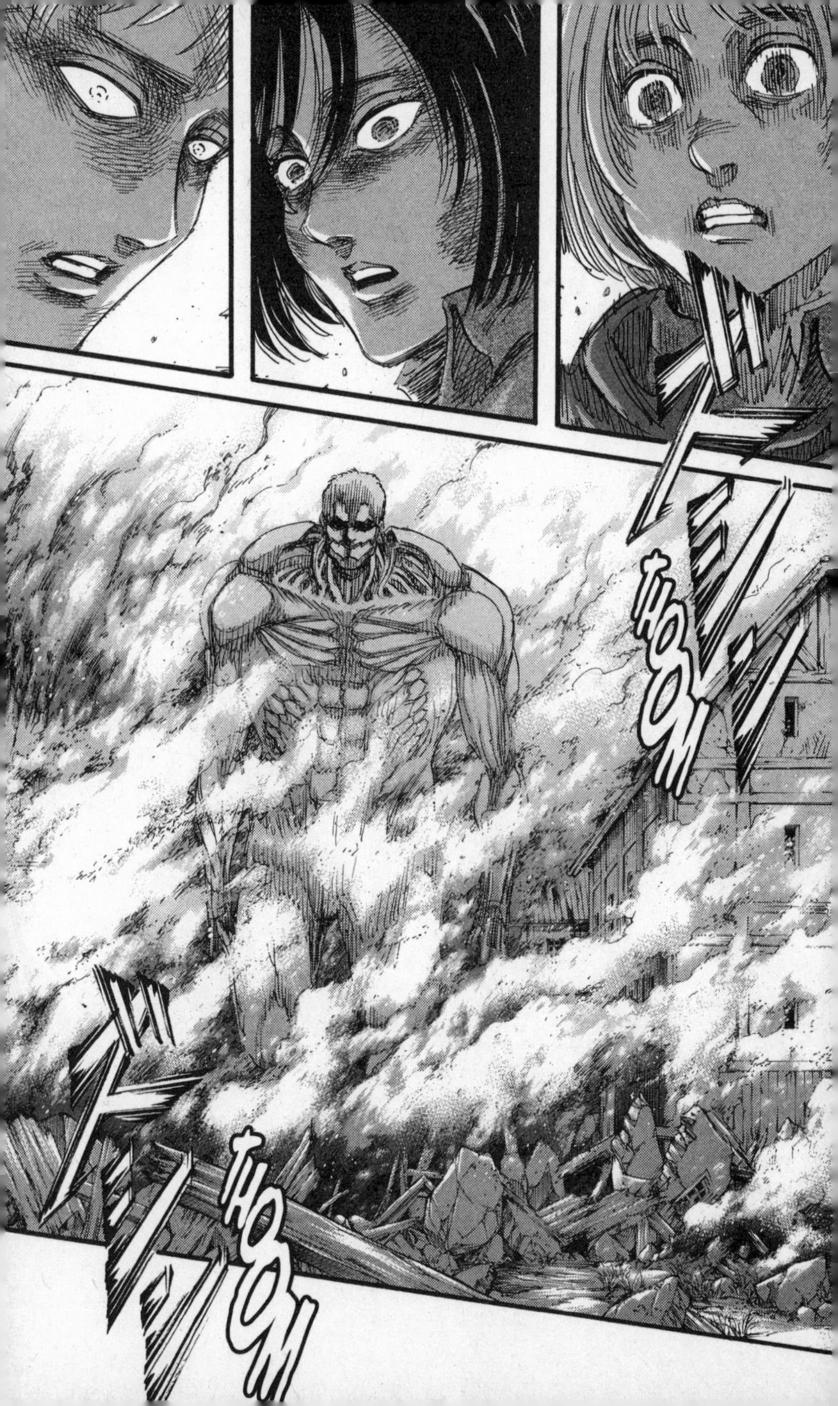
THOOM
THOOM

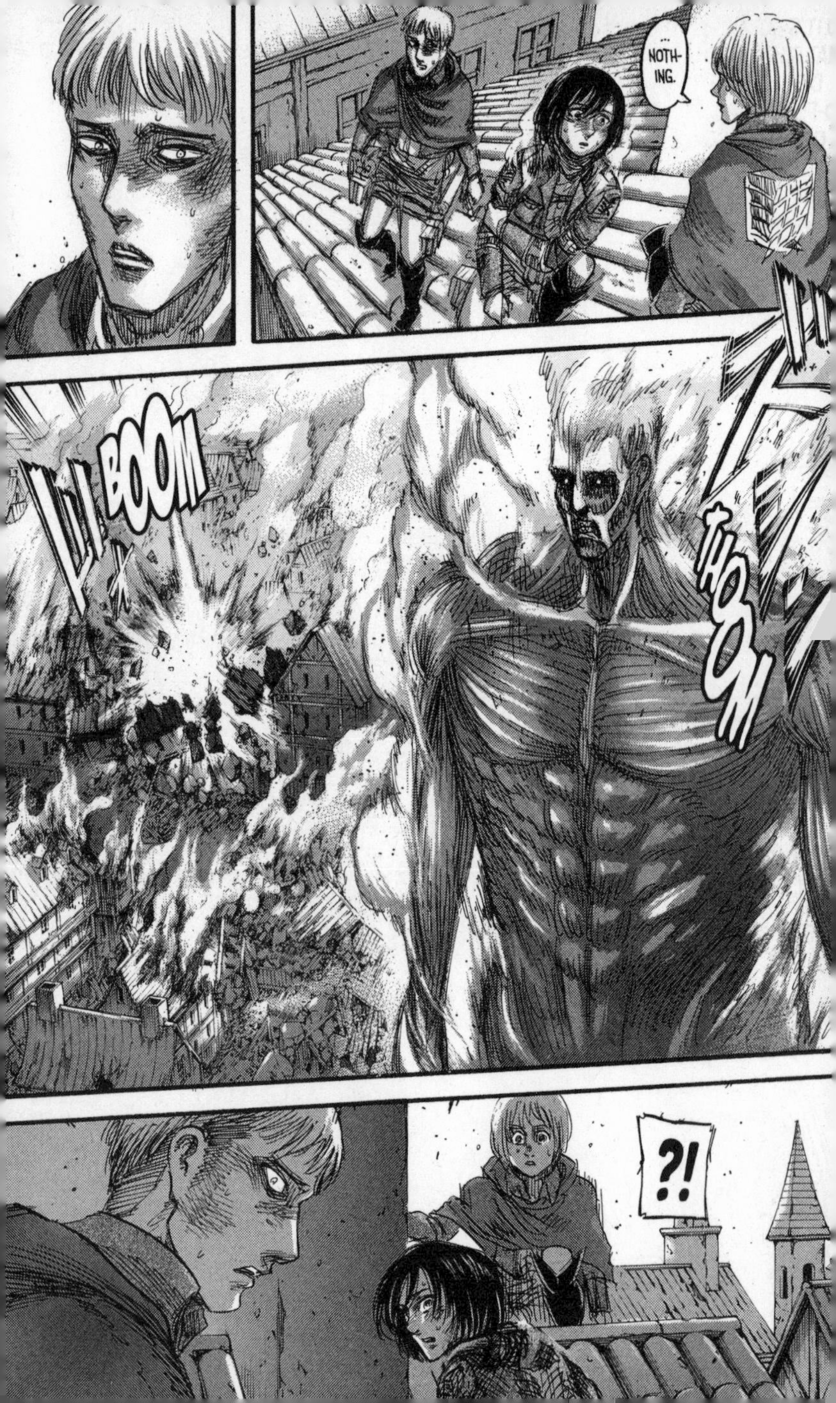
... NOTHING.
THOOOM
BOOM
?!

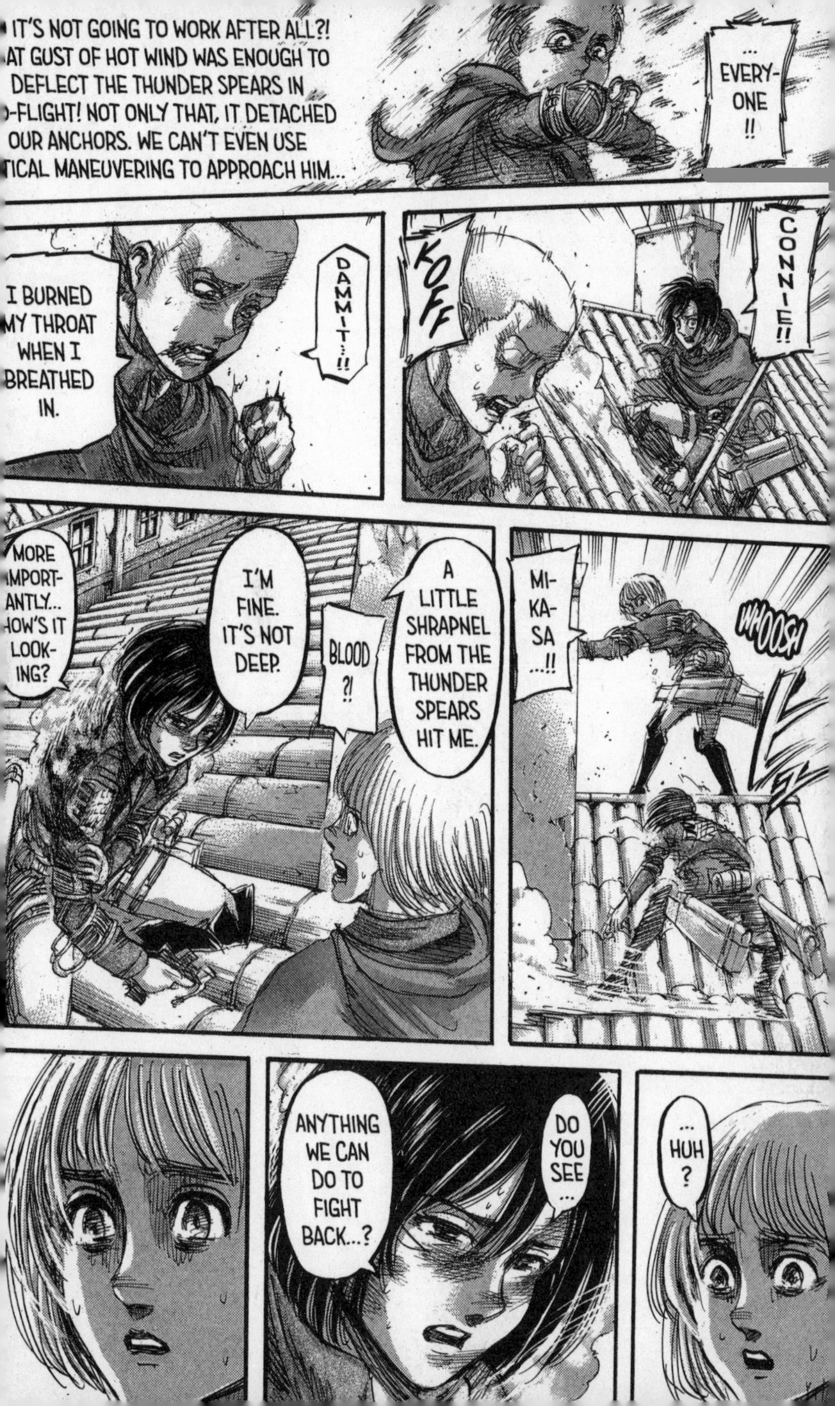

... EVERY-ONE !!
IT'S NOT GOING TO WORK AFTER ALL?! AT GUST OF HOT WIND WAS ENOUGH TO DEFLECT THE THUNDER SPEARS IN -FLIGHT! NOT ONLY THAT, IT DETACHED OUR ANCHORS. WE CAN'T EVEN USE TICAL MANEUVERING TO APPROACH HIM...
CONNIE!!
KOFF
DAMMIT...!!
I BURNED MY THROAT WHEN I BREATHED IN.
MI-KA-SA...!!
WHOOSH
BLOOD?!
A LITTLE SHRAPNEL FROM THE THUNDER SPEARS HIT ME.
I'M FINE. IT'S NOT DEEP.
MORE IMPORT-ANTLY... HOW'S IT LOOK-ING?
... HUH ?
DO YOU SEE ...
ANYTHING WE CAN DO TO FIGHT BACK...?

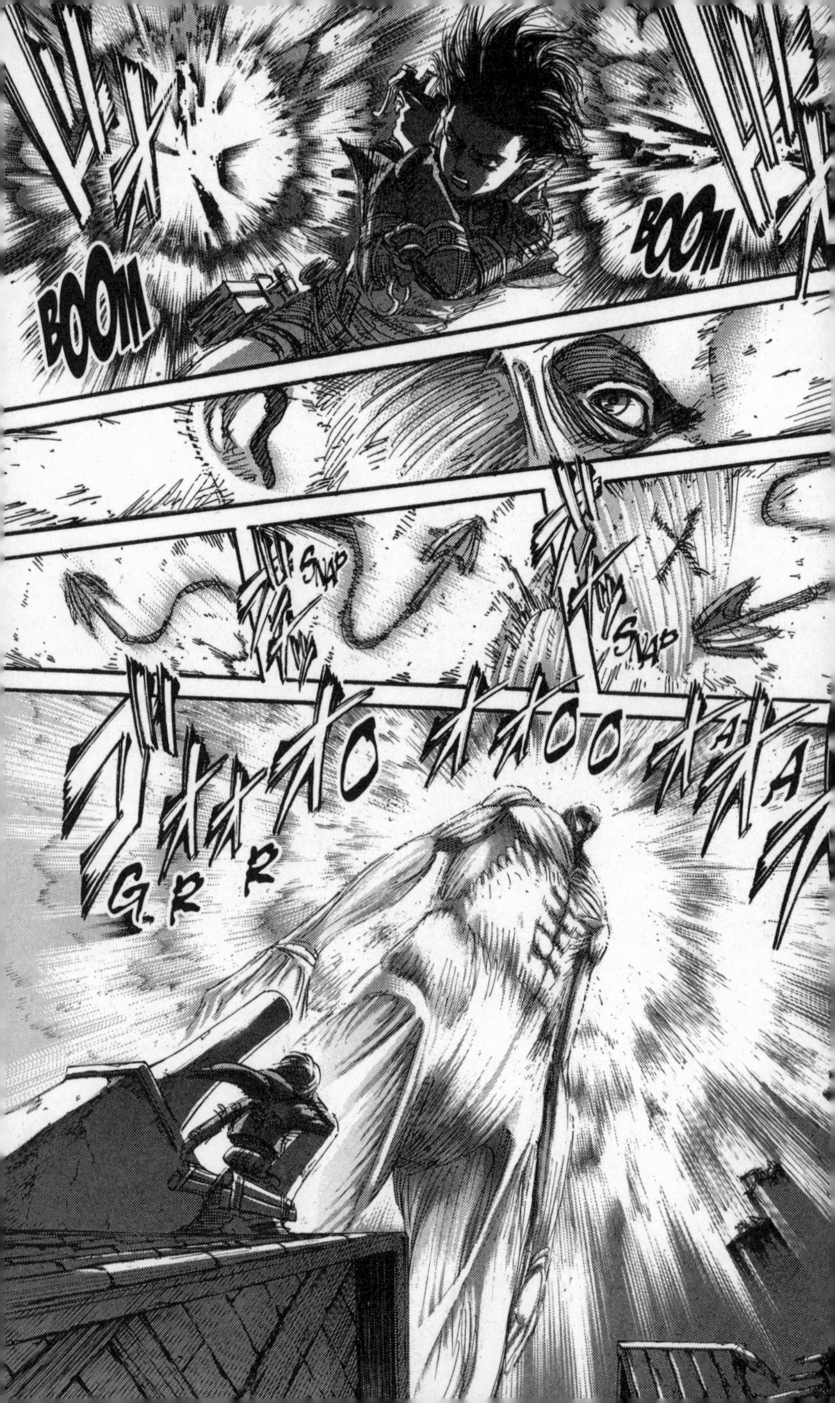
BOOM
BOOM
SNAP
SNAP
GRR

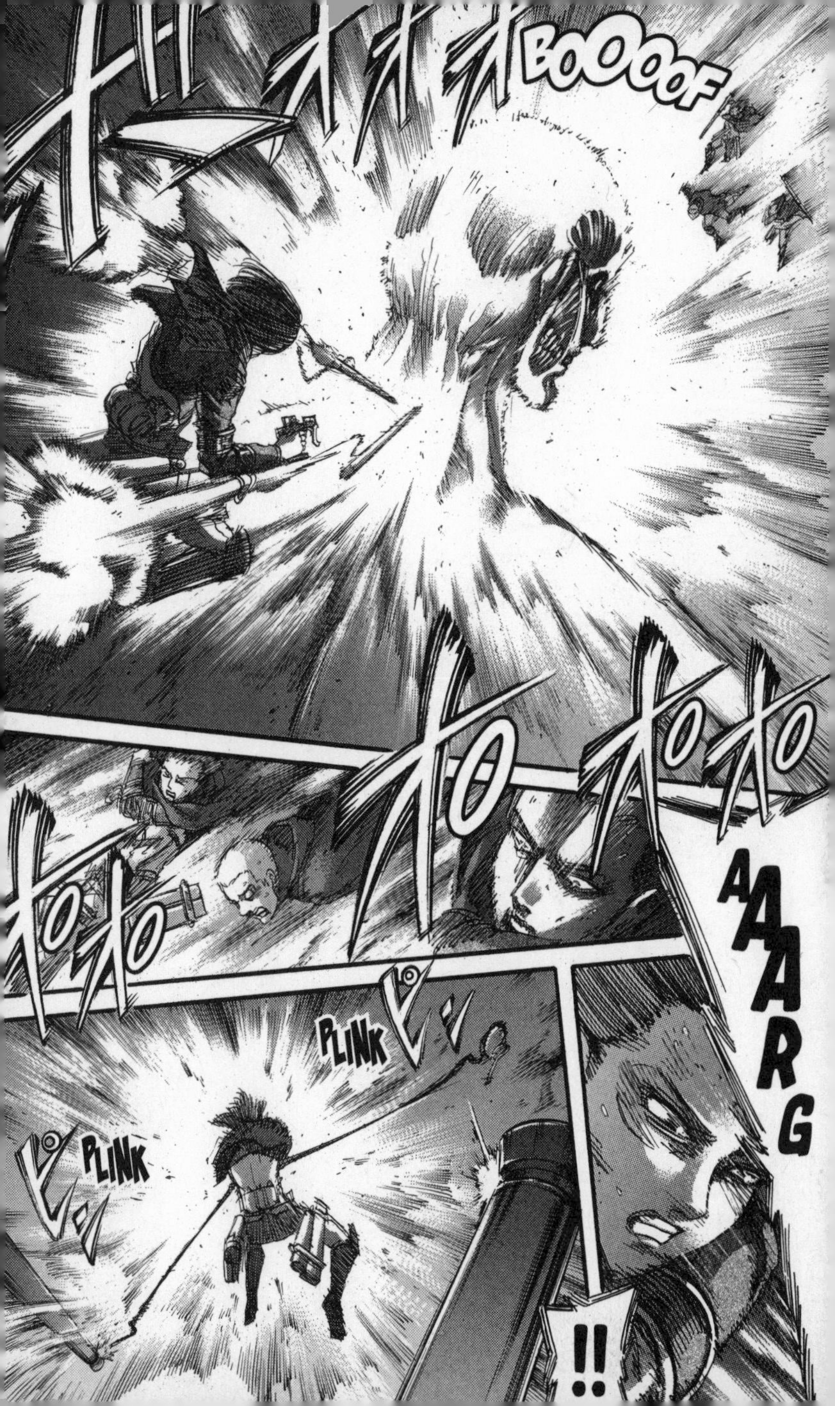
BOOOOF
AAARG
!!
PLINK
PLINK

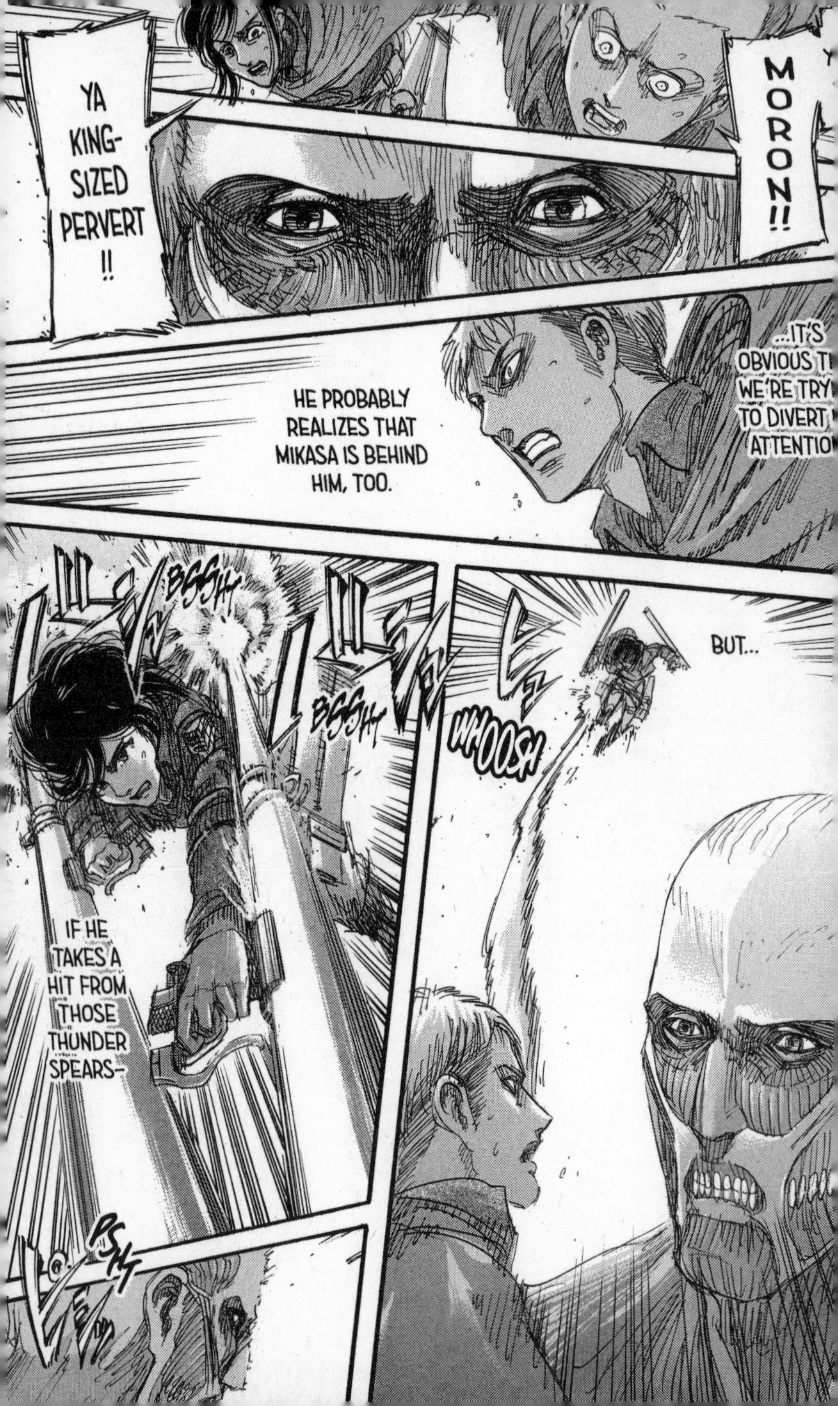
MORON!!
YA KING-SIZED PERVERT !!
...IT'S OBVIOUS T
WE'RE TRY
TO DIVERT
ATTENTIO
HE PROBABLY REALIZES THAT MIKASA IS BEHIND HIM, TOO.
WHOOSH
BUT...
BSSH
BSSH
IF HE TAKES A HIT FROM THOSE THUNDER SPEARS-
PSSH

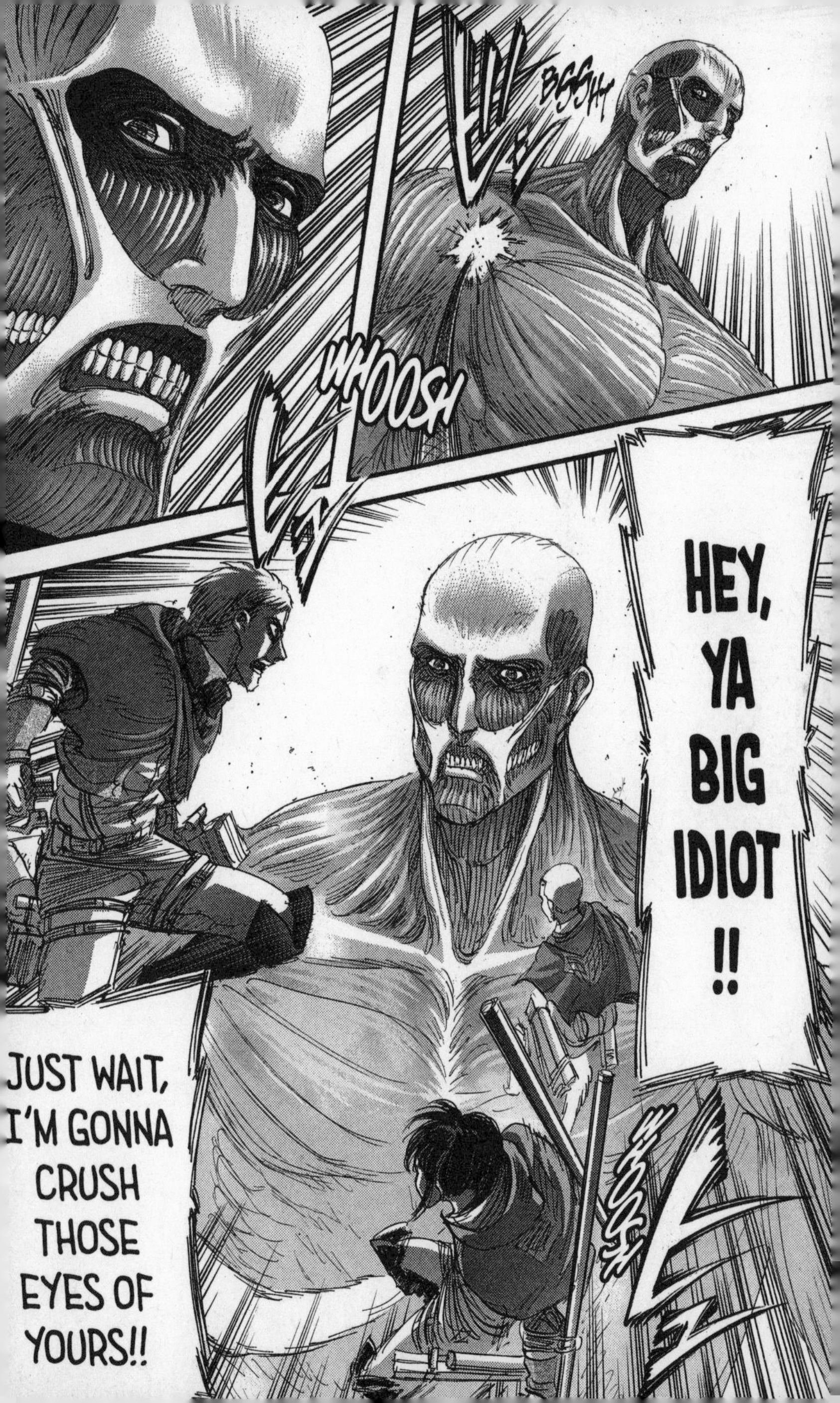

WHOOSH
HEY, YA BIG IDIOT!!
JUST WAIT, I'M GONNA CRUSH THOSE EYES OF YOURS!!

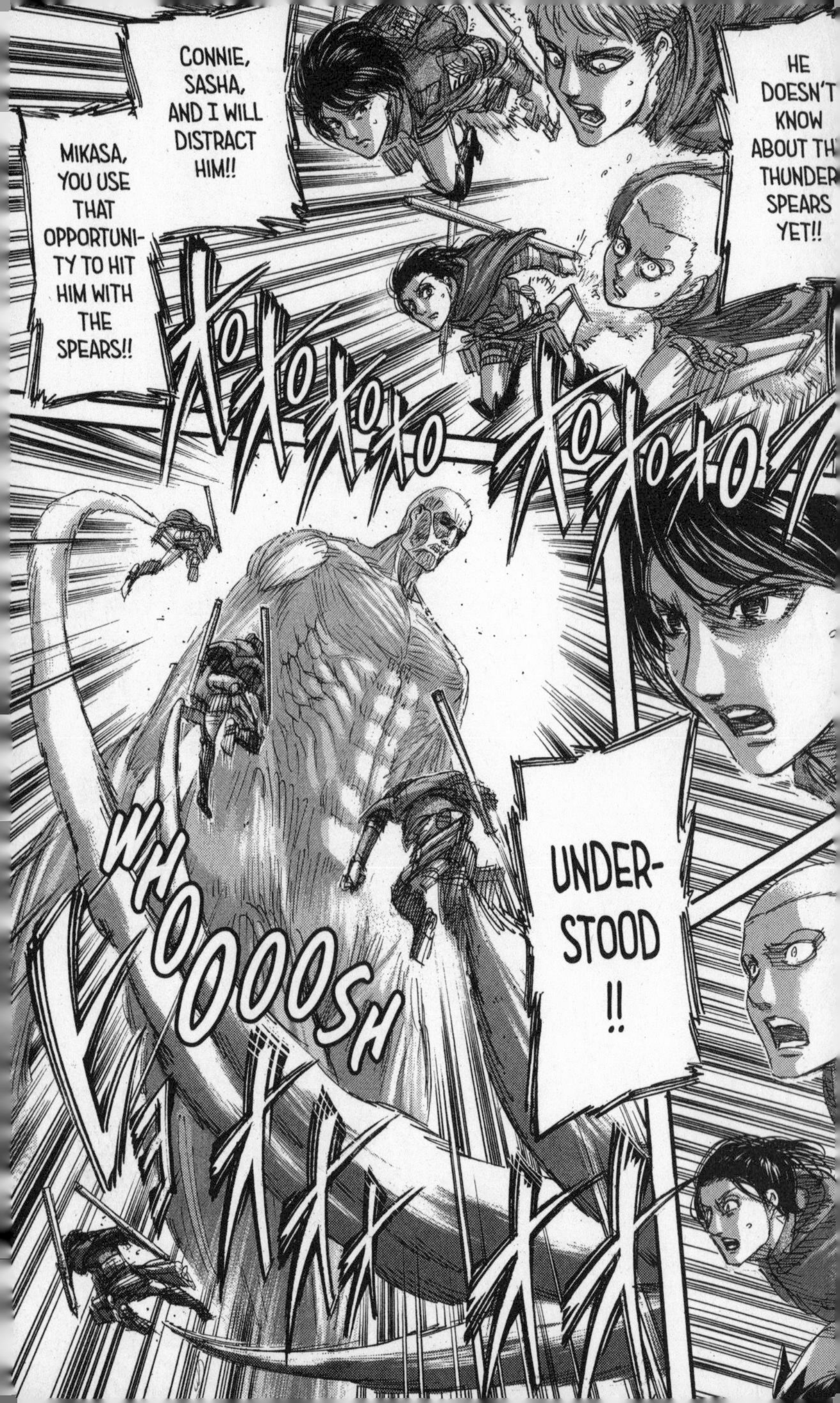

HE DOESN'T KNOW ABOUT TH THUNDER SPEARS YET!!
CONNIE, SASHA, AND I WILL DISTRACT HIM!!
MIKASA, YOU USE THAT OPPORTUNI-TY TO HIT HIM WITH THE SPEARS!!
UNDER-STOOD !!
WHOOOOOSH

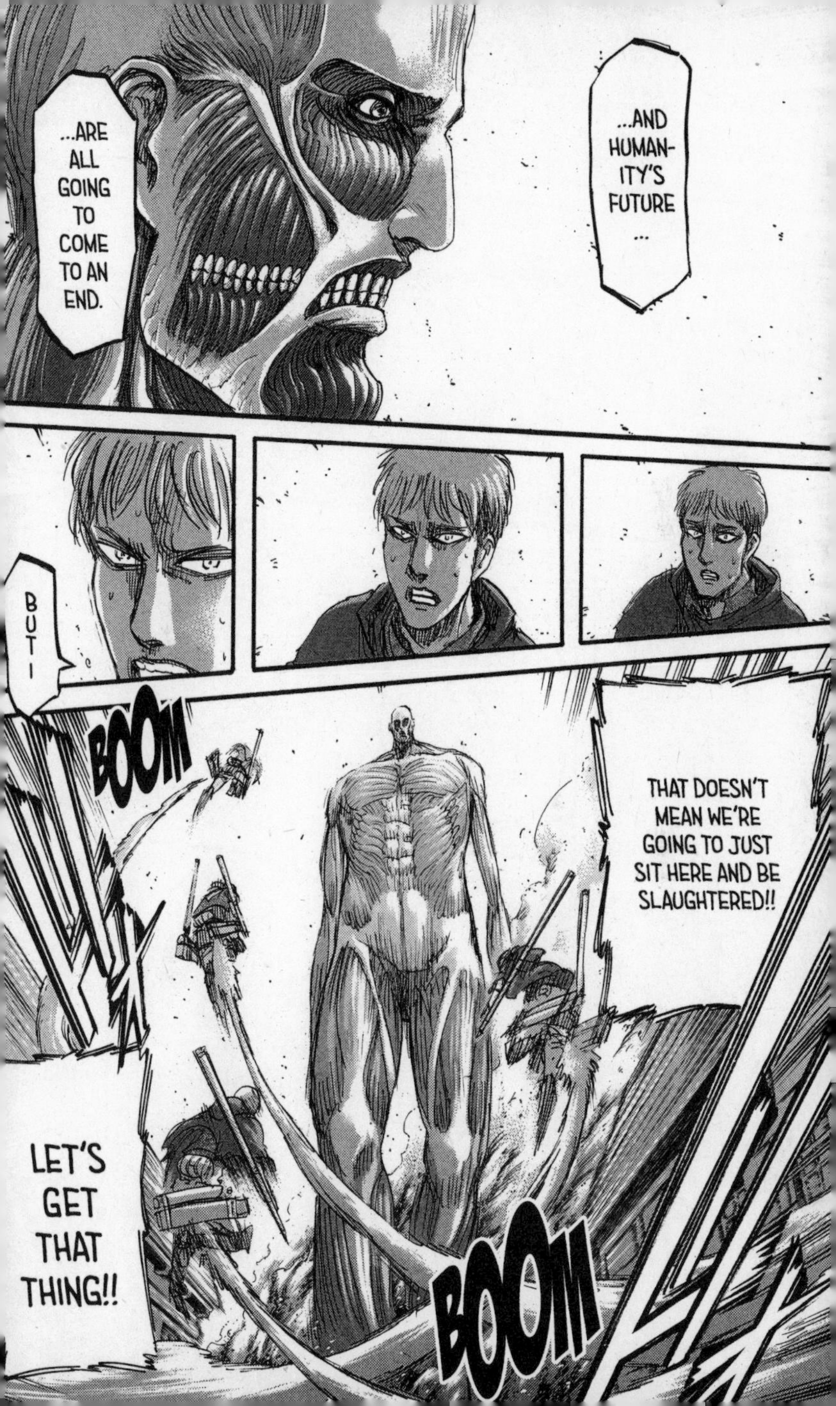
...AND HUMAN-ITY'S FUTURE ...
...ARE ALL GOING TO COME TO AN END.
BUT I
THAT DOESN'T MEAN WE'RE GOING TO JUST SIT HERE AND BE SLAUGHTERED!!
BOOM
BOOM
LET'S GET THAT THING!!

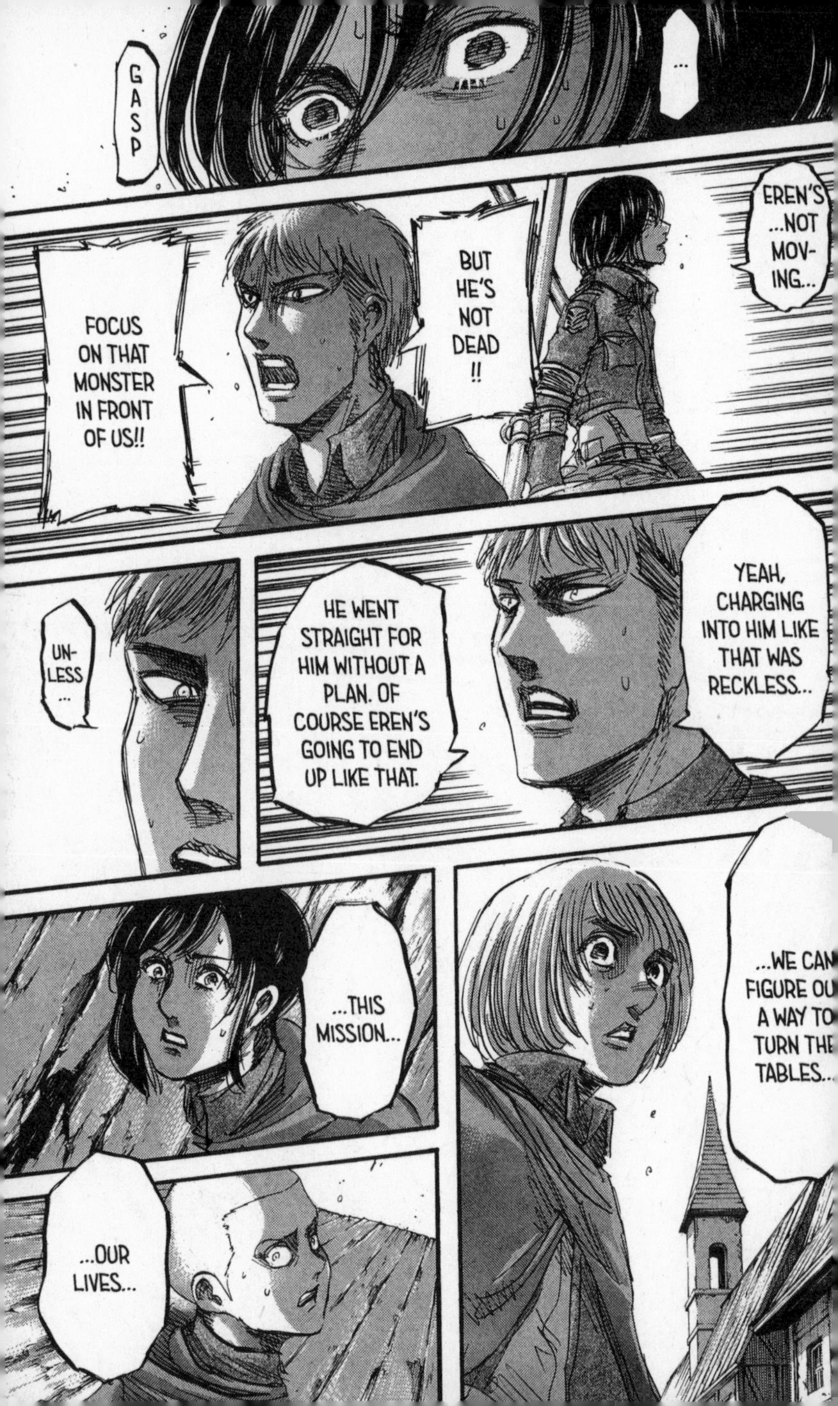
...
GASP
EREN'S ...NOT MOVING...
BUT HE'S NOT DEAD!!
FOCUS ON THAT MONSTER IN FRONT OF US!!
YEAH, CHARGING INTO HIM LIKE THAT WAS RECKLESS...
HE WENT STRAIGHT FOR HIM WITHOUT A PLAN. OF COURSE EREN'S GOING TO END UP LIKE THAT.
UNLESS...
...WE CAN FIGURE OU A WAY TO TURN THE TABLES...
...THIS MISSION...
...OUR LIVES...

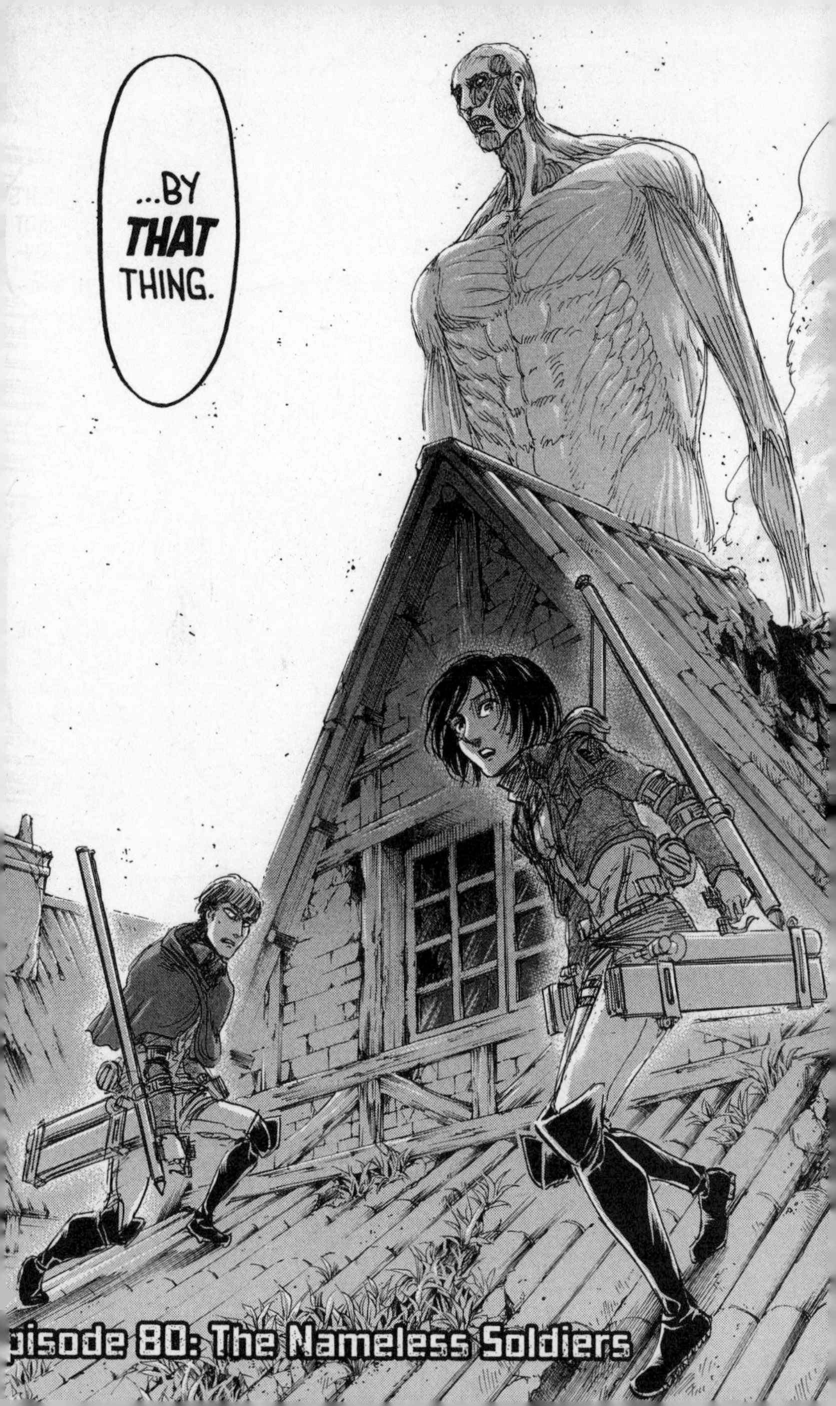

...BY THAT THING.
pisode 80: The Nameless Soldiers

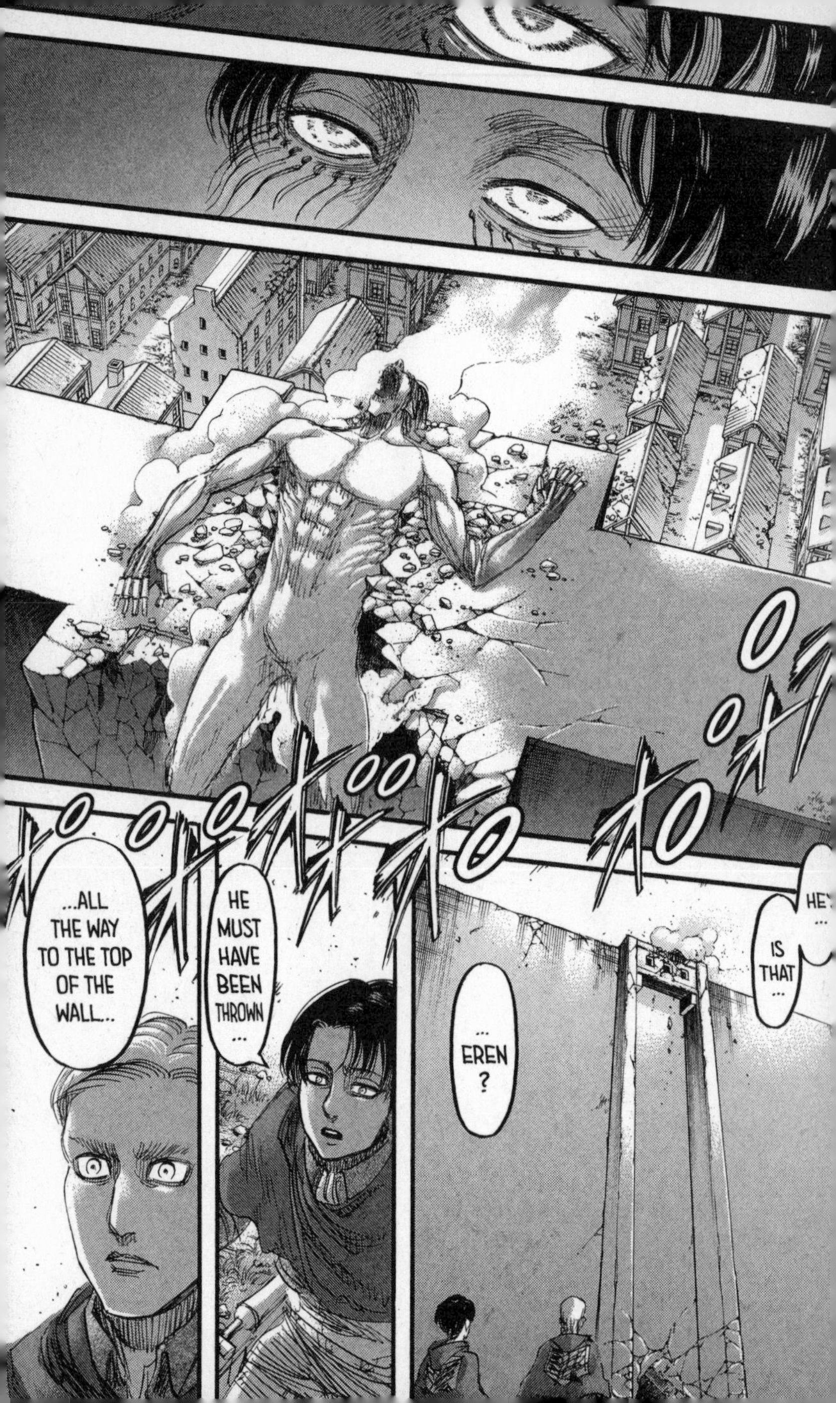
HE'...
IS THAT...
...EREN?
HE MUST HAVE BEEN THROWN...
...ALL THE WAY TO THE TOP OF THE WALL...

ATTACK on TITAN

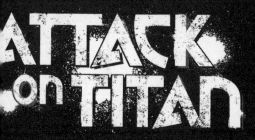

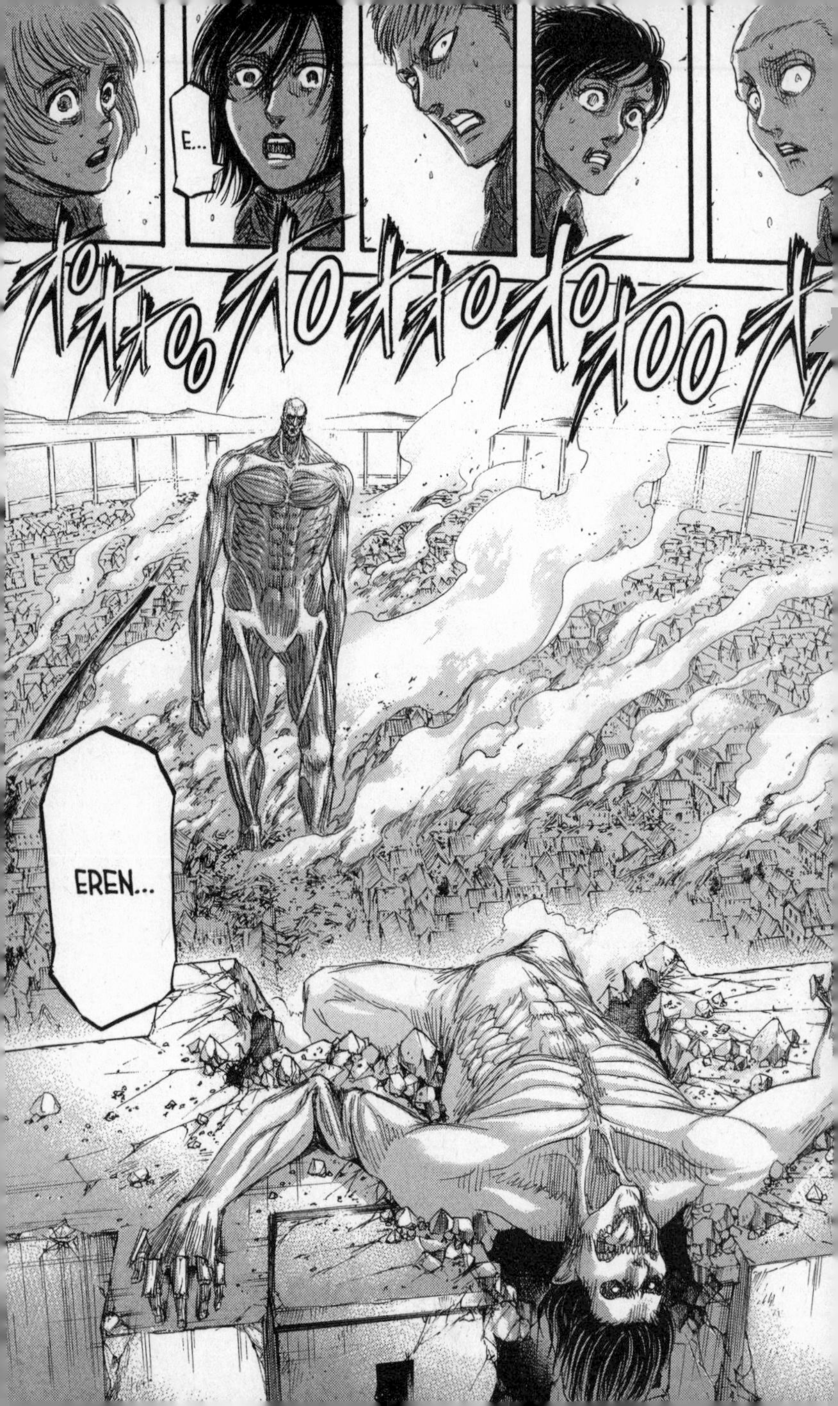
E...
EREN...

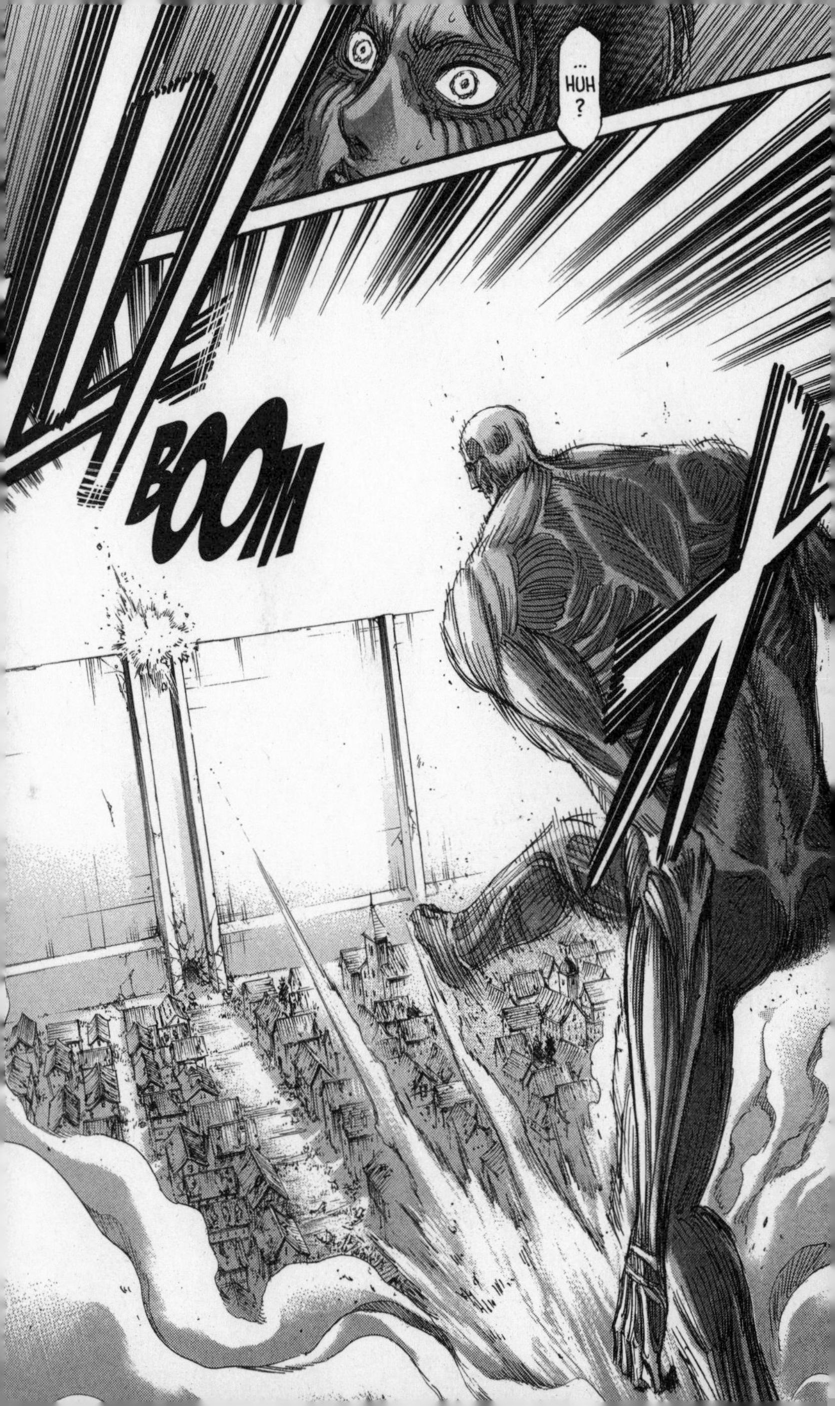
... HUH ?
BOOM

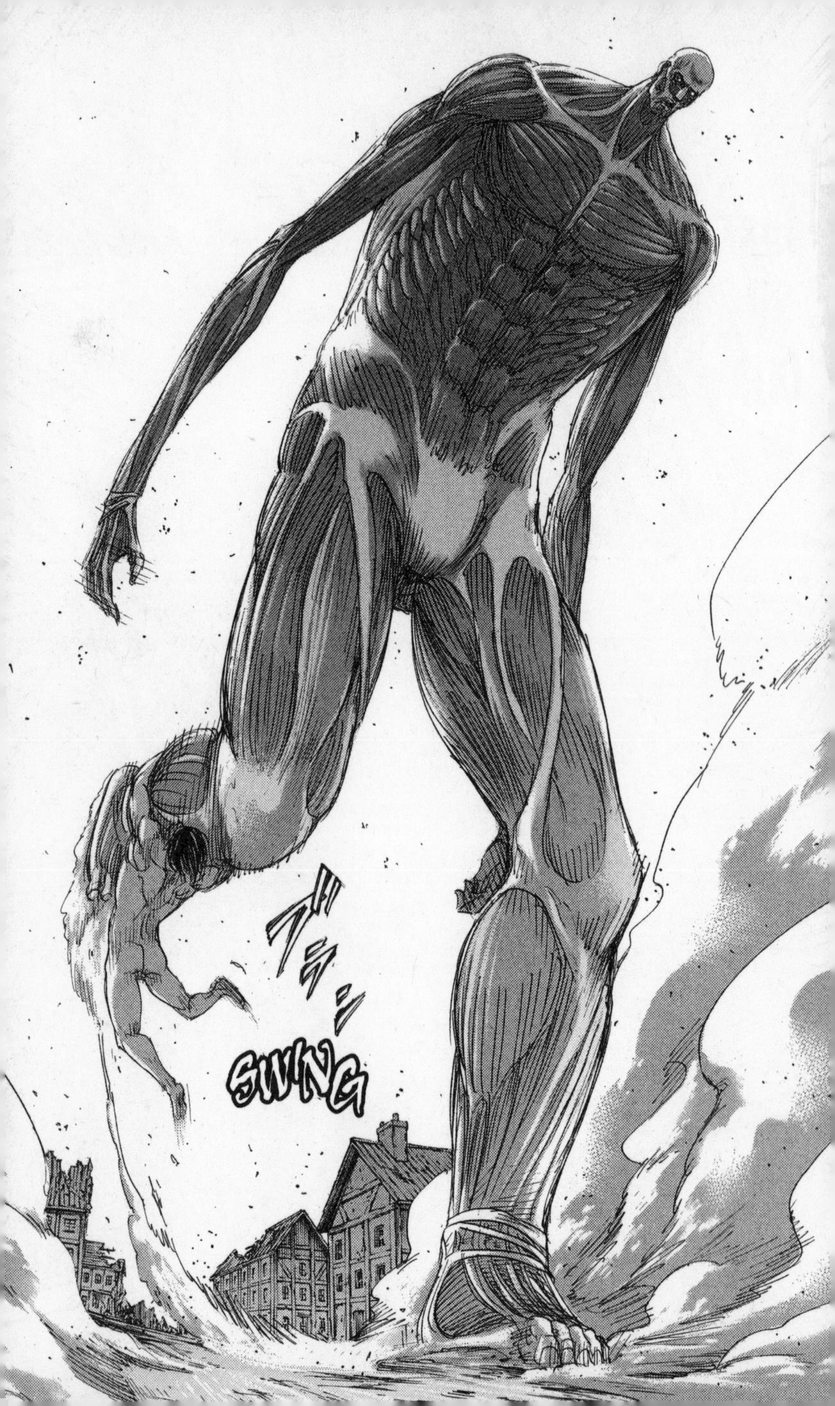
SWING

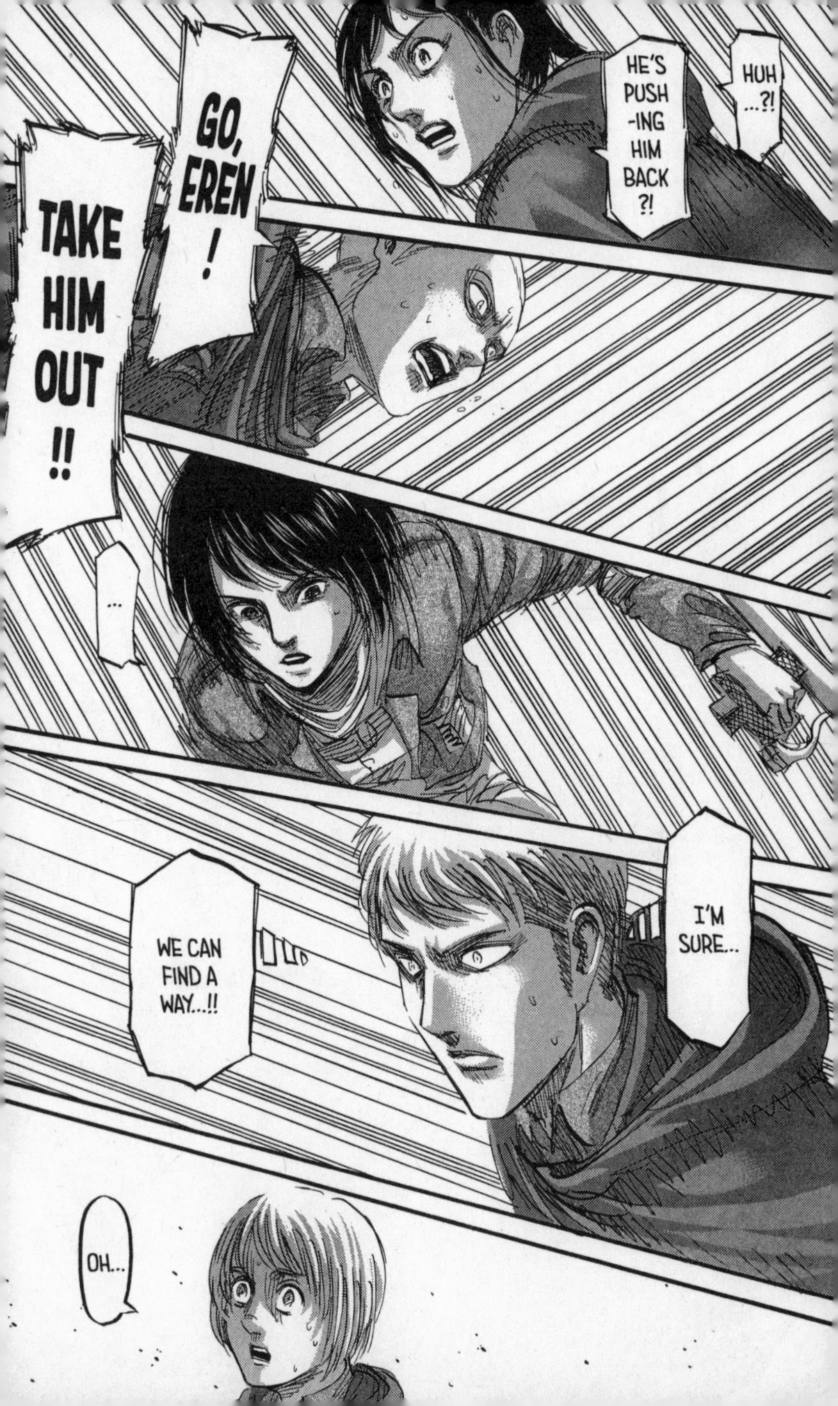

HUH ...?!
HE'S PUSH -ING HIM BACK ?!
GO, EREN !
TAKE HIM OUT !!
...
I'M SURE...
WE CAN FIND A WAY...!!
OH...

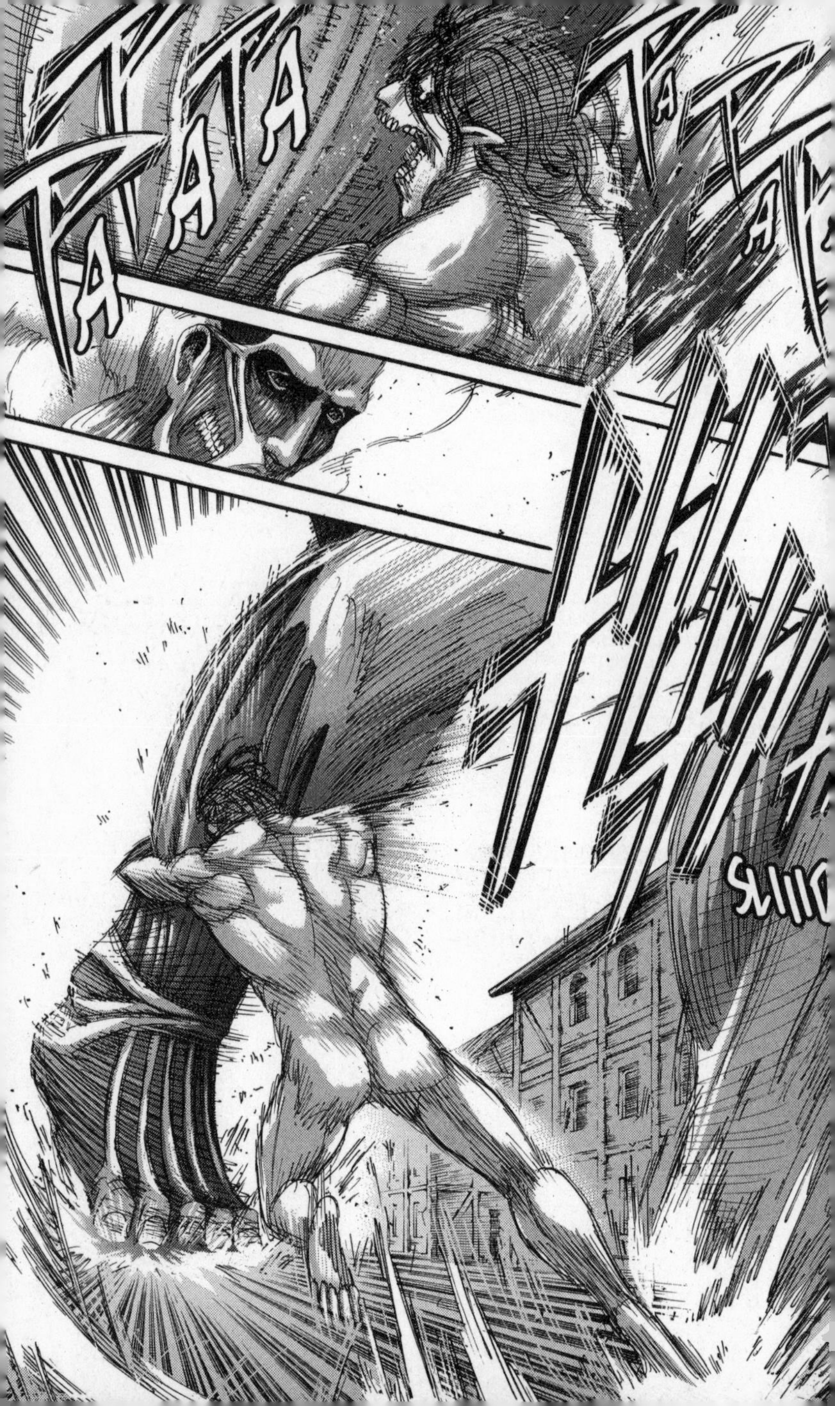

TA TA TA TA
TA TA TA
SLIIIC

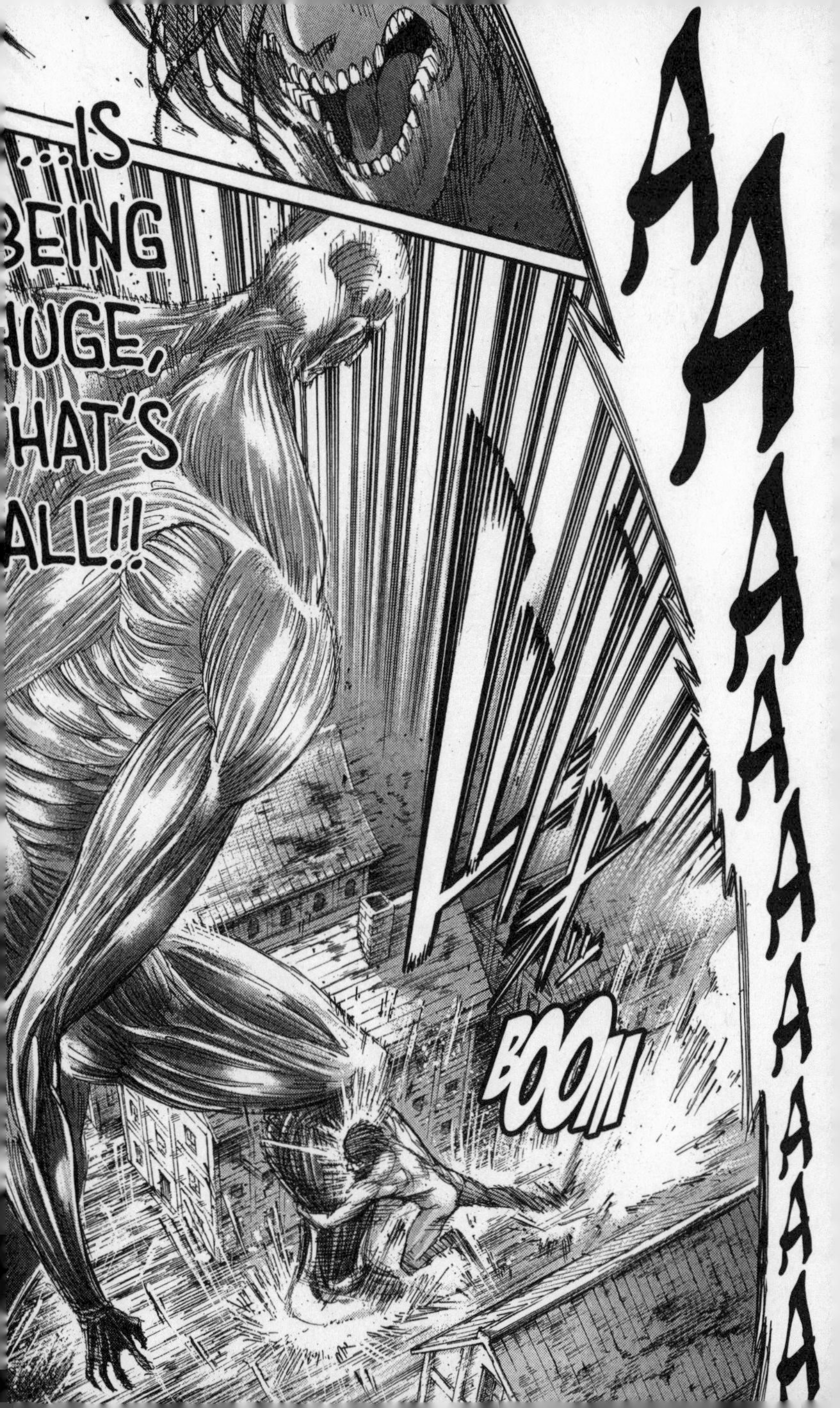
AAAAAAAAAAAA
...IS BEING HUGE, HAT'S ALL!!
BOOM

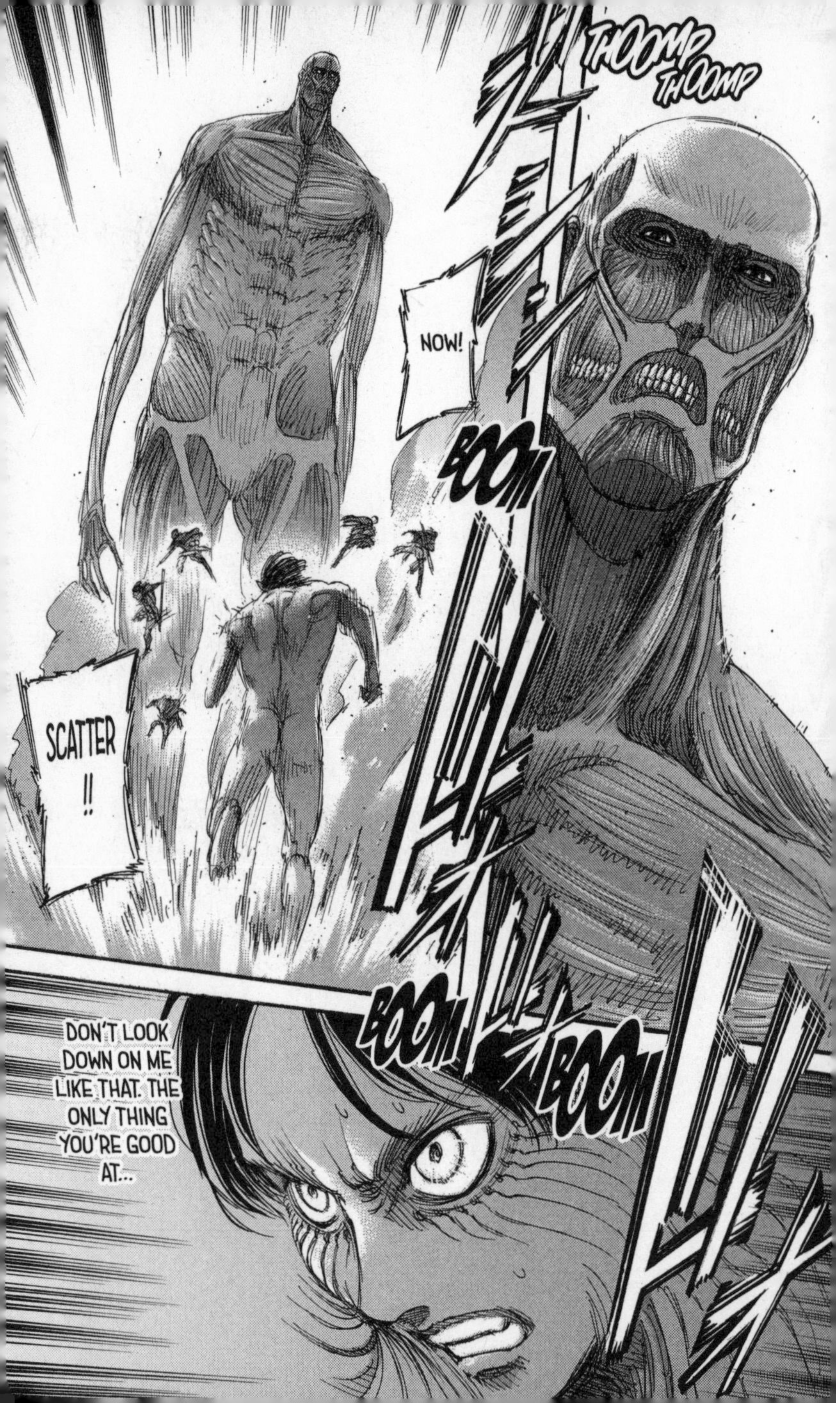
THOOMP THOOMP
NOW!
BOOM
SCATTER !!
BOOM
BOOM
DON'T LOOK DOWN ON ME LIKE THAT. THE ONLY THING YOU'RE GOOD AT...

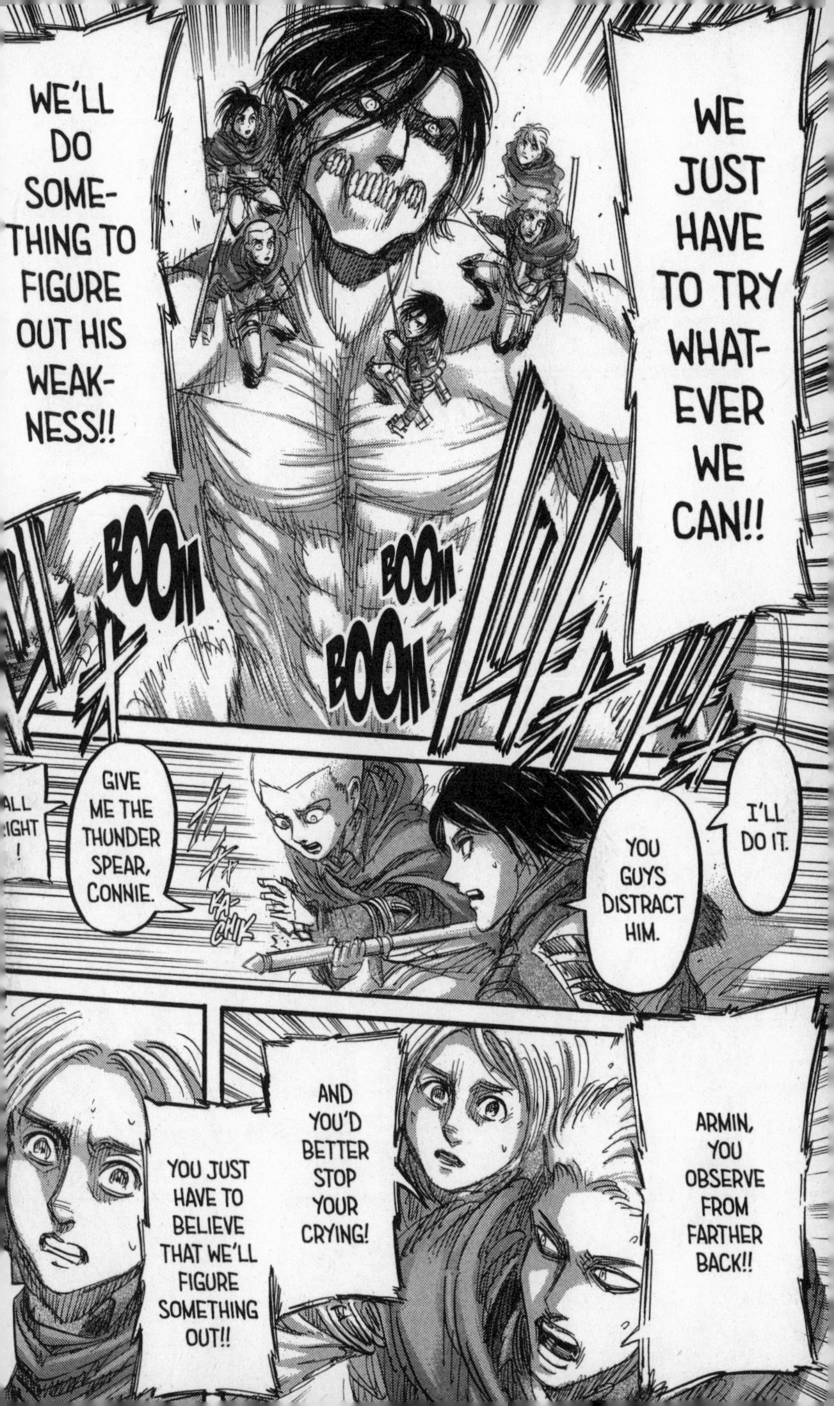
WE JUST HAVE TO TRY WHATEVER WE CAN!!
WE'LL DO SOMETHING TO FIGURE OUT HIS WEAKNESS!!
BOOM
BOOM
BOOM
I'LL DO IT.
YOU GUYS DISTRACT HIM.
GIVE ME THE THUNDER SPEAR, CONNIE.
KA-CHIK
ALL IGHT !
ARMIN, YOU OBSERVE FROM FARTHER BACK!!
AND YOU'D BETTER STOP YOUR CRYING!
YOU JUST HAVE TO BELIEVE THAT WE'LL FIGURE SOMETHING OUT!!

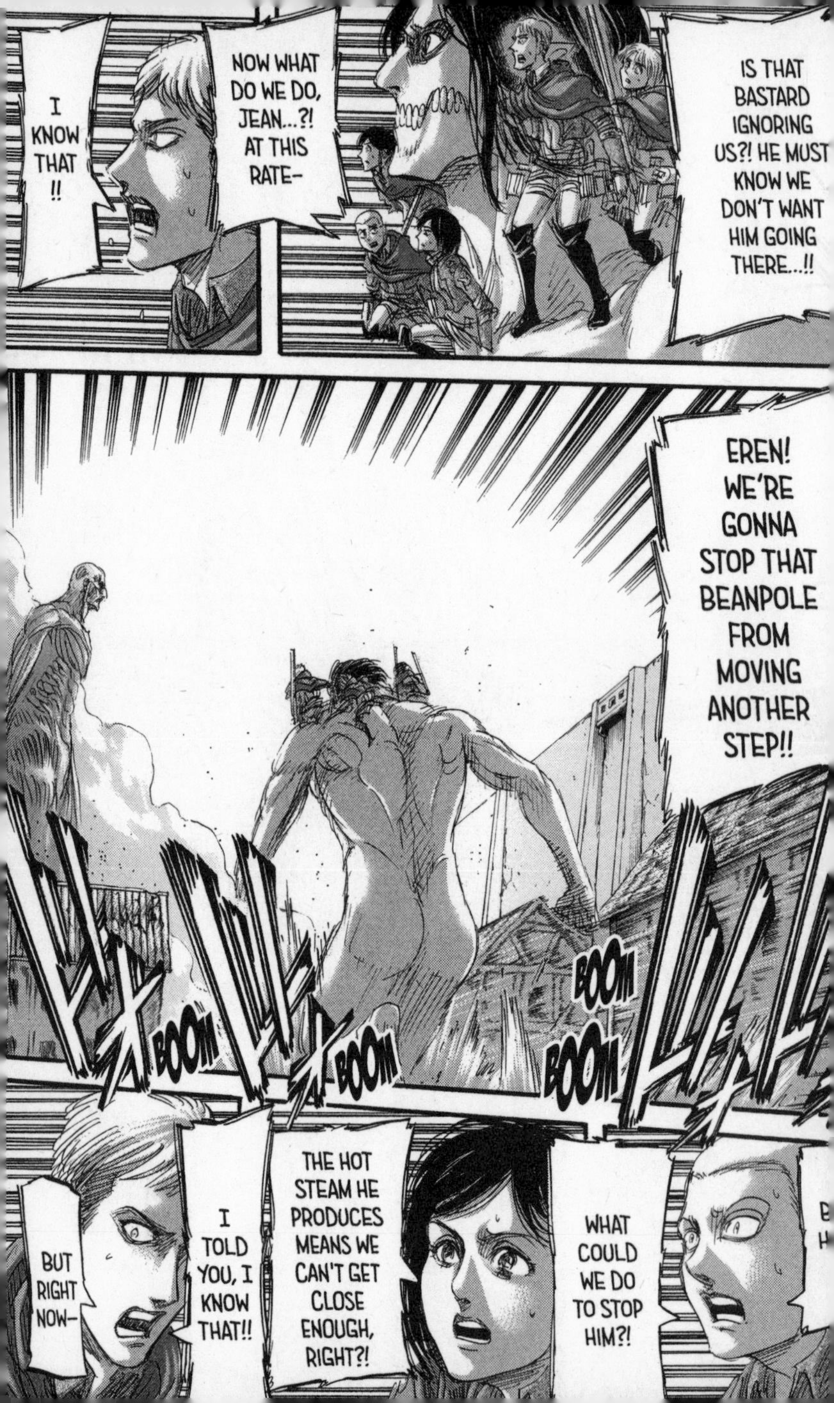
IS THAT BASTARD IGNORING US?! HE MUST KNOW WE DON'T WANT HIM GOING THERE...!!
NOW WHAT DO WE DO, JEAN...?! AT THIS RATE–
I KNOW THAT !!
EREN! WE'RE GONNA STOP THAT BEANPOLE FROM MOVING ANOTHER STEP!!
BOOM
BOOM
BOOM
BOOM
WHAT COULD WE DO TO STOP HIM?!
THE HOT STEAM HE PRODUCES MEANS WE CAN'T GET CLOSE ENOUGH, RIGHT?!
I TOLD YOU, I KNOW THAT!!
BUT RIGHT NOW–

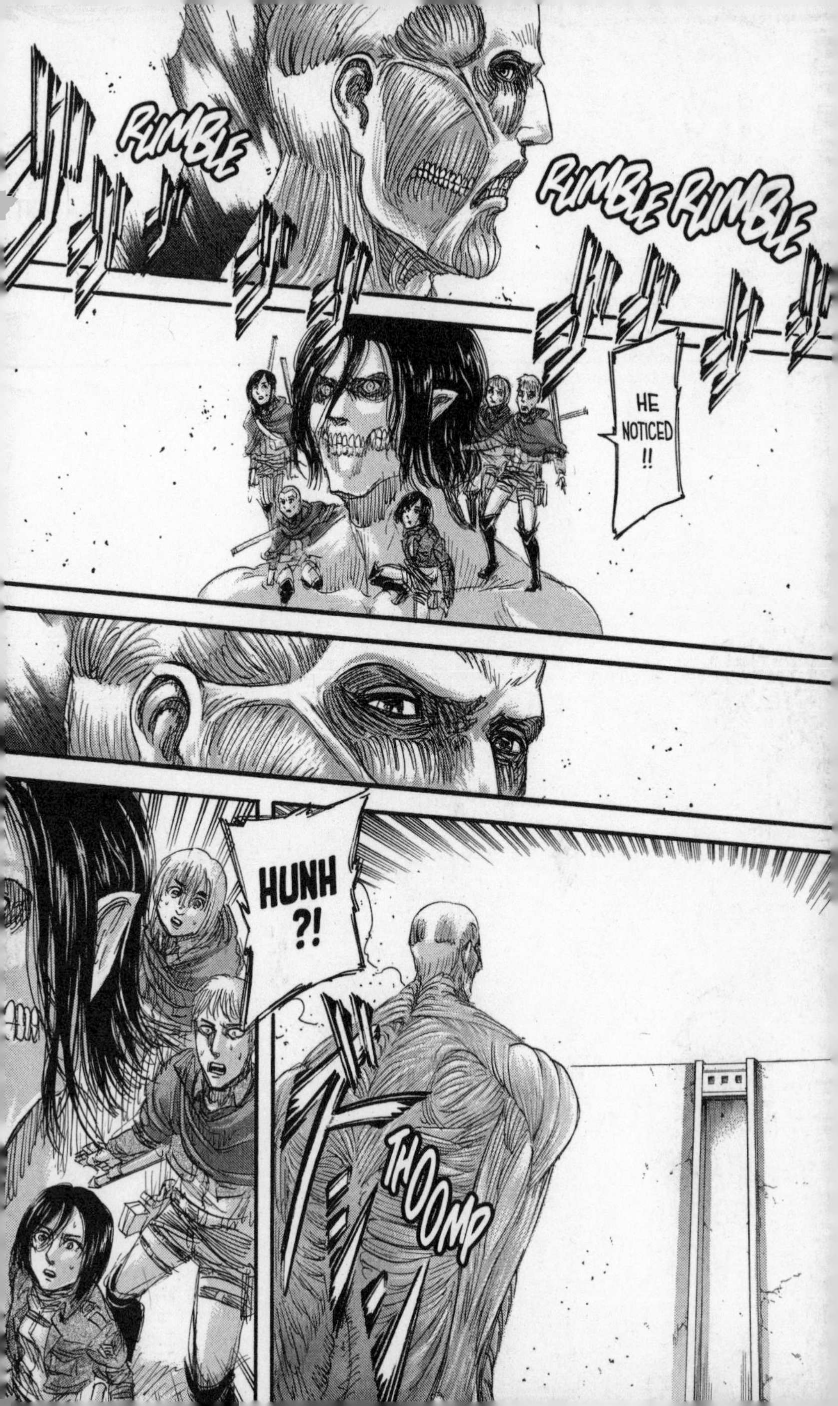
RUMBLE
RUMBLE RUMBLE
HE NOTICED !!
HUNH ?!
THOOMP

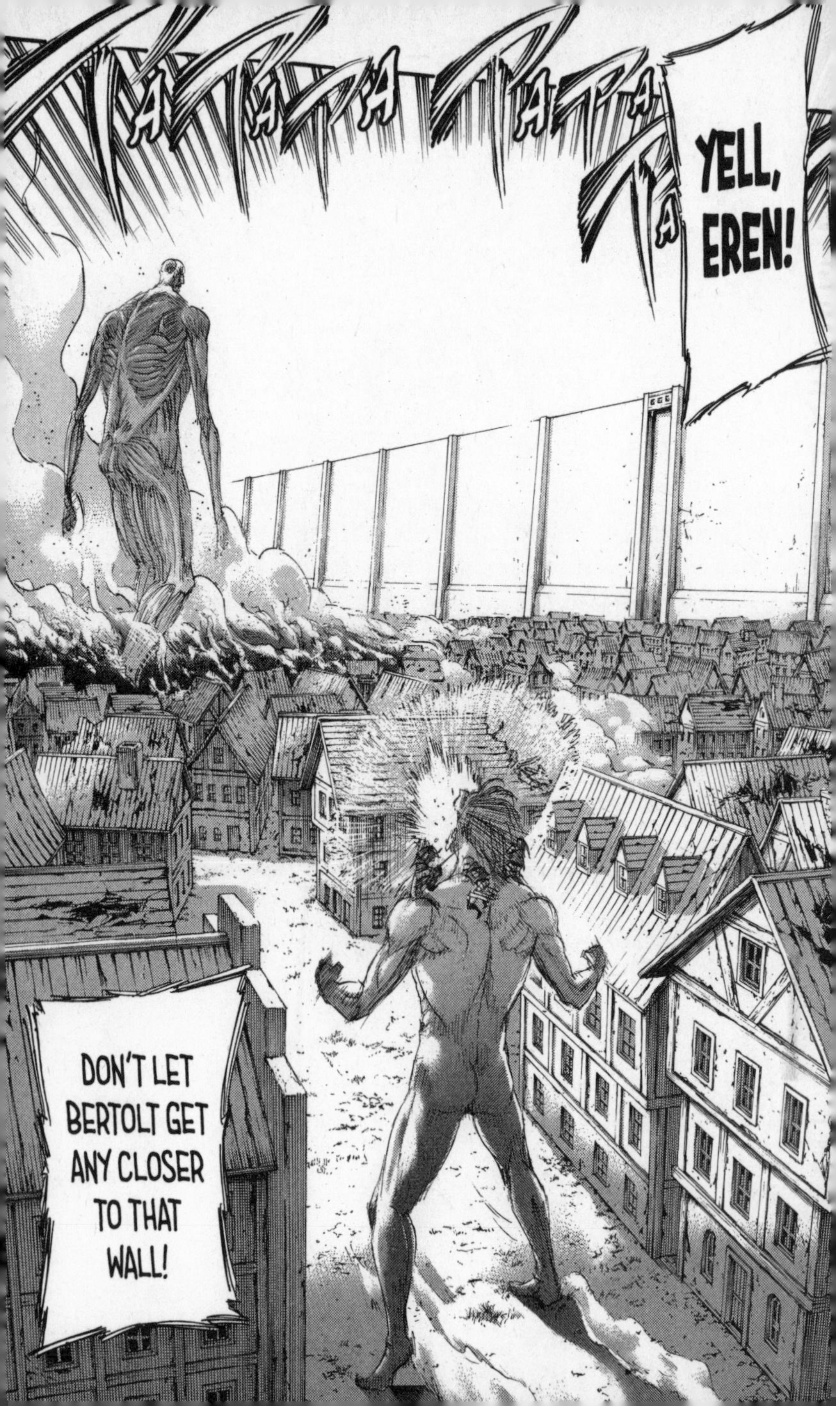
YELL, EREN!
DON'T LET BERTOLT GET ANY CLOSER TO THAT WALL!

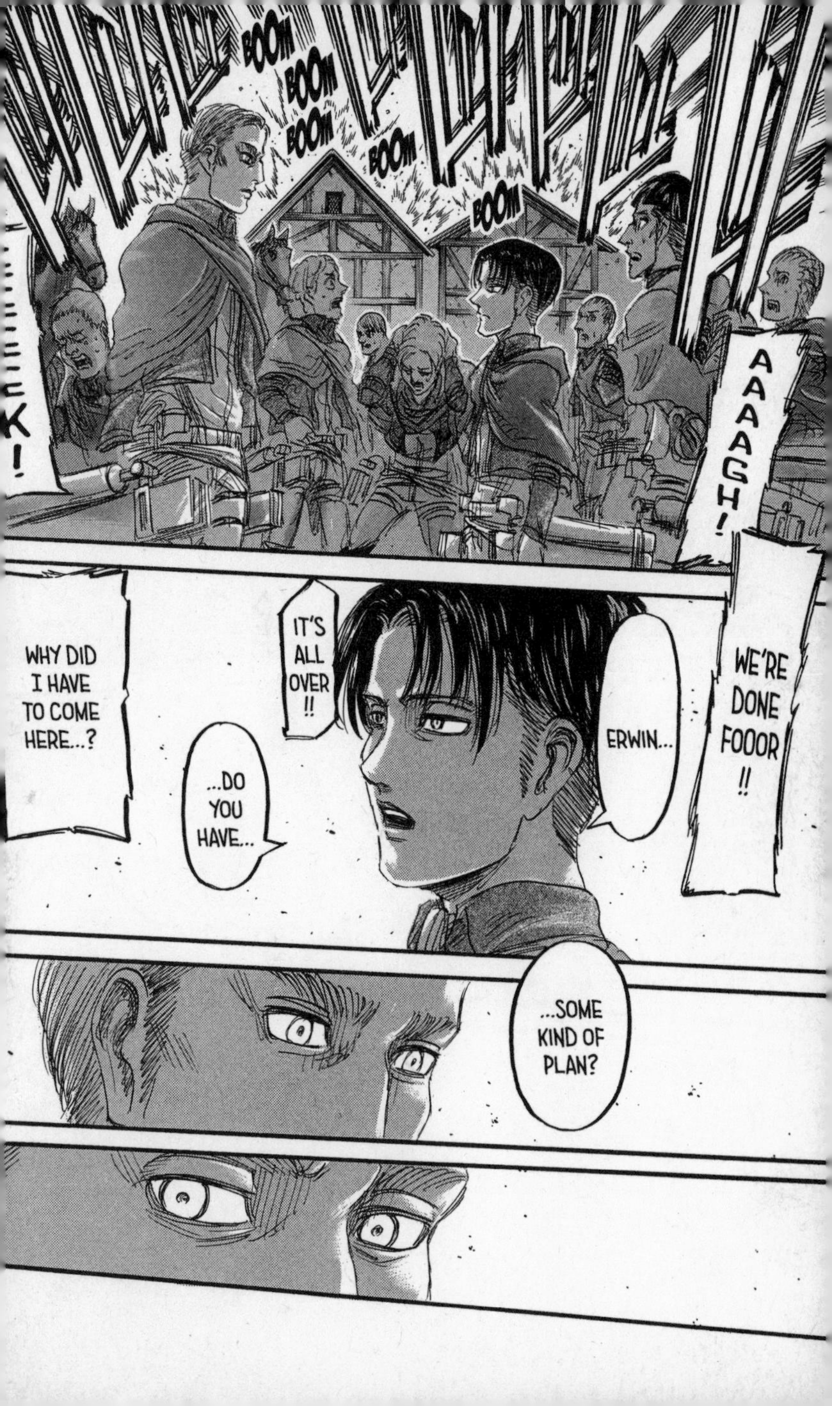
AAAAGH!
BOOM
BOOM
BOOM
BOOM
BOOM
BOOM
K!
WE'RE DONE FOOOR !!
ERWIN...
IT'S ALL OVER !!
...DO YOU HAVE...
WHY DID I HAVE TO COME HERE...?
...SOME KIND OF PLAN?

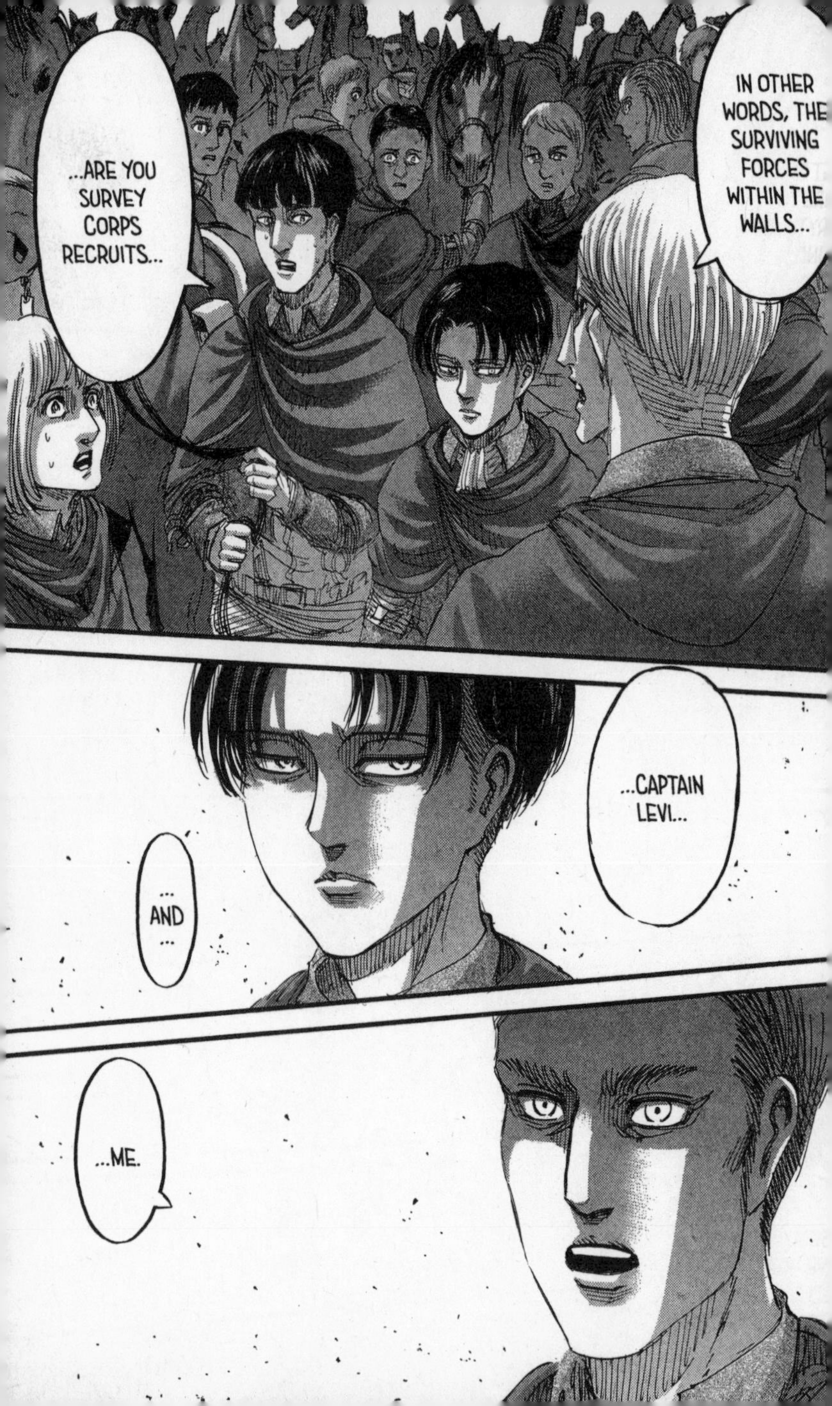
IN OTHER WORDS, THE SURVIVING FORCES WITHIN THE WALLS...
...ARE YOU SURVEY CORPS RECRUITS...
...CAPTAIN LEVI...
... AND ...
...ME.

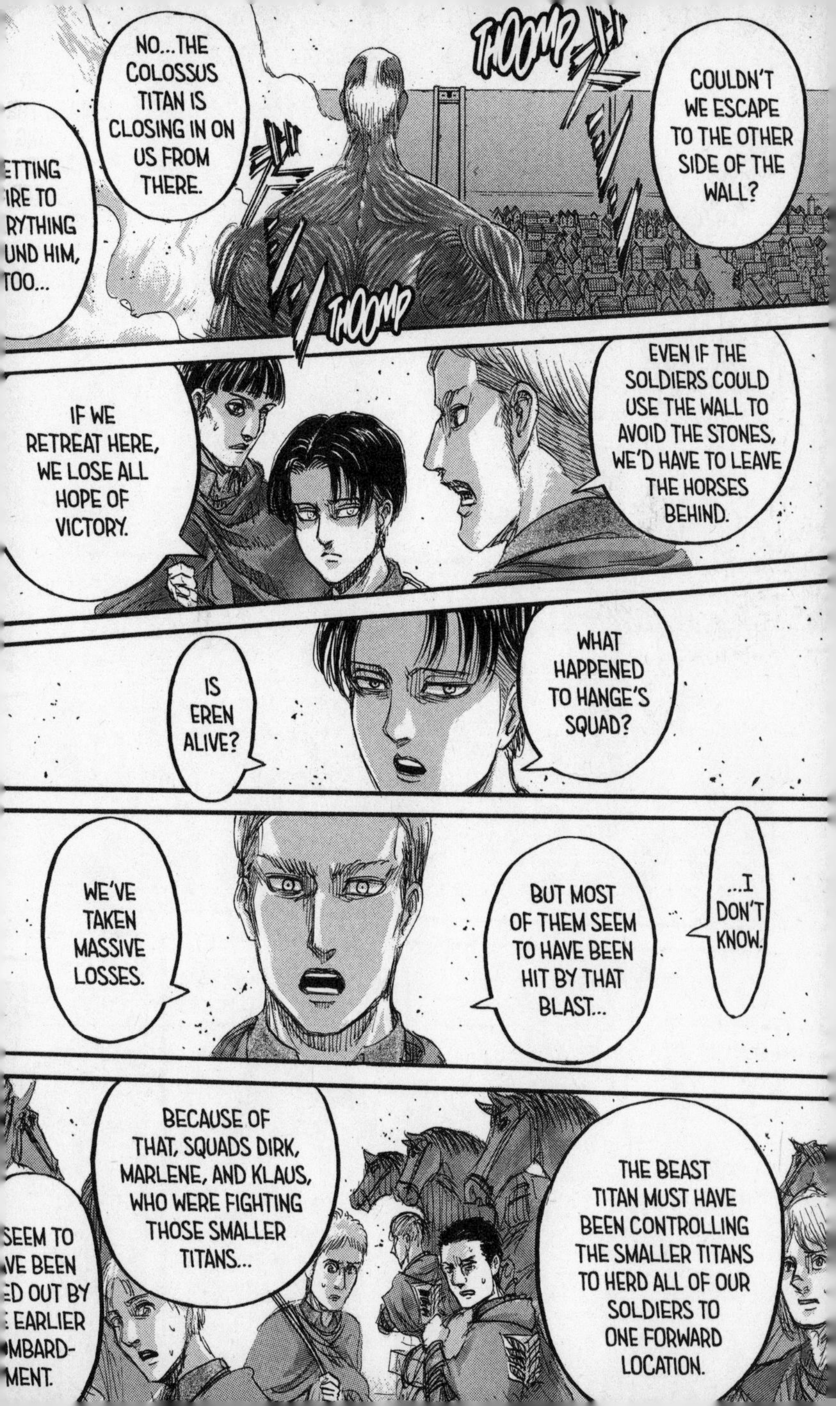
COULDN'T WE ESCAPE TO THE OTHER SIDE OF THE WALL?
THOOMP
NO...THE COLOSSUS TITAN IS CLOSING IN ON US FROM THERE.
THOOMP
ETTING IRE TO RYTHING UND HIM, TOO...
EVEN IF THE SOLDIERS COULD USE THE WALL TO AVOID THE STONES, WE'D HAVE TO LEAVE THE HORSES BEHIND.
IF WE RETREAT HERE, WE LOSE ALL HOPE OF VICTORY.
WHAT HAPPENED TO HANGE'S SQUAD?
IS EREN ALIVE?
...I DON'T KNOW.
BUT MOST OF THEM SEEM TO HAVE BEEN HIT BY THAT BLAST...
WE'VE TAKEN MASSIVE LOSSES.
THE BEAST TITAN MUST HAVE BEEN CONTROLLING THE SMALLER TITANS TO HERD ALL OF OUR SOLDIERS TO ONE FORWARD LOCATION.
BECAUSE OF THAT, SQUADS DIRK, MARLENE, AND KLAUS, WHO WERE FIGHTING THOSE SMALLER TITANS...
SEEM TO VE BEEN ED OUT BY EARLIER MBARD- MENT.

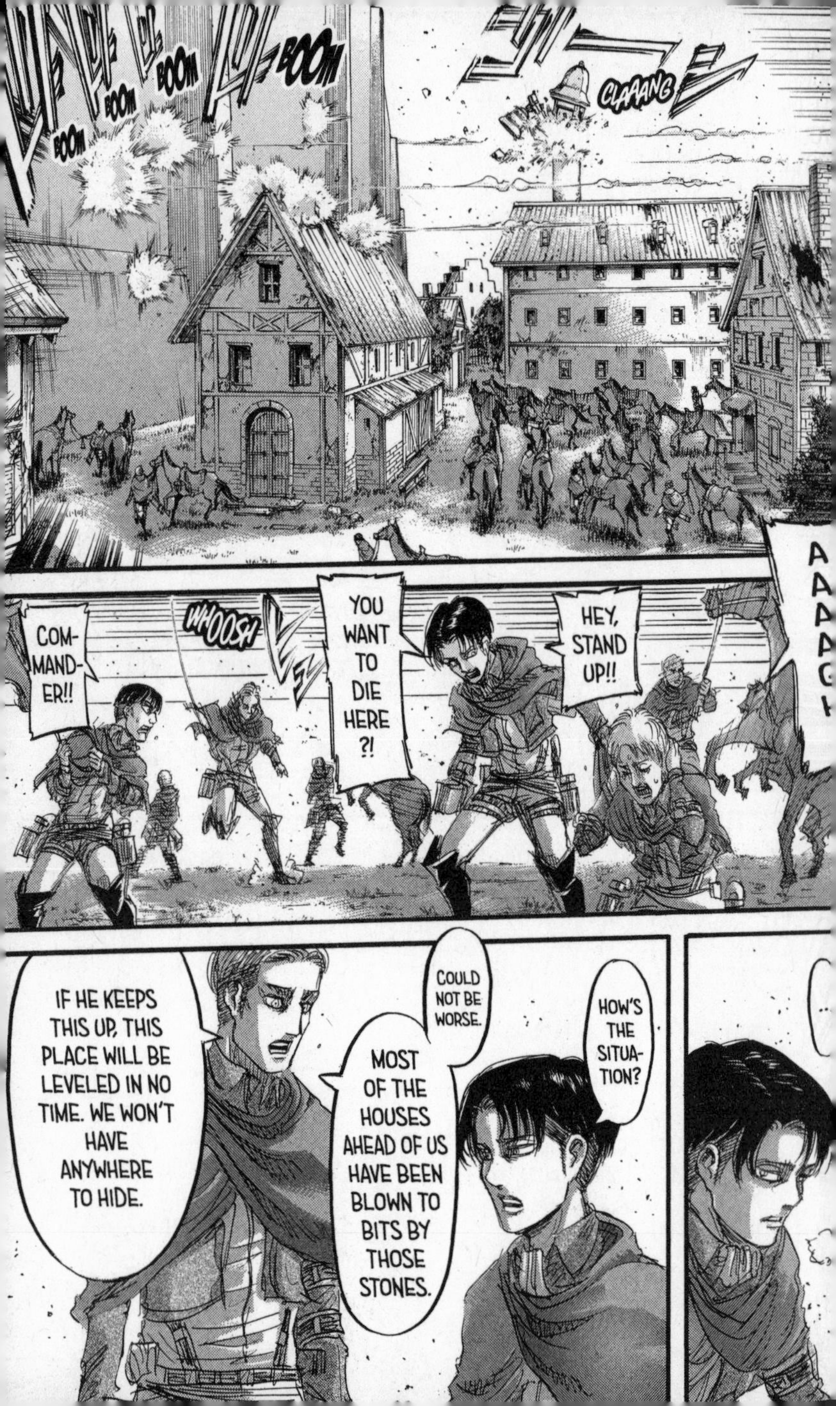

CLAAANG
BOOM
BOOM
BOOM
BOOM
AAAAGH
HEY, STAND UP!!
YOU WANT TO DIE HERE?!
WHOOSH
COMMANDER!!
HOW'S THE SITUATION?
COULD NOT BE WORSE.
MOST OF THE HOUSES AHEAD OF US HAVE BEEN BLOWN TO BITS BY THOSE STONES.
IF HE KEEPS THIS UP, THIS PLACE WILL BE LEVELED IN NO TIME. WE WON'T HAVE ANYWHERE TO HIDE.

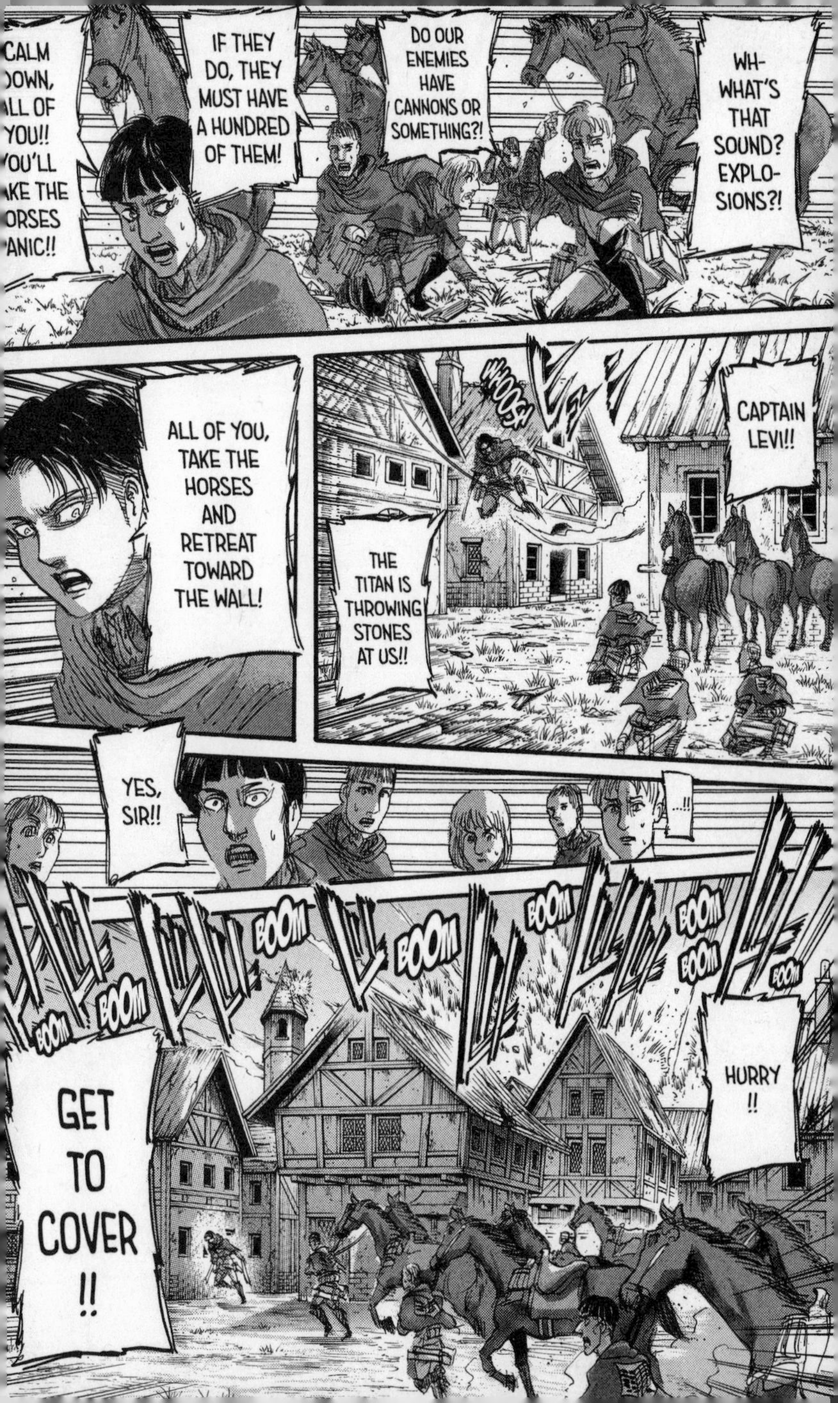
WH- WHAT'S THAT SOUND? EXPLOSIONS?!
DO OUR ENEMIES HAVE CANNONS OR SOMETHING?!
IF THEY DO, THEY MUST HAVE A HUNDRED OF THEM!
CALM OWN, LL OF YOU!! OU'LL KE THE ORSES ANIC!!
WHOOSH
CAPTAIN LEVI!!
THE TITAN IS THROWING STONES AT US!!
ALL OF YOU, TAKE THE HORSES AND RETREAT TOWARD THE WALL!
...!!
YES, SIR!!
BOOM
BOOM BOOM
BOOM
BOOM
BOOM
BOOM
BOOM
BOOM
HURRY!!
GET TO COVER!!

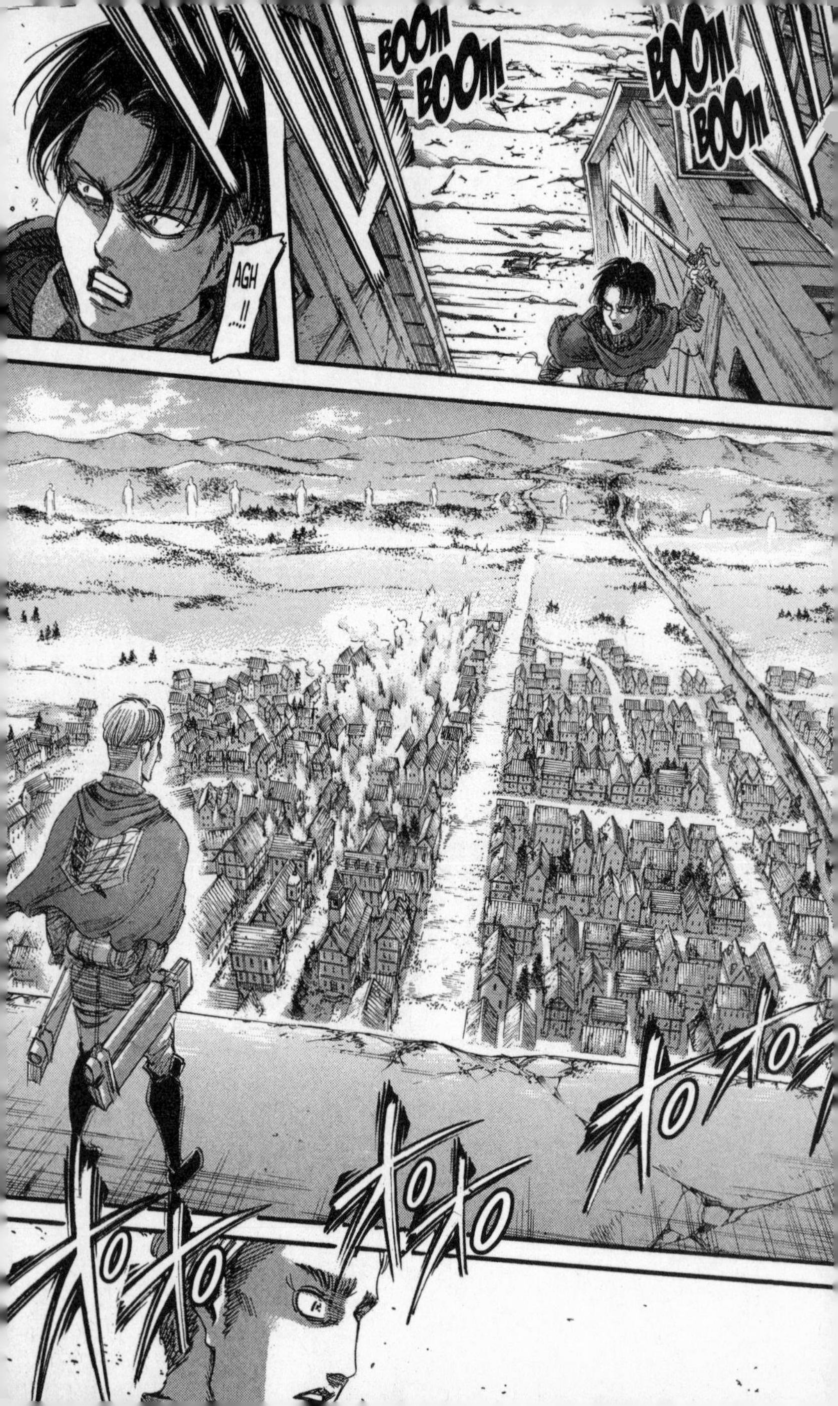
BOOM
BOOM
BOOM
BOOM
AGH
...!!

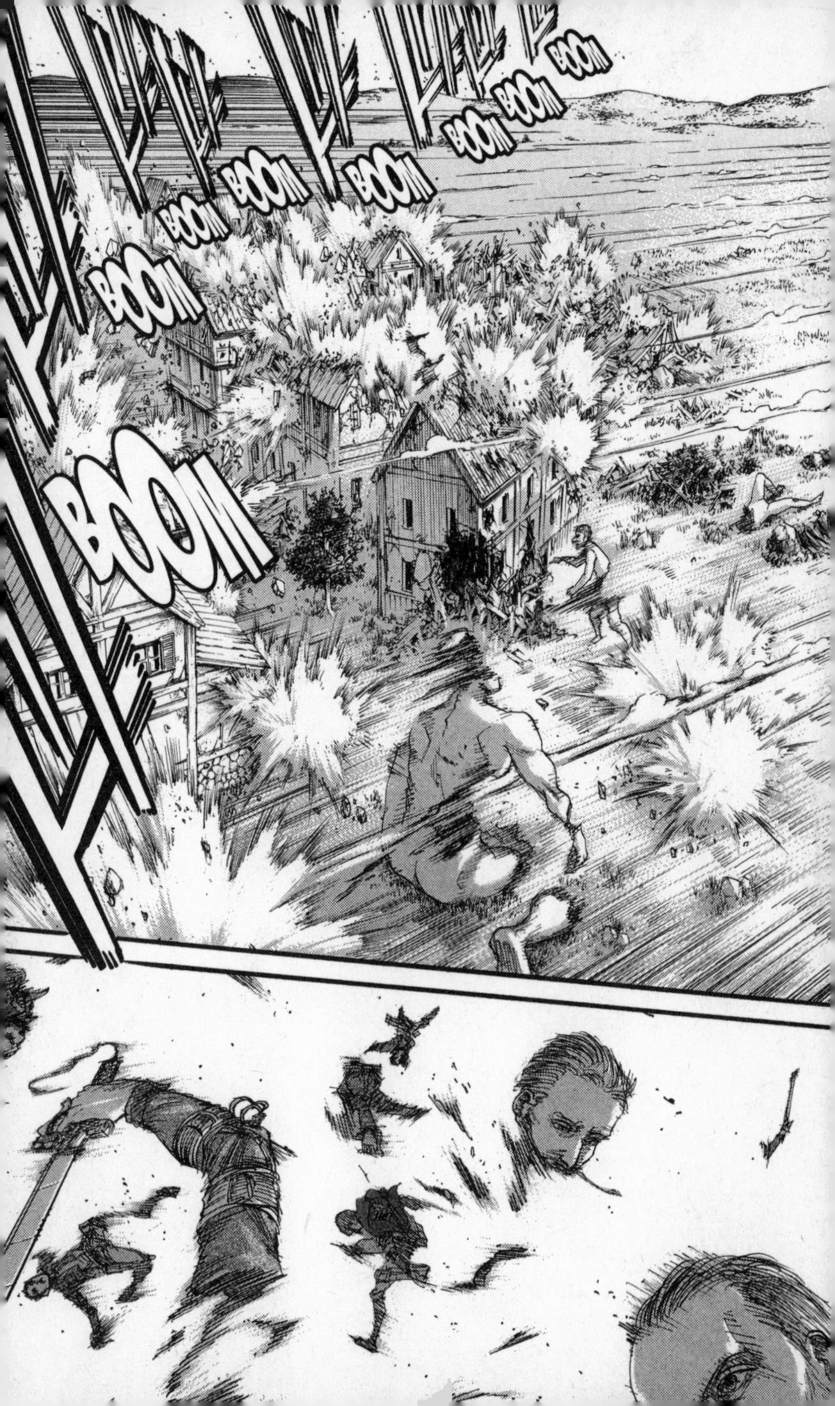
BOOM
BOOM
BOOM
BOOM
BOOM
BOOM
BOOM
BOOM

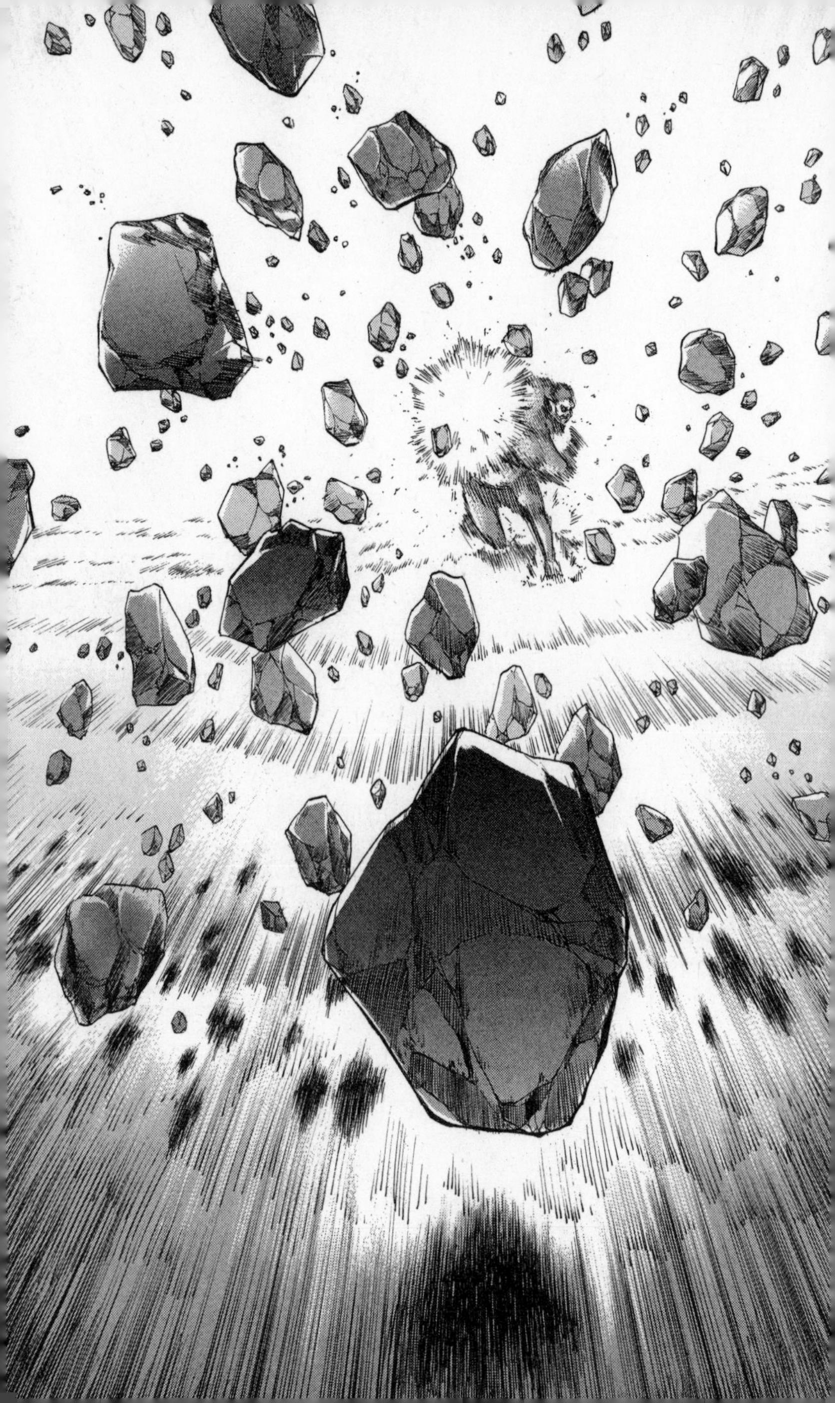

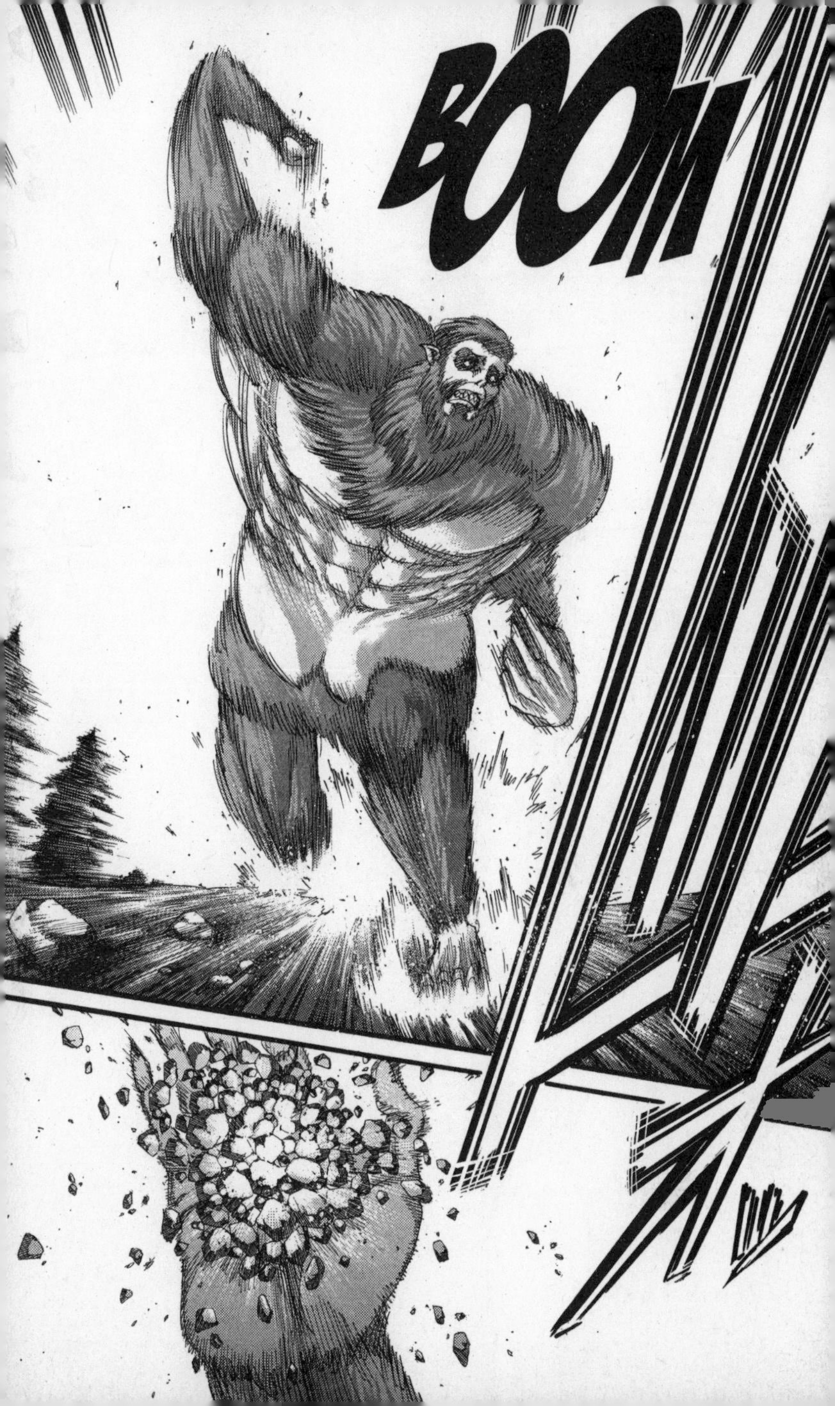
BOOM

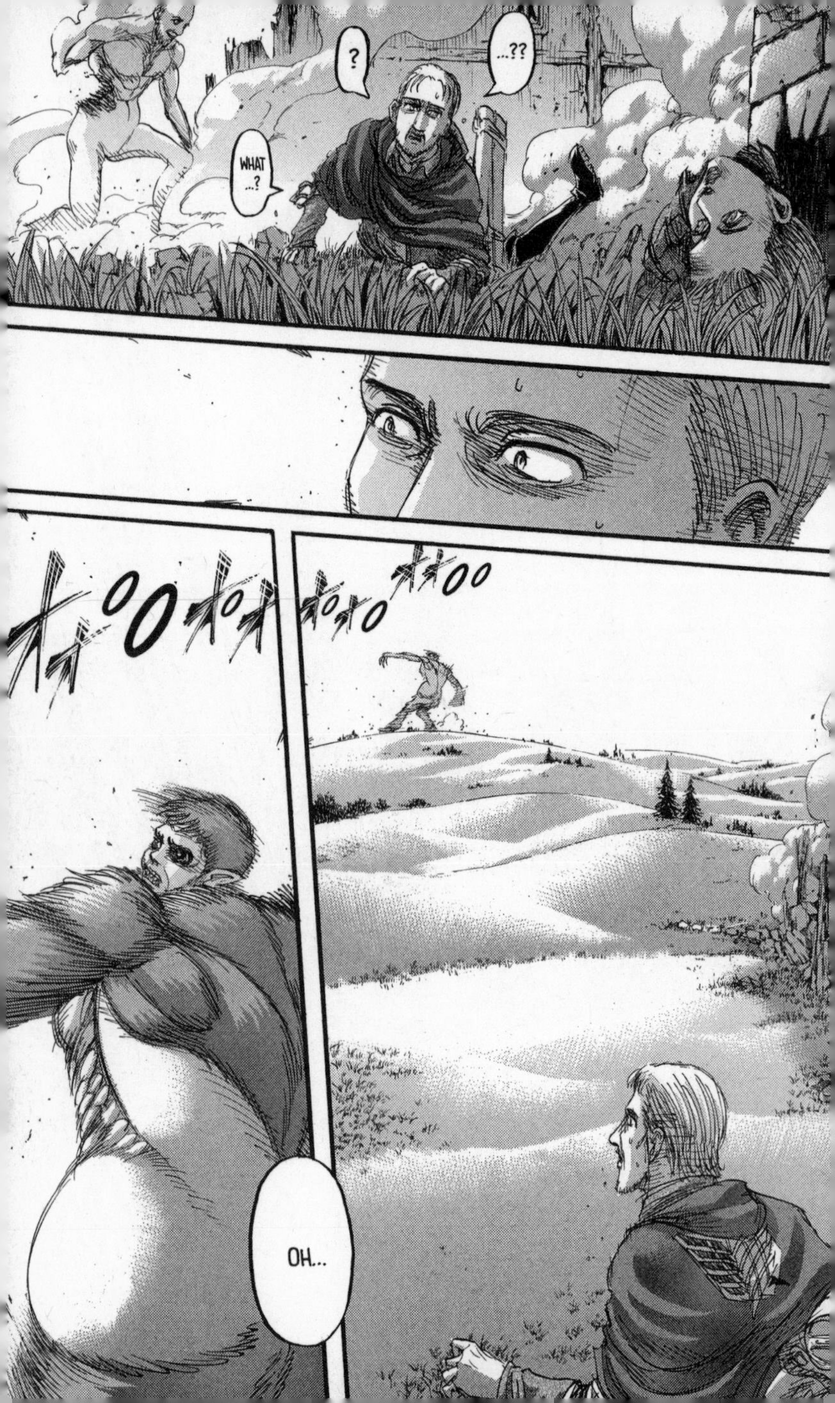
...??
?
WHAT ...?
OH...

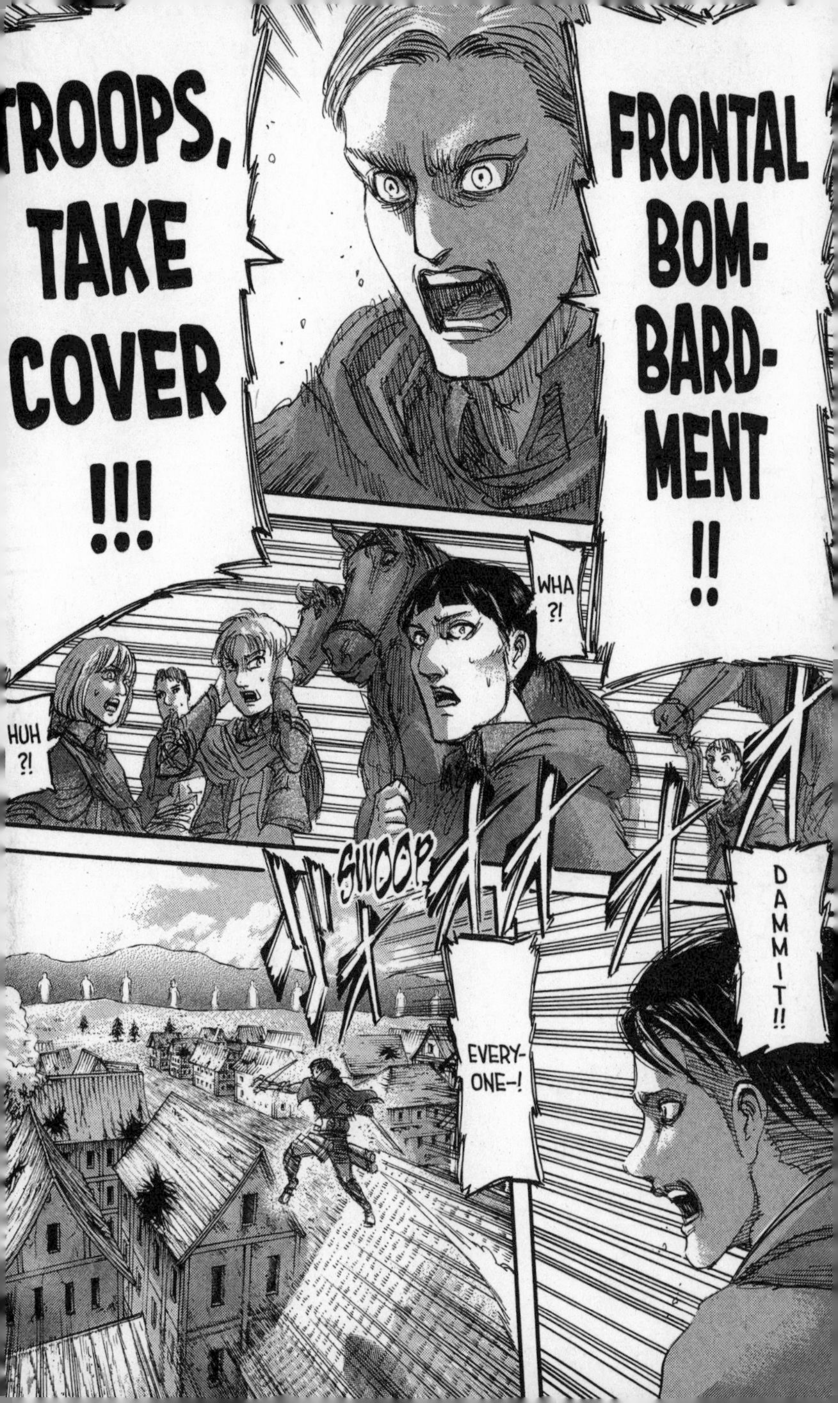
FRONTAL BOM-BARD-MENT !!
TROOPS, TAKE COVER !!!
WHA ?!
HUH ?!
DAMMIT!!
EVERY-ONE-!
SWOOP

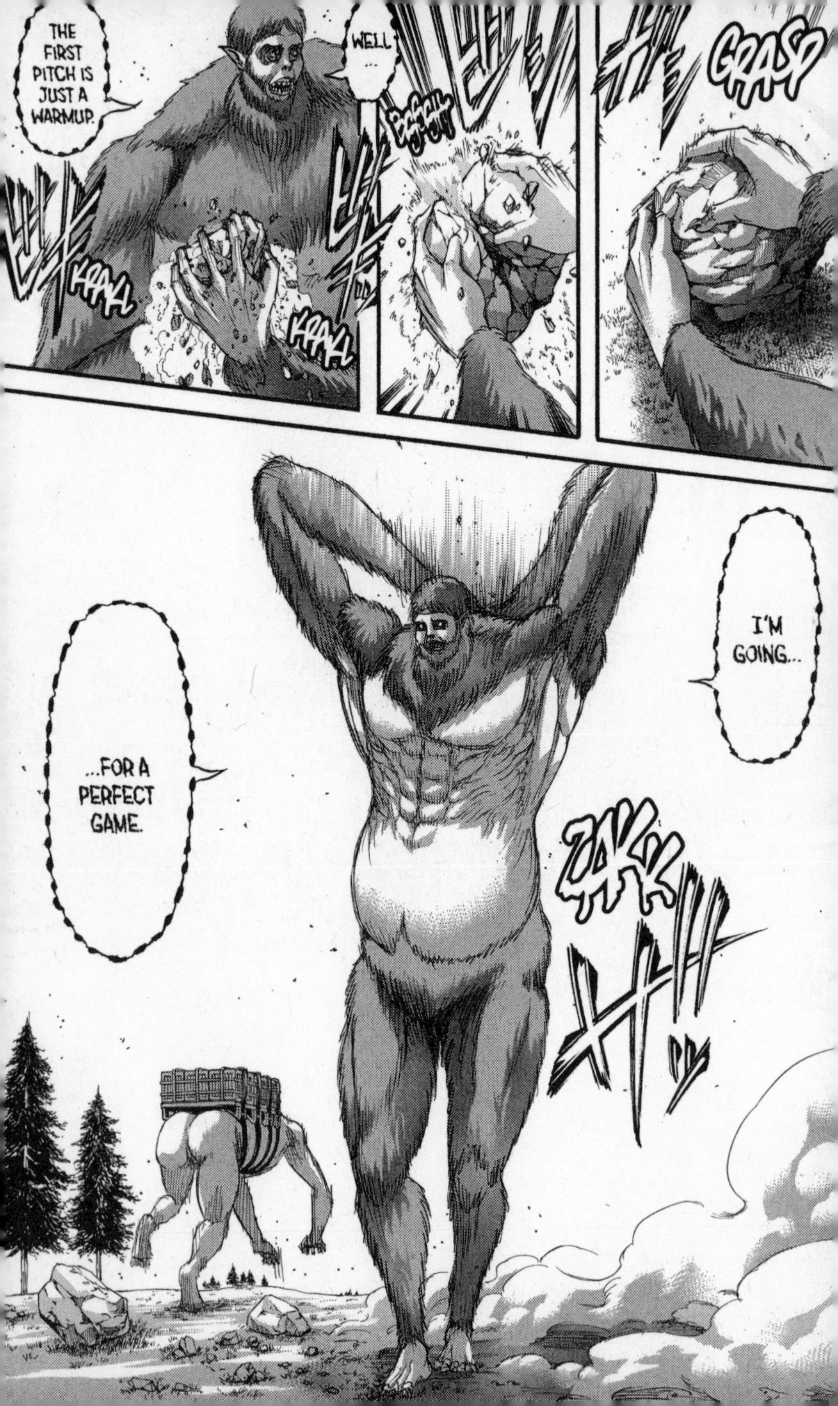
GRASP
KRAK
KRAK
THE FIRST PITCH IS JUST A WARMUP.
WELL ...
I'M GOING...
...FOR A PERFECT GAME.

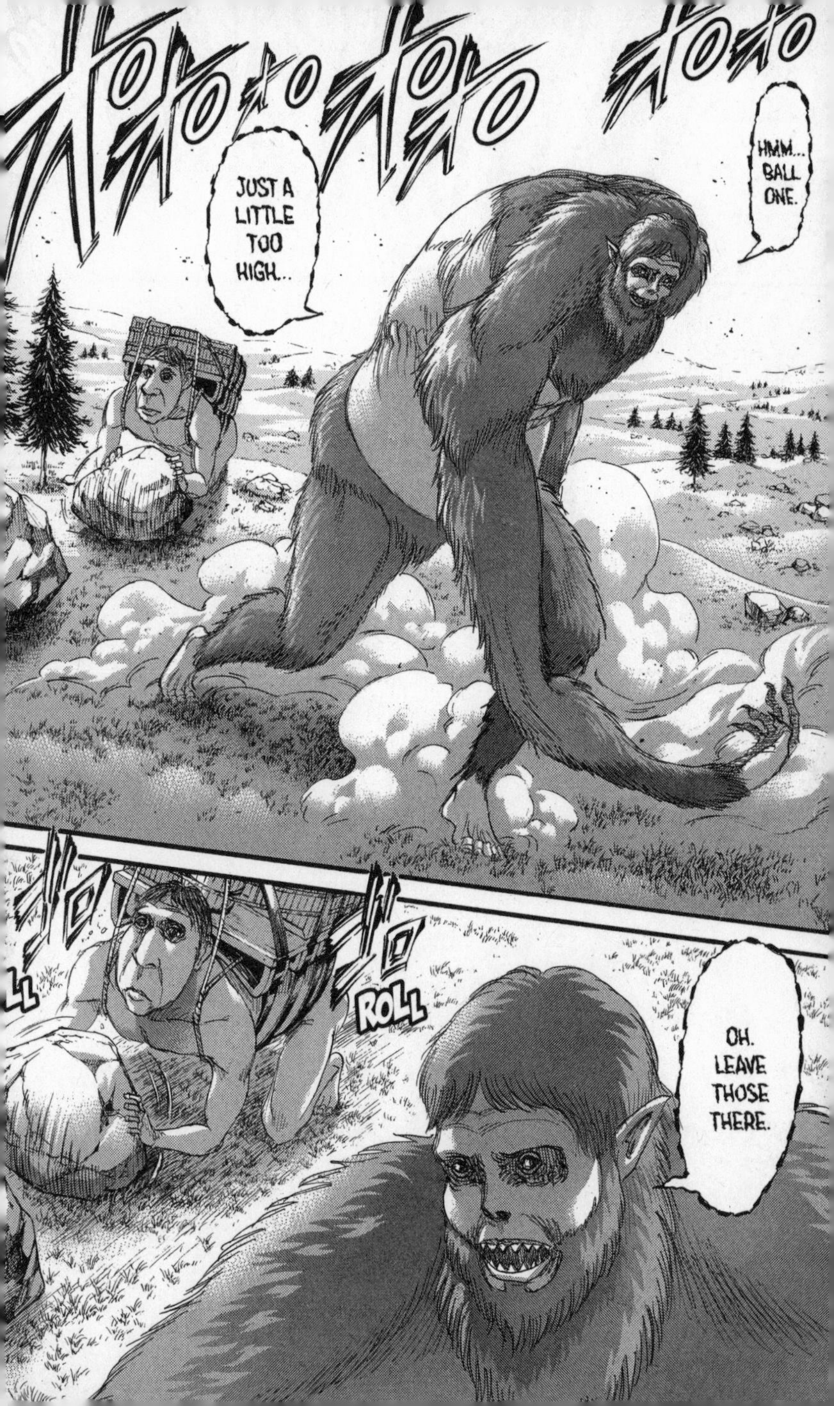
HMM... BALL ONE.
JUST A LITTLE TOO HIGH...
OH. LEAVE THOSE THERE.
ROLL
LL

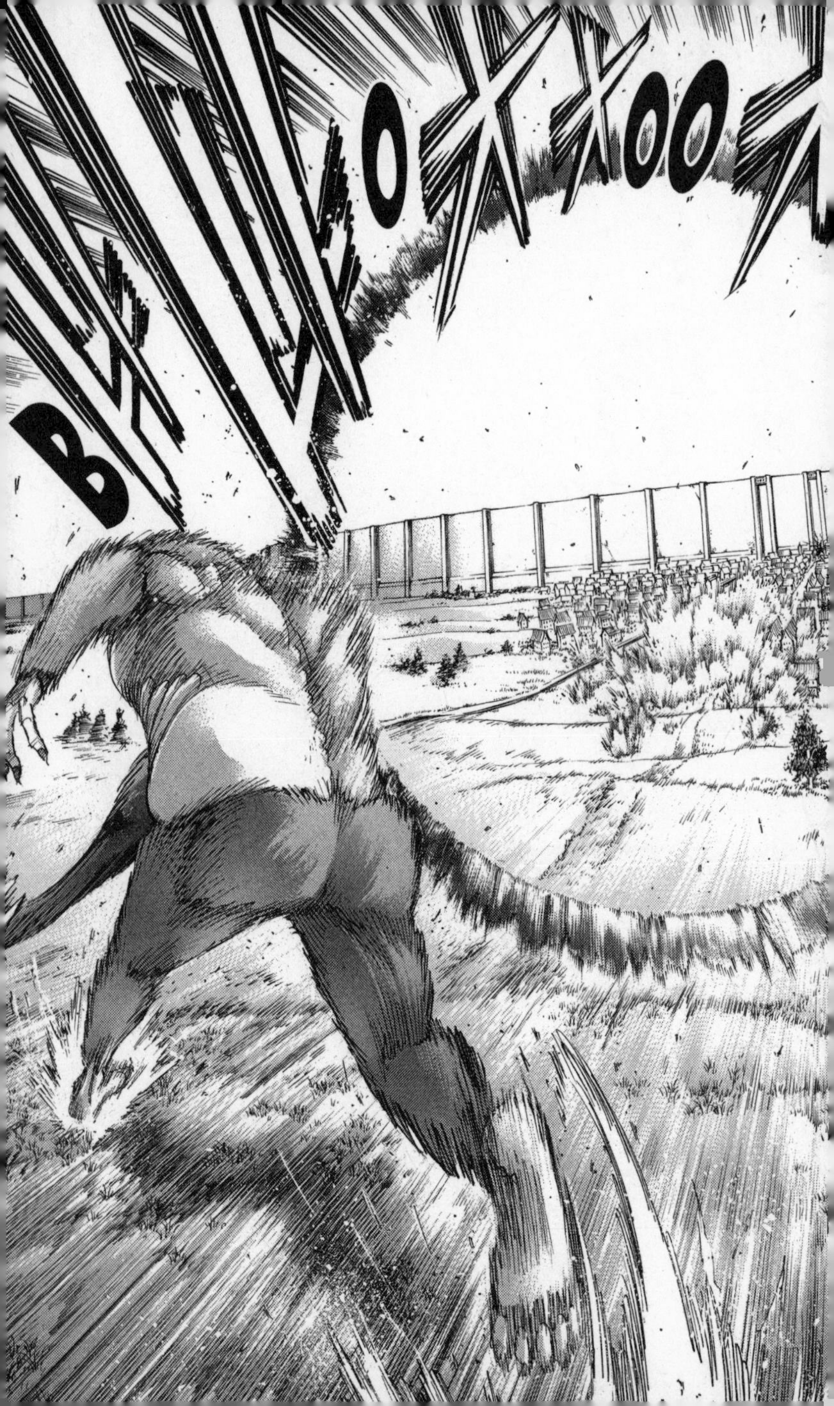
BOOO

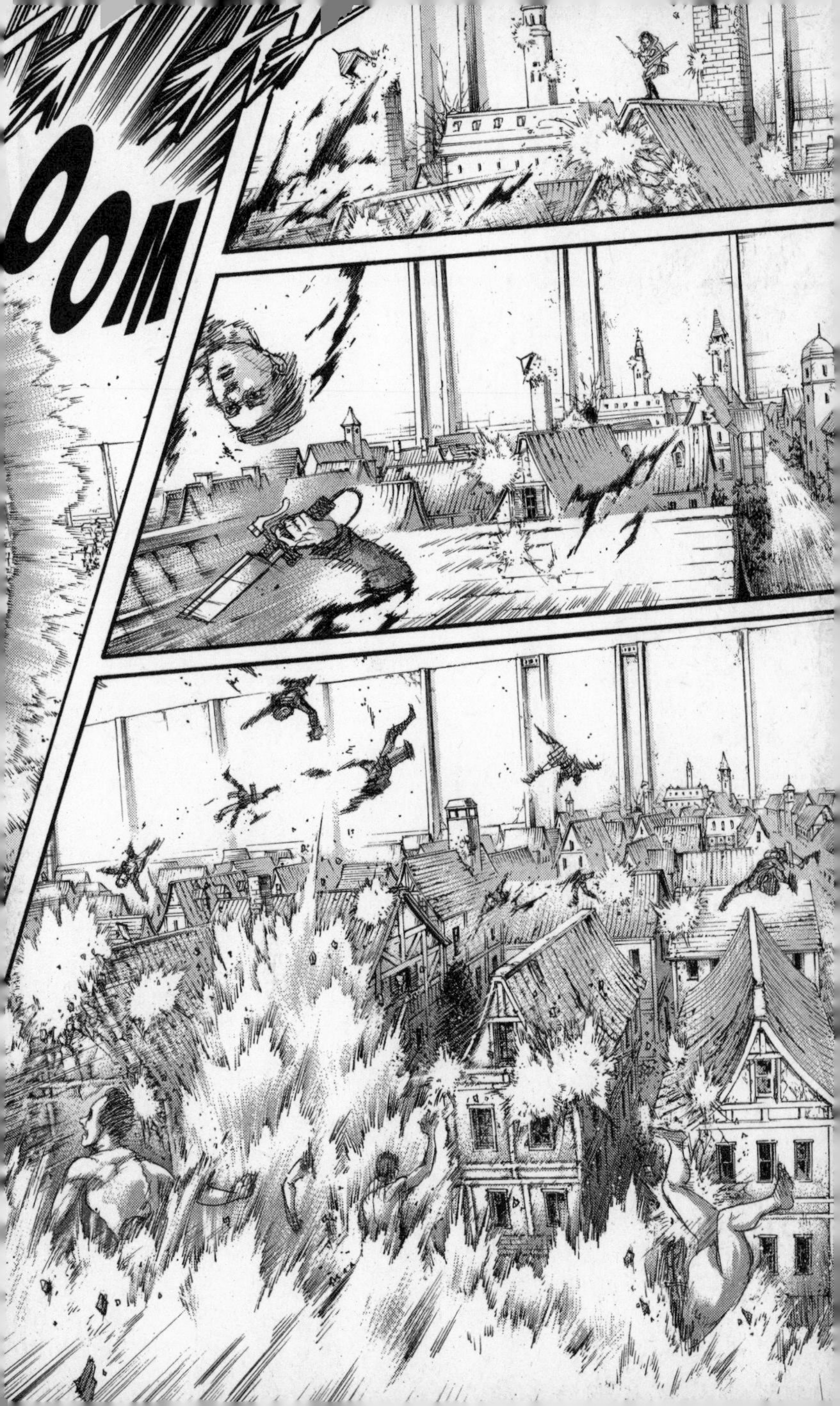
OOM

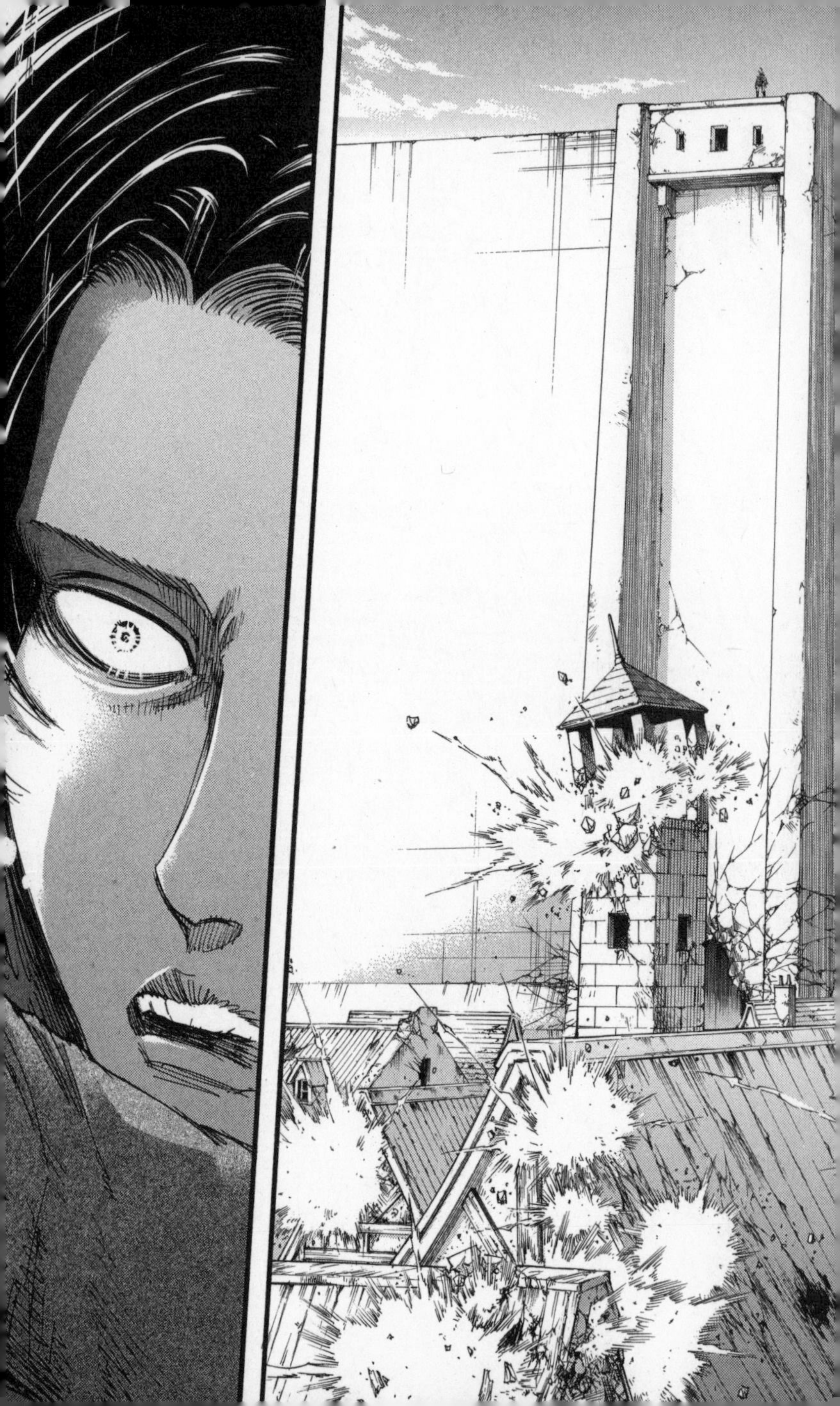

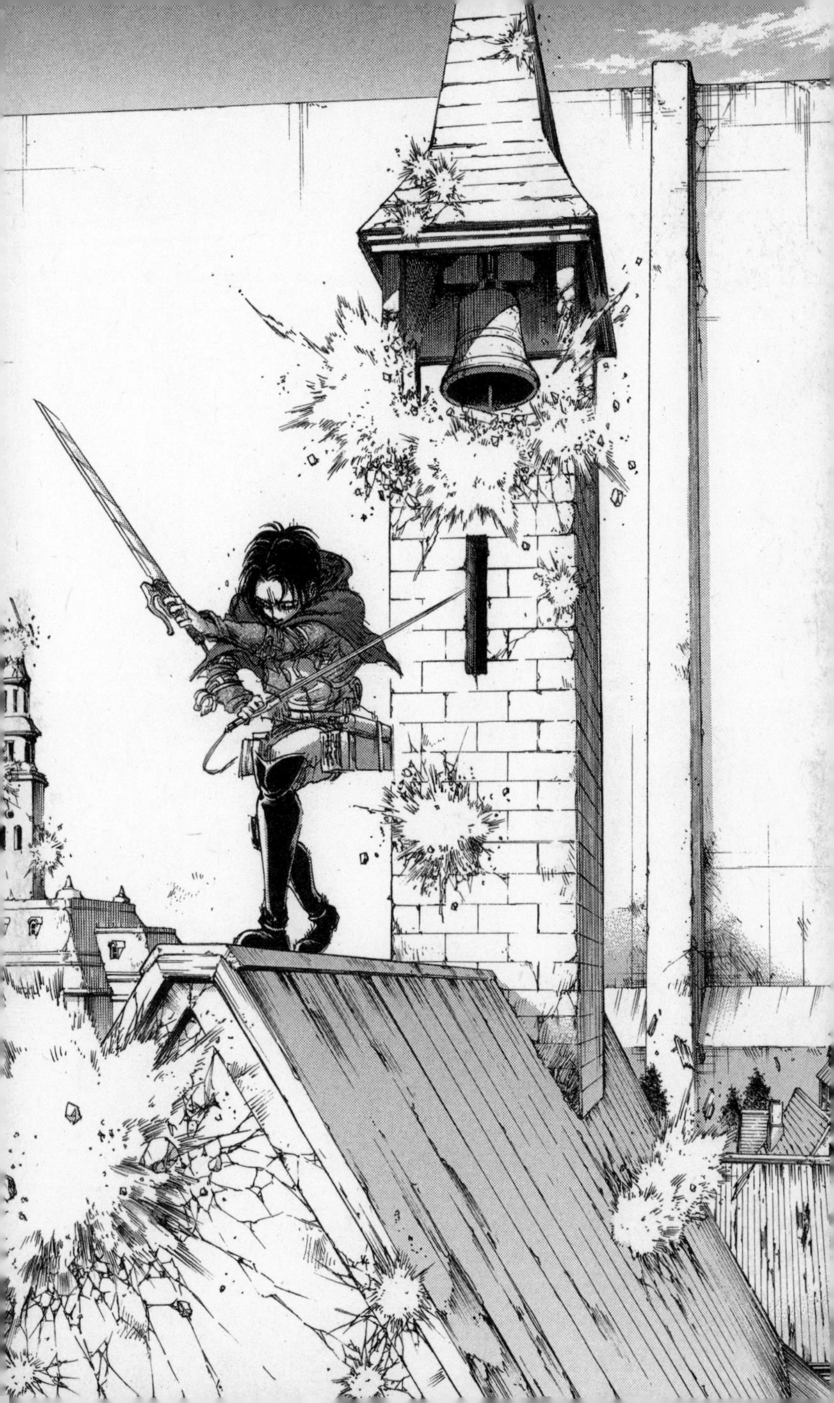

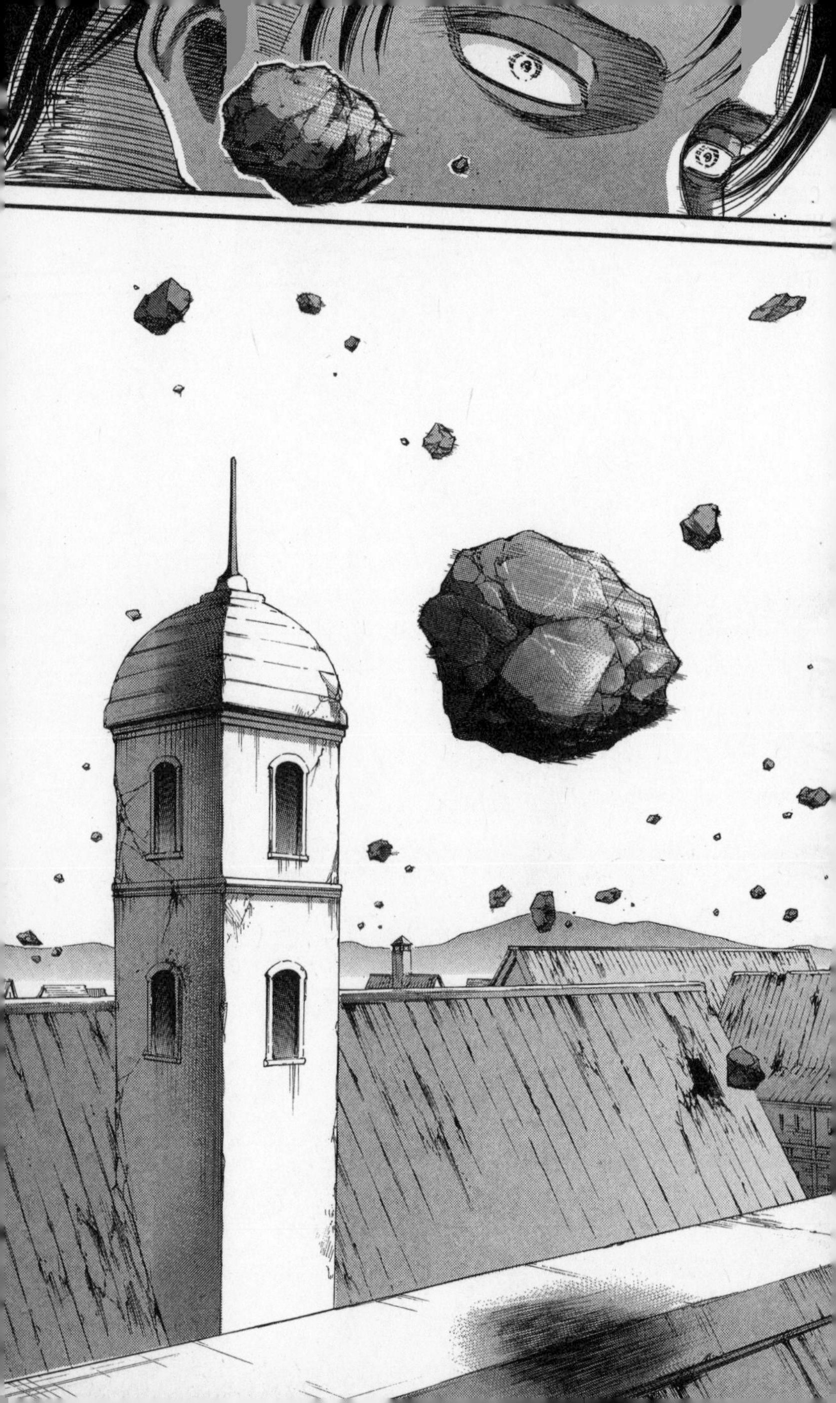

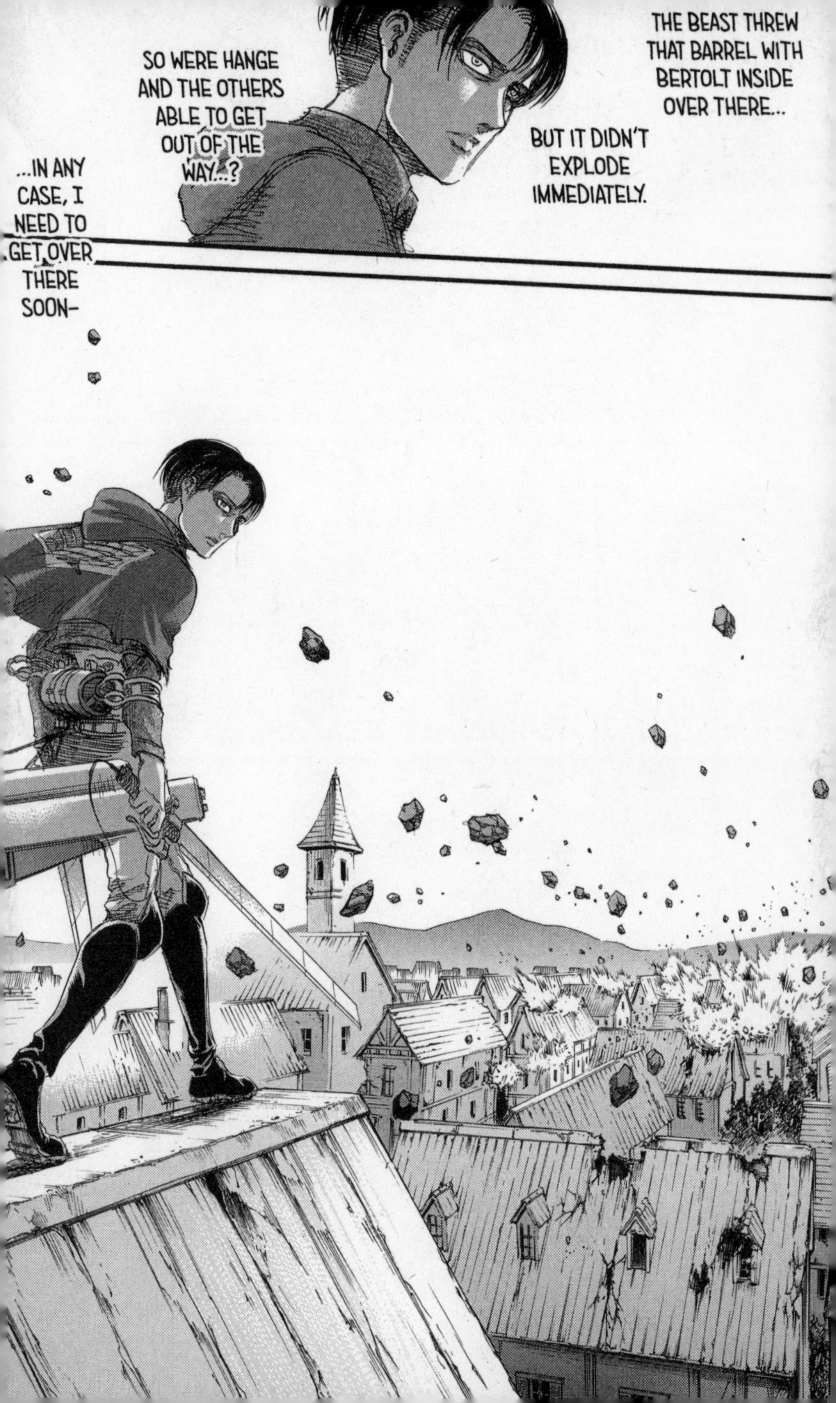
THE BEAST THREW THAT BARREL WITH BERTOLT INSIDE OVER THERE...
BUT IT DIDN'T EXPLODE IMMEDIATELY.
SO WERE HANGE AND THE OTHERS ABLE TO GET OUT OF THE WAY...?
...IN ANY CASE, I NEED TO GET OVER THERE SOON-

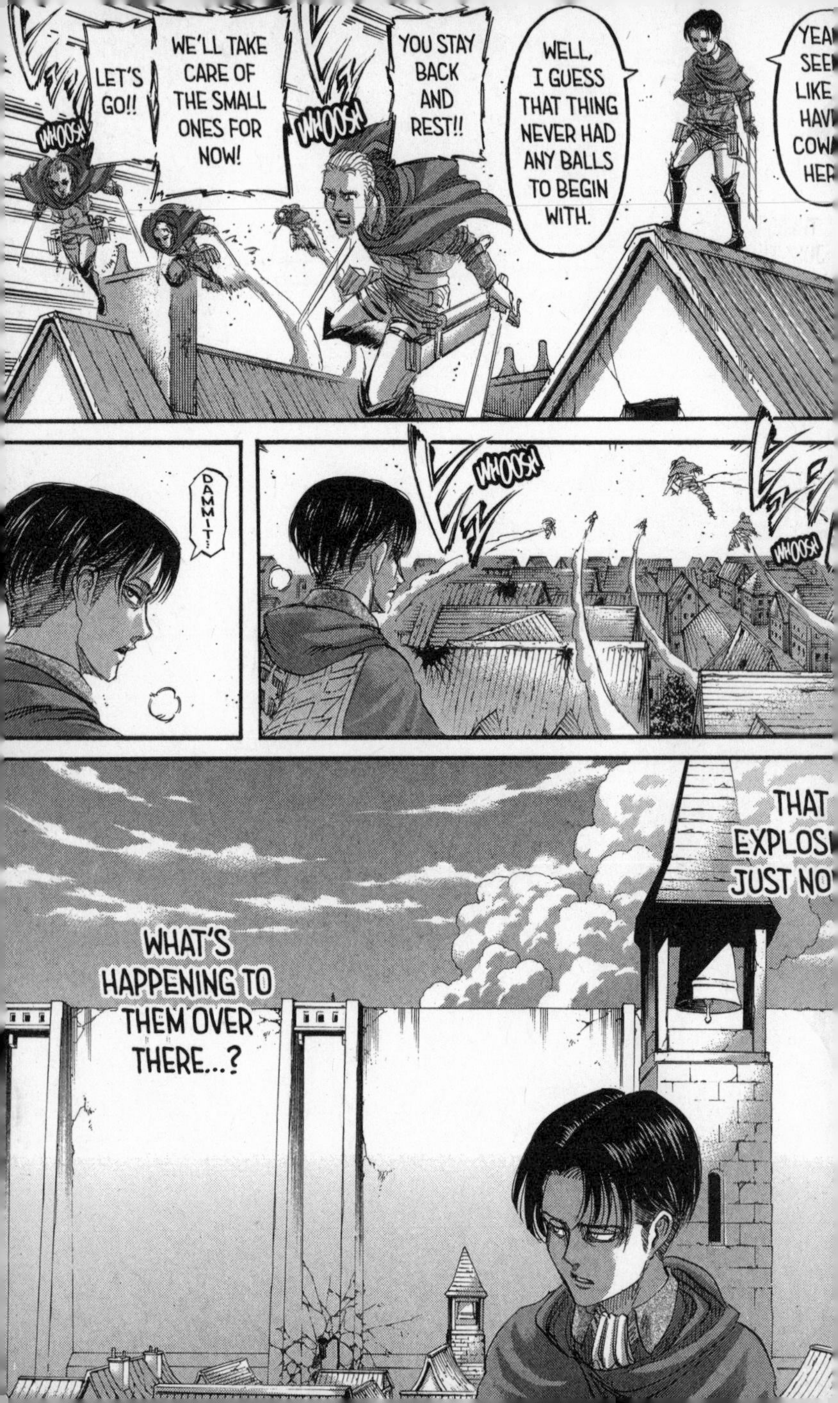
YEA
SEE
LIKE
HAV
COW
HER
WELL, I GUESS THAT THING NEVER HAD ANY BALLS TO BEGIN WITH.
YOU STAY BACK AND REST!!
WHOOSH
WE'LL TAKE CARE OF THE SMALL ONES FOR NOW!
LET'S GO!!
WHOOSH
WHOOSH
WHOOSH
DAMMIT...
THAT EXPLOS
JUST NO
WHAT'S HAPPENING TO THEM OVER THERE...?

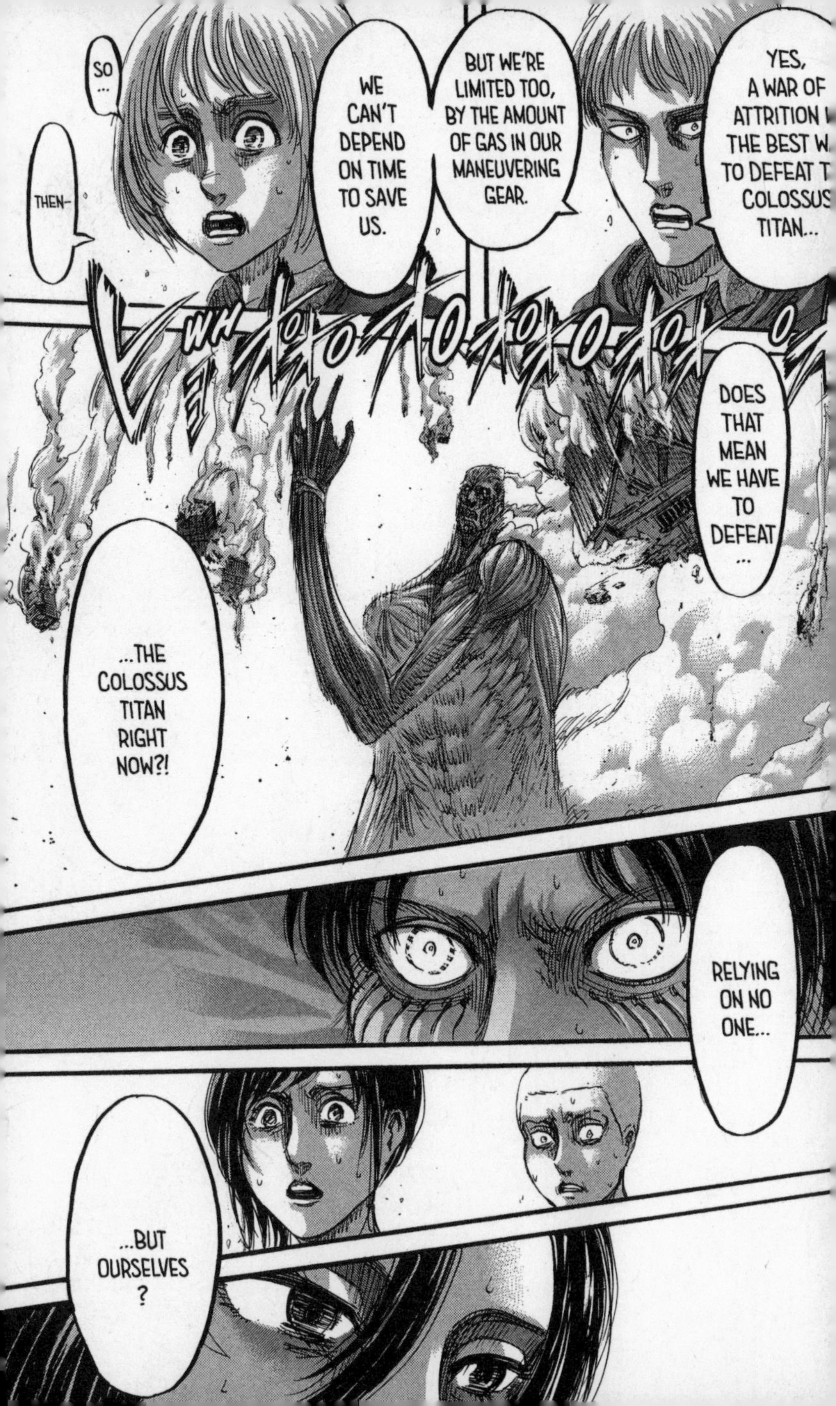
YES, A WAR OF ATTRITION I THE BEST W TO DEFEAT T COLOSSUS TITAN...
BUT WE'RE LIMITED TOO, BY THE AMOUNT OF GAS IN OUR MANEUVERING GEAR.
WE CAN'T DEPEND ON TIME TO SAVE US.
SO ...
THEN-
DOES THAT MEAN WE HAVE TO DEFEAT ...
...THE COLOSSUS TITAN RIGHT NOW?!
RELYING ON NO ONE...
...BUT OURSELVES ?

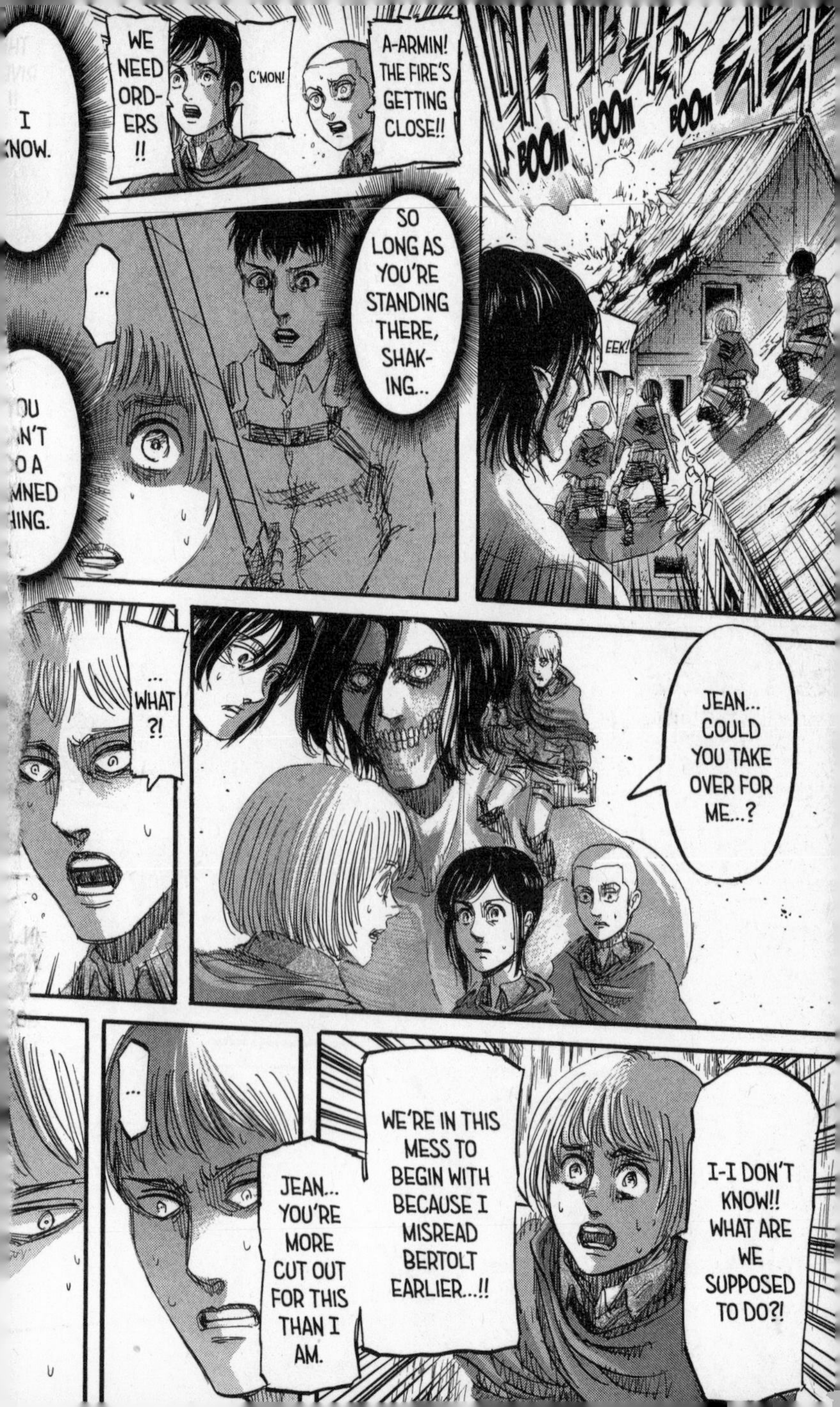
BOOM
BOOM
BOOM
EEK!
A-ARMIN! THE FIRE'S GETTING CLOSE!!
C'MON!
WE NEED ORD-ERS!!
I
NOW.
SO LONG AS YOU'RE STANDING THERE, SHAK-ING...
...
OU
N'T
O A
MNED
HING.
JEAN... COULD YOU TAKE OVER FOR ME...?
... WHAT?!
I-I DON'T KNOW!! WHAT ARE WE SUPPOSED TO DO?!
WE'RE IN THIS MESS TO BEGIN WITH BECAUSE I MISREAD BERTOLT EARLIER...!!
JEAN... YOU'RE MORE CUT OUT FOR THIS THAN I AM.
...

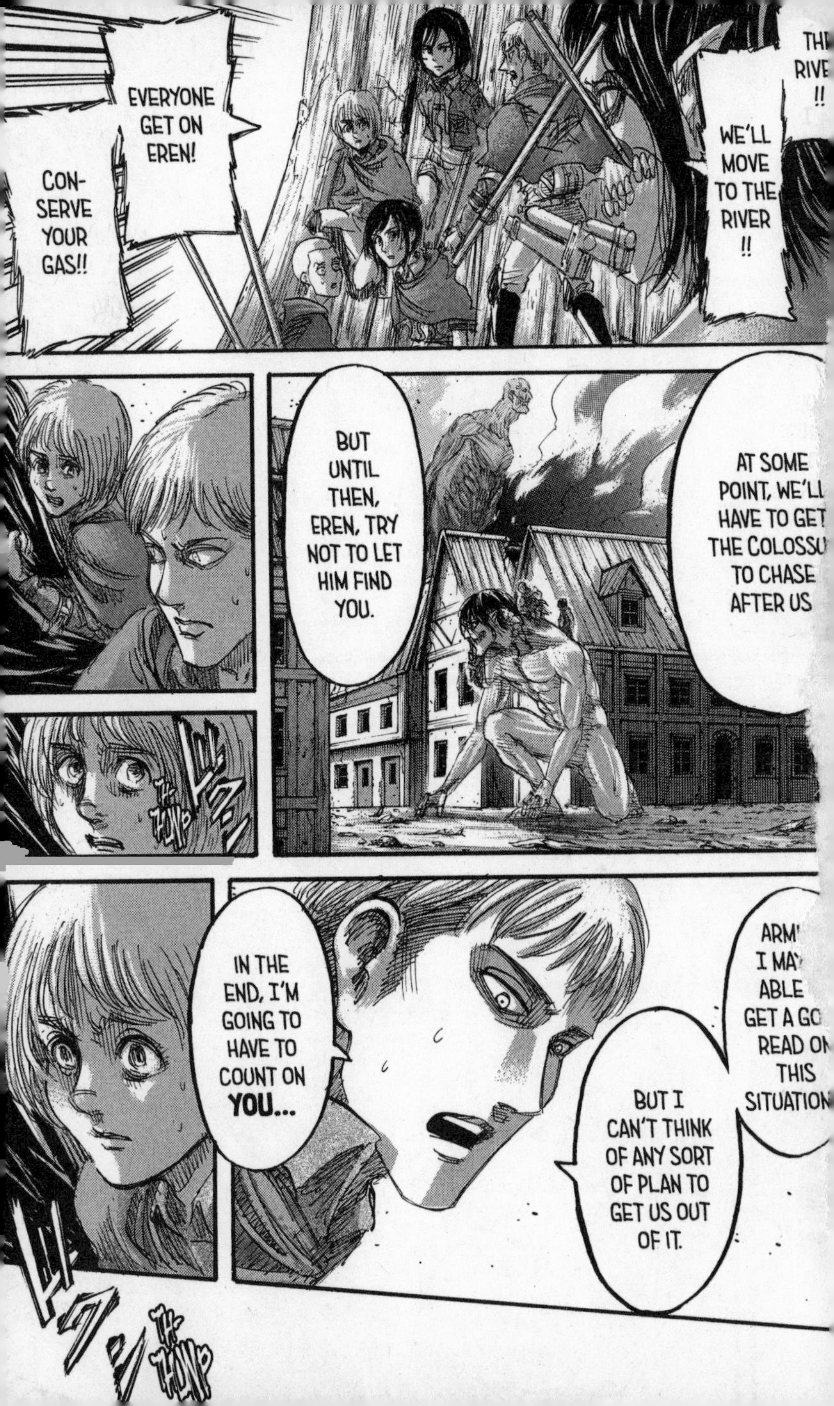
THE RIVE !!
WE'LL MOVE TO THE RIVER !!
EVERYONE GET ON EREN!
CON-SERVE YOUR GAS!!
AT SOME POINT, WE'LL HAVE TO GET THE COLOSSU TO CHASE AFTER US
BUT UNTIL THEN, EREN, TRY NOT TO LET HIM FIND YOU.
ARM I MA ABLE GET A GO READ ON THIS SITUATION
BUT I CAN'T THINK OF ANY SORT OF PLAN TO GET US OUT OF IT.
IN THE END, I'M GOING TO HAVE TO COUNT ON **YOU...**

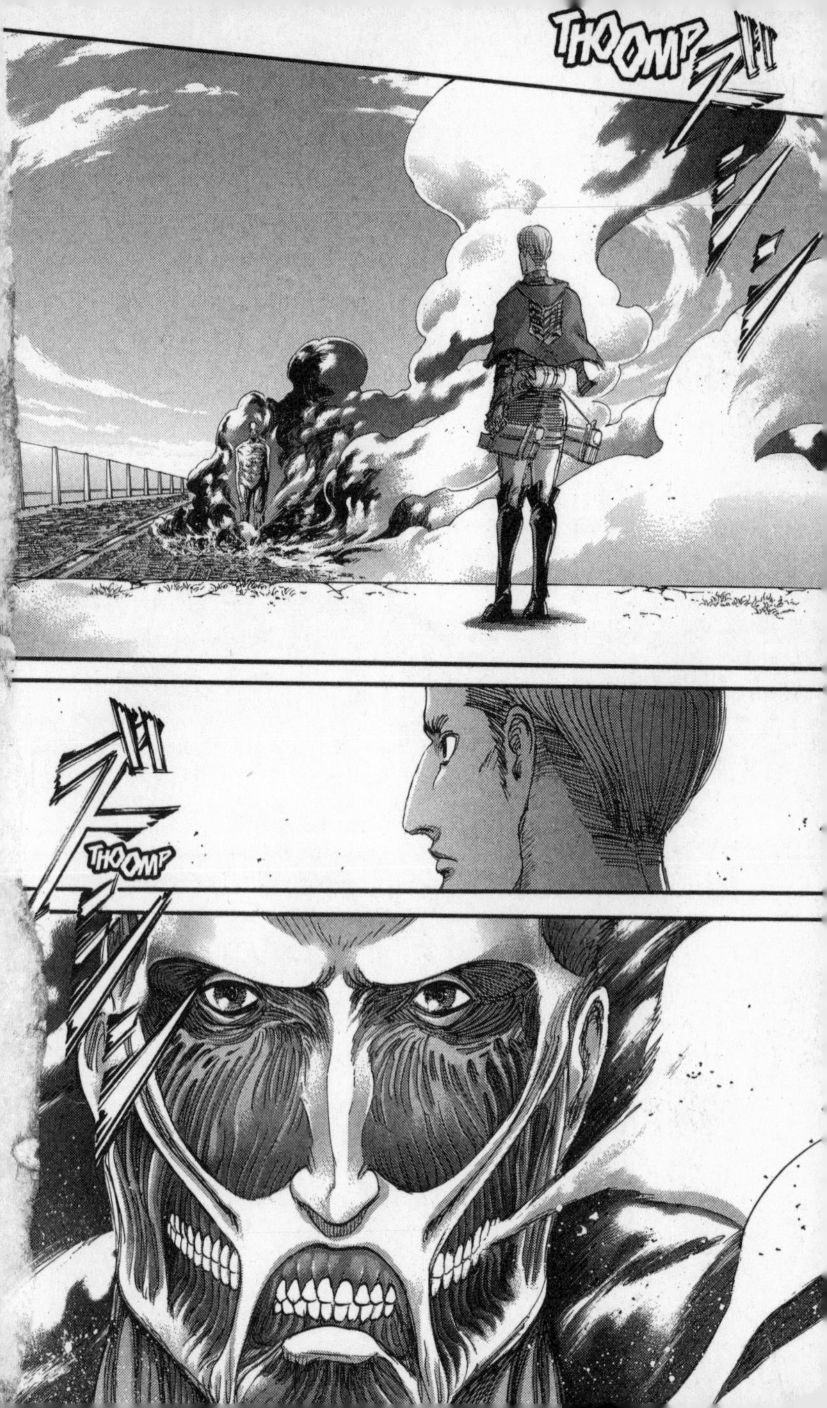
THOOMP
THOOMP

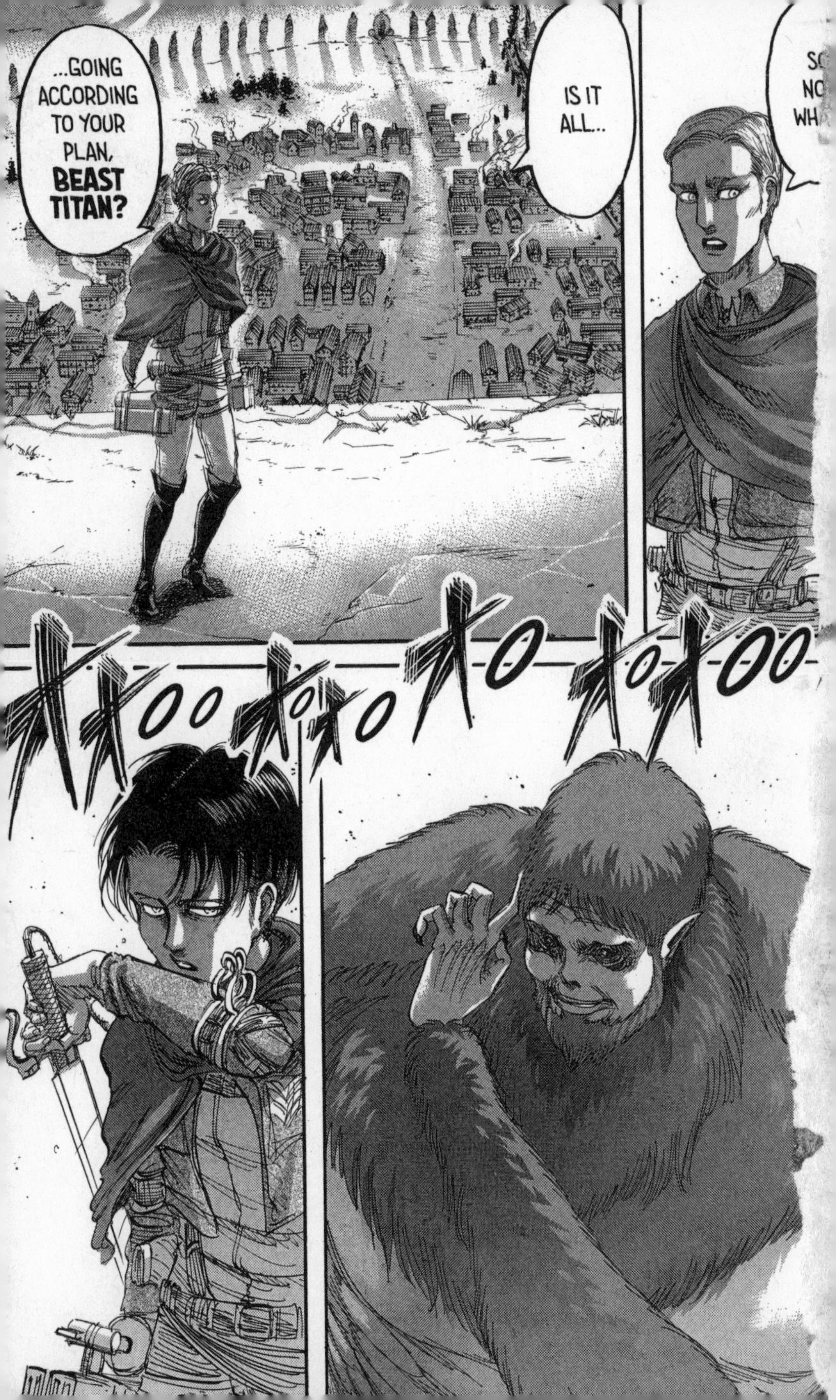
IS IT ALL...
...GOING ACCORDING TO YOUR PLAN, BEAST TITAN?

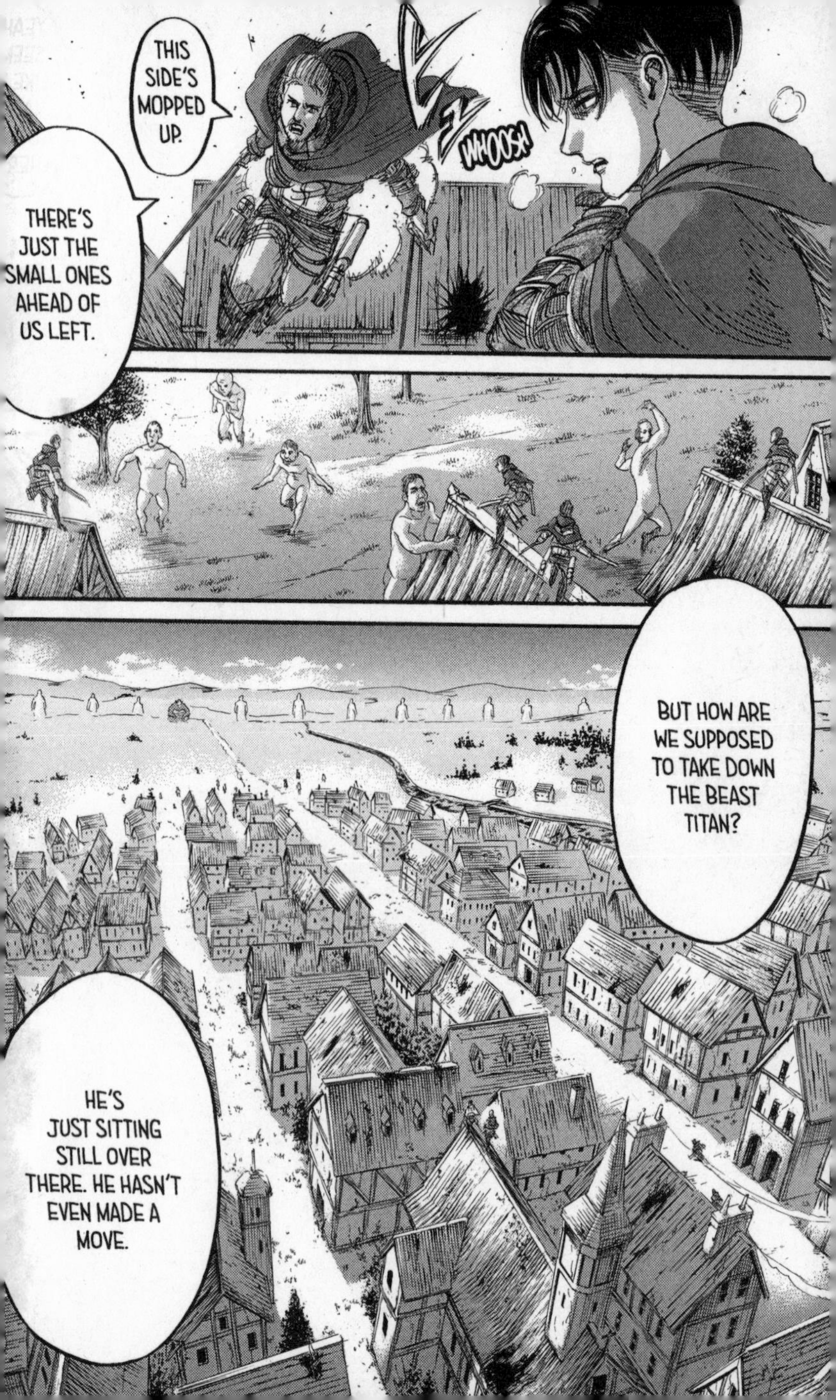
WHOOSH
THIS SIDE'S MOPPED UP.
THERE'S JUST THE SMALL ONES AHEAD OF US LEFT.
BUT HOW ARE WE SUPPOSED TO TAKE DOWN THE BEAST TITAN?
HE'S JUST SITTING STILL OVER THERE. HE HASN'T EVEN MADE A MOVE.

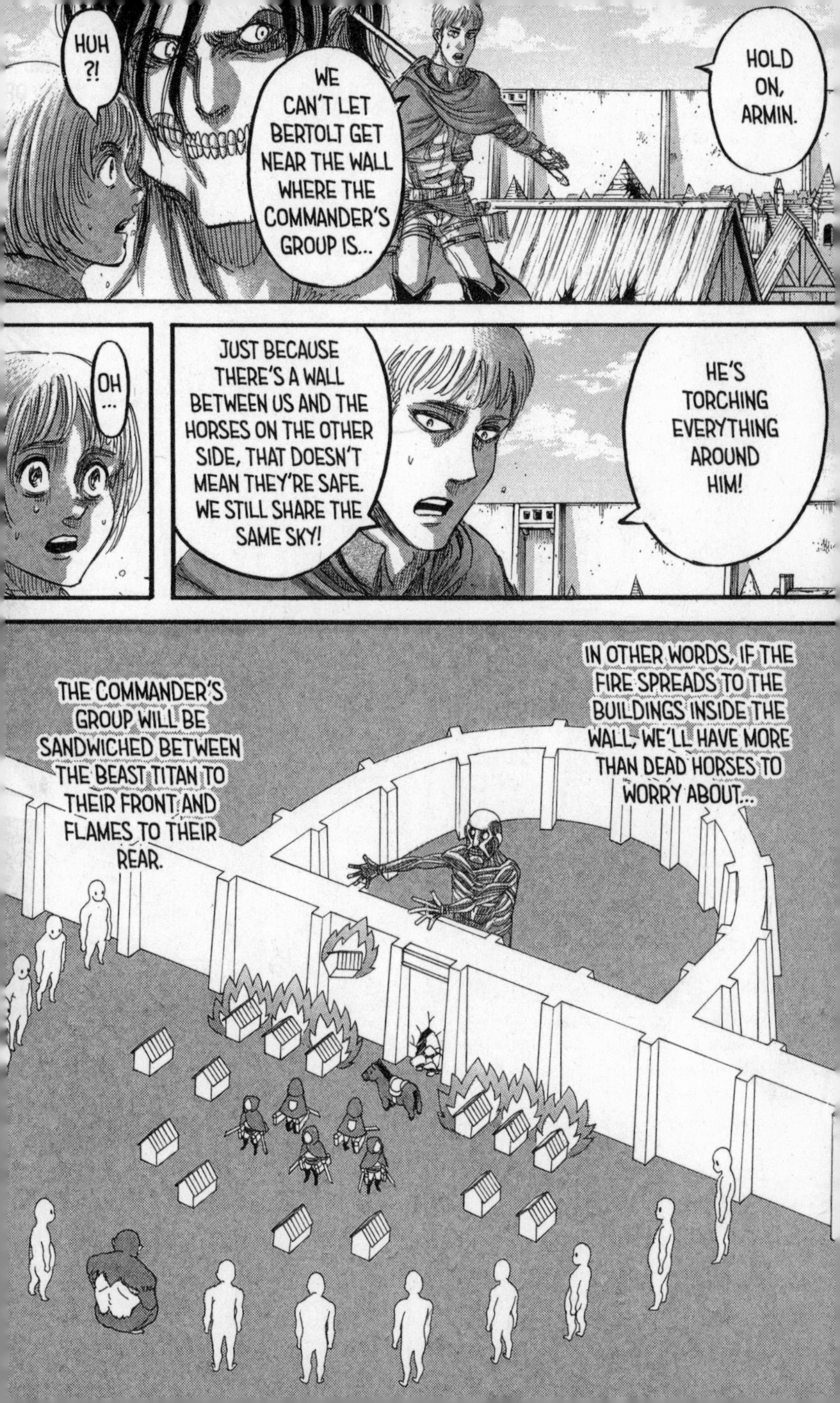
HOLD ON, ARMIN.
WE CAN'T LET BERTOLT GET NEAR THE WALL WHERE THE COMMANDER'S GROUP IS...
HUH ?!
HE'S TORCHING EVERYTHING AROUND HIM!
JUST BECAUSE THERE'S A WALL BETWEEN US AND THE HORSES ON THE OTHER SIDE, THAT DOESN'T MEAN THEY'RE SAFE. WE STILL SHARE THE SAME SKY!
OH ...
IN OTHER WORDS, IF THE FIRE SPREADS TO THE BUILDINGS INSIDE THE WALL, WE'LL HAVE MORE THAN DEAD HORSES TO WORRY ABOUT...
THE COMMANDER'S GROUP WILL BE SANDWICHED BETWEEN THE BEAST TITAN TO THEIR FRONT AND FLAMES TO THEIR REAR.

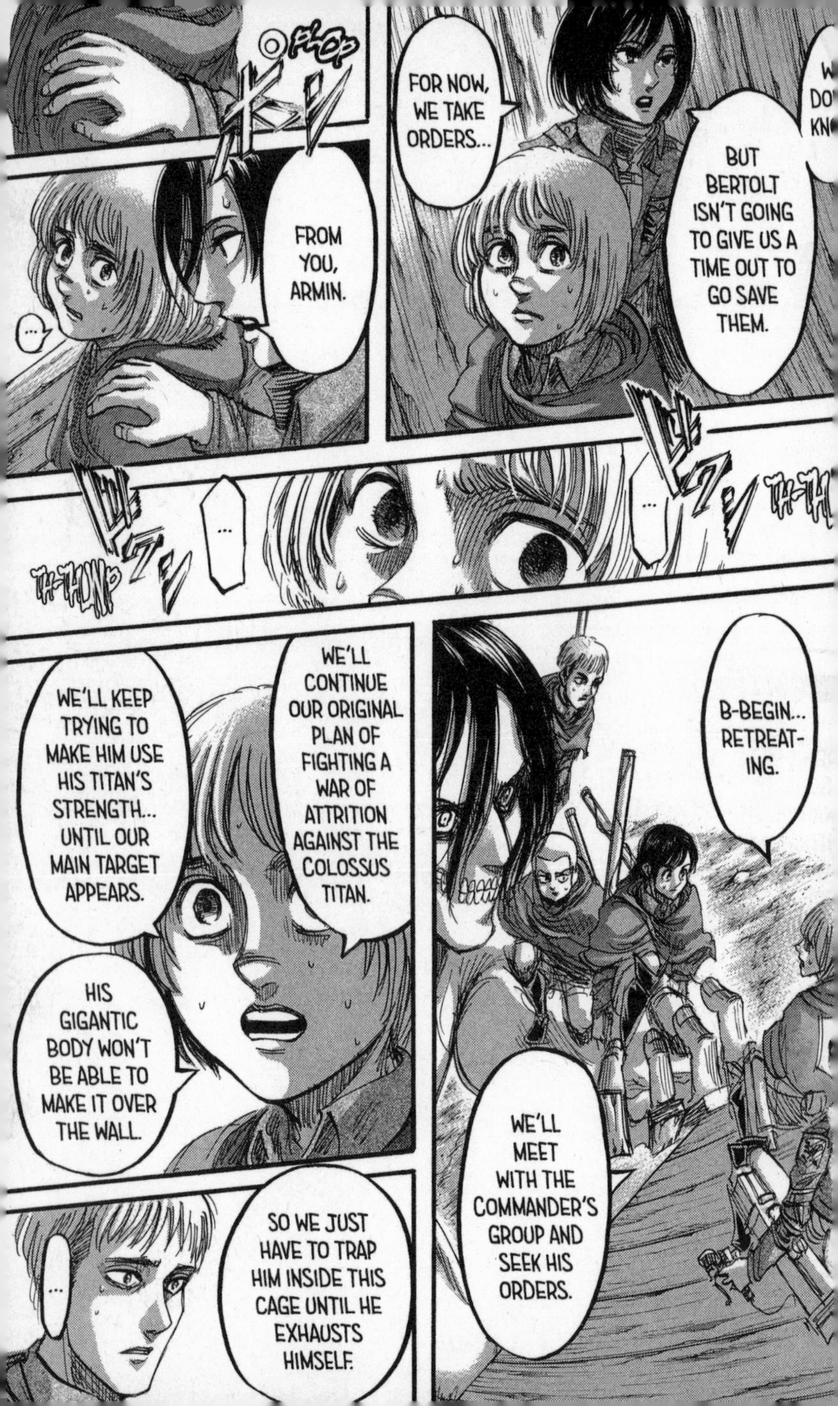
BUT BERTOLT ISN'T GOING TO GIVE US A TIME OUT TO GO SAVE THEM.
FOR NOW, WE TAKE ORDERS...
PLOP
FROM YOU, ARMIN.
...
...
TH-THUMP
...
TH-THUMP
B-BEGIN... RETREAT-ING.
WE'LL MEET WITH THE COMMANDER'S GROUP AND SEEK HIS ORDERS.
WE'LL CONTINUE OUR ORIGINAL PLAN OF FIGHTING A WAR OF ATTRITION AGAINST THE COLOSSUS TITAN.
WE'LL KEEP TRYING TO MAKE HIM USE HIS TITAN'S STRENGTH... UNTIL OUR MAIN TARGET APPEARS.
HIS GIGANTIC BODY WON'T BE ABLE TO MAKE IT OVER THE WALL.
SO WE JUST HAVE TO TRAP HIM INSIDE THIS CAGE UNTIL HE EXHAUSTS HIMSELF.
...

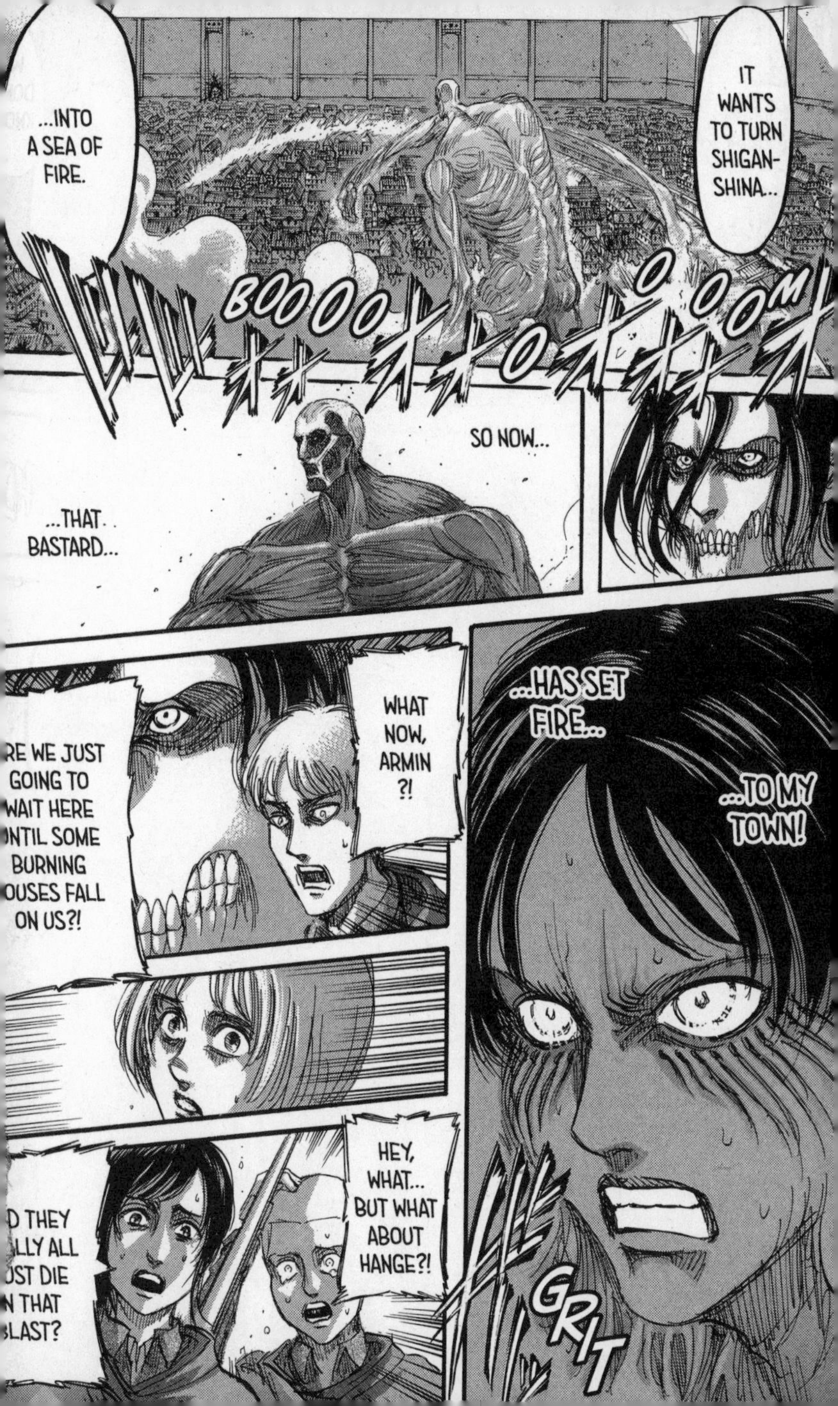
IT WANTS TO TURN SHIGAN-SHINA...
...INTO A SEA OF FIRE.
BOOOOOOOOOOM
SO NOW...
...THAT BASTARD...
...HAS SET FIRE...
...TO MY TOWN!
GRIT
WHAT NOW, ARMIN?!
RE WE JUST GOING TO WAIT HERE NTIL SOME BURNING OUSES FALL ON US?!
HEY, WHAT... BUT WHAT ABOUT HANGE?!
D THEY ALLY ALL UST DIE N THAT LAST?

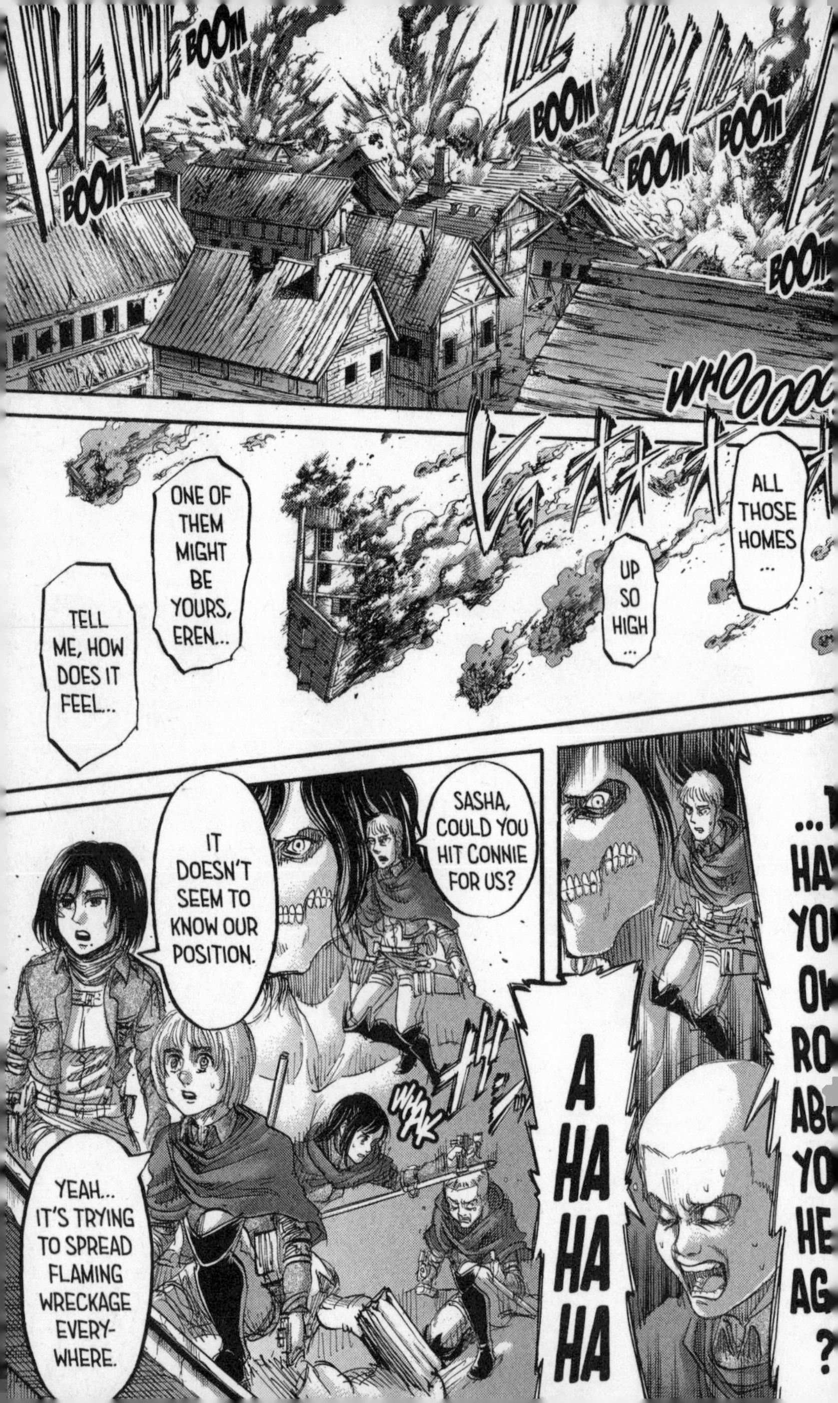
BOOM
BOOM
BOOM
BOOM
BOOM
BOOM
WHOOOOO
ALL THOSE HOMES ...
UP SO HIGH ...
ONE OF THEM MIGHT BE YOURS, EREN...
TELL ME, HOW DOES IT FEEL...
A HA HA HA HA
SASHA, COULD YOU HIT CONNIE FOR US?
IT DOESN'T SEEM TO KNOW OUR POSITION.
WHAK
YEAH... IT'S TRYING TO SPREAD FLAMING WRECKAGE EVERY-WHERE.

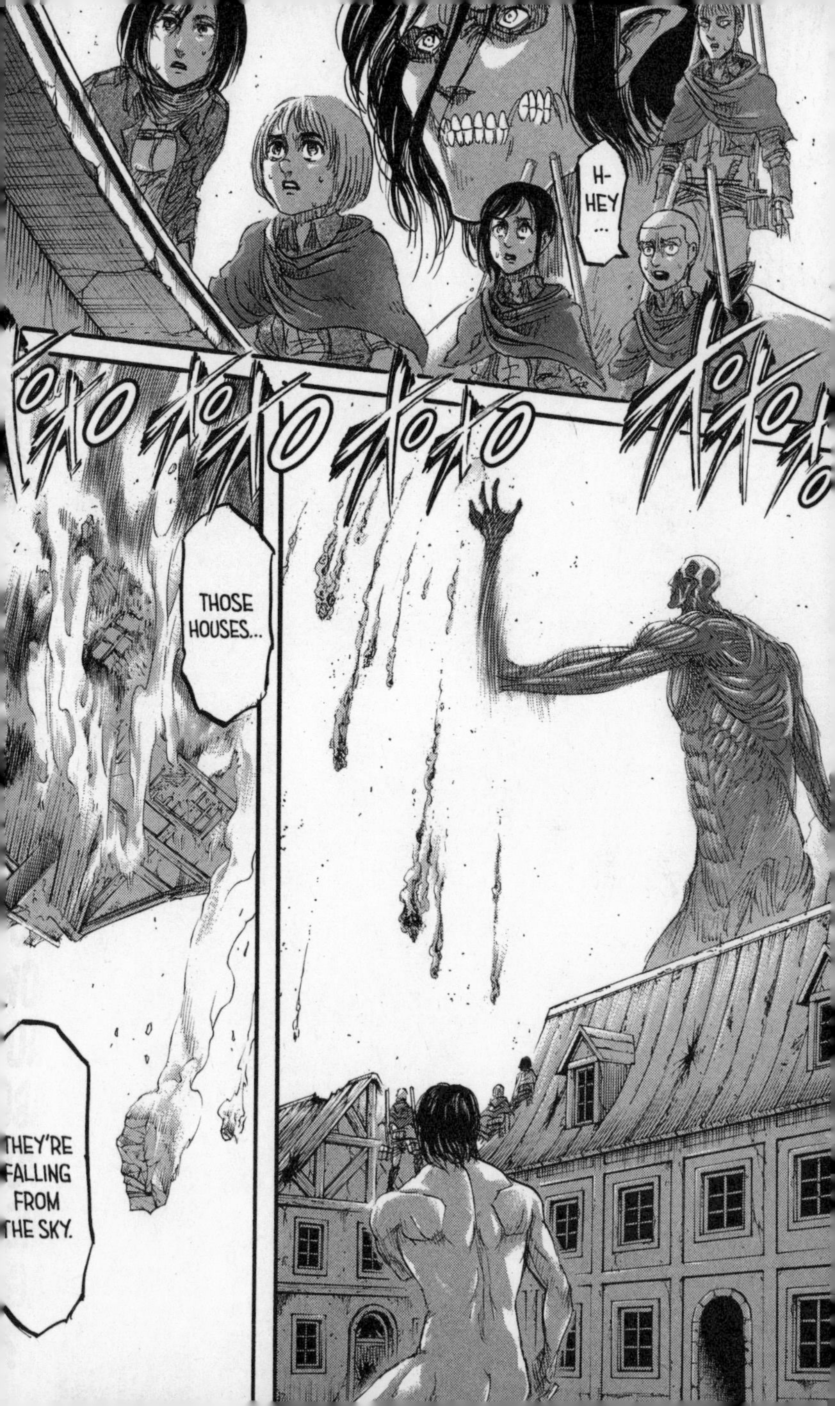
H- HEY ...
THOSE HOUSES...
THEY'RE FALLING FROM THE SKY.

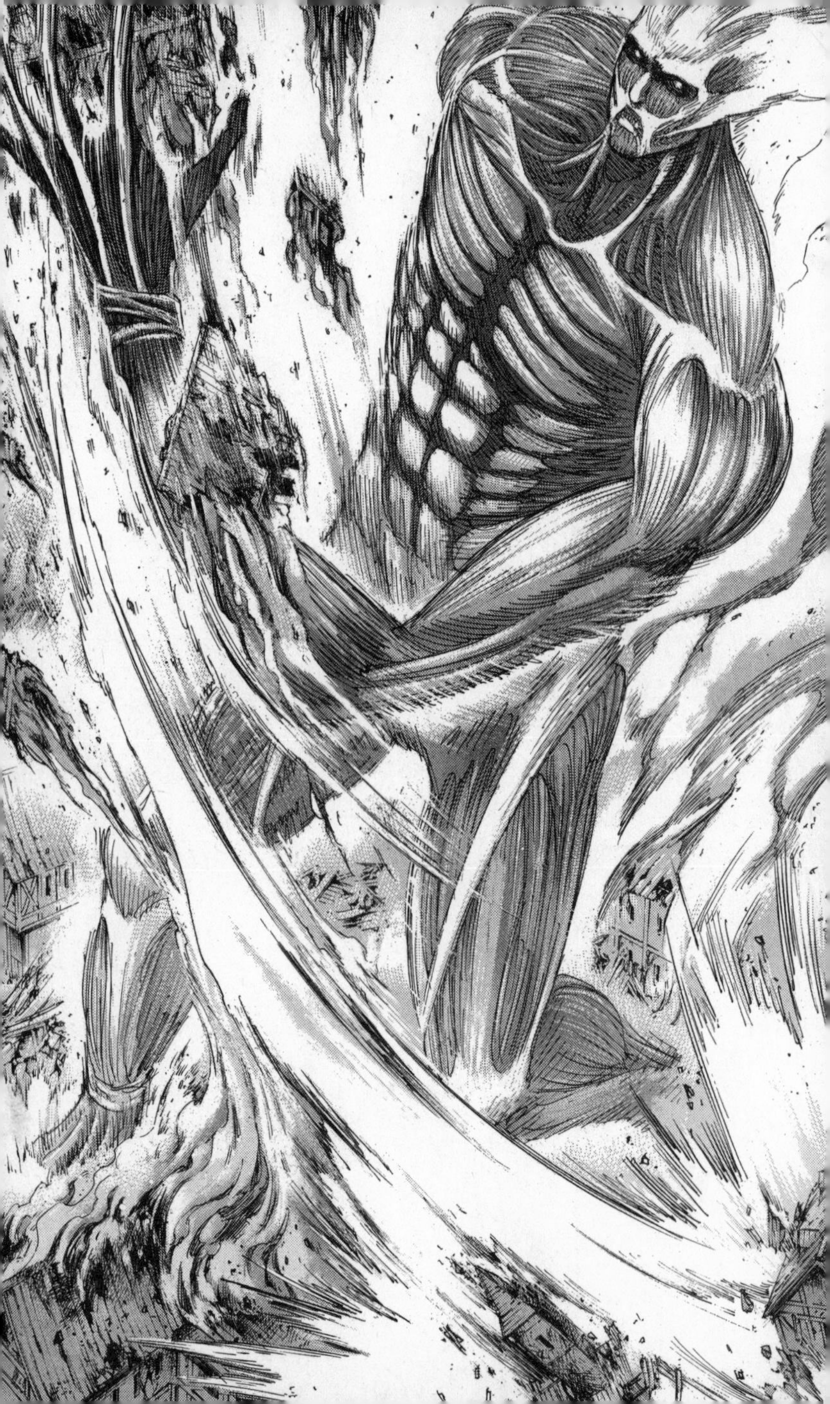

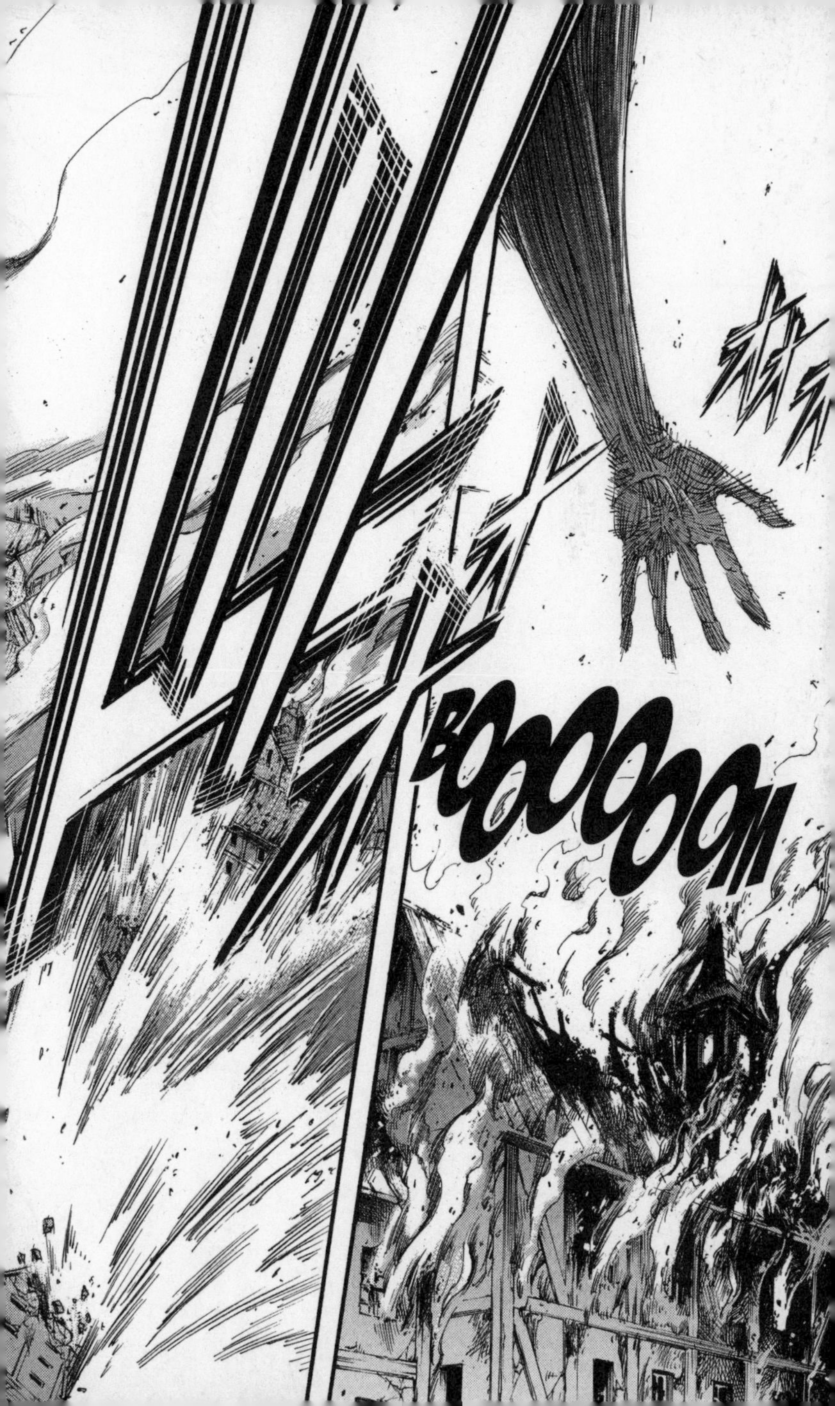
BOOOOOM

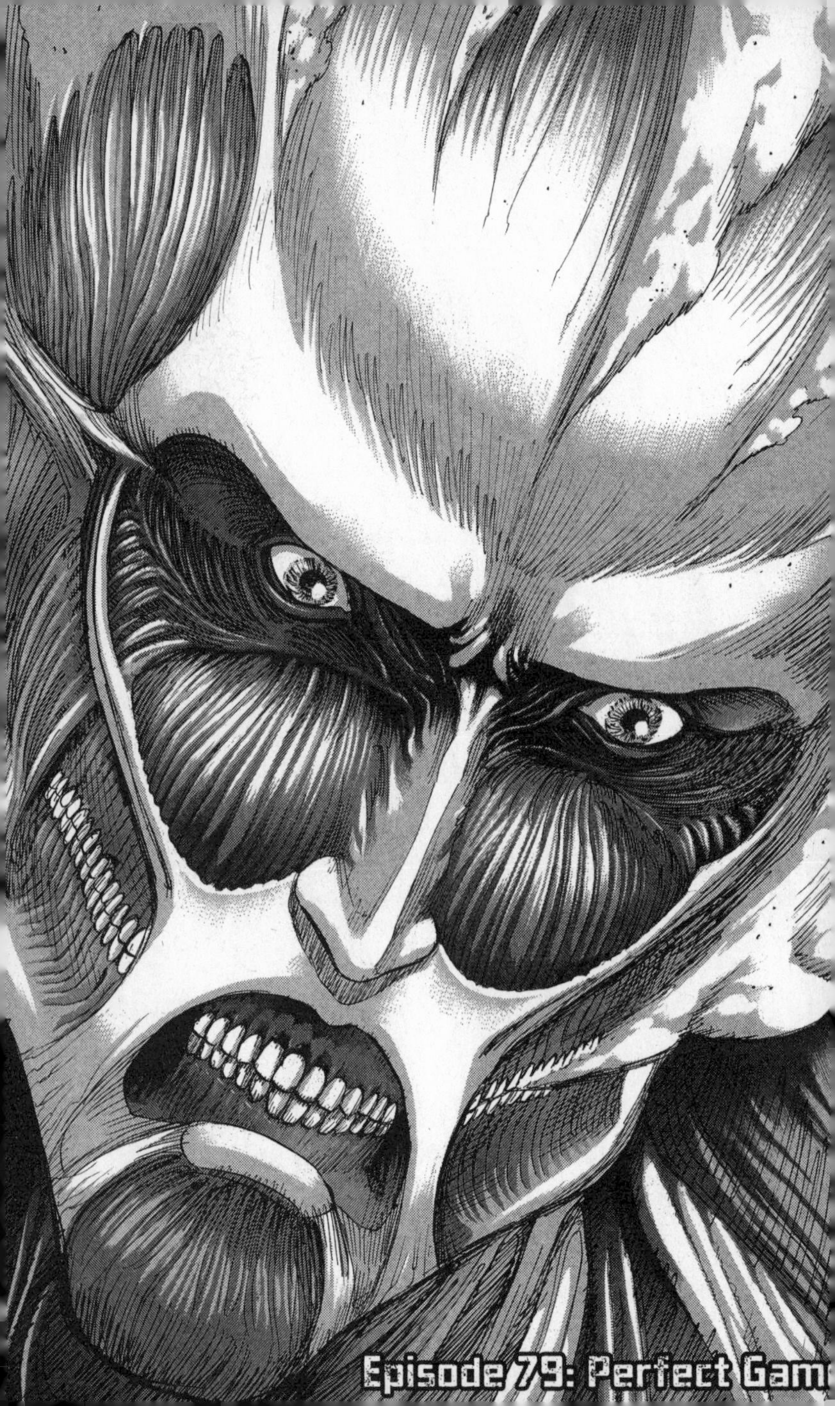
Episode 79: Perfect Gam

ATTACK
on TITAN

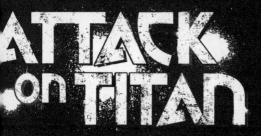

Survey Corps

Soldiers who are prepared to sacrific[e] themselves as they brave the Titan territory outside the walls.

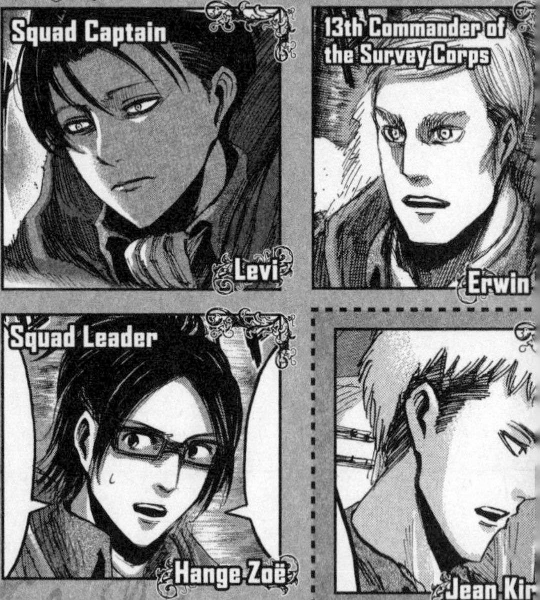
Squad Captain
Levi
13th Commander of the Survey Corps
Erwin
Squad Leader
Hange Zoë
Jean Kir

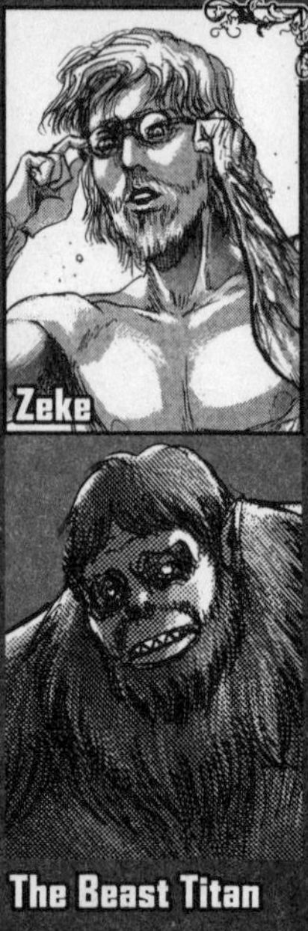
Zeke
The Beast Titan

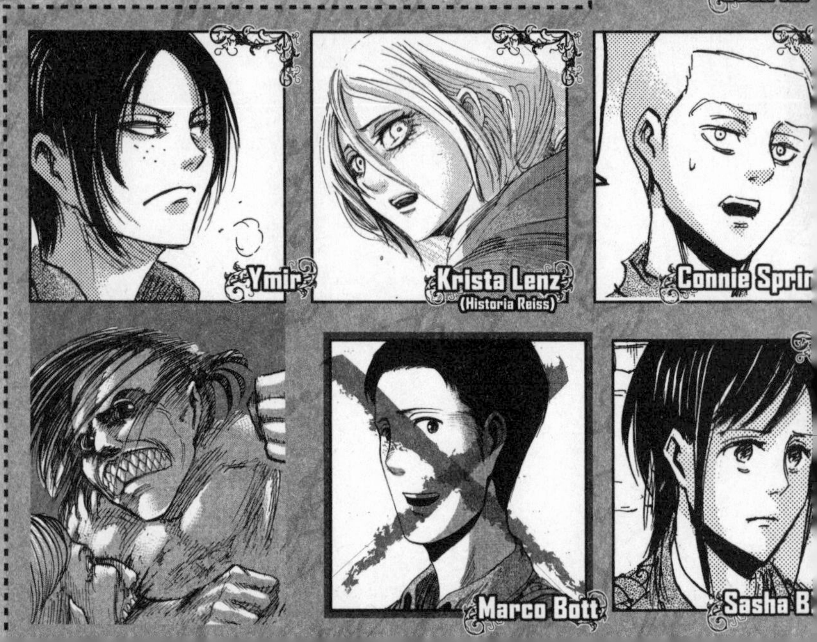
Ymir
Krista Lenz
(Historia Reiss)
Connie Sprin
Marco Bott
Sasha B

"Attack on Titan" Character Introductions

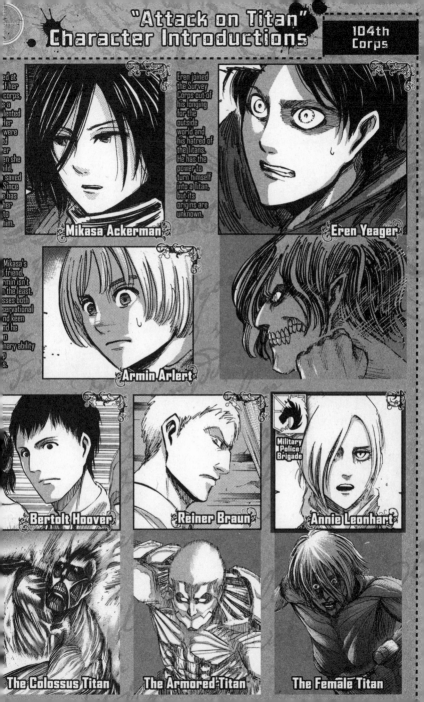

104th Corps

Eren joined the Survey Corps out of his longing for the outside world and his hatred of the Titans. He has the power to turn himself into a Titan, but its origins are unknown.

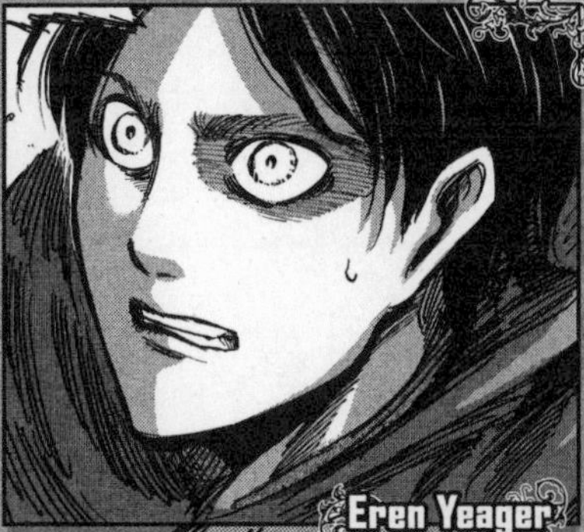
Eren Yeager

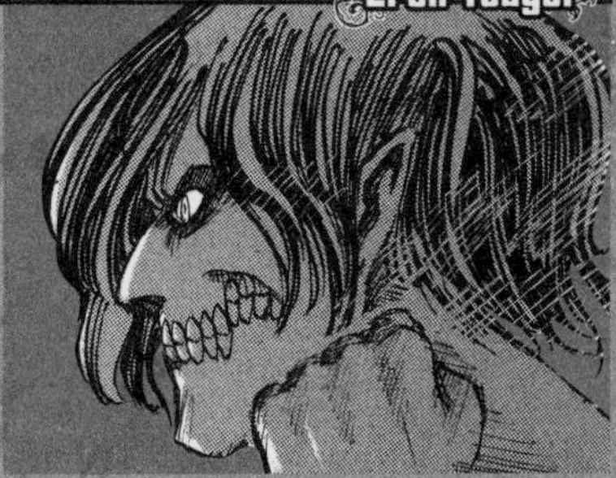

ed at
f her
corps,
s a
lented
Her
were
d
er
en she
hild,
saved
Since
e has
her
to
him.

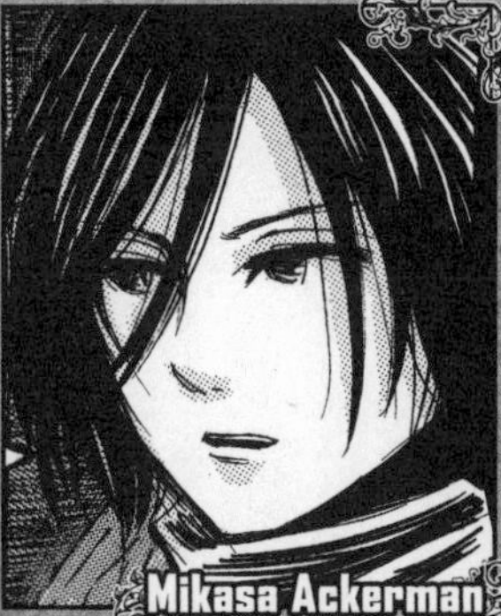
Mikasa Ackerman

Mikasa's
l friend,
rmin isn't
n the least,
sses both
servational
nd keen
nd he
n
nary ability
p
s.

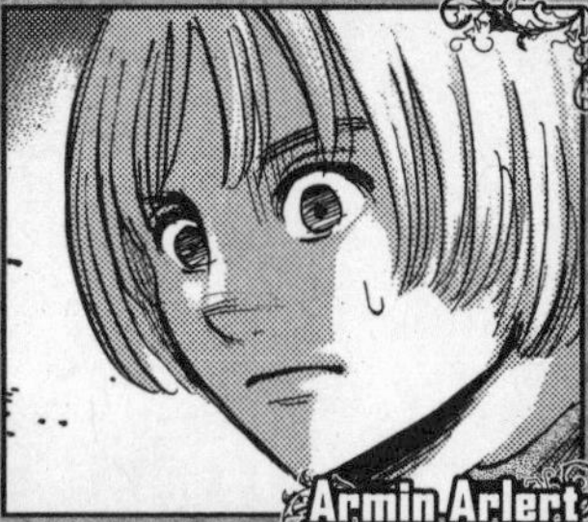
Armin Arlert

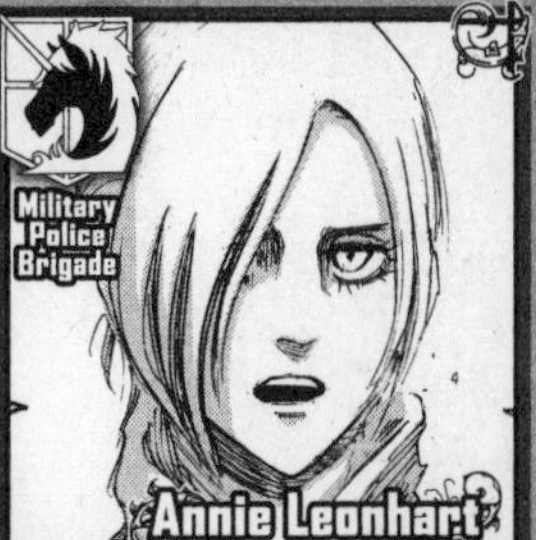
Military Police Brigade
Annie Leonhart

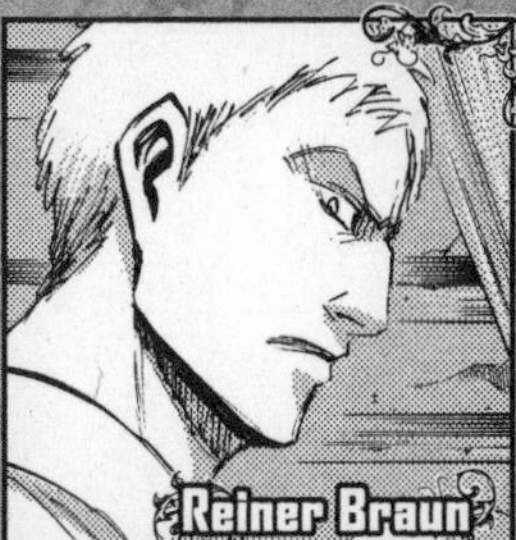
Reiner Braun

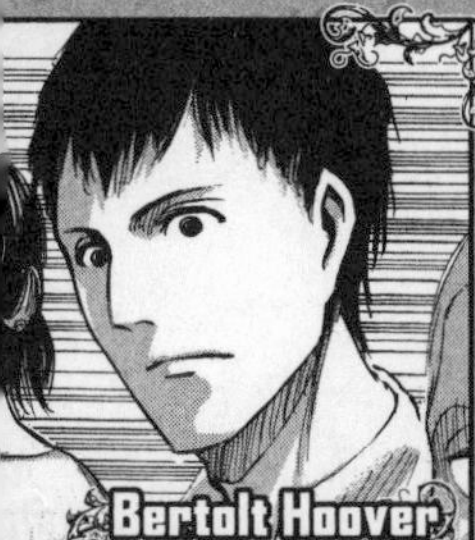
Bertolt Hoover

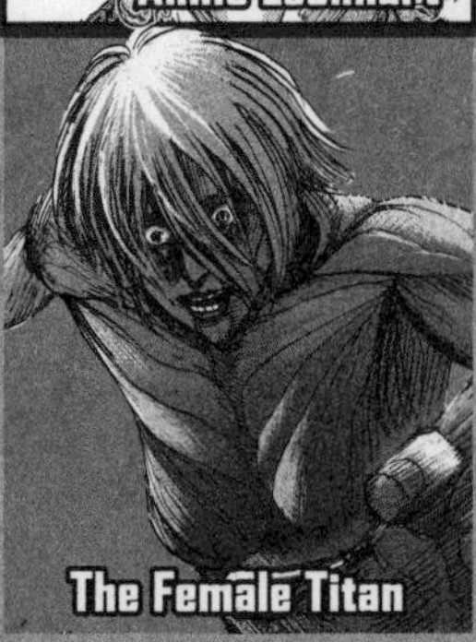
The Female Titan

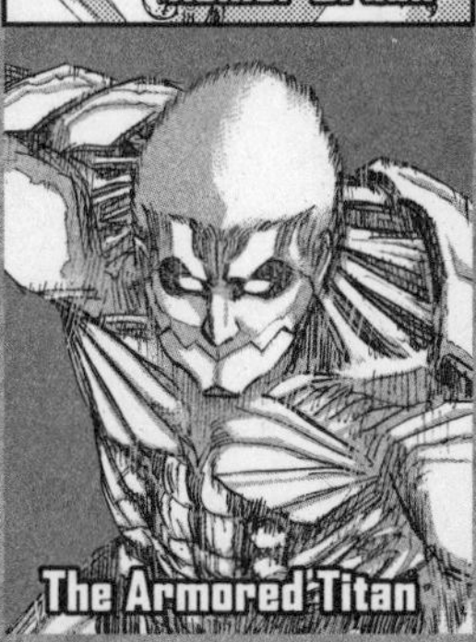
The Armored Titan

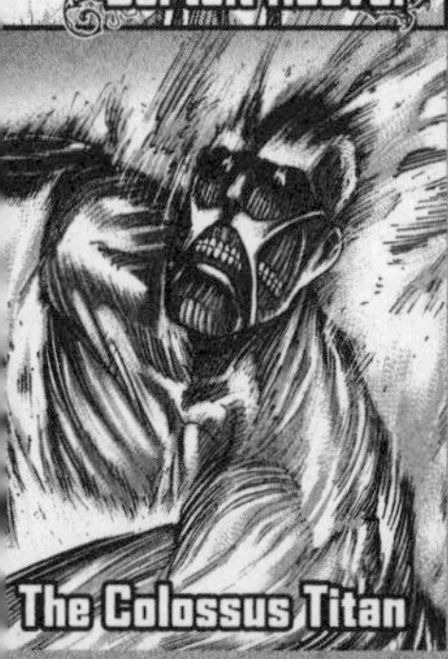
The Colossus Titan

ATTACK ON TITAN

20

HAJIME ISAYAMA

Episode 79:
Perfect Game
5

Episode 80:
The Unknown
Soldiers
51

Episode 81:
Promise
97

Episode 82:
Hero
143